MAKERS AND TAKERS

Other books by the author:
THE MANIFESTO OF INDIVIDUALISM (1968)
THE TROJAN PROJECT (1997)

MAKERS

AND

TAKERS

HOW WEALTH AND PROGRESS ARE MADE

AND

HOW THEY ARE TAKEN AWAY OR PREVENTED

by

EDMUND CONTOSKI

with a Foreword by

John Chamberlain

American Liberty Publishers
Minneapolis, Minnesota

American Liberty Publishers
P.O. Box 18296
Minneapolis, MN 55418

Publisher's Cataloging in Publication
(Prepared by Quality Books, Inc.)

     Contoski, Edmund.
       Makers and takers : how wealth and progress are made and how
    they are taken away or prevented / by Edmund Contoski ; with a foreword by
    John Chamberlain.
       p. cm.
       Includes bibliographical references and index.
       ISBN 0-9655007-4-8

       1. Individualism—United States. 2. United States—Civilization
    —Philosophy. 3. Civil Society—United States. 4. Capitalism.
    5. Economics. 6. Environmentalism. 7. Pollution. 8. Environmental
    policy. I. Title.

    JC599.U5C66 1997   320.5'12
                              QBI96-40556

Cover design: Paul Kielb

Library of Congress Catalog Card Number 96-78787
Printed and bound in the United States of America.

CONTENTS

Foreword

Ludwig von Mises has made the classic case against government interventionism. He did it in terms of logic. But never, till now in Edmund Contoski's *Makers and Takers,* has there been a book to document the Mises points with examples that span the entire gamut of State interference as it has affected the energies of creative individuals.

Mr. Contoski begins by asking a simple question: was it a politician who invented the automobile, the electric light, or even Kentucky Fried Chicken? He notices that there have been two dominating but competing forces in history, the first embodied in the creative mind, the second in the presumption of politicians who, in the name of a "greater good," simply seize a portion of the "maker's" products for their own purposes, which includes feeding those who keep them in power.

Mr. Contoski's thematic beginnings are reminiscent of the anthropology of Franz Oppenheimer, who established the gangster origin of the State. The early inhabitants of Jericho, in Mr. Contoski's example, learned how to farm. They distributed their products among themselves, grain for wool, without having to pay tribute to anybody. But there were "takers" over the horizon waiting to move in on Jericho. What they had was the force of arms. The "makers," not yet initiated into the secrets of defense, gave way.

Since Jericho, the world has seen centuries of see-saw between the two forces of the creative mind and forcible expropriation of what free thinking has brought into being. In the days of William the Conqueror outright military seizure prevailed. Since then there have been the various degrees of taxation. In mercantilist times there was regulation, raised to a fine point more recently in America. Finally, there have been the big inflations, whether sparked by Cortez's seizure of the Aztec gold at gunpoint or, as in modern times, by simple overworking of the government printing presses.

Having cleared the ground by making his clear distinctions, Mr. Contoski moves in on all the current excuses for government intervention. Regulation in all its phases is a prime culprit. Environmentalism has spawned a hundred bugaboos, all of which are demolished by Mr. Contoski's studies.

Mr. Contoski's book ends by becoming a paean to an older America whose philosophy of individualism liberated the human mind. Deregulation measures have had a healthy effect, but government spending continues on an horrendous scale. "Functional socialism" is still with us. It won't be changed until there are thousands of angry listeners to Mr. Contoski's dramatically illustrated reasoning.

John Chamberlain

PART I
PROGRESS or POLITICS

Chapter One
WHAT HATH GOVERNMENT WROUGHT?

> *An essential fact that stands out*
> *in all history is that the real sources of*
> *well being are scientific and economic,*
> *not political and social.*
> —Carl Snyder in *Capitalism the Creator*

Think for a moment about our standard of living, about all the things that make our lives so comfortable and enjoyable, telephones, television, automobiles. Think about all the things which have enhanced human existence from the wheel to the airplane, the printing press to polaroid photography, the microscope to penicillin. Consider the electric light, the flush toilet, nylon, gasoline, rubber, the sewing machine, the refrigerator, and the safety pin. How many of these were the result of government anywhere in the world?

None. All these and many more were created by a process having nothing to do with political power or methods.

What is this mysterious creative process, and why has there been such a strong tendency to look instead to political action for human advancement? Why has it been so popular to believe that it is progressive to place under political control the production of material goods which governments everywhere have been incapable of creating in the first place? Was it a politician who invented the automobile, the telephone or the electric light? Did government give us Kentucky Fried Chicken or television—or has government merely interfered with such things, as, for example, when the Federal Communications Commission for years delayed licensing television in order to protect the public's investment in radio?

All progress in our standard of living has been due to man's ability to control the materials in the world around him, to grow food, to make tools, to manufacture luxuries. Political action, on the other hand, aims to control people. When the control of materials has brought us where we are, why has there been such willingness to believe the control of people will take us where we want to go? The societies where men have been most controlled have been those in which it has been least desirable to live, societies without freedom.

Every step of progress throughout the centuries has always broadened man's horizons and extended the scope of his actions. Every advancement has been a *breakthrough* of previous limitations, yet throughout the world governments generally have *imposed* limitations—reduced freedom—in their efforts to advance society. To the extent they have succeeded in their means, they have defeated their end. Progress is consonant with freedom, not control. This conclusion is not surprising or original. What is surprising is how reluctant the world has been to accept it. Throughout history there have been very, very few societies that have been even relatively free. Why weren't there more imitators of these few shining examples? Even within those few prosperous and progressive societies the secret of their success was so little understood that freedom was more often lost from within than by external aggression.

And what of those governments that even today have pursued failing policies of economic interventionism year after year, decade after decade? Why have they been so reluctant to adopt the successful measures of freer nations? Or even to learn from their own mistakes? What is so appealing about government direction of human affairs that nations which employ it extensively are reluctant to abandon it despite its failures—while nations that are free and prosperous commonly relinquish successive degrees of their freedom in order to employ government direction more extensively?

There is plenty of evidence, both contemporary and historical, of the efficacy of freedom and, conversely, of the failure of government controls or intervention. Let's look at some wide-ranging examples.

THE SOVIET UNION

When Mikhail Gorbachev announced his policy of *Perestroika*, or restructuring, he demonstrated that the most controlled economy in the world was failing. Henceforth the Soviets would begin to relax controls, introduce some free market incentives and ideas, and in general move toward a more open society—but not any more than necessary. Government would retain as much control as practicable, allowing just enough freedom to make the system function.

When first announced, this restructuring was greeted with much surprise by the outside world. Even more surprising, however, is that such reform was so long in coming, for the evidence was plain, and had been accumulating for decades, that the Soviet system was inimical to progress.

Under the oldest and strongest communist government in the world the Soviet people couldn't produce enough food for themselves—in a country that was once an exporter of food at a time when there were no tractors or other modern machinery and no chemical fertilizers. In 1953 Nikita Khrushchev admitted the country had fewer livestock than in 1913 even though there were 60 million more people to feed. In 1973, after more than a half-century of government effort, agricultural production was still such a failure that the Soviets set a record by importing more food than any nation in history. Of the 22 million tons of grain they imported that year, most came from the United States even though the Soviet Union had more arable land than the U.S. and was cultivating three times the wheat acreage. In the U.S., moreover, only three percent of the labor force was devoted to agriculture, compared to 20 percent in the Soviet Union. And it was not only the Soviets whom the United States' abundance was feeding. American farmers, comprising one-tenth of one percent of the world's population, were feeding twenty-five percent of the world's people.

In the 1980s the Soviets had to import still more food despite 30 percent of total Soviet investment being devoted to agriculture. In 1984 the Soviet Union imported 55 million tons of grain—two and one-half times the record imports of 1973!

Even more food imports would have been needed if it weren't for the few small agricultural plots the government allowed to remain in private ownership. As far back as 1975 *Pravda* published an article by scientist Yuri Yoloviev stating that these private plots accounted for 4 percent of Soviet farmland but produced 25 percent of the country's meat, 37 percent of its vegetables, and 63 percent of its potatoes. The article admitted that this remarkable production was achieved with only spare-time labor and obsolete tools.

Still the government persisted year after year in its failing agricultural policy. Meanwhile, side by side with the giant collectivized farms the small private plots continued to produce abundantly. A visitor to the Soviet Union in 1987 wrote:

> From Leningrad to Tashkent, it seemed as if every woman carried a tote bag, every man a briefcase, on the off chance they will come across a scarce item they need. Meat is in chronic short supply. This fall in Leningrad and Moscow, supplies of fruits and vegetables also are inadequate....

> In Tashkent, a farmers' market offers a bounty of fruits and vegetables…. The market is supplied wholly from private plots cultivated in spare time by cooperative-farm families….
>
> Tashkent consumers appear willing to pay the private market's high prices rather than purchase food from subsidized state-owned markets. Fruits and vegetables from state farms move so slowly through processing that they often are inedible when they arrive at the state market.[1]

Health care statistics are even more shocking than the agricultural ones. Life expectancy declined, and mortality rates for infants and for the total population rose. No other industrialized country in the postwar period has experienced a sustained adverse movement in even one of these indicators.

Life expectancy in the Soviet Union was lower in the 1980s than in the 1960s, and infant mortality was two and one-half times the U.S. rate. In 1987 35 percent of rural hospitals had no hot water, 27 percent were without sewer systems, and 17 percent lacked running water. Even in Moscow 12 of 33 maternity hospitals lacked basic sanitation. *Pravda* reported that these unsanitary conditions plus negligence have been "killing so many mothers and infants that administrators have been trying to hide their institutions' mortality rates."[2] For 14 years—until Mr. Gorbachev's *glasnost* (openness)—the U.S.S.R. Central Statistical Board didn't even publish life-expectancy figures.

After more than seven decades of government-managed health care, Soviet hospitals were experiencing chronic shortages of such simple items as sterile bandages and even diapers. Needles, rubber gloves, intravenous tubing, and catheters were used over and over. They were too limited to be considered disposable.

The reforms initiated by Gorbachev were advanced much further by his successor, Boris Yeltsin. He undertook the world's largest privatization program, bringing 75 to 80 percent of Russian industrial production into some form of private ownership. More than 11 million apartments were privatized, and some 40 million citizens became shareholders in 15,000 companies.

When the Soviet Union was dissolved, it seemed as though communism was dead for good and the road lay open to political liberty and a free economy. But in the Russian parliamentary elections of December 1993 Yeltsin received a stunning defeat. The Communists won more seats in the Duma (parliament) than any other party, and other parties opposed to Yeltsin, including that of the ultra-nationalist Vladimir Zhirinovsky, elected a surprising number of representatives. The future of the reform movement was placed further in doubt in early 1994 with the resignation of the key architect of Yeltsin's economic reforms, Yegor Gaidar, and the minister of finance, Boris Fyodorov, another key player in the reforms. Both men quit because they believed the recent election results meant that parliament would no longer allow them to carry out those reforms.

On March 15, 1996 Russia's parliament—by an overwhelming vote—declared that the breakup of the Soviet Union in 1991 was illegal and rescinded. It demanded concrete steps to restore the old political entity. The lopsided vote of 250 to 98 indicated that the measure received widespread support beyond that of its Communist backers. Yeltsin indicated he would block the move and it would have little effect. But what will happen after he leaves the scene?

On March 27, 1996 *The Wall Street Journal* wrote:

> From the Soviet wreckage, Communist leaders working with underdog zeal have salvaged a leaner, more dedicated party. They have rebuilt it into the most powerfully organized political machine in Russia. And the renewed party's aim, before Russia clicks too firmly into the ways of market democracy, is to set the country back on the track of the Bolshevik revolution sparked in 1917 by Vladimir Lenin.
>
> As many party leaders describe it, Russia's 74 years of Soviet rule were just a rehearsal in which Communists had a chance to learn from their mistakes. Now they mean to get the revolution done right....
>
> Now, with communism waging a comeback, former [party] members have been flocking to re-register.

In July 1996 Yeltsin won a run-off election against his Communist opponent. It was a remarkable victory, considering he trailed by huge margins in public opinion polls early in the campaign. Nevertheless, he was left in the position of having to deal with a parliament where the largest number of seats were held by Communists.

CHINA

A decade before Gorbachev's *Perestroika,* Deng Xiaoping introduced capitalistic reforms in the People's Republic of China. The country was unbelievably backward, had a gargantuan population of over one billion people, and a history of food shortages. There had been particularly harsh famines during the "Great Leap Forward" of Deng's predecessor, Mao Tse-tung, a virulent Marxist, when 25 to 30 million people died of starvation.

Deng dissolved the communes and gave the peasants small private plots of land, along with considerable freedom in what to plant. Part of their production was to be sold to the state, but the rest could be sold on free markets. These reforms allowed 450 million farmhands to become farmers and triple their incomes.

As recently as 1983 China had been a net importer of corn and soybeans. In 1987 she became the world's third-largest exporter of both crops despite the fact that corn was still picked by hand and grain collected in horse-drawn carts. This remarkable increase in productivity occurred in the face of a drop in government investment! In 1986 agriculture received 3.3 percent of government investment, compared to 10.6 percent in 1978, the year the reform began.

By 1990 China was producing so much grain that her granaries were overwhelmed. That year's record harvest of 462 million tons surpassed the previous record by a whopping 55 million tons. Premier Li Peng called for "emergency measures" to handle the overflow, such as the erection of temporary storage tents and the renting of warehouses and empty buildings.

Deng's reforms were not limited to agriculture. He encouraged private enterprise and urged individuals to "get rich." In a decade both China's gross national product and per capita income more than doubled. By 1989 there were more than 5 million private companies employing 75 million workers. A bond market opened in Shenyang (1986) and stock markets were opened in Shanghai (1986) and Beijing (1987).

By 1995 entrepreneurs and small enterprises were producing more goods, employing more workers and providing more foreign trade than the state industries. The government reported that state industries, which produced 40 percent of industrial output—down from 60 percent three years earlier—showed little growth and were $200 billion in debt. Meanwhile, private companies increased their output by an astonishing 24 percent over the previous year. "State companies are just getting swamped," said Elichi Watanabe of the Asian Development Bank. "Private or basically private companies are flourishing. I think the socialist sector will just fade away."[3]

Yet, incredibly, many government leaders were clinging tenaciously to the tenets of socialism that produced decades of unmitigated failure. On July 20, 1995 *The Wall Street Journal* reported:

> As the economy moves toward capitalism, official China clings ever-more dearly to socialism, pledging to revive state industries and "achieve communism." To slow the changes, recent edicts forbid the sale of "state assets," or factories, to private investors.

We should not leave the example of China without mentioning Hong Kong. Located only a few miles from mainland China, it is densely populated and has none of the mainland's natural resources. Nevertheless, it has become a thriving center for trade, banking, and manufacturing because of its freedom. Since 1980, it has had the world's fastest-growing economy. Though containing only 405 square miles, it is now the world's eighth-largest trading nation. Per capita income in Hong Kong is higher than in Great Britain, and it's twenty times that of the People's Republic of China. And the top personal tax rate is only 15 percent.

ARGENTINA

In the 1920s Argentina had a democratic government, a literacy rate of nearly 90 percent, an extensive system of universities, and one of the world's highest credit ratings. It was the fifth most productive nation in the world. Now it is 70th and has one of the world's largest debts. In 1929 its per capita output of goods and services was four times that of Japan. Now it's only one-third.

Argentina was once widely regarded as more promising than Canada or Australia. Almost as large as India, endowed with fertile soil and two billion barrels of proven oil reserves, it faced the future with just about everything. Everything but a free economy.

Communism has never been a serious threat in Argentina, but government intervention doesn't have to be of the communist variety to be detrimental. In Argentina the government intervened in the economy on behalf of both labor and industry. It created a powerful union movement to favor workers, and it resorted to protectionism to favor local industries. Both measures made the country uncompetitive. Government muscle enabled the unions to raise labor costs beyond market levels, but the protectionism raised the cost of doing business, too. For example, in 1986 no less than 90 percent of the country's 12,000 categories of imports faced tariff or other restrictions, which added to the costs of manufacturing practically anything. Former Undersecretary of Commerce Jorge Bustamente said, "Show me the Martian who wants to invest here, and I'll show him the government regulation that guarantees he loses money."[4]

The system also made bribes and other forms of corruption inevitable. Inefficient producers were protected; waste became institutionalized.

Because of its central role in the economy, government grew. As it did, the people grew more dependent. "Individuals became accustomed to asking the state for all solutions,"[5] says Jorge Tiaca, a labor unionist. Welfare spending ballooned.

The government's efforts to finance its bloated budgets created hyperinflation, which destroyed savings and investment capital or drove them from the country. Economic and political uncertainties resulting from a succession of military coups also discouraged private investment and intensified the need for government borrowing. The nation was saddled with a huge debt and had regressed to the status of an underdeveloped country. In the words of Harvard economist Nick Eberstadt, it was "the most dramatic case of a country heading back from the First to the Third World."[6]

But in 1991 President Carlos Menem sought to rebuild Argentina's ravaged economy by turning away from the decades-old policies of government intervention. He favored deregulation, privatization of government industries, and a sound, fully convertible currency. The results were dramatic. In 1993 the economy grew 9 percent, and the annual inflation rate was down to 10 percent, compared to 4,200 percent in 1989. In 1995 inflation was down to single digits and the nation's economic growth had averaged 7 percent per year for four years.

INDIA

A democracy since becoming independent almost a half-century ago, India is a poor, large country that for decades has had nearly half of the world's food shortages. Surprisingly, despite its massive population, it has about as much arable land per capita as France—a country known for the luxuriousness of its cuisine, rather than for starvation. But India has had a government which, in the words of one authority, "has irrationally thwarted the progress of food production."[7]

In its policy of fixing food prices low to please the masses, the Indian government created powerful disincentives for farmers to produce food and distributors to market it. Price fixing also delayed adoption of new high-yielding strains of wheat and rice. Government compounded the problems of agriculture and of all industrial progress with an elaborate system of controls. Virtually all economic enterprise was smothered by a huge bureaucracy that was not only inefficient but reflected the government's xenophobic hostility to foreign capital. Fertilizer plants, oil refineries, and agricultural equipment factories for many years couldn't even be built because of the government's stubborn and doctrinaire rejection of "exploitation" by foreign investment.

When India became independent in 1947, her annual steel production was 1.2 million tons. Twenty-five years later it had risen to only 6.6 million tons despite India's abundance of iron and coal. During the same period Japan increased her steel production from less than one million tons to 106.8 million tons despite the fact she had to import both iron and coal. Japan chose a private enterprise economy while India opted for government enterprise. In 1962 Prime Minister Nehru rejected an American offer to build the Bokaro steel mill as a private venture. As a government enterprise, the Bokaro mill took eleven years to produce its first ingot.

India entered the 1990s as one of the world's poorest countries, with an annual per capita income of only $335. Its 850 million people were producing fewer exports than tiny Hong Kong with its mere 6 million people.

LIECHTENSTEIN

The people of Liechtenstein enjoy the highest per capita income in Europe and are among the wealthiest in the world. They are also among the world's least taxed; the average individual income tax is only about 6 percent. Poverty and unemployment are virtually nonexistent. Only about a dozen people are out of work. (The principality has 27,400 citizens, 61.8 square miles.)

Such success is a relatively recent achievement. Though independent since 1806, Liechtenstein as recently as World War II was "an impoverished backwater with high unemployment and more than a third of the population eking out a bare existence from the land."[8]

That the country emerged quickly from almost feudal poverty to a modern industrial nation is due largely to one man, Prince Franz Josef, who became the reigning monarch in 1938. He turned the nation to classical principles of free market economics with low taxes and little or no interference in business. As one observer put it, the guiding principle seems to be "to tread lightly where fools rush in to regulate."9

Liechtenstein is best known to Americans for its bank secrecy and easy business climate. These features have attracted so many corporations that the country now has more corporations than people. What most outsiders fail to appreciate is that Liechtenstein is fully competitive in world markets and is one of the most highly industrialized countries in the world—even more so than that part of Germany that used to be known as West Germany. Nearly 54 percent of its labor force is in industry, compared to 40 percent for the West German sector. Liechtenstein exports machines and instruments, chemical products, textiles, artificial teeth and ceramics.

"What we have tried to do," says Crown Prince Hans Adam, successor to his father, Prince Franz Josef, "is to see that the small-business man, the entrepreneur, has the opportunity to start up his business without too much interference from the state." And, he says, "Our country did not take taxes from those businesses who are doing well and give them to those who are not."10

Even with minimal taxes the state operates in the black. Its people live in relative harmony, and the country is politically stable. Prince Franz Josef died in 1989, but he had ceded all but ceremonial duties to his son five years earlier. The succession has not altered the direction of national policy. There is every indication that this tiny nation's prosperity will continue.

SWITZERLAND

Just before Liechtenstein vaulted into first place, Switzerland held the distinction of having the highest per capita income in Europe and second highest in the world. Only oil-rich Kuwait had a higher figure. The Swiss remain one of the most prosperous people in the world.

How has Switzerland, a landlocked country with almost no natural resources, achieved such prosperity? Certainly not through government power or efforts. The outstanding characteristic of Swiss government is its virtual insignificance. An article in the West German weekly *Die Zeit* says that government is so unimportant in Switzerland that most people there do not even know the name of their president.

The Swiss would much prefer to have no head of government at all. A president in office must behave accordingly.

And truly it would be a bad sign if one day most Swiss citizens could without more ado tell their president's name. It would be more troubling still if they stopped being proud not to know the name. Such ignorance is definitely a mark of distinction and a privilege of the Swiss—not shared by the unhappy Germans, miserable French and pitiable Americans for whom it is impossible to overlook their leaders. People who don't know their president's name thereby certify his utter insignificance or—more positively—his wholly harmless nature. Anyone who finds that a president causes problems gets the name in mind.

What's true of Switzerland's head of state is largely true also of the whole Swiss government. It also must act, as far as possible, as if there were no government. Idle ministers are usually more popular than those who believe they ought to do something. The best hope for a councilor who does things is that no one will notice.

There is, to be sure, little cause for concern. The Swiss government does not make waves. It seldom offends. According to a recent Zurich newspaper poll, no fewer than 85 percent of Swiss men and women are content with the regime....

What a fortunate people! And what a more-than-lucky government that is praised precisely for governing so little, with a president who wins unheard of acceptance almost incognito.[11]

SOCIALIST SASKATCHEWAN

The Canadian province of Saskatchewan had a socialist government from 1944 to 1964. After 18 years there were fewer jobs in manufacturing than in 1945—in spite of government investments of $500 million. Twelve of the twenty-two corporations established through government funds had gone bankrupt or been disposed of, and others were operating at a loss. Welfare measures, which the government expanded greatly, were to have been paid for by the profits from the government businesses. Instead, the welfare costs plus the business losses had to be paid for through taxes. More than 600 new taxes were introduced during this period, and 650 others were increased. No wonder 270,000 people left Saskatchewan.

UNITED KINGDOM

In the 1970s Great Britain—the birthplace of the Industrial Revolution—saw its economy slip to last place among the industrialized nations. Its industrial output was actually shrinking. Its gross national product, which fifteen years earlier was larger than that of West Germany, by 1975 was less than half its size. One by one virtually all of the countries of Western Europe overtook Great Britain in per capita income. Only Spain and Portugal still lagged behind her—and they were gaining.

A major news magazine, *U.S. News & World Report,* stated, "The standard of living is falling, almost day by day it seems."[12] That observation was written not by an American but by the magazine's bureau chief in London, Mr. Robin Knight, an Englishman. In *The Wall Street Journal* Vermont Royster wrote, "The standard of living of its people is lower than comparable countries in Europe, vastly lower than in the U.S. And it is a shrinking standard of living for all."[13]

Here is a list of Britain's economic woes from an article of that period in the *Chicago Daily News.*

> LONDON, England—Britain's nationalized steel industry is losing money at the rate of five million pounds—about $11 million—a week and is headed for a $550 million loss this year.
>
> The nationalized gas industry lost $97 million in its just-ended fiscal year.
>
> The nationalized railroads lost $350 million in the last year despite two major fare increases. The nationalized electric power industry lost $565 million. The nationalized coal mines lost $8.5 million. The nationalized airlines lost an estimated $22 million in the first five months of this year alone. The post office lost $675 million last year and is well on the way to duplicating the disaster again this year.
>
> Altogether the country's nationalized industries, in figures reported in the last week or so, have turned in losses exceeding $1.7 billion. All of this has contributed significantly to Britain's deepening economic crisis, an inflation rate of more than 25 percent, and the steady and frightening slump of the pound sterling to record lows on foreign exchanges.[14]

How was Great Britain ever able to attain the position it once held as the leading nation of the world? Great Britain became "great" *before* it became a welfare state. British industries were profitable *before* they became government industries. The British people were prosperous *before* their government tried to make them so. Here is a description of the rise of the British Empire from *The Mainspring of Human Progress* by Henry Grady Weaver:

> The only able Tudor was Queen Elizabeth, whose father Henry VIII, had left England so uncontrolled that it took all her energy and wit just to hold on to her throne. There was no time

left for her to rule, and never was a realm so loosely governed. She built up the British navy by doing nothing for it. She told her sea captains to act on their own responsibility and at their own expense. She wouldn't even pay for the powder and lead they used in defending England against the Spanish Armada. Her plan was to do no planning. With great firmness of character and consistency of purpose, she always decided to do nothing. By this highly intelligent means, she let her subjects found the British Empire.[15]

And what about the Industrial Revolution? The distinguished British historian Paul Johnson says:

> It is no accident that the Industrial Revolution took place in late 18th century England. It was a period of minimum government. Of all the periods of English history, indeed of European history, it was the time when government was least conspicuous and active.... As a matter of fact, the Industrial Revolution—perhaps the most important single event in human history—seems to have occurred without the English government even noticing. By the time they did it was too late; happily—otherwise they would probably have stopped it.[16]

As time passed the British government was not content with its minimal role. It tried to do more for its people. It substituted centralized planning for individual planning, government control for freedom. In a word, it turned socialistic. Public debt grew. The economy slowed, then stagnated, then fell behind as the government increased efforts to improve it. The standard of living, which had been rising without the government's efforts to elevate it, began to fall as those efforts rose.

Following World War II, a succession of Labor Party governments nationalized British industry. When Margaret Thatcher took office in 1979, the government dominated the transportation, energy, communications, mining, steel, shipbuilding and health care industries. The government also owned about 35 percent of all housing in the country.

The pride of the British welfare state was the National Health Service. Socialized medicine. In 1979 there were 750,000 Britons—a 40 percent increase in two years—on the waiting list for hernias, hemorrhoids, plastic surgery, gallstones, hip replacement, varicose veins, tonsillectomies, and other "elective" operations. In several cities "elderly patients must now wait for two years for hip replacements, and children must wait three years for tonsillectomies."[17] There were fewer hospital beds in Great Britain than in 1948 when the National Health Service began. By contrast, in the years 1900 to 1938, before the National Health Service, the number of hospital beds increased 400 percent. The government took over nearly 3000 hospitals; after more than four decades of socialized medicine, scarcely half that number remained. In 1993 more than one million patients were waiting for hospital admission, and the number waiting for more than a year was rising steeply.

British socialism was once highly touted as an example of the utopia of socialism without the violence associated with the communist varieties; but peaceful socialism, too, proved to be an economic failure. To better understand how the turn to socialism produced a national disaster for Britain, let us examine one important British industry, the coal industry.

Coal has been a vital element in the British economy since the early 19th century. Under free enterprise coal exports approached 100 million tons a year. There was plenty of coal. Even Labor Party Leader Aneurin Bevan admitted this, saying, "This island is almost made of coal; only an organizing genius could create a shortage."[18] Yet in the years following nationalization of the coal mines in 1947 there were constant shortages. Coal was rationed. From an exporter of coal, Britain actually became an importer. One observer wrote,

> You have heard the expression "Taking coals to Newcastle." Well, ships have been taking coals to Newcastle since the nationalization of the British mines and they had to land it with the assistance of barges because the derricks on the wharves were made only to handle coal outwards, not inwards. Probably nothing epitomizes the failure of the British nationalized coal industry so as those coals to Newcastle.[19]

But there is more. The real clincher in the British coal story

> lies in the fact that when the National Coal Board took over there were a few Welsh mines that were not nationalized because the board considered them so uneconomical that they would be liabilities. It left these mines in the hands of the owners to struggle with as best they could…In 1960 these were the most productive mines in Great Britain. Their workers produced more coal per man than the workers in the nationalized industry, and they received higher wages than the nationalized mines paid

their employees. These were the mines, it must be remembered, that the National Coal Board considered too difficult to work.[20]

The government response to such productivity was typical. More restrictions. If government couldn't raise its own production, at least it could lower that of the competition. In 1960 the National Coal Board decided that the licenses of the privately owned mines would be renewed only if they *cut* production by 40 percent!

Despite the dismal record of the government mines, despite the economic absurdity of forcing cutbacks at the most efficient mines, there was something so attractive about government power that the British people continued to favor its management of the coal industry. Here was an example very much like that of the small private plots in the Soviet Union outperforming the government's collective farms; the small private British mines were outperforming the government's coal mines. Yet the British government and the British people doggedly stuck with the socialist approach. Fifteen years later the government mines were still losing money, and what was happening in the coal industry was happening throughout the British economy.

Of course, the Soviet people had no choice about their political system. The same cannot be said for the British. Their undoing was their own doing. It was the direct result of deliberate, popular policies of a government chosen by the voters.

Finally, more than three decades after British socialism began, the trend was reversed, thanks to Margaret Thatcher. She began to "privatize" the nationalized companies—sell them to the public. Madsen Pirie, President of the Adam Smith Institute in London, a think tank that acted as a behind-the-scenes advisor in the administration's privatization campaign, has written,

> We follow a simple rule of thumb: If you can sell, sell it. If you can't sell the whole, sell part of it. If you can't sell any of it, give it away. And if you can't give it away, contract it out. Almost any government program can be turned around in this manner.[21]

Five years after Prime Minister Thatcher took office, the government had sold British Telecom (the world's fourth largest telephone company), British Aerospace, British Petroleum, the National Freight Company, various subsidiaries of British Rail, British Steel, and British Airways, and certain other holdings. These sales transferred almost a half million jobs to the private sector. Per capita income was now growing on a par with Japan's and well ahead of the rates in the United States, France and West Germany. And the nation's worker-productivity gains had been the highest in the developed world for the previous three years.

By 1986 the British Treasury had received $28 billion from the sale of government industries. The Thatcher Administration also sold 873,000 public houses to private individuals, bringing about $10 billion more to the treasury. Britain was easily able to repay the International Monetary Fund the almost $4 billion emergency loan she was forced to borrow in 1977. And the nation's inflation rate was only four and one-half percent.

Privatization continued. In 1987 alone it brought the treasury $20 billion.

Despite the success of the program and her own personal popularity, Prime Minister Thatcher was cautious about trying to reform the nation's socialized medicine, for political reasons. The National Health Service was the largest employer in Europe, and its one million employees—strongly unionized—were a formidable political foe. In addition, the institution remained popular with the voters, regardless of its poor performance, because they had gotten to like the idea of "free" medical care and were fearful of the cost of private alternatives. By 1988, however, something had to be done. Despite huge cash injections, the National Health Service was reported

> on the brink of chaos. Wards are closing for lack of cash or nursing staff. Doctors are complaining of run-down facilities and equipment shortages. Newspaper headlines are shouting about delayed surgery for desperately ill children and long waiting lists for others. English nurses struck for a day earlier this month—for the first time ever—and disgruntled patients are marching and suing.[22]

The waiting list for elective surgery stood at 660,000. The Kidney Patient Association estimated that 1,500 Britons were dying every year for lack of kidney treatment. Only one-third of the people needing coronary bypass operations were receiving them.

The Thatcher Administration announced the most sweeping study of the health care system in its history, followed by the introduction of various market-oriented changes. Unfortunately, Mrs. Thatcher did not remain in office long enough to see these reforms carried through.

Meanwhile, the rest of the British economy continued to prosper. Worker productivity was rising at 7.7 percent, more than any major competitor except Japan. Average worker earnings were growing at an annual rate of 8.75 percent. In 1989 *The Wall Street Journal* reported, "Private economists expect the growth rate to reach 10 percent this year, and to remain about 8 percent through 1990. Earnings in Britain's major overseas competitors, the U.S., Japan, France and West Germany, are rising at half Britain's current rate."[23]

When Margaret Thatcher left office in 1990, more than a million former tenants of public housing now owned their own homes, and 900,000 jobs had been transferred from the public to the private sector. Two-thirds of the state-owned companies had been sold or were scheduled for sale, bringing in $77 billion; and these companies, which had been costing the taxpayers billions, were now becoming profitable. British Steel, for example, a perennial loser as a government enterprise, made the *Guinness Book of World Records* in the late 1970s for the greatest loss ever suffered by a United Kingdom company; but in 1993, as a private company, it was the only profitable major steel producer in Europe. In 1995 British Steel was producing a ton of steel with 4.7 labor-hours—among the best productivity in the world—compared to 14 labor-hours in the late 1970s. The same positive effects were evident in other privatized British industries:

> Overstaffed, underperforming companies that cost taxpayer £50 million ($80 million) a week back in 1981 now *contribute* £55 million a week to the Treasury in taxes and dividends. Profits, productivity and stock prices have soared.[24]

Still, the nationalized coal mines, despite a horrible record for nearly a half century, were among the last businesses to be privatized, in 1995. Moreover, despite the obvious and ever-growing success of privatization, which by then had covered 48 major businesses and brought the government $95 billion, there was still something so attractive to the British public about government ownership of business that "public support for privatization is at its lowest in 20 years."[25]

WEST GERMANY AND JAPAN

The postwar successes of these two nations are too well known to require documentation here. There are two points, however, which deserve to be mentioned. First, the "German miracle," in which West

Germany became by far the strongest and wealthiest nation in Europe in a single generation after World War II, was not the result of American foreign aid. West Germany and Japan actually received less foreign aid from us than Great Britain and France, who had suffered far less war damage. In fact, American aid to West Germany was actually reduced *because* the Germans rejected American advice for socialistic reforms and insisted upon capitalism. Meanwhile, our government sent billions to England to subsidize socialism.

Second, the reconstruction of Japan was shaped by a man with extraordinary powers, who happened to be a staunch advocate of free enterprise, Douglas MacArthur. His biographer William Manchester, concludes he was "in effect an absolute monarch" and "omnipotent."[26] Given a free hand, MacArthur was not only responsible for the new Japanese constitution—even writing key sections himself—but laid the foundations for economic recovery. He said that from the outset as the civil administrator of Japan one of his policies was, "Encourage a free economy."[27] Later, in a letter to Prime Minister Yoshida, he summed up his political philosophy, urging "restraint and frugality in the use of the public purse," "avoidance of excessive centralization of political power," and cautioning against "paternalism in government." Then he wrote, "The preservation inviolate of the economic system based upon free, private, competitive enterprise alone maximizes the initiative, the energy and in the end the productive capacity of the people."[28]

UNITED STATES

While Japan was building a free and prosperous nation, the United States pursued policies exactly opposite to those MacArthur established in Japan. We engaged in more public spending, centralization of political power, and government paternalism. From the 1930s until 1980—when Ronald Reagan, who promised to cut back government, was elected—the voting public turned increasingly to the federal government as the means for human advancement. So the government naturally mushroomed.

In 1933 when Herbert Hoover left office, the entire budget of the federal government was less than $5 billion. In succeeding decades total spending not only exploded; it was directed to vastly different purposes. Back in 1902, for example, 87 percent of federal spending went for defense, veterans' benefits, the Post Office, and similar government functions. In 1952 these functions still accounted for 81 percent—but just twenty years later they were only 47 percent of federal outlays. Domestic programs had swollen to 53 percent of the federal budget by 1972. "Between 1952 and 1972," writes Roger A. Freeman, "as much was added to federal outlays for domestic purposes every two years as had been in the preceding 163 years."[29] In 1980 only 24 percent of the budget went for defense, and the budget was 156 percent larger than in 1972.

What did this colossal government spending for domestic purposes do for the prosperity of our country? Well, for the decade of the 1960s our economy grew at an annual rate of 4 percent—the lowest of any major industrial nation except Great Britain. For the decade of the 1970s our growth rate was only 2.5 percent. In both decades our rate was less than half Japan's, below even Iceland's, and about equal to Ireland's.

Per capita income in the United states, once the highest in the world, had fallen by 1975 to fifth place, behind Kuwait, Switzerland, Sweden and Denmark. By 1980 six more countries had moved head of us: Belgium, Canada, Luxembourg, Norway, Saudi Arabia and West Germany.

According to the Tax Foundation, real purchasing power of Americans declined every year from 1975 to 1981. In terms of constant dollars the after-tax income of the typical U.S. family in 1981 was $1,485 lower than in 1973.

In the 1960s our productivity grew at a rate of three percent per year. In the early 1970s it slipped under two percent. In the middle of the decade it averaged only one percent. In 1979 it turned negative, dropping to minus 0.9 percent. And in the second quarter of 1980 the rate plunged to minus 3.1 percent—the steepest drop since the government began issuing reports in 1947.

By any measure, then, our economic growth was diminishing as our government was expanding. Is it surprising, then, that in 1980 the country was ready to turn to Ronald Reagan with his philosophy of less government?

The American experience with expanding government was not unusual but typical. We could have learned from other countries, but we didn't. The inverse relationship between economic growth and government growth had been documented by a number of academic studies. Former U. S. Secretary of the Treasury William E. Simon summarized European studies on this subject as follows:

> Hudson Institute, Europe, has done a revealing study of
> the relationship between the growth of the public sector and real

economic growth in fourteen countries. The findings show that
overall growth is the lowest in countries where the government
sector is the largest. These findings have been supported by
other studies conducted in Britain by economists Robert Bacon
and Walter Eltis and by David Smith, using a nineteen-nation
sample during the sixties. *All such studies conclude that the
expansion of government in the Western industrial nations
results in shrinking profits, falling investment, and plunging
growth rates.*[30] (Italics added)

While America's economic performance was slipping, federal
regulations were proliferating. In the 1960s the *Federal Register,* which
publishes the direct regulations on industry, was about 15,000 pages. In
1970 it was 20,000 pages. But in the next decade it more than
quadrupled, ballooning to 87,000 pages in 1980. By comparison, the
Encyclopedia Britannica contains 32,000 pages.

Prior to 1914 the United States had only one federal independent
regulatory agency, the Interstate Commerce Commission. By the 1970s
no one—not even the office of Management and Budget—knew how
many regulatory agencies there were, let alone how many regulations.
Just one agency, the Occupational Safety and Health Administration,
issued 15,000 regulations and 100,000 safety standards in only the first
year of its existence. These took a mere 250 pages in the *Federal
Register*—but single copies of all rules, warnings, notices, explanations
and similar documents issued by OSHA in its first year would make a
stack 17 feet high. Now contemplate the restrictions of the other 86,750
pages of the *Federal Register;* it doesn't take much imagination to see
that the United States was clearly and rapidly moving away from a
free economy.

In Great Britain government control had taken the form of
nationalizing the industries. In the United States the ownership of
industries was left nominally in private hands while control of them was
being passed to Washington. The tightening network of regulations
deprived the citizenry of freedom in economic activities while enabling
government to escape the responsibilities of ownership and the
horrendous costs of the regulations. Those costs were borne by the
people through a slowing economy that meant lower profits for business
and lower real wages for workers.

All this occurred as science and technology were bringing
fabulous benefits to our way of life, benefits undreamed of only a few

decades earlier. Why as we benefited more and more from science, did we come more and more to rely on the politicians to manage our lives? Were the politicians scientists? Offhand I can think of only one in our history who was, Ben Franklin, and his scientific achievements were not the result of his government office or the political process. Why in our scientific age did we become so dependent upon anything so unscientific as political action? What was so appealing about politics that we assigned it superiority over science by subjecting even the most scientific industries to political regulation?

Were the politicians any more qualified in the arts than in the sciences? None with any artistic credentials or achievements comes to mind. Yet we extended government intervention in the arts. A 356-page pre-Reagan government guidebook lists 250 federal programs for the arts.

What was it about political power which led millions of people to believe that by possessing it those who had no particular qualifications for anything suddenly became qualified to deal with everything, no matter how diverse or highly specialized? What was the nature of this mysterious power in which so many had such confidence?

Political power, at least in the United States, is said to represent the "power of the people," but power to do what? In a democratic form of government the "power of the people" quite clearly implies the power of numbers, the "will of the majority." But the power of human numbers, even in a free society, is not the power of progress. The electric light, the telephone, the automobile were not invented by the "will of the majority." Human numbers did not create the transistor, quartz watches or Scotch tape nor raise them to prominence in our society through political action. Why is it that human numbers are regarded as so important in the American political system while human progress seems to lie outside the realm of both?

Americans are said to have "faith in democracy." But Hong Kong is extremely prosperous, and it has no democracy at all. India is extremely poor, and it has had democracy ever since becoming independent in 1947. Argentina had both democracy and prosperity when it began its economic slide toward the Third World. Liechtenstein rose from poverty to the highest per capita income in Europe under a monarchy with considerable authority. Great Britain voted for national economic suicide under democracy.

Within our own country there has always been plenty of evidence that even our respected democratic government is unable to perform economic functions as well as the free market. Just like the examples of the private agricultural plots in the Soviet Union or the coal mines in Great Britain, we have had examples of government inefficiency and incompetence side by side with superior performance by the private sector. Here are a few examples:

Postal Service

Government postal operations have been remarkably consistent in losing money and providing poor service throughout a long history. In the 19th century there were thousands of private mail carriers, whose service was "almost laughably superior"—even when they rode the same steamships and rail cars as the government postmen. One such carrier, Henry Wells, established a sizable business carrying letters between Philadelphia and New York in the 1840s for 6 cents while the government was charging 25 cents. He even offered to carry the government mail for a nickel, but the government declined. As a result of such private carriers,

> In five years private competition captured between a third and half of the American letter-carrying business, drove postage down to one-eighth of its former maximum, and brought the United States Post Office within sight of extinction.[31]

In response the government increased restrictions. When legislative prohibitions against private horse and foot posts were circumvented by carrying mail on the railroads, Congress closed that freedom loophole. When courts held that the private delivery of mail within large office buildings and between connected buildings was legal because carriers did not utilize post roads, Congress passed additional restrictions to "correct" that situation.

Since packages aren't considered mail, private companies are allowed to deliver them. How has the package delivery service of a private company, United Parcel Service (UPS), compared with that of the United States Postal Service's parcel post? Here's a candid answer by the head of the Postal Service's bulk-mail processing division:

> As a result of our poor performance, they [UPS] offered better service at better prices with less damage. While we were reading regulation books and discouraging business, they were accommodating customers.[32]

Postal Service officials admitted the breakage rate of their service was five times that of UPS. In the 1960s the government was delivering about three-fourths of all packages in the United States. By 1989 UPS had ninety percent of the business.

Furthermore, UPS had to pay taxes and still made a profit while the Postal Service did neither. In 1975 the U.S. Postal Service ran a deficit of $415 million while UPS made a $30 million profit. In 1980 the Postal Service deficit was $306 million while UPS netted $198 million. In 1985 the Postal Service lost $251 million while UPS profits were $567 million. For 1990 the UPS figure is unavailable, but the Postal Service lost more than $1,277 million. In 1995 the Postal Service found it necessary to raise the price of first-class postage to 32 cents—the tenth increase since 1971—because it had lost $1,300 million the previous year while UPS made a record profit of $943 million for the same year.

Despite postal rate increases that have outpaced inflation, postal delivery has actually gotten slower during a time when everything else in our world seems to have been moving faster. The speed of first-class service has declined 25 percent since 1960 according to the Postal Service's own measurements. The goal is 95 percent on-time delivery for first-class mail, but no city in the Postal Service's 1994 survey achieved it. According to the *Business Mailers Review,* only 82 percent of letters that were supposed to arrive in one day actually did so—down 2 percent from the previous year. And only 71 percent of letters with destinations within 600 miles arrived within two days. That's a rate of 13 miles per hour.

Perhaps the most damning evidence of Postal Service inefficiency is the fact that some federal offices hire private companies to deliver the mail. The General Services Administration unit in Atlanta, for example, has admitted it pays UPS $200,000 annually to deliver mail because of its "better service and cheaper rates."[33] GSA bulletin FPMR B-63, entitled "Reducing Mail Costs," says, "Use commercial small parcel carriers as a cheaper alternative to priority mail and U.S. Postal Service insured parcels."

Public Education

From 1946 to 1962 scores on the College Board Scholastic Aptitude Test (SAT) rose every year. Then they declined eighteen years in a row. Scores plummeted for both verbal and mathematical skills, even among the brightest groups of children.

Can it be coincidence that the decline began with the much-publicized drive by the federal government to "improve" primary and secondary education, and that test scores dropped just as consistently as federal spending rose? By 1975 federal expenditures for education were 1,500 percent greater than in 1960—and 1975 saw the largest drop ever recorded in SAT scores.

The SAT results are borne out by other tests, including the National Assessment of Educational Progress and the American College Testing Program (ACT). A report by the Hudson Institute says the decline in test scores cannot be blamed on changes in the student population, such as changes in the numbers of minority students. The percentage of minority students actually remained fairly constant during most of this period. Meanwhile, the pupil-teacher ratio dropped from 25 to 18.

While the public schools were flunking, the non-government schools were earning much better grades. In 1978 Victor Solomon, Director of Educational Affairs for the Congress of Racial Equality, testified before a senate subcommittee,

> At the same time we see…parochial and private schools, often the neighborhood Catholic school, doing an adequate job, day in and day out, in the same areas as the failing public schools.[34]

The Association of Christian Schools International reported that the scores of eighth graders in its 1,200 member schools were 12 months above the national average.

In a Dallas school district 535 new faculty members took a competency test for persons 13 years of age or older. Half of them failed. The school administrators who were tested did even worse than the teachers. But a cross-section sample of high school students from a local private school outscored the public school teachers and principals.

After a few years of minimal improvement in the early 1980s, SAT scores of public school students again started to slide. By 1991 the average score had fallen four years in a row; scores on the math portion of the test were the lowest since 1984, and scores on the verbal portion were the lowest on record. Yet the decade of the 1980s was "the most ambitious period of school reform in the nation's history," says John E. Chubb, co-author of a Brookings Institution study of America's schools. In the 1980s nearly all states passed laws ordering stiffer course requirements, and educational spending increased 30 percent beyond inflation. After studying 20,000 students, teachers and principals at 500 schools, Chubb and Stanford Professor Terry Moe concluded that "government has not solved the education problem, because government *is* the problem."[35]

In 1990 the average annual operating cost per student for kindergarten through 12th grade was $4,841 in public schools, compared to $1,902 in private schools. Yet private school seniors taking the SAT test in 1990 scored 12 percentiles higher than public school seniors. Michael Barone, author of the *Almanac of American Politics,* notes that New York City's Catholic Schools, with a central bureaucracy of 35 people, outperform the public schools with their 20,000 central bureaucrats.

On March 28, 1991 *The Wall Street Journal* reported:

> Based on the latest available comparisons, students in Catholic school beat public school students by an average of 4.5% in science, and 12.5% in reading in the three grade levels of the federal government's National Assessment of Educational Progress test.

In view of the record it is absurd that private schools must constantly fight for their independence from government regulation. Federal and state agencies unceasingly try to force them to comply with government standards for teacher qualifications, labor practices, and curricula, as the public schools do. If there is any benefit to such regulations, it is certainly not evident in the educational results of the school system where they are most comprehensively applied.

Nor has government power been effective in school desegregation. In *Phi Delta Kappan,* an educational journal, two experienced researchers, Bilione Whiting Young and Grace Billings Bress, concluded what many Americans already suspected and what other researchers have since verified: the government's powerful attempt at school desegregation has been futile, even counterproductive. Bress and Young noted that while it did little for educational minorities, "mandatory busing has *contributed* to the racial and economic *segregation* of our cities...to the extent that in many there are no longer enough white pupils to integrate."[36] (Italics added) Curiously enough, private schools—which have no mandatory busing policy—are more likely than public schools to be racially mixed, according to Chubb and Moe.

There have been hundreds, if not thousands, of studies over several decades documenting the continuing failure of public education—even studies by the government itself. A study by the U.S. Department of Education released in September 1993 says there are 90 million Americans who are "functionally illiterate," who can't read a newspaper or buy groceries without the assistance of pictures on the labels. In 1994 two and one-half million high school students graduated, and according to the U.S. Department of Education, one million of them were unable to read their diplomas.

Social Security

For years the social security system has been so poorly managed that on several occasions the government had to increase rates to ward off insolvency. The latest of these was in 1983, following which the Social Security Trust Fund is now accumulating a surplus. However, even with the lower rates that existed before 1983 young workers could obtain from private insurance more than twice the benefits of Social Security for the same cost. The much-praised 1983 "reform" may have postponed insolvency of the system, but it has only widened the discrepancy with private insurance. Now young workers are unlikely even to get back the money they put into Social Security.

> The Congressional Research Service of the Library of Congress and the Social Security Administration's own "intermediate-range" projections point to the fact that today's younger Americans will pay much more in taxes and receive less in benefits.... Those who were age 65 in 1984 will, on the average collect Social Security benefits worth more than two and one-half times the value of their contributions. Their 21-year old counterparts in 1984 can expect to receive less than 98 cents on the dollar for their contributions.[37]

These younger participants will receive no interest on all the money they have paid in and nothing to compensate for depreciation of the dollar over all those years until they retire. And by the time they retire—if not before—the system will once again be facing insolvency.

Near-term surpluses in Social Security are due to demographic factors which over the long term will reverse far more powerfully. Social Security expert Peter J. Ferrara explains:

> The "baby boom" generation is entering its prime earning years, swelling tax payments, while the relatively small generation born during the Great Depression and World War II is

entering retirement, minimizing Social Security obligations…
[But when] the baby-boom generation enters retirement, [it will
impose] enormous benefit obligations, while leaving in the work
force to pay the taxes the relatively small generation born in the
low-fertility years since the mid-1960s.[38]

Carolyn L. Weaver, Director of the American Enterprise Institute's
Social Security and Pension Project says:

> Under current projections, Social Security will run
> surpluses for the next 30 years or so, and deficits every year
> thereafter. A period of saving is thus followed by an indefinite
> period of dissaving. By the year 2050, when the baby-boom
> generation's children are entering retirement, the program is
> projected to be insolvent—despite a continuing liability on the
> order of…about $1 trillion annually in today's dollars.
> Should we have fewer babies or live a bit longer than the
> actuaries assume, the surpluses will be smaller and the reserve
> fund depleted more quickly. Should Congress take the now
> familiar route of increasing benefits or bailing out Medicare
> when there are a few extra dollars in the trust funds, the
> condition of the trust funds will be even worse.[39]

If you think we need not concern ourselves about something so far
into the future, that Social Security will be secure for many years,
consider what happened when the system was "saved" in 1977.
Congress passed a $227 billion tax increase which "Mr. Social Security,"
the venerable Claude Pepper, Chairman of the House Select Committee
on Aging, said would "strengthen the Social Security System, not just for
the immediate future, but far into the next century." The trustees of the
Social Security Trust Fund flatly proclaimed the program would be
sound till the year 2030. But in just *six years* it was again facing
bankruptcy, and the 1983 legislation was needed to "save the system."

The Social Security system has continuing problems because it
has not been accumulating reserves as true insurance or pension plans
would do. Instead it has been operating on the principle of an endless
chain letter. It disburses current revenue and always hopes to pay
current contributors with future collections from new members.
Anyone operating in this manner in the private sector would be
arrested. In 1989 recipients of Social Security were receiving along
with their monthly checks a card explaining that Social Security is not
"savings" but "a pipeline. Revenues collected by today's workers flow

into one end of the pipe, and payments to today's beneficiaries flow out the other end."

Thus the Social Security Administration does not even acknowledge that the contributor has any right to the money he pays into the system. He has no contractual claim to the premiums he pays; he has no policy, as he would with private insurance. The Supreme Court has ruled (in *Flemming v. Nestor,* 1960) that an individual has no right to the money he has paid into Social Security. His only claim is to such money as Congress may from time to time authorize for the particular classification into which he falls. And, "You should remember," says Robert J. Meyers, former Chief Actuary for the Social Security Administration, "that Congress can decrease as well as increase."[40] Which, of course, a private insurance company cannot do.

Transportation and Fuel

Here, as everywhere else, those functions performed by government are characterized by inadequacy while those performed by free enterprise are marked by abundance and efficiency. For example:

There is no shortage of airplanes built and flown by private companies, but there are frequent backups at the public airports. Are we to believe it is less difficult to build complex aircraft and operate them in the air than to arrange landing space for them on the ground?

The same situation can be observed in land transportation. There is never a shortage of private automobiles, but we never seem to have enough public highways, which are frequently overcrowded.

American private automobiles are operated on public roads with great freedom as to frequency, destination, choice of routes, time of departure, length of time an individual may drive, etc. With railroads the situation was reversed: government had come to dictate these operational options on tracks and rights-of-way under private ownership. So the results were now reversed. Instead of overcrowding on tracks and inadequacy of routes—as is the case with highways—the railroads had more trackage than they could use; for many years they tried to pare unprofitable routes. Meanwhile, government control of train operations created a "shortage" of rail transportation; the government made it so uneconomical that most of the industry disappeared in a few decades. But after substantial deregulation in 1980 and 1982, the railroads staged a remarkable comeback. They reversed years of declining freight haulings and now carry more freight than 35 years ago, when they had four times as many employees but were less efficient. Analysts report the industry is in better shape financially than it's been for a very long time.

Federal involvement in the oil industry is also illustrative. In all the decades before we had an energy department in Washington the United States never experienced a peacetime shortage of oil. According to Yale Brozen, Professor of Business Economics at the University of Chicago, the real reason for the long lines at gasoline stations in 1974 was not the Arab oil embargo but our federal government. Says Professor Brozen:

> All during the period of the embargo, crude oil and other petroleum products in storage kept increasing.... It came from Canada, Indonesia, Venezuela, and Nigeria.... The oil companies did a massive and heroic job of redirecting world trade.... But the Federal Energy Office overemphasized heating-oil production at the expense of gasoline, then underallocated gasoline to metropolitan areas and overallocated to rural areas. City residents wasted gasoline by driving far into rural areas to fill their tanks.[41]

In 1995 a former deputy administrator of the Federal Energy Administration admitted that the energy shortages of the 1970s were "a direct result of the government's price and allocation controls."[42]

After the establishment of a federal energy agency—which was supposed to achieve energy independence—the percentage of oil that we import more than doubled. Meanwhile, West Germany and Japan, which had to import all of their oil, did not experience the empty gas pumps, waiting lines at gas stations, and odd-even-day rationing that took place in the United States in 1979.

By 1980 the American people were finally ready to elect a president who unequivocally promised them less government rather than more. They got a mixed bag. They got somewhat less government regulation but even more government spending.

When Reagan left office in 1988 the *Federal Register* was "only" 53,000 pages, down 39 percent from when he took office but still more than two and one-half times its size in 1970. The national debt, meanwhile, had ballooned to $2.6 trillion, from $914 billion.

The so-called "Reagan Revolution" was a disappointment to many who had expected dramatic, across-the-board reductions in the federal government. Realistically, it was probably not politically possible to do much more than Reagan did. Unlike Margaret Thatcher, whose party controlled sizable parliamentary majorities, Reagan had to deal with congresses controlled by the opposition party, the Democrats. As he himself used to point out, only Congress could appropriate money, not the executive branch. And Congress showed far less enthusiasm for trimming government and far more for pleasing factions favoring government regulations and programs. In 1982 President Reagan agreed to a $98 billion tax increase in return for Congress' promise to cut three dollars in spending for every one dollar in new taxes—but far from cutting spending as promised, Congress spent an additional $200 billion. Between 1982 and 1989 there were a total of five "budget summit agreements" between the president and Congress, and in every case Congress failed to cut spending as promised even though tax increases were included in four of the agreements.

While senators and congressmen are sensitive to the local political effects of economic regulations, they are far more sensitive to social programs. These can directly impact far greater numbers of voters. The result was that even under the Reagan Administration a far higher percentage of government spending went for social programs than was the case in France under Francois Mitterand's socialist government, which included communists as well as socialists in its ministries.

In an article in *The Wall Street Journal* Mr. Maurice Cranston of the London School of Economics drew a distinction between structural socialism and functional socialism. Structural socialism fits the standard definition: government ownership of the means of production. For a definition of functional socialism, Mr. Cranston quoted from Janet's "Le Socialisme": "Any doctrine claiming that the state has the right to alter the inequality of wealth existing among men, and to introduce an equilibrium by taking away from those who have and giving to those who have not." Under this definition the United States is noticeably more socialistic than Francois Mitterand's government, an example of structural socialism. Mr. Cranston said:

> The French give proportionally more to defense and only a fraction of the U.S. percentage to health and income transfers. It is these social and equalizing purposes that account for the fact that the American taxpayer carries a heavier burden than the French.

Noting that Mrs. Thatcher had denationalized various British industries, Mr. Cranston concluded that it is easier to reverse structural socialism than the functional variety:

> Even a government that is fully aware of what is
> happening and has the will to change it is to a large extent
> trapped by the momentum of flow. We can see in America today
> that too many interests rally around the handouts, too many
> bureaucratic habits have accumulated and too much public
> information is controlled by adherents of left-liberal ideology
> for the tide to be turned swiftly.[43]

The "momentum of flow" has not been stopped. The tide has not
been turned. Federal spending actually accelerated during the
administration of a president dedicated to reducing it. So much of the
budget is "uncontrollable." There are so many spending commitments
from previous congresses, so many "entitlements," so many
expenditures that are politically untouchable. Much has been made of
the large defense buildup during the Reagan years, yet when he left
office defense accounted for only about one-third of the federal budget.
So-called "entitlements" accounted for 47 percent of the budget.

Federal spending increased further under the Bush Administration with domestic spending accelerating most dramatically. In
constant dollars the average annual domestic spending increase under
George Bush was fifteen times larger than it was under Ronald Reagan
and nearly three times larger than under Jimmy Carter. By 1992 federal
spending for "entitlements" was twice as large as spending for national
defense.

According to the Congressional Budget Office, the budget plan
President Clinton presented in early 1995 would have increased total
government spending by $328 billion in five years—with 97.3 percent
of that increase due to higher domestic spending. The CBO projected
that domestic spending would grow 91 percent faster than needed to
offset inflation.

Most Americans will be shocked to learn that their government,
once renowned for its capitalism, has become more socialistic than that
of Francois Mitterand, the president of France for fourteen years, until
1995, who openly proclaimed his socialism. Still fewer will understand
how it got that way—just as few understand how government
regulations with the best of intentions could virtually strangle the
American economy.

The sad fact is that most Americans have never really understood
the American system. They were fortunate enough to have been born
into it and benefited from it, but they didn't really understand it and so

couldn't defend it. And they have been gradually losing it without ever knowing why, many without even realizing it was disappearing. That is the way freedom generally disappears. It is lost a little at a time, traded for good intentions that are to be achieved by government.

The wave of welfarism and government interventionism that swept America from the 1930s on was variously called by such names as the New Deal or the New Frontier. The names conveyed the idea of newness, of something never existing before. The word "progressive" became a favorite for describing these schemes as the mode of the future. President Kennedy used to talk about "getting America moving again," implying that the move would be forward. Then there was the Great Society—as though greatness was to be created by government. But there was nothing new about the governmental approach behind these slogans; it was a throwback to policies as old as government itself, policies that failed to move even primitive societies forward, much less make them "Great." Welfarism, economic controls, even government regulation had all been tried countless times over the centuries. King James I of England, for example, regulated even such small items as pins; he made it a penal offense to sell pins other than those "doubled-headed, and their head soldered fast to the shank, and well smoothed; and the shank well shaved; and the point well and round-filed and sharpened."

Our government merely attempted to apply these age-old methods to a society in which science and human enterprise were bringing unprecedented progress independent of government efforts, by means of the freedom available. As government grew, freedom was displaced. Voters traded it for promises, hopes and handouts. Never understanding how freedom actually worked, neither the public nor political leaders could understand why other countries began moving ahead of us.

Since the policies government pursued were not new, neither were the results. It was just one more rerun of history, this time in a modern setting. While the past offers ample evidence of such governmental failures, it also furnishes evidence of the success of freedom. Here are three historical examples.

SPAIN PRIOR TO 1700

I cannot improve on this succinct and dramatic description by Rose Wilder Lane in *The Discovery of Freedom*. So I quote it directly:

> For almost eight hundred years, human energy in Spain
> had produced such an abundance of food, comforts and luxuries

as the world had never before imagined. After Granada fell, human energy continued to operate in Spain and through Spain upon the New World and Europe, for two more generations. The third generation no longer knew that men are free, and energy weakened in Spain. The fifth generation could no longer support the government, and their children died of starvation.

In 1699 the British Minister to the Spanish Court could not buy bread in Madrid. Like everyone else, he had to ask the Government for bread. The Corregidor gave him an order for bread, and he was obliged to send men conspicuously armed with "long guns" two leagues from the city to get bread and bring it back, for only armed men could protect bread in the streets of the capital of Spain.

Twenty thousand starving peasants came into Madrid that day, from the country where the plows were rotting in the weedy fields.[44]

THE DUTCH REPUBLIC, 1579-1750

This tiny nation with few natural resources, and even land in short supply, became Europe's greatest economic power through commerce on the seas. Holland was the center of world trade, buying commodities all over the globe and redistributing them according to market demands. By 1625 it was engaged in more shipping than the rest of the world combined.

The economic opportunities of Holland's free trade attracted so many people that by 1685 half of its population was immigrants. Dutch business helped to foster one of history's greatest eras of art. Merchants, shopkeepers, even peasants bought paintings for pleasure and for investments. Rembrandt, Hals, Vermeer, Steen, Ruysdael, Van Goyen, Hobbema and deHooch emerged here. Besides these master painters there were such famous thinkers as Descartes, Huygens, Leeuwenhoek, Spinoza and Grotius—to whom we are indebted for the first formulation of the doctrine of freedom of the seas, for the unhindered flow of Dutch trade. Many of these artists and thinkers were themselves involved in business. Jan Steen operated an inn and was a brewer. Van Goyen was an auctioneer, an art appraiser and sold tulips. Vermeer supported himself more from his business as an art dealer than from his painting. The philosopher Spinoza was a lens grinder.

Because of its sea-based economy, Holland produced the best ships, maps, telescopes, spectacles, and navigational instruments. Dutch investments, ideas and industry went wherever their ships went, enriching the far corners of the world with knowledge of building canals, reclaiming land, clearing forests, rotating crops, opening mines, and providing capital for these endeavors.

In writing about this nation Robert A. Peterson notes,

> Unlike many other nations, her prosperity was not built on military adventurism or expropriation from others, but on an underlying philosophy of freedom.... [T]he Dutch allowed only the most limited of governments. The new government was limited to protecting life and property."[45]

ANTWERP, 15TH AND 16TH CENTURIES

Before Columbus discovered America there existed a thriving commercial center, like Switzerland or Hong Kong today but even more prosperous by contemporary comparison. Antwerp doubled its population between 1450 and 1500 and doubled it again by 1560. In a world that had not yet seen the affluence created by science and technology—the Industrial Revolution was three centuries away—Antwerp nevertheless displayed an abundance of English cloth, Portuguese spices, German silver and copper, and countless other commodities. Visitors to the city were overwhelmed by the opulence, the variety, the seemingly endless supplies of material goods. What was the secret of such affluence?

> The trade in Bruges had been free in comparison with the restrictions prevalent in other cities of the Middle Ages, but in comparison with the absolute freedom enjoyed by foreign merchants in Antwerp, Bruges seems medieval.... In Antwerp...in the city's prime there were practically no restrictions on the trade in money, precious metals, and bills. The city authorities gave trade all the freedom possible, and such regulations as existed originated almost entirely with the merchants themselves.... In the course of four decades Antwerp became a trading center such as Europe has not witnessed before or since.[46]

THE UNIVERSAL BASIS OF PROSPERITY

Wherever we look, whether in America, Europe or Asia, whether in our own time or hundreds of years ago, whatever progress we find within the society is the result of something other than political action, regardless of the form of government. There is something universal about governments, whether they be monarchies, democracies, communist dictatorships, or anything else, that is inimical to progress; it's not the form of government but the very nature of government that is the limiting factor. The relatively free countries have been more progressive because they have had less of this universal limiting factor. Their progress has come from the degree of its absence—freedom. Unless one believes that an absence, a void, can produce material wealth, then there is some other process which produces it, a process that doesn't operate at the political level or in the presence of government action.

Yes, freedom "works," but why? Freedom is the state of political liberty, the absence of government restraint or interference. Strictly speaking, freedom doesn't cause progress; it's a condition of it, a necessary condition, but the actual process is something else. It's a process that is universal to all human advancement, whether in agriculture, industry, commerce or anything else. When a man understands this process, he will know why governments can't perform it. And when he knows what is universal to all governments, he will know why they can only limit it.

Chapter Two
THE PATH OF PROGRESS

ORIGINS

Man is the product of millions of years of evolution. Millions of genetic changes have been made along the way. Yet none of these occurred simultaneously throughout the species or in even a majority of its members. Each genetic change began as a singular divergence from other members of the species. Through reproduction and natural selection the alteration eventually became widespread.

Somewhere in man's evolutionary past he began to discover ways of satisfying his needs other than by physical prowess. While other animals continued to develop greater strength and speed, man's mental development made it unnecessary for him to compete on their terms. Thinking became the distinctive mode of man's survival and the key to what we call progress.

The evolution of human ideas has followed the same pattern as the evolution of the human form. Every intellectual advance has begun with one man's thinking diverging from that of other men in the same way that biological advances have begun through individual genetic divergence. New ideas do not originate throughout the species or in a majority of its members. Every idea begins in the mind of some lone individual who makes a mental connection which others did not make. Through communication, ideas are "reproduced" for others; and through the exercise of human choice, selected ideas eventually become widespread.

Where survival depends upon physical struggle, numerical strength is important. Even lesser animals utilize the advantage of their numbers in fighting. A pack of wolves, for example, can bring down an animal they would have no chance of conquering if they hunted separately. But once man began to live by the productive power of his mind, his survival and advancement depended upon a process to which numerical strength was no longer relevant. Fighting is an external activity that can be done cooperatively, but thinking is an internal process that must be done alone. No massing of human numbers, no collective action can make the mental connections within an individual's brain which constitute thinking.

THE CRUCIAL IDEA

All of the progress we think of as human civilization has occurred in less than one percent of the time man has inhabited the earth. Man has been around for upwards of a million years, but civilization began only little more than 10,000 years ago. All of the men who lived in the first 99 percent of human history were unable to come up with the one idea which was to become the springboard for human progress, the idea which lead to so many others. This crucial idea, which more than any other made civilization possible, was the invention of agriculture. It happened in the Fertile Crescent of the Middle East, near the ancient town of Jericho, the oldest city of which we have any record.

The agricultural revolution relieved man of the necessity of spending all his time just to obtain food. Now he could even build up food surpluses. He had time to develop various crafts, simple technology. Cultivation allowed—even required—man to settle, which meant he could not only accumulate goods but, at least as important, he could plan ahead and make them for future use. The nomad could do neither; he simply couldn't carry such things. Permanent settlement, a result of agriculture, was a prerequisite for the advance of civilization.

But agriculture meant still more. Among tribes living by hunting and gathering there was previously no incentive for a large-scale interaction of human efforts. Exactly the opposite. It was easier for small scattered tribes to sustain themselves since large concentrations of people would quickly exhaust the available food. By vastly increasing the amount of food that could be obtained from a given land area, agriculture permitted not only permanent settlement but greater population density. Cities could now develop. Large numbers of people living closely together led to the specialization of labor and the development of commerce. Under these conditions men were able to undertake large and increasingly complex projects, such as the building of fortifications for defense or canals for irrigation.

How did the invention of agriculture come about? Did an entire society, or a majority of its members, suddenly receive a flash of insight and decide to commit themselves to some new method of survival? Hardly likely. There must have been someone who mentally connected his observations of plants in such a way as to conclude they sprouted from seeds. We don't know the circumstances of his thinking or who he was, but he realized something that no man in the 99 percent of human existence which preceded him had known. No doubt his only concern was filling his own belly, but others learned from him. They and all mankind that followed benefited from his selfish pursuit. Like agriculture, every other human achievement has come from individuals using their minds for their own interests.

MAN BECOMES A MAKER

Two million years ago a predecessor of man—not yet man— discovered how to produce a rudimentary tool by striking a stone to give it a sharp edge. The shaping of a stone was a demonstration not only of skill but of foresight. This early thinker prepared the stone for future use. To do so, he had to grasp the cause-and-effect relationship of his actions in shaping the stone, but he also had to think across time. He had to mentally connect his present activity with the prospect of future gain, when the tool would be employed. No other animal had a brain that could do that. It was man's ability to think which enabled him to elevate his existence beyond that of the animals. The production of material values is the basic demonstration of that ability. Crude stone tools, for chopping and cutting, were the first examples, or at least the earliest examples of which we have record.

For at least the next million years this basic invention remained unchanged. The next significant advance in tool making is one which Professor George R. Stewart ranks with the steam engine or the airplane.

> It was the first example of a basic idea of manufacturing. It could not have happened very well by accident. I cannot see either how it could have evolved slowly over centuries, bit by bit. The simplest way to explain such a discovery is to credit it to the creative moment which comes to the gifted individual.
>
> This individual's tribe, we may assume, had fire-hardened wooden spears, and also used sharp stone points for scrapers or knives. In a brilliant flash he saw the two combined into something new under the sun—the heaviness and sharpness of stone joined with the length and lightness and strength of wood.
>
> The idea itself was not enough. Afterward he had to work out some way actually to fasten stone point to wooden shaft. This again did not happen slowly over the course of centuries. The mere idea would not be passed from one generation to another. So we almost need to assume that the original discoverer worked out the practical side....
>
> Anyone looking back from modern times at what seems to him this very simple implement may be inclined to pooh-pooh it. But in it lay all the idea of the most complicated modern machines, built up by joining hundreds and thousands of parts.[1]

Thereafter man began to make better tools, tools with sharper edges, tools of different types for special needs. For example, he developed the harpoon, then the barbed harpoon. The most advanced tool of primitive man, developed much later, was the bow and arrow. Of this, Professor Stewart writes:

> It is difficult to see any series of developments by which it could have evolved bit by bit. There were not even many materials at hand to suggest a bow. The tribesmen must have learned about thongs and the tying of knots to be able to fasten spearhead to shaft, but a much stronger and longer thong was needed for a bowstring. And a springy stick was hardly part of the common stock; a spear shaft should be stiff, not limber. So again, as with the spear itself, the simplest way out is to suppose the sudden flash in the creative mind.[2]

In all this time man was still a hunter and a forager. He lived by what he could take from nature. The tools he made only improved his ability to take what he needed. But with the invention of agriculture man was able to produce food, not merely take what he found. He shifted from a "taker" to a "maker" of his own sustenance. In this respect he was now markedly different from other forms of life, a reflection of his unique mental development. Every other organism sustains itself by being a "taker." Man alone is a "maker."

The production of food depended upon the same kind of mental process as the production of the earliest stone tools, only greater in degree. Man again had to grasp cause-and-effect relationships, first between the seed and the plant and then between his own actions and their result. And he had to act for a gain well into the future. A stone tool might be used within a matter of days, but it took far longer before a man could reap a harvest from the seeds he planted.

Agriculture marks the beginning of civilization because it marks the beginning of production as a way of life. The production of food was the basic step, but others quickly followed. Men now began to produce many other things which they would not have used or could not have carried with them as nomads.[3] They made clay pots, bricks, permanent dwellings. They made heavy stone implements for grinding the wheat and baskets for carrying and storing it. The weaving of baskets led to the weaving of cloth. Men were learning to utilize more materials and were reshaping them more and more radically in order to make them useful. In short, men were becoming increasingly productive.

UNEXPECTED HARVEST: IDEAS CROSS-FERTILIZE, MULTIPLY

One advance led to others. A progressive idea by one man was not inimical to the progress of other men but seemed to create conditions enabling them to advance even further. Though men were simply pursuing their own interests, their achievements benefited others in ways which were not intended and could not have been foreseen. Innovations created secondary effects. Ideas interacted in unexpected ways. Often the combining of seemingly unrelated ideas would provide a practical and intellectual base upon which some new idea would be pyramided.

Grain was grown for the seeds, but farmers found themselves with plenty of straw. This could be woven into mats, used as fodder for some animals, or used for bedding. Sheep and goats were the earliest domesticated food animals, but their coats furnished the material with which men first learned to weave cloth. The earliest cloth was probably plaited from goat hair.

The domestication of animals for meat quickly led men to another source of food—milk. Then from milk itself came a whole string of unexpected and valuable products: curds, butter, cheese and, much later, casein paints and glues.

The keeping of animals and the raising of grain worked together in ways which no one expected. Manure aided the growth of crops, and the extra grain enabled man to feed the animals. But there were even more surprising and far-reaching consequences. The domestication of food animals led to the domestication of draft animals. This achievement, in turn, led to an invention by which these animals could be used to multiply agricultural output many times over: the plow.

Though this was one of man's most important inventions, it was not the only consequence of the draft animal. In the remarkable way in which ideas build and branch in more than one direction, another supremely important invention grew from the use of the draft animal: the wheel.

Agriculture was invented more than once: in Thailand not long after its occurrence in the Middle East, and at least once later in the New World. But the plow and the wheel were invented only once, because the other agricultural inventors lacked the draft animal. Incredible as it seems, in view of their many splendid achievements, the Incas of Peru and the Aztecs of Mexico cultivated maize and potatoes for centuries without the plow and built magnificent cities, even roads and bridges, without knowing the wheel.

The wheel was invented for transportation, apparently by someone in what is now southern Russia, but other people found a host of new applications for it. Again a new idea by one man proved to be a base for diverse and unpredictable advances by others. The wheel was turned into an instrument for making pottery, another for grinding wheat. The principle of the wheel led to the ancient bow-lathe. And the engineers of Sumer and Assyria used the wheel to develop a pulley system for drawing water.

The multiple effects of new inventions were not confined to their practical applications. While new inventions led to others, they also led to something else: theoretical science. "Every stage in the domestication of plant and animal life," says Dr. Jacob Bronowski, "requires inventions which begin as technical devices and from which flow scientific principles."[4] He illustrates as follows:

> The most powerful invention in all agriculture is, of course, the plow. We think of the plow as a wedge dividing the soil. And the wedge is an important early mechanical invention. But the plow is also something much more fundamental: it is a lever which lifts the soil, and it is among the first applications of the principle of the lever.[5]

In this matter settled agriculture created the technology from which all physics, all science grew.

In the same way that new inventions were often applied in unexpected ways, the mental process men were employing in itself began to be applied in an unexpected way. Just as men found they could obtain things from nature through the use of their minds, they found they could obtain things from each other by the same process. This was the beginning of commerce, of economic exchange. It followed from the specialization of the various crafts.

After the invention of the potter's wheel, pottery making became an occupation of specialists. Other crafts, too, were becoming more complicated. Metalwork from the very beginning was beyond the ordinary farmer. Even farming itself was becoming more elaborate.

Specialists in each of these lines of work found they could obtain what others were producing by offering products of their own specialty in return. They obtained what they wanted from others by being "makers," not "takers," by producing for indirect gain. In this respect they were using their minds in the same indirect manner as their forebear who chipped the first stone tool. He made it because it enabled him to get something else which he wanted, namely food. The specialists made artifacts because these enabled them to trade for things which others produced. The stone tool maker fashioned his product to get what he wanted from nature; they fashioned theirs to get what they wanted from other men.

Like the tool maker, who produced for his own self-interest, the specialist craftsmen and farmers produced and traded for their self-interest. They entered into trades with each other only when they thought they could gain. If a farmer didn't think it was to his advantage to exchange some of his excess grain for a fancy clay pot or a metal tool, he wouldn't do so. After all, men had gotten along without those things from time immemorial. He would have, too, unless he thought he could better his condition by trading for them.

The craftsman, of course, wouldn't trade his pots or tools unless he, too, could gain. If he couldn't trade his product for at least as much grain as he could have raised by spending his time farming instead, he would probably give up his craft and return to farming. After all, that's what he was doing before he became a craftsman.

Everyone, then, was using his mind in choosing occupations and transactions to best serve himself. But to get others to do business with him, he had to appeal to their *minds*; he had to offer something they considered in *their* interests. A transaction, therefore, would occur only when it was *mutually* advantageous. When people invented such things as stone tools, the plow and the wheel, they acted for their own interests and yet incidentally benefited others. Now people were trading for their own interests—and yet incidentally benefiting those who traded with them.

Everyone could perform the work he did best and through it obtain that which others could do better and probably preferred to do. No doubt the farmers preferred to work in the fields rather than in crafts with which they were unfamiliar. The craftsmen, too, preferred their specialties. So people were both better off and more content than they otherwise would have been. Civilization was advancing because people were applying their minds more and more to the world around them and to their dealings with each other. Brute force couldn't have invented agriculture or the wheel, nor could it have brought the prosperity that resulted from specialization of labor and economic exchange.

CONTINUITY THROUGH THE CENTURIES

All human progress has occurred in the same manner as those early advances. In the same way that civilization began at Jericho with an idea—agriculture—it has continued to grow as men's ideas have grown. What we see is the visible evidence of civilization; we don't see the invisible process of thinking that created it. We see the cities, the skyscrapers, the machines, the luxuries; but everything man makes—just as with the earliest stone tools—he makes because he thinks.

Because of the way ideas are built upon each other, it is sometimes assumed that civilization just "takes off" once it gets started, as though the process becomes more or less automatic. But there is nothing automatic about it. We have seen the progression of early civilization, how ideas developed in a logical sequence, but their continuation at any point was never inevitable. Every later step in the sequence was just as dependent as the first upon someone conceiving a new thought. The domestication of food animals didn't automatically lead to the draft animal; whole civilizations, such as the Incas, arose having the former but not the latter. Many peoples adopted the wheel but never progressed to certain applications of it, such as the pulley. When no mind was able to think of the next advance, the sequence stopped.

From the manner in which a whole culture seems to advance, with many new ideas working together in complex and complementary ways, it is sometimes easy to lose track of the singularity of thinking. Regardless of the multiplicity of consequences an idea may have, regardless of how widely others in society may accept it or react to it or benefit from it, every idea originates in the mind of one man. No matter how complex and advanced the culture, no matter how educated or otherwise select a group of people may be, they can never perform collectively that crucial function which takes place silently within the individual mind.

Throughout history the line of progress has been continued by creative individuals, men who built upon previous knowledge, extended it, combined it in new ways, or opened up totally new fields to human understanding. We are as indebted to men such as Cyrus McCormick and Henry Ford, for inventing the reaper and mass-producing the automobile, as earlier civilizations were to the individuals who invented the plow and the wheel. Though the process of thinking has become increasingly complicated, its nature remains the same, whether for the simplest practical idea or the most profound theoretical insight.

When John B. Tytus of Armco Steel introduced the continuous rolling of wide-strip steel in the 1920s, he was performing a mental operation not unlike that of the individual who first attached a wooden handle to a stone tool. That primitive mentally connected two separate bits of knowledge to produce something new. Tytus, the son of a paper manufacturer, mentally connected his knowledge of steel with his memory of huge rolls of paper emerging from his father's mill. That mental connection, though not a strikingly profound one, was an idea that had never occurred to anyone else. It was a big step forward for the steel industry.

In the same way that some thinker thousands of years ago discovered how to use copper, with consequent benefit to the rest of mankind, Charles Martin Hall in the 19th century discovered the secret which led to the everyday use of aluminum throughout the world.

The wheel was invented for ground transportation, but, as we have seen, it was adapted to serve other purposes, ancient and modern. Robert Fulton, in still another adaptation of this basic device, combined the paddle wheel with an engine to provide a means of water transportation—the steamboat.

When Elias Howe constructed his first sewing machine, he had to grasp the cause-and-effect relationships involved in assembling materials in a specific way so that they would serve a new purpose. But that was the same kind of mental operation the maker of the first bow-and-arrow had to perform.

Our complicated, advanced civilization hasn't changed the fact that progress depends upon thinking—and that means the individual mind. Things such as the electric light and the telephone, which are probably as representative of our civilization as pottery and the plow were of ancient cultures, are far more complex; yet they can still be traced to the minds of single men, such as Thomas Edison and Alexander Graham Bell. Everything we have, everything that characterizes our high standard of living, we still owe to that basic mental process which produced every advance since man began to walk upright.

Though human progress has always depended upon the individual, we have increasingly structured society toward mass action. Since thinking is inherently an individual process, we are obviously orienting our culture to some other process. We are increasing the number of issues determined collectively through political action and decreasing the number that the individual can decide by his own thinking. We have given the majority increasing power to stifle the individual (and the mind), and we look upon the participation of the masses in ever-more-powerful political action as a *progressive* development! When all human advances have come from a small minority of thinkers, why is there such optimism about entrusting our future to the "wisdom" of the majority? The majority—even a select majority—have never come up with a new idea. In fact, they have usually been slow to accept or even recognize one when faced with it.

The Wright Brothers' first flights weren't considered newsworthy even in their own hometown. Only three newspapers in the nation bothered to mention them.

In England Darwin was ridiculed for his work on evolution, which even the scholars of the prestigious Linnaen Society failed to appreciate. The annual report of the society's president stated:

> The year which has passed…has not, indeed, been marked by any of those striking discoveries which at once revolutionize so to speak, the department of science on which they bear.[6]

Ignaz Semmelweiss was hounded out of Vienna and went insane because he couldn't convince doctors to wash their hands when "cadaveric material" on them was the source of fatal infections in patients. Fearing the ridicule of fellow astronomers, Copernicus delayed publishing his work until the very end of his life—the first printed copy was brought to him on his deathbed—but the mere one thousand copies printed never even sold out and went unnoticed for fifty years.

When Charles Kettering offered General Motors the plans for an electric self-starter to replace the hand crank on automobiles, the company called for expert opinions from General Electric, Westinghouse, and a German electrical trust.[7] These experts unanimously concluded it wouldn't work.

A century ago when the electrical genius Nicola Tesla revealed to the world his ideas on alternating current, he encountered almost universal opposition from the leaders of science and industry, who favored direct current. Lord Kelvin, the famous English scientist, came out flatly against the Tesla concept. The great Thomas Edison even tried to get it outlawed. But though the vast majority of experts failed to grasp the worth of the new system, one individual did and acted accordingly. George Westinghouse bought Tesla's ideas and hired him to supervise

the construction of new dynamos, motors, and transformers, which led
to electric power development throughout the world. Tesla's inventions
permitted the long-range transmission of electricity—not feasible with
direct current—and they remain the basis for power transmission even
today. Few scientific or technological advances would have come into
being if they had required majority approval, even a majority of scientists
or men of the relevant industry.

THE ROLE OF SELF-INTEREST

Whoever chipped the first stone tool, or planted the first seed, or
made the first wheel did so for his own self-interest. He saw how he
could benefit from his idea, so he acted upon it. Thinking is an individual process—and it is motivated by individual satisfaction. The two
go together: thinking is the means; the individual's own interests, the
purpose.

In the same way those early thinkers employed their minds for
their own gain, succeeding men achieved further progress in the same
manner. Their thinking, of course, was more complex and their gains not
always so immediate, but the intellectual nature of their advance and its
motivation were the same.

Not every thinker's interests were the same. But that was always
true. The first tool maker and the first agriculturist had the same interest,
namely food, but the inventor of the wheel had a different concern. He
was simply trying to make it easier for himself to move things. In
addition to food and convenience, the progressive ideas of later men
have been motivated by money, comfort and various other individual
concerns. Copernicus, a priest, seems to have had no worldly ambitions
at all, his only interest apparently being truth. But whatever their
concerns, all thinkers have pursued what they regarded as their interests,
their own satisfaction.

Elias Howe deliberately set out to make a fortune. As a machine-
shop apprentice, he overheard his boss and some visitors arguing about
the possibility of inventing a sewing machine. A large fortune was
mentioned if it were possible. The fortune didn't come easily for Howe.
It took him five years to hit on the key idea, an eye in the head of a
needle which made an interlocking stitch with a second thread. But
success was still a long way off. After loss of his financial backer and a
string of other disappointments in America, Howe decided to pursue
his idea in England. There he was so destitute he had to pawn his

clothes for cab fare to take his ailing wife to the dock so she could return home. Later he had to borrow the money to visit her on her deathbed. Then he had to fight a string of lawsuits against infringement on his patent. In spite of all the obstacles Howe persevered, and in the end he made his fortune.

A century ago Charles Martin Hall, a student at Oberlin College, heard his chemistry professor say a fortune would be made by anyone devising an economical method of extracting aluminum from bauxite clays. Hall set out to do just that, and he succeeded. By the time he died some thirty years later, he had received 23 million dollars in royalties.

Whatever their interests, the men who advanced the human race created their own satisfactions. There was no one from whom they could have taken them. From whom could the first farmer have taken the secret of agriculture or Charles Martin Hall the secret of aluminum? From whom could the first stone tool maker have taken his achievement or Edison his light bulb? Such men were exploiters of nature, not of other men.

Edison, Hall, Howe, Fulton and others like them amassed fortunes, the money coming from other men. But what other men received in return was of *greater* value to them. Otherwise they would have kept their money. Nobody was forced to buy light bulbs, aluminum articles, sewing machines or steamboat tickets. Men had gotten along without these things from time immemorial. They would have continued to do so unless they thought they could improve their condition by purchasing them. Like the early men who traded for clay pots, copper tools and other primitive items, people were now trading for more sophisticated products because they found it *in their interests* to do so. Buyers, like the inventors, were using their minds for their own personal satisfaction. Both producers and consumers were acting for their own aims, yet each was benefiting the other. If not, there would have been no sales. The fortune that went to Elias Howe and the $23 million that Charles Martin Hall received were not measures of their exploitation of other men but rather measures of the benefits others received from them.

So it is with the fortunes of all producers in a free society. Far from being the enemies of the consumer, those making the largest fortunes are those who incidentally provide the greatest benefits to others. John D. Rockefeller, who made a fabulous fortune through his Standard Oil Company, did so by offering people values. In *The Enterprising Americans* John Chamberlain writes:

Just why the first industrial giant should have been so hated is a mystery if the question is tackled from the standpoint of the consumer. Buyers always liked the company's product—they proved it by rushing to substitute petroleum kerosene for the old coal-oil and whale-oil illuminants. And buyers did not have any particular reason to complain of Standard's pricing policy; not only did kerosene cost less than the older fluids, but it had to meet the competition of the Welsbach gas burner and Mr. Edison's carbon-filament electric light bulb.[8]

Chamberlain adds that "Standard Oil could not have imposed a lighting monopoly even if it had tried," despite the fact that at its peak it controlled ninety percent of the industry.

In appealing to the consumer's self-interest Rockefeller and other productive men relied on the buyers' minds to recognize the value of their products in comparison with any alternative available. In such a system the consumers live by their own minds just as do the producers. Thus does a free society become a society of men of the mind, a society where all transactions are by choice rather than by force. In a free society all men are at liberty to pursue their own interest, but no one can compel anyone to deal with him in any way, as buyer, seller, employer, employee, consumer, producer, or any other way. All relationships are only by the voluntary consent of the participants.

The world has not yet seen a totally free society, but 19th century America came closest to it. Enormous fortunes were made by some; but whenever they were made without force, by men living by their minds and dealing with others on the same basis, such fortunes always brought corresponding values to other people. Thus there was a general advance in the standard of living throughout society. A rich, complex, modern society emerged in the same way as the first primitive civilization, by people employing their minds in tasks and trades for their own gain. Everyone was thinking for him*self*.

Well, not quite everyone. There were a few such as John Fitch. Like anyone else using his mind, Fitch conceived of something by himself which men could never have devised collectively. But he was seeking collective benefit, not individual gain. He wanted to use his mind for the good of others, not be selfish. Instead of trying to profit from his invention, he tried to give it to the government for the benefit of the whole country. On August 30, 1785, more than two decades before the voyage of Fulton's *Clermont*, Fitch wrote to the United States

Congress about his plans for a steamboat, a small model of which he had already tested successfully. Congress read his letter and referred it to a committee. The matter died in committee. Fitch petitioned Congress continually for five years. He also tried the legislatures of Virginia, Maryland, Delaware, New Jersey and Pennsylvania. He contacted George Washington, James Madison, James Monroe, Patrick Henry and Ben Franklin. They listened to him and referred him to other politicians. Spain offered to buy his invention, but Fitch was too patriotic to sell it to a foreign country. In his petition to Congress in 1787 Fitch wrote:

> I do not desire at this time to receive emoluments for my own private use, but to lay it out for the benefit of my country. I do not wish any premiums to make a monopoly to myself.[9]

Poor John Fitch. Fulton came later, but he wasn't handicapped by Fitch's altruism and political dedication. Hoping to reap profits for himself, Fulton did more for his country incidentally than Fitch did by intention and years of self-sacrificing perseverance.

Far from being surprising, the government's action in Fitch's case was characteristic. Perhaps the only surprise is that even with some of the greatest political leaders in all history, the political system functioned little differently than with men of other times or places. But why, then, with lesser men in office, is there even now such a willingness to resort to political action as the means of human betterment?

All Western governments were given a chance to participate in the great idea of a Frenchman named de Lesseps. He offered them shares in the Suez Canal "expecting that they would leap at the opportunity."[10] But they didn't recognize a great idea when they saw one. The Suez Canal was to become the world's busiest waterway, but political leaders couldn't envision that. The British government, despite its command of the seas and the importance of British trade in the East, refused to buy any of the 80,000 shares it was offered. The United States bought none. Finally the Egyptian government took a seven-sixteenth interest. But that was not enough. The canal project would have been stymied but for private investors who hoped to make a profit and had more foresight than the politicians. More than half of the remaining shares went to 21,000 Frenchmen, mostly small investors. Only 188 persons bought more than 100 shares, and the average was only nine.

Once the canal was opened, the British leaders changed their minds. Political mismanagement in Egypt gave them a second chance.

In 1875 the profligate Khedive of Egypt, who almost bankrupted his country, offered to sell his shares in the canal because of his debts. Britain quickly made the purchase before the French government did. But that was all after the fact. A major international project had been accomplished in spite of the shortsightedness of not one but several governments. It had been conceived by a private individual, financed in large measure by private funds, and carried out under private supervision.

The Suez Canal project demonstrated that even gigantic undertakings were feasible through the system of individual economic choice. Thousands of people made independent decisions to participate in a venture larger than most public works projects. The promoter didn't force anyone to buy shares, nor did anyone force him to sell. Those private investors who did not wish to invest didn't; the minority who thought it a worthwhile venture did. Each could follow the thinking of his own mind. The people did not need government management of their money or regulation of their transactions. All they needed was the freedom to act according to their own judgment. Given that, even small investors could participate in projects of worldwide significance and profit from them. And though profit was their only motive, they helped create a facility that benefited the whole world for a century—until governments closed it.[11]

INDIVIDUALISM AND PROGRESS

Scientists tell us that man hasn't changed in any biologically significant manner for at least 10,000 years. Yet human progress has been far from uniform throughout that time. In fact, since the early beginnings of civilization, there have been only three periods of great progress: the Golden Age of Greece, the Renaissance, and the 19th century, particularly in America.

If human potential has been relatively constant, then there is some factor that either restrains or releases that potential. When we look for a factor which we can correlate with the prolific mental achievements of those three periods, we find it in a spirit of individualism. The flourishing of human thought goes hand in hand with the status of the individual.

The importance of the individual in Ancient Greece, the birthplace of freedom, can be seen in this passage by an authority on Greek culture:

> The conception of the entire unimportance of the
> individual, which had persisted down from earliest tribal days
> and was universally accepted in all the ancient world, has given
> place in Greece to the conception of the liberty of the
> individual.[12]

Citizens in Ancient Greece lived in a free market economy. The
law allowed them to live as they saw fit and scrupulously protected
private property. Civilization advanced faster here in two centuries than
in all the preceding millennia. The free men of Greece were pioneers in
logic, mathematics, physics and ethics. They made fundamental
advances in architecture, astronomy and literature. Educated Greeks
knew the earth was round seventeen centuries before Columbus. Indeed,
Eratosthenes in that ancient time calculated the circumference of the
earth to within one percent.

Roman civilization was built on the intellectual foundations of the
Greeks. And when Rome fell, most of the knowledge of the civilized
world disappeared with it. The Dark Ages had arrived.

Not until the Renaissance, a thousand years later, did civilization
again reach its former peak. Then all at once amazing advances were
made in every branch of science and art, all in a relatively short span of
time. And with these phenomenal achievements we find once again the
rise of individualism. The Swiss historian Jacob Burckhardt, the
preeminent authority on the Renaissance, in his classic *Civilization of
the Renaissance in Italy,* cites individualism as the central characteristic
of the Renaissance. In his view, "the development of the individual"
made possible "the discovery of the world and the discovery of man."

The Humanism of the Renaissance brought a new concern for life
in the here and now rather than in the hereafter. People lived life for its
own sake. They began to be more concerned with their own interests
than with those of Church or State. The power of the old institutions
broke down, and people began to assert themselves and think for
themselves. They began to seek answers from nature rather than from
authorities. They even dared to learn Greek, the forbidden language of
heresy, and learned things that further weakened the control of contemporary institutions over them. The individual was breaking free. The
mind was picking up strands of progress left centuries earlier by the free
men of Greece. It was a passage about an idea of Aristarchus that led
Copernicus to hypothesize a heliocentric universe. It was the work on
conic sections by Appolonius of Perga that led Kepler to the idea that the

orbits of the planets were elliptical. It was a problem by Pappus that led Descartes to create analytic geometry. Men were building on the knowledge of a previous civilization in the same way that men in the first civilization built upon each others' achievements in agriculture, basketry and later the technology of the wheel, etc.

The emergence of individualism was never complete in Ancient Greece or during the Renaissance. Men were still only partially free. And in the succeeding periods much of the freedom which had been achieved was lost again as the individual was subjugated and forced to serve purposes other than his own interests.

But the spark of individualism lighted in the Renaissance was never completely extinguished. It was yet to burn its brightest. In time it was carried by John Locke's philosophy across the ocean to the New World, where it inflamed the colonists with a burning passion for individual liberty. It led for the first time in all history to the founding of a government upon the principle of the supremacy of individual rights. In the language of the Founding Fathers, those rights were "unalienable." There was nothing, not royalty, government, majority rule, society, the "public interest," or anything else to which individual rights were to be subordinated.

It's revealing that the British people, now as in former times, refer to themselves as "British subjects." The government *subjects* the people. Americans even today do not consider themselves "American subjects," though the term would not be as inappropriate as in the early days of the republic. Then it wasn't the people who were subjected. The government was subjected to the principle of individual rights by the Constitution. The government served the people; the people didn't serve the government—they served themselves! That famous phrase the right to the "pursuit of happiness" is nothing less than a statement of the individual's right to serve *his own interests.* Is it any wonder, then, that the achievements of men such as Edison, Howe, Hall, Westinghouse, Goodyear, Fulton, McCormick, Whitney, Bell, the Wright Brothers and Henry Ford should emerge in the one country where men enjoyed unparalleled freedom to pursue their own interests and to profit from them? In the Old World men were always suppose to serve the king, the Church-State, the pharaoh, the feudal lord. But in America they were free to serve themselves.

Mind and self go together. Through most of history the potential of the mind wasn't realized because the self was repressed. The real meaning of individualism, in terms of human progress, is that it permits the functional relationship between the mind and the self to flourish.

Now, as an illustration of how Americans have failed to understand their own success—and are moving away from its source—consider the widely-quoted and much-admired statement of President Kennedy: "Ask not what your country can do for you; ask what you can do for your country." The man who best exemplified that view was John Fitch! What President Kennedy should have said was, "…ask what you can do for your*self.*" Fitch and the country would both have been better off with that approach. The same principle applies today because the process of progress is universal.

As with the Renaissance and Ancient Greece, America's progress has stemmed from the individual. "Whenever we seek the real sources of America's strength," writes Dr. Felix Morley, an authority on American government,

> we find them, in the last analysis, resting on the belief that the individual is at least potentially important, and that he fulfills himself through voluntary cooperation in a free society.

It is only in a society where individual fulfillment is permitted that the power of the individual mind is unleashed. In a free society men deal with each other voluntarily, according to their own thinking, and for their own interests. Throughout history societies have violated this process because the dominant belief has been that force was more efficient, powerful or "practical" and that, furthermore, it was the only way to keep men from acting for themselves. The prevailing moralities have invariably held that man should act for some "higher purpose" than his own interests.

From man's earliest achievements, the nature of thinking has remained the same even though man's ideas have grown increasingly complex. In the same way, the nature of human force has remained constant from its most primitive application to the most modern. In this chapter we saw how civilization began and advanced by men thinking for themselves. In the next we shall examine the origin of organized force among men. Then we shall turn to the more complex applications of this type, which men are employing against each other today.

Chapter Three
THE WARPATH:
THE POWER OF ORGANIZED FORCE

The invention of agriculture, as we have seen, was the crucial achievement which marked the beginning of civilization; but it was crucial for human history in another respect, too. While further progress flowed as a result, something entirely different also began to develop.

> All at once at that time Jericho is transformed. People come and soon become the envy of their neighbors so that they have to fortify Jericho, turn it into a walled city, and build a stupendous tower....[1]

What was happening? Before the invention of agriculture, no society had any surplus, hence virtually nothing for any invader to seize. But now there was an objective for conquest. "War," says Dr. Bronowski,

> is a highly planned and cooperative form of theft. And that form of theft began ten thousand years ago when the harvesters of wheat accumulated a surplus, and the nomads rose out of the desert to rob them of what they themselves could not provide.... That is the beginning of war.[2]

A large, organized operation was required for seizing the grain because Jericho was a sizable settlement and well defended. There had never been any large-scale organization among the surrounding nomadic people, only small scattered tribes, because the hunting-and-gathering way of life necessitated the dispersal of people over large areas. It seems unlikely, therefore, that one of these nomadic bands would have been able to conquer the agricultural community, whose way of life could support a greater concentration of population. More likely two or more of them combined in some sort of political alliance. This would permit planning of a massive assault and give them numerical superiority over the defenders of Jericho. Since combat in a fortified defensive position would have favored the defenders, numerical superiority would have been essential for the invaders, particularly when only primitive weapons were used and when there couldn't have been much difference in the weaponry of the two sides.

From archeological evidence it is apparent that Jericho was besieged again and again in those early years. Sometimes the defense

56

held. Sometimes the attackers were victorious.

What excuse did the invaders have for attacking Jericho? Did they believe that the fruits of the earth belonged to everyone?—that the grain was a resource in which all mankind should share, not just those few who produced it? Did they think that simply because they were the "have-nots" they had a right to take from the "haves," or that the "haves" were wealthy and didn't need so much grain? Did the invaders believe in majority rule and, being the majority, think that they were entitled to determine the disposition of the grain? Did they think that because they were "underdeveloped" or "underprivileged" that their needs took precedence over other people's rights to the grain? Or did they use arguments of uniformity and equality to call for "redistribution" of the wealth from the few to the many? Perhaps they justified their hostility by arguing that planting, irrigation and urban development were destroying the environment.

Regardless of how firmly the invaders may have believed in their cause and how vigorously they pursued it, their method produced nothing. They simply took what others produced. Even if they were victorious beyond their most ambitious hopes, there would still have been no more grain than before. The very nature of their method precluded it from being productive. Agriculture was a mental achievement—that's why no other species was capable of it—but the seizure of the grain was an act of physical force against other men. A physical process could never duplicate the results of a mental one; fighting could not produce that which depended upon thinking. Force could only destroy or seize, never create.

Notice also that human numbers were irrelevant to the mental achievement but vital to the conflict. The size of the population had nothing to do with the invention of agriculture, but the size of the attacking force had a great deal to do with the success of the invasion.

CAUSALITY: THE LOGICAL BASIS OF PROGRESS AND PROPERTY

Man's progress has depended upon recognition of the cause-and-effect relationships in the world around him. This is what enables him to use the materials of the earth—seeds, metal ores, etc.—in such a way as to produce consequences of benefit to himself. But in doing so men themselves become part of a cause-and-effect sequence; and civilization depends not only upon recognition of the causal relationships which give men the science to master their physical environment, but also upon recognition of the same scientific principle in their own actions. This recognition, of man's role as a causal agent of material values, is expressed in the concept of ownership. Thus, in the same way that man's early productive achievements led to various other unexpected advances, they also led unexpectedly to still another: property rights. The grain belonged to those who produced it—by recognition of the same principle of cause and effect which they had to understand to grow it. And just as the invaders ignored or failed to grasp this principle by which others were able to produce grain, so also did they ignore or fail to recognize to whom the grain belonged.

THE PROPER ROLE OF FORCE

People start a war to obtain something which belongs to others. So those who have something had better be prepared to defend it. Self-defense is a basic principle of survival, and force is the only answer to force; unopposed loss is the alternative. It's not hard to imagine what would have happened to the people of Jericho if they had chosen to demonstrate a peace-loving nature by unilateral disarmament—as some modern "doves" have advocated—instead of self-defense. If they weren't massacred, they would have starved. On the necessity for protection John Stuart Mill eloquently wrote:

> Insecurity of persons and property means uncertainty whether they who sow shall reap, whether they who produce shall consume, and they who spare today shall enjoy tomorrow. It means not only that labor and frugality are not the road of acquisition, but that violence is.[3]

Refraining from force in defense doesn't eliminate violence. It rewards and encourages it and makes it the "road of acquisition."

The proper use of force is in *defending* values, not in *obtaining* them. Obtaining any value by physical force means overriding the mind of the owner, negating his choice. In physically defending a value one responds to an aggressor with the method of his own choice: force. Any force the aggressor receives is the justice of his own choice. Any value he obtains is an injustice. The invaders of Jericho sought to obtain something; the defenders, merely to protect what was theirs. If they had wanted anything from the invaders, the people of Jericho could have traded for it peacefully. They had something valuable to offer in return.

Because an aggressor wages war to gain something, the strongest deterrent to war is the probability that he will fail and incur destruction in the process. The greater that probability, the less likely war becomes. Peace is brought about not by a balance of power but by its imbalance: when one power is strong enough to enforce peace and insure destruction of a possible aggressor. (Consider, for example, the periods of peace backed by the imbalanced power of the British navy during the height of the British Empire or the nuclear power of the United States in the years after World War II.)[4]

A balance of power leads to war, even to extended wars or a succession of wars, as all history from Jericho onward demonstrates. The destruction of a potential aggressor is less probable when power seems balanced; hence he is more likely to be tempted by war. Moreover, it is when power seems balanced that miscalculations are most likely to occur; it is then that a false prospect of victory may appear inviting and the risk of destruction may be underestimated. And when wars are fought between evenly matched powers, they are likely to be indecisive—and therefore prolonged and frequently repeated. The latter is what happened at Jericho. It is apparent from the many, many wars there that its people were not strong enough militarily to discourage invasion or to settle the issue once and for all by destroying the invaders.

THE CROSSROAD

Ancient Jericho was the site of an important crossroad in human history. Agriculture marks the beginning of both civilization and warfare, and these have been major directions for human endeavor ever since. Men still till the earth. The principle is the same, but the methods are more complicated, more numerous, and the yields higher. Warfare, too, is still the same in principle, but the weapons are more complicated, numerous, and their yields higher. The natures of both activities have been consistent for thousands of years but are perhaps easier to identify in the simple, uncomplicated example of Jericho.

The early battles at Jericho typify the struggle for thousands of years between two kinds of people, those who produce wealth and those who seize it, the "makers" and the "takers." The one lives by the mind; the other by physical force. The first exploit nature; the second exploit other men.

Even the most successful invasions couldn't grow a single grain of wheat—much less invent agriculture. If even the first and most basic development of civilization couldn't be produced by force, how much more ridiculous it is to expect to advance human welfare by this method in our scientific age. Guns are more efficient than clubs or spears only for destruction or theft, not for the production of human values. Man can't dig a furrow with a bullet, much less build a computer with one. The advance of civilization has required greater rather than less use of man's mental ability.

It is the increasing use of man's mind which has expanded his productivity, his ability to utilize the materials of the earth to satisfy himself. And as greater material wealth is produced, there is proportionally greater need for recognition of ownership and for the defense of property. The people of Jericho had little to defend besides their grain. We, who have immensely greater material wealth, are no less entitled to what we have produced and to defend it against those who would take it from us. Now, as then, those who would "redistribute" wealth they themselves cannot create, who do not understand the process of production, have likewise failed to grasp the corresponding principle of property.

Production and property have a common origin and are interdependent. Production creates property—but without protection of property there would be no point in producing. Would the people of Jericho have bothered to cultivate the grain if they knew it would go to invaders? Of course not. In the same way, every other labor requires the expectation of its fruits or it would not be undertaken. The creation of material values is dependent upon men's minds, and men won't employ their minds without the prospect of reaping the harvest themselves. Only the recognition and protection of property makes this possible. It's only in a society where property is honored and defended that the distinctively human potential for producing values can be achieved because the concept of property sanctions the relationship between the self and the mind.

In 1707, exactly a century before Robert Fulton's fame with the *Clermont*, a steamboat was operating on the Fulda River in Germany. The other boatmen on the river burned it, almost killed the inventor, and drove him into exile, where he died, starving.

A similar incident occurred with the sewing machine. Elias Howe didn't develop his machine until 1845, but a Frenchman, Barthelemy Thimmonnier, had a successful one in 1829. He had several in his shop when a mob of angry French tailors, like the German boatmen, broke in and completely destroyed them.

Is the concept of property any different for the complicated machines of these inventors than for the grain of the people of Jericho? No, the principle is the same, whether it involves food or any other material value, whether it applies 10,000 years ago, a century ago or today. The need for protection of property is no less consistent, nor has the passage of time made it any less essential for the motivation to produce. Would these inventors have been any more likely than the early farmers to have pursued their labors if they could have foreseen that they would not be allowed to benefit?—if they could have foreseen the loss of their property?

The first inventors of the steamboat and the sewing machine, like the first farmers, sought to benefit by thinking. The mobs of German boatmen and French tailors, like the early invaders, sought to benefit by force. But whereas the invaders attempted to gain by seizing values, the modern barbarians attempted to gain by destroying them. What they sought was not the inventors' products but rather the business they would receive.

The boatmen and the tailors were acting for what they regarded as their common interests. But by the very nature of their method, force, they could only seize or destroy values, not create them. The power to create lay within individual minds, not mass action. No matter how large their numbers, no matter what their good intentions, the mobs' only power was physical. The inability of physical force to create values means that the *only* way anyone can gain by force is if someone else loses. Like the invaders of Jericho, the boatmen and tailors gained by inflicting losses on others.

Now, it might be asked if society didn't benefit when the business that would have gone to the two inventors was distributed instead to the many other boatmen and tailors. Didn't many people benefit that way rather than just those two? And weren't there then more workmen's families who were better cared for? So wasn't society as a whole better off in each case? Certainly not. When the mobs destroyed the inventors' properties, they also destroyed future economic choices for customers who would have gained from them. So all the people who would have purchased these goods and services were less well off for their being made unavailable. It wasn't from the inventors' losses but from those of other people—in terms of getting less for their money—that the mobs of boatmen and tailors gained. It wasn't just the inventors who lost—it was the whole buying public! So society as a whole was much worse off.

INSTITUTIONALIZED FORCE

Government is force. Everything it does depends upon its power to seize or destroy. Behind every law lies a gun.

Many people fail to recognize the true nature of government power because for the most part government doesn't act violently. It doesn't need to when the mere threat to do so is sufficient. But what if the invaders of Jericho had obtained the grain by merely threatening to use their power unless it was handed over. Then no violence would have occurred either, but the outcome would have been the same in every other respect. No grain would have been produced; it would simply have been transferred. And force, by way of threat, would still have been the basis for the transfer. The nature—and the results—of government power are no different when employed for economic gain.

The belief that government can advance society is simply a belief that human progress can be achieved by force against other people. It is often assumed that because government represents the organized power of society that that power is somehow different from that of the invaders of Jericho or the mobs of boatmen and tailors. But social organization doesn't make the power of human force productive; it merely permits society to function through a system of organized, orderly threats rather than outright violence.

Each side in the conflicts at Jericho demonstrated an organized effort, the one side being organized for common defense; the other, to gain something by force. Since it's proper for any individual to use force in self-defense, it's proper for any number of people to organize for that purpose. However, since it's improper for anyone to use force to *gain* values, it's no less improper for any number of people to do so. The act of organizing merely compounds the force; it doesn't change its nature or the justification for its use. Accordingly, the only proper function a government can have is defense.

Force, either individually or through organized action, simply cannot produce the results of thinking. Being force, government does not and *cannot* create values. So it can't bestow on its people anything it doesn't take from somebody. Its wealth is inherently ill-gotten, obtained by plundering people either at home or abroad.

It's easy to see the similarity between the invasions of Jericho and the use of government power to invade and plunder foreign nations. And it's easy to recognize that no wealth can be produced by the process. But the essence of a government's power is the same with respect to its own citizens; the difference is simply that a government must usually exercise its force to gain values from other countries whereas among its own citizens, who are under its jurisdiction, the mere threat of violence is usually sufficient.

It's not hard to see the depravity of plundering foreign nations, but is it any less wrong to use the force of government to obtain wealth from one's own countrymen? In a democracy we delude ourselves that the people (rather than a king, for example) are the beneficiaries of wealth taken by force from the populace. But wealth is nevertheless taken from *some* people for the benefit of *others*. Some gain, others lose. Wealth is transferred just as effectively, and on the same principle, as in the invasions of Jericho or any other invasion in history. No matter how sophisticated or complicated the form of government, its revenue is obtained by force or the threat of force. The Internal Revenue Service is no different in this respect than the collection agencies or invading armies of any other government in history. Behind the tax collector stands the threat of armed force, to be used against the recalcitrant and to seize his property, violently if necessary.

Picture some barbarian, such as a leader of one of the invasions of Jericho, promising wealth to his people by seizing it from others, assuring his people they are entitled to a better life at other people's expense. Now picture some politician, such as a leader of one of our political parties, promising wealth to groups of voters by seizing it from others through taxes, assuring his people they are entitled to a better life at other people's expense. The principle is the same in both examples. Both involve the use of organized physical force against some people in order to transfer material benefits to others.

Furthermore, the more government is used for the transfer of wealth, the more it fails in its defensive function. Government can't be protecting a man's wealth while simultaneously seizing it for another. Thus a government that attempts to perform "generosity" by force actually destroys its only proper function, defense.

Nor is that all that is destroyed. Such "generosity" destroys the motivation essential to progress and the creation of wealth. Here the deadly force of government produces a double casualty. The recipient of government plunder loses the motivation for productive effort because the government has removed the need for it, and the victim loses his motivation by being deprived of the fruits of his labor. Would Elias Howe have spent years in poverty and hardship working on his sewing machine if today's income taxes had existed in his day? Some creative thinkers worked even longer and under even more trying conditions. Charles Goodyear, who spent ten years developing the vulcanization of rubber, worked in such poverty that many of those years were actually spent in debtors' prison, where kindly jailors allowed him to continue his experiments. Politicians and social reformers who call for the democratic distribution of wealth blithely ignore the motivation that productive achievements require. As government destroys that motivation, it replaces it with the appetite for legalized plunder. But as more and more people obtain wealth through the force of government, fewer and fewer concern themselves with producing it. They have continually less incentive for doing so.

THE NEGATIVE MOTIVATION OF GOVERNMENT

Men are motivated to produce by the prospect of gain from their efforts. Government, on the other hand, attempts to motivate them by the fear of loss, the fear that the authorities will take away their wealth or their freedom, by fines or jail sentences, unless they comply. Of course, this is exactly the motivation one should expect from the institution whose power is to seize or destroy.

Government can't force people to produce because it can't force them to think. No amount of force could have compelled Goodyear to make the mental connections he made voluntarily even while in prison. Such thinking occurred in spite of government force, not because of it. Productive thinking is voluntarily initiated for value. Agriculture, the plow, the wheel, the steamboat, the automobile weren't produced because of men fearing what they would lose; nor were other people motivated to trade for them on that basis. All scientific and economic progress has come about from men envisioning what they could gain, from men seeking fulfillment rather than shrinking in fear, from the pursuit of happiness rather than the threat of pain. Value, fulfillment, happiness are the incentives of production. Loss, fear, pain are the "incentives" of government.

DEMOCRACY REPRESENTS BRUTE FORCE—NOT MINDS

Most Americans would agree that the number of inhabitants in a large country would be no justification for it to invade and plunder a smaller one. Yet Americans generally accept the idea that numbers justify the forced transfer of wealth within their own country. For many people the mere fact of political organization seems to legitimize actions that would be reprehensible on any other basis. If nine men decide to rob a tenth man, their majority decision wouldn't make it right. But the same thing happens every day under a political system calling itself democracy, and hardly anyone objects except the victims.

Different forms of government establish different ways of constituting and employing force. Democracy institutionalizes numerical strength as the basis for seizing the "grain"—wealth—of some for the benefit of others. What makes democracy seem the ideal form of government to so many people is the fact that there is a correlation between brute force and numerical strength. So, if one accepts physical force as the basis for human affairs, there is a certain logic in having such affairs decided by democratic vote, in having the actions of government—the agency of force—determined by human numbers.

The more human affairs are determined by government, even democratic government, the fewer are the issues to be decided by the minds of individual citizens. The trend to greater government is an atavistic trend, a throwback to prehuman existence when survival depended on force rather than mind, on the brute strength of muscular size and animal numbers rather than thinking.

Some proponents of democracy argue that, although expanding other forms of government would replace thinking with force, democracy is different. They argue that democracy represents everyone's thinking and that subjecting more of the issues of society to democratic vote expands rather than reduces the role of the mind in society. Hence they favor expanding government—growing socialism—as long as it is democratic. This, they say, is an "intellectual" as well as "progressive" approach. There are several errors in this line of thought.

First, expanding the number of issues voted upon, or the number of voters, does not alter the fact that the resulting government action is force. Participatory government allows the citizens to participate in force; it doesn't confer cerebral power upon government policy. Enlarging the size of a coercive force doesn't make its actions any more intelligent. Enlarging the size of an army makes it stronger, not wiser; and even allowing all its soldiers to vote on its operations wouldn't confer intelligence upon them. This is a difficult point for the advocates of greater government to grasp because they haven't grasped the difference between mental power and physical force. Since they think in terms of physical force, they try to measure thinking in the same way, by the physical strength of numbers; but the validity of an idea is determined by its relationship to reality, not by the number of its adherents. The world was round even when the vast majority believed it to be flat.

Second, since democracy is based on physical quantity rather than mental ability, in practice the system maximizes not the power of minds but the power of fools. In the voting booth the fool is equal to the wise man. As there are always more fools than wise men, the former become far more powerful politically than the latter. Democracy allows numbers of people to determine the outcome of issues on which they have little or no knowledge—hardly an "intellectual" approach. Democratic voting, far from maximizing mental ability, places it under the thumb of ignorance and incompetence. An extreme but illustrative example is the case where a judge ruled that 1200 inmates in a mental institution had a right to vote in local elections in a New Jersey town with a population of 400 residents.

Third, democracy is inherently nonprogressive. Because it is geared to the majority, democracy is geared to the *status quo* rather than to progress. Progress requires that the small minority of geniuses be free from the restraint of the majority, but that restraint increases as democratic political power expands. How long would the development of the steamboat have been delayed if Robert Fulton had had to obtain majority approval first? John Fitch spent years trying to get just a few politicians to approve his. And how long would it have taken a majority to approve Kettering's electric starter for the automobile, the Wright Brothers' first flights, or the building of the Suez Canal? All human progress has been the result of men following the truth of their own thinking, not the will of the majority as democracy requires. Progress requires uncommon thinking, but democracy enforces conformity.

Fourth, the outcome of a democratic vote represents at *most* the thinking of only the majority since the thinking of the losing minorities becomes irrelevant. Fifty-one percent of the voters can determine the outcome for all the citizens, regardless of what the other forty-nine percent think. If a majority approves a new public school, for example, everyone pays for it. If the figures are reversed and the school is voted down, the minority who want it will have to do without it. In a free market, however, the thinking of the minorities is not obliterated since they may still implement their views. For example, if the building to be constructed is not a public school but a bank or store, it will be paid for only by those who wish to do so, no matter how small a minority. No one will be forced to pay for it against the judgment of his own mind. Other people may even invest in competitive enterprises if they wish. Thus, though an area has only one public school it may have several banks or stores, each paid for by different minorities, and the consumers can use their minds on which banks or stores to patronize—which they cannot do regarding public schools. It isn't democracy but the absence of political control which allows people to act on their thinking, even when they are in the minority.

Fifth, the outcome of a democratic vote often doesn't represent anyone's thinking, much less everyone's or even the majority's. Often an issue becomes so compromised by efforts to obtain the necessary votes that it represents no one's thinking and satisfies no one. The resultant democratic "victory" may well represent a grotesque package-deal of the worst features of all sides of a given issue.

Sixth, democracy, in giving everyone an equal share in the determination of any issue voted upon, ignores the fact that not everyone has equal *rights* to the determination of all issues—any more than everyone, invaders included, had equal rights to the grain at Jericho. Democracy assigns physical quantity supremacy over the intellectual principle of causality, from which the concept of rights is logically derived. Although proponents of democracy clamor loudly about rights, the system is based on numbers, not rights: it allows some people, if they are numerous enough, to vote away the rights of the others. That they do so under slogans of "equality" doesn't mitigate the injustice and illogic of the process.

GENERAL CONSEQUENCES OF SUBSTITUTING FORCE FOR MINDS IN THE ECONOMY

The sheer impracticality of a pure democracy, where people vote directly on the issues, has led to representative democracy, where people elect representatives who in turn vote on the issues. In order to overcome some of the other difficulties with democracy, various offices in our country have been made appointive rather than elective, and some agencies, such as the Federal Reserve Board and the various regulatory commissions, have been made deliberately independent of the functional control of elected officials. These measures mitigate democracy, but they don't mitigate the coercive nature of government. Government is still force, and the expansion of government activities beyond the defensive function, whether by indirect election, appointed officials, independent agencies, or any other political mechanism correspondingly reduces the role of the mind in society. To the citizen there is no difference whether the exercise of his judgment is prohibited by elected officials, bureaucrats or a pure democracy. What's important in any case is that government can violate his mind, that organized force replaces individual thinking in human affairs. Since wealth and progress are produced by man's mind, any reduction in the role of the mind has adverse economic consequences and inhibits human advancement.

An economic system is made up of billions of transactions. A voluntary transaction constitutes a gain in the minds of *both* parties or they wouldn't make it. The aggregation of such mutually profitable transactions, therefore, ought to add up to a prosperous economy. In fact it does. Countries with free economies, or relatively free ones, are indeed prosperous.

But this doesn't tell the whole story. A free economy is prosperous not just because it's the sum of individually profitable transactions, but because, just as in the earliest civilization, production and trade create positive economic consequences which aren't intended or foreseen. For example, market pricing allocates resources most efficiently, stimulates the production of goods and services most in demand in society, and rewards the most efficient producers. Prices develop into an intricate system of relative values which becomes the self-adjusting regulator of economic activities throughout society. The price mechanism develops without anyone attempting to create it, and it performs all these functions without anyone's supervision. It comes into existence and operates continuously simply as a by-product of individuals acting for themselves.

Finally, and perhaps most importantly, a free economy is prosperous because people are motivated to productive effort by the knowledge that they can thereby purchase things they desire from others on *terms they themselves consider favorable*. Individual satisfaction is the basis of each man's economic actions and the self-motivating energy of the economy.

Now let's consider what happens when the government intervenes in the economy. In a voluntary exchange both parties offer values to each other. Government intervention, on the other hand, consists of substituting force for value. Instead of value the government offers loss or the threat of loss: jail and/or confiscation of your property, at the point of a gun if necessary. A coercive transaction violates the thinking of one side instead of representing the thinking of both; for when a man is faced with the threat of physical force by government, he is compelled to part with a value at a loss, against his judgment. And just as a prosperous economy is an aggregation of countless profitable transactions, a government controlled economy is an aggregation of losses, a disastrous economic system, such as occurred for decades in Argentina, the Soviet Union, or Great Britain under the socialist policies of its Labor governments.

We have seen that gains through production and trade create unexpected secondary benefits for others. We also noted, in the examples of the German boatmen and French tailors, that losses inflicted by force against particular individuals caused indirect secondary losses to others, those who would have benefited from the new products and services. In the same manner, the losses in production and trade which government inflicts on some people produce a ripple of secondary losses throughout society.

Not the least in the chain of losses resulting from government intervention is the loss of satisfaction from economic transactions. Participants in free trade are satisfied with the terms of their transactions—as evidenced by the fact they voluntarily agree to do business! But whenever the government dictates the terms of any transaction, at least one side, sometimes both, are dissatisfied—as proven by the fact they wouldn't accept them if given a free choice. Dissatisfaction is no motivation for productive effort. And in the same way that human satisfactions have positive consequences in a free market, human dissatisfactions created by government intervention generate negative economic effects. For example, if price controls force producers to sell a product at a price they think unsatisfactory, they will stop producing it and a shortage develops; the more severely the government tries to hold down prices for the benefit of the consumers, the more shortages it creates for them. On the other hand, if government fixes the price level above the market value of any product, overproduction will result; energy and materials will be misallocated for producing a commodity in excess of the demand, and production of other commodities in greater demand will suffer accordingly.

Any economic intervention is necessarily detrimental to the economy. All government has to offer is force, and force doesn't make anything economic. Quite the contrary. The fact that any economic objective requires force is proof that people consider it uneconomic. Otherwise they would accomplish it voluntarily. Government intervention can only force people to take actions they consider uneconomic or to refrain from taking actions they consider economic. Expanding government intervention can only mean forcing more actions of more people to be either unprofitable or less profitable. Thus, the government's only power is to create a less profitable, less productive economy. With diminishing prospects for profit the motivation for productive effort drops proportionately, and the whole economy spirals downward. It's no coincidence, moreover, that this whole process occurs as government increasingly prevents people from acting on their own judgment. What the proponents of economic intervention have never understood is that economic progress is a result of man's mental faculty and any attempt to forcibly displace the role of the mind in the marketplace is economically counterproductive *because* it is anti-mind.

Those who propose so-called progressive government programs in attempting to advance human welfare have never grasped the nature of human advancement and the nature of government. If they did, they would know that the phrase "progressive government" is a contradiction in terms. Force and thinking are opposites. Progress necessitates thinking, and government is necessarily force. Any attempt to substitute force for thinking in human affairs is not progressive but barbaric as well as futile.

Since government can't create wealth, every economic benefit that results from it is someone else's loss. Just like the invasions of Jericho. Government economic policies merely determine who benefits at whose expense and whether the benefits are acquired directly, as at Jericho, or indirectly, as with the mobs of German boatmen and French tailors.

To carry out these policies, the government has three economic weapons in its arsenal: taxation, regulation and inflation. In the next three chapters we shall examine each of these and show why it is anti-mind and why its economic effects are no different from the violent examples of force we have discussed.

Chapter Four
THE TRADITIONAL WEAPON: TAXATION

TAXATION AS INVASION

There are many forms of taxation, but the essence of all of them is the surrender of money to organized force. Taxation, like war, is a "highly planned and cooperative form of theft." Taxation is a method of seizing values within a country just as invasion is of seizing them beyond national borders. People part with their tax money not in return for value but in response to a threat of physical violence. They are compelled to act against their minds rather than by them. They are coerced into what they consider an unprofitable exchange, an exchange counter to their interests.

In some cases tax money is simply handed over to others, "redistributed," as in domestic welfare programs and foreign aid. Such exchanges are as one-sided as the invasions of Jericho. Like the people of that ancient town the taxpayers surrender values and receive nothing in return. Government is used to transfer wealth the way a robber uses a gun or a club.

In other cases tax money is spent in ways for which the taxpayers supposedly receive something in return. This return may be in the form of public works projects, government services, or the subsidization of certain enterprises deemed socially desirable. Here again, however, the benefits usually go to certain groups of citizens at the expense of others. For example, the employees on public works projects, the corporations receiving government subsidies, and the passengers riding the federally-funded Amtrak all benefit at the expense of the rest of the taxpayers. Such programs are merely another means of using the force of government to transfer the wealth of some people into benefits for others.

In a few cases it can be argued that all or nearly all of the taxpayers benefit in some way from certain government expenditures. But the essence of any such case is that what the taxpayers receive is always of less value to them than the money it requires. That's why they won't pay for it without being forced.

WHY GOVERNMENT SPENDING IS ALWAYS A LOSS

The advocates of public spending always point to the projects they favor, anything from public housing to moon rockets or research on Yugoslavian lizards, as though these projects represent the creation of value, as though they add something to humanity. On balance they subtract from it. Even though many government projects have some positive worth, that worth is always less than its cost. It's only by overlooking the cost that government spending seems to be beneficial, and by considering the cost that it can be seen to bring a net loss to society. All public projects are paid for by the people. For every dollar that the government spends, the people have one less dollar to spend for themselves. If people were allowed to keep their money, they would spend it on things of greater value to themselves, whether clothes, food, appliances, entertainment, or anything else. Government spending simply preempts countless private expenditures and substitutes those of the politicians, frequently for grandiose public projects. The Soviet government, for example, undertook gigantic public projects, even an elaborate space program, while its people suffered shortages of consumer goods. India is another example. For years the Indian government spent tremendous sums of money to develop heavy industry and even nuclear power while the people's greatest want was food. Government spending doesn't create wealth; it simply transfers it to projects which are of less value to the people who pay for them. Any public project, though it may seem beneficial, is a monument to the loss of things more valuable. This is true of the best of government spending, let alone the worst.

One of the reasons it's difficult for some people to understand why any government expenditure represents an economic loss rather than a gain is that many public projects are easily identified and visible whereas the alternative private expenditures are not. If the government buys a new post office or a lunar landing program, the project becomes visible. But if instead the taxpayers retain the money, they will utilize it in diverse and not readily apparent ways. Some of the money will be used for household expenses, some for recreation, etc., and some will be deposited in saving accounts where, in turn, the banks will "spend" (invest) it. But no one will know how much of the money went where. People will simply be a little better off because each in his own way has quietly employed his share of the money in his own interests. Not only are such private expenditures diverse, unquantified, and inconspicuous, but they will never even come into existence if preempted by public spending. The people never see what their money could have bought. They see only what they have been forced to buy through taxes—and that's bad enough.

In our country the taxpayers have been forced to purchase a bowling alley on Whidbey Island for $269,000, a study of bats in Morocco for $238,000, a study of the frisbee for $375,000, and a study of the mating calls of Central American toads for $29,324. How do the taxpayers benefit from these expenditures? No wonder they pay for them only because they are *forced* to do so!

In a free market people exchange their money for goods and services they consider of greater value. But which taxpayers think research on wild boars in Pakistan is of greater value than the $70,000 the American government spent for this purpose? Which is worth more in the minds of the taxpayers: $15,000 or a study of hitchhiking?—or $46,000 or a dictionary of witchcraft? Would the taxpayers rather have $4.3 million or another military band—in addition to the 143 existing military bands? Wouldn't the taxpayers prefer to keep their money or else to spend it in ways which they could see bringing them some benefit in return? How can it be argued that it's in the taxpayers' interests for the government to give $600,000 of their money to a single beekeeper in Washington? What value did the taxpayers receive in return for the $68,000 the American government paid the Queen of England for not growing cotton on her plantation in Mississippi? Obviously the taxpayers did not voluntarily "purchase" these items. Government forced them to exchange their dollars, in the form of taxes, for items of *lesser* value—or no value—to themselves.

The National Foundation on the Arts and Humanities has spent the taxpayers' money on everything from old political cartoons to the archives of Malta. The National Science Foundation has expended $122,000 to study the climate of Africa during the last ice age and $135,000 to see if chimpanzees can learn to talk. The Smithsonian Institution and eight other federal agencies have funded research on such exotic subjects as the semen of the Ceylon elephant, a bisexual Polish frog, Egyptian skulls, and numerous other projects of equally little value to the people forced to pay for them.

Not all government purchases are as obviously lacking in value to the taxpayers as those just cited, but all are of less value than their cost. Otherwise people would make such purchases voluntarily in the same way that they buy automobiles, television sets, fishing trips, haircuts, and theater tickets. A profitable exchange doesn't require force; an unprofitable one does. Do you see now why free trade builds a prosperous society and why increased taxation and government spending impoverish the citizenry? In a free market every dollar is exchanged for *greater* worth whereas every tax dollar is exchanged for *lesser* worth—as proven by the fact that one is done willingly while the other requires the threat of physical violence.

FUNCTIONAL DIFFERENCES IN PUBLIC
AND PRIVATE SPENDING

The buying public doesn't make purchases for the sake of supporting particular industries; people buy for their own selfish interests, but in doing so they unintentionally and unavoidably enrich the enterprises they patronize. Thus any enterprise which is valuable to other people will be sustained by them voluntarily even though incidentally.

In a free economy all enterprises obtain their money voluntarily, either from customers, who benefit from the exchange, or from investors or lenders, who anticipate future profits. In this manner wealth is used to build further wealth by enriching others, not by impoverishing them. The process utilizes the minds of all who participate, not force. It's the minds of men throughout society which control the flow of money, which direct it to enterprises they regard as valuable and withhold it from those that are not. The money each enterprise receives is in exact proportion to its value to other members of society. The process creates gradations of value so fine, so numerous, and interrelated so intricately as to be hopelessly beyond the most ambitious and optimistic "fine tuning" by government economists.

In the same way that free minds operate to build wealth, they operate to safeguard it and to stop any dissipation. In a free economy any enterprise that can't justify itself to the minds of men in the marketplace goes out of business, thereby stanching the waste of financial resources within the society. Government enterprises, on the other hand, can continue losing money because their funds are obtained by force, not mind. Whenever government needs money, it can launch another invasion against its people: more taxes. The marvelously intricate economic mechanism by which free minds interact to control the flow of money in the marketplace, which would shut off the waste of financial resources, is supplanted by crude force, and wealth is instead seized and dissipated. As Richard Gould, senior assistant postmaster general in charge of finances, said of the Postal Service, "If you were to look at the balance sheet right now and this was a private corporation, you'd be out of business. You wouldn't be allowed to operate. You couldn't operate."[1] The same is true of Amtrak. Here's a description of its financial dissipation:

> Some Amtrak routes lose so much money the government could actually save money by halting the trains and buying bus tickets for each rail passenger. And on one route, between New Haven, Connecticut and Springfield, Massachusetts via Hartford, the government could come out ahead by sending people by two's in a cab—and tipping the driver $5.[2]

In the first ten years of its history, Amtrak's passenger revenue increased by over 200 percent while its operating expenses rose by 300 percent and its deficits by 400 percent. Its operating loss went from $150 million in 1972 to $720 million in 1981 as its loss-per-passenger rose from $9.48 to $38.30.

Amtrak's losses continued with no prospect of profit. Even Amtrak's chairman, Donald Philip Jacobs, confessed: "I must say, in all honesty, that the probability of Amtrak ever being profitable approaches zero. It's hard to believe that we'll be able to provide passenger service at a profit in the United States."[3]

He was right. In 1989 *Business Week* noted, "Amtrak still loses nearly $600 million a year before subsidies."[4] Its losses for the previous five years totaled $3.179 billion.

Despite the infusions of billions of tax dollars, Amtrak service actually worsened. In 1988 30 percent of Amtrak trains were late—the worst performance since 1980—and consumer complaints were up 15 percent. In addition to the tardiness, riders complained about dirty coaches, broken air conditioners, clogged toilets, and even mice.[5] By 1994 Amtrak trains were running late almost 40 percent of the time, and there were 70,000 complaints on everything from dirty toilets to rude personnel—100 percent more than in 1988.

In twenty-five years Amtrak soaked up $18.7 billion in taxpayer subsidies and never had a profitable year. Faced with the prospect of budget slashing from the new Republican-controlled Congress, Amtrak in December 1994 announced it was laying off 5,500 workers and cutting service by 21 percent in an effort to stem its losses. Yet, despite all the rhetoric about cost cutting, the new Congress proposed Amtrack subsidies of $1.035 billion for fiscal 1996, up from $1.012 billion in 1995.

In the same way that every profitable enterprise is supported voluntarily, though incidentally, by others because they benefit from it, every enterprise that can't make a profit is providing less benefit to society than its cost. It is doing more to consume wealth than to enrich the lives of others. But it's precisely to such enterprises and individuals that tax money is allocated, to those who offer *less* value in return than they receive. Profitable enterprises don't need tax support, and those that aren't profitable don't deserve other people's money. By subsidizing the unprofitable, government acts against the minds and interests of free men. In the case of Amtrak, for example, the government has forced the tax-payers to "buy" billions of dollars worth of passenger rail service which their lack of patronage already indicated they didn't want. Just as profits enable productive enterprises to build wealth, tax funds enable dissipative enterprises to keep on losing it. These opposite effects illustrate the practical difference between mind and force in the utilization of wealth.

And who pays the taxes? Those who are not only providing for themselves but in the process are supplying even greater values to others. In the same way that consumers incidentally benefit the enterprises they patronize, producers, though they act for their own selfish interests, incidentally enrich the lives of those who buy their products and services. Taxation, by inflicting losses on the productive members of society, hurts not only those individuals but all who benefit from their enterprises. Thus the attempts to create prosperity through taxation and government spending accomplish the exact opposite: every tax robs the productive elements of society, which enrich the lives of others, and funnels the money into dissipative outlets, which consume rather than produce wealth. Society becomes poorer, not richer.

The intent of allocating money through taxes is to distribute it differently, and supposedly more beneficially, than free market transactions would do. But if men voluntarily direct their money to those enterprises which offer the greatest value to them in return, any other distribution will necessarily be of less value to them. The forced result is always less satisfactory. And the more force displaces the minds of men, the less satisfactory the result becomes, which is no coincidence. Wealth is a product of the human mind, but taxation is a means of thwarting people's minds, of using their money against their judgment. As taxation increases, the people have less and less opportunity to use their minds regarding their own money. Foolish tax expenditures, a few of which we've mentioned, as well as the vast waste which characterizes even the least foolish government programs are simply evidence of the inferiority of force as a substitute for the mind.

MORE FORCE, MORE LOSSES

Unfortunately, the advocates of tax-supported programs don't connect the disappointing results of these programs with their coercive, anti-mind nature. Instead they blame an *insufficiency* of force and call for more tax money to fund more and larger government programs. More force, they say, will correct everything. That's why all levels of government have been expanding and the federal level has grown the most. It has been argued that: programs which were in trouble at the state level would somehow be successful if taken over by the federal government; programs which were unsuccessful at the municipal or county level would surely be effective if administered by the states; Project X would have succeeded if more tax money had been available; Plan Y would have worked if everyone had been forced to comply; Program Z was not comprehensive enough, or restrictive enough, or punitive enough. Always the advocacy of greater force. Always the belief that greater force can accomplish what lesser force could not. In a free market an idea must first prove itself on a smaller scale, where success in turn justifies its growth. With government programs, however, larger programs have frequently been "justified" by smaller-scale failures. Consider, for example, the argument which has been used for so much federal legislation, "The cities have failed, the states have failed, therefore the federal government must do something about_____." In the one case an idea grows from its success; in the other, from its failure. Such are the opposite ways in which mind and force operate.

Ironically, the belief that more force will succeed where lesser force has failed has validity—in contests of force. For example, an invasion which has failed from insufficient force may well succeed with a larger force. The example at once reveals both the futility of trying to advance mankind through this approach and the mentality of those who advocate it.

In an invasion one side can never gain more than the other loses. Generally the gain is less because of the cost of the battle and because some of the spoils may be consumed in the fighting. But invaders are never concerned with the economics of the total system; their only concern is what they gain, not what other people lose. One can imagine an invader of Jericho holding a basket of grain and saying, "See, isn't this a good thing? Isn't it good that we have enough to eat? Before we had nothing, and now look." Yes, the basket of grain is a good thing. Yes, they are better off than before. Force, however, has not created anything, for other people are now worse off. But their losses aren't considered. Whenever the modern beneficiaries of force point to their basket of government benefits and say, "See, isn't this a good thing?" there are always people somewhere who are now worse off as a result, but their losses aren't considered. When people say, "Isn't it good that we have food stamps or tax-supported school lunch programs?" remember this "grain" is taken away from unseen victims, the taxpayers.

"But," some will say, "We are needy. We *need* the free food." Well, the invaders of Jericho could have said the same thing. After all, they were in need of food, too. The argument of need, in fact, can be applied to any invasion. It's because an invader doesn't have something which others do, which he asserts he "needs," that he attacks them. If he weren't needy, if he already had what others had, there would be no need for invasion. And if need does not justify invasion, how can it justify taxation? What makes invasion deplorable is the use of force for taking values from others, but why isn't the same standard applied to taxation?

Now, would it make any difference if the invaders voted on the matter before they attacked? They could even afford to let the people of Jericho vote as long as they were outnumbered. Would a "one-man, one-vote" decision really be justice? Or is justice based on something other than organized force, on some principle more significant than human numbers or the physical strength to seize what any group of men wants or "needs" from any other? Is popular approval an adequate justification for either invasions or tax programs that inflict mounting losses on peaceful, productive people?

Once the principle of obtaining values by force is accepted, even once, there is no logical way to limit its further application. Any argument that appears to justify force once can be used again and again. If it were granted that the invaders of Jericho should be allowed to take not all the grain but only enough to permit them a "minimum sub-sistence," this concession would simply become a justification for further invasions. Would it be acceptable if, instead of emptying the granaries at once, the invaders returned again and again, each time taking only a little, and would it be possible to limit them to a little? Once it is conceded that the invaders should have *any* of the grain, the protection is removed from the rest of it, both physically and morally. Once the right of the people of Jericho to *all* of their grain is breached, how can their right to any of it be defended? It can't, not any more than the invaders could have been limited to "minimum subsistence" or "basic needs" once they had breached the defenses of Jericho.

Taxation empties the taxpayers' pockets just like the invasions emptied the granaries of Jericho. Once it's conceded that outsiders have a right to any portion of another man's earnings, there is no logical way to limit taxation—the moral, natural line of defense is broken. If taxation, like invasion, is rationalized for obtaining anything, then it can be rationalized for obtaining everything. If obtaining values by force is acceptable for minimum subsistence, why isn't it acceptable for moderate subsistence? Or even luxurious living? If food can be obtained by force, then why not scientific research projects or social programs? The invaders simply return again and again, as they develop more and more new "needs," until the granaries, or the taxpayers' pockets, are empty. But instead of pointing to a basket of grain, or food stamps and school lunch programs, the neo-invaders point to a $220,000 research program on plant life in the Fiji Islands, or a $159,000 grant to teach mothers how to play with their children, and say, "See, isn't this a good thing?"—ignoring the fact that other people are now worse off for every one of these items.

METHODS AND EFFECTS FLOW FROM THE VALUE OF THE INDIVIDUAL

Force is the means by which some people are made to serve others rather than themselves. Seizing the grain from the people of Jericho was a way of turning their labors to the service of the invaders just as much as if they had been enslaved and forced to grow grain for their captors. There's no difference in principle, and no significant difference in outcome, between using force to seize other people's property and using force to deprive them of their freedom. In either case the invaders end up with the grain. By force. Against the minds of the producers.

Taxation, like the invasions of Jericho, is a method of forcing some people to serve others by seizing the wealth they have produced. It preempts people from using their money for themselves just as the invasions 10,000 years ago preempted people from using their grain.

It is the primacy of the individual, of every man's right to live his life for its own sake—not in involuntary servitude to others—that is the basis of the principle that men must not obtain values by force. The absence of force leaves each man free to serve his own interests. Instead, taxation commits people to involuntary servitude not only to feed others but to support countless social programs and exotic research projects on everything from Fiji plants to Polish frogs. Once the primacy of the individual is destroyed, there is nothing to prevent the interests of the taxpayers from being subordinated to the needs of others, the aims of politicians, so-called national interests, or any other "higher purpose."

If the individual is to be considered inferior to some higher purpose in one instance, others will follow. More and more higher purposes will be "discovered." If one scientific project can be deemed more important than the individual interests of the taxpayers, then countless others will be justified in the same manner. If scientific projects on earth can be thus justified, so can those in outer space, which is exactly what happened. If a film on how to brush teeth properly can be rationalized once as more important than what the taxpayers themselves would do with the money, then it can be rationalized a dozen times. So twelve different films on brushing teeth are authorized by a dozen federal agencies. If films can be justified on one subject, they can be justified on others. The federal government makes an average of 2000 films annually and has files of 1.4 million films under 58,000 different titles.[6] And if seizing money from some Americans to benefit others is considered more noble than men using their money for their own benefit, then taking money from all Americans to benefit still other people will be justified as an even more noble cause, which is what happened with foreign aid. This kind of squandering is called "transcending the national interest."

It's important to realize that government expenditures for wasteful, foolish purposes are invariably the result of the good intentions of government officials. They appropriate money for what they regard as worthwhile causes. It's just that they have such a low opinion of the individual as to rank his interests below even the study of Polish frogs and Fiji plants. Government spending necessarily displaces spending for private interests regardless of anyone's good intentions; and as government officials assign lower and lower values to the individual, they are willing to exchange his interests for less and less in return. Their opinion of the individual being low enough, they have even considered a documentary film on the history of the toilet as more important than what the individual taxpayers would do with the $46,000 spent for that item.

It's the downgrading of the individual that leads to the systematic exchange of greater values for lesser ones and to a chain of unfortunate economic consequences. Waste, shortages, inefficiencies, the penalization of the productive, and the subsidization of the non-productive all follow from displacing individual spending with public spending. These are the results of "assigning the public sector priority over the private sector," as they say.

On the other hand, it's the importance of the individual that leads to the upgrading of values and to a chain of beneficial economic consequences in a free market. It's because each man considers himself important that he acts for his own interests in the marketplace, that he seeks to obtain greater values for himself in exchange for lesser ones. It's a consequence of each side in a voluntary transaction acting for its own interests that both sides benefit. It's a consequence of individuals acting selfishly that free enterprises are rewarded in proportion to their value to other people. It's a consequence of individuals acting for themselves that waste is limited, that efficiency is promoted, and that such affluence is created for satisfying the needs and wants of others. But deny the individual the freedom to serve his own self-interest, and you deny the consequent benefit to others. Negate the value of the individual, and you stop the complex economic machinery of progress. That machinery is fueled by individual motivation and operated by individual economic decisions. It's run by human thought, not human force. It's the machinery for creating values, not implementing invasions.

Chapter Five
THE NEW WEAPON: REGULATION

By *regulation* I mean all laws or other governmental restrictions on any human action (including the use of property) that does not involve initiating physical force against other persons or property. While some regulations are intended to protect man from his own solitary actions, most regulations involve man's actions with other men. It is this type of economic regulation upon which we shall concentrate.

REGULATION AS INVASION

Through *taxation* government forces people to make economic transactions with their government. Through *regulation* government forces the terms of exchange upon people in their transactions with each other. These terms may be either the prices or the specifications of goods or services to be exchanged. Under *taxation* people surrender material values to the government, which, in turn, may convey them to other people. Under *regulation* people surrender values directly to other people. In both cases values are transferred by means of organized force. The principle, therefore, is once again the same as in the invasions of Jericho. Some people obtain material benefits by employing force against others.

Since the terms of a regulated exchange are forced, they are contrary to the judgment of one or both of the participants. If the terms of an exchange are identical to what the participants would accept without regulation, the regulation is superfluous, meaningless. The intent of any regulation is to force at least some people to act against their minds.

People will voluntarily agree to transactions they consider beneficial. The whole purpose of regulation is to have government intervene on one side in order to obtain an exchange that would not be struck in a free market—because detrimental to the other side. In a free exchange both sides gain. In a regulated exchange what one side gains through coercion is what the other is forced to lose; there is no net gain. Force cannot create a net gain. It can only create a loss. Increased regulation can only increase the number of losses. The trend from a free society to a regulated one is therefore distinctly uneconomic. Mankind can never advance through regulation any more than through any other employment of force.

Politicians have been quick to recognize the political appeal of regulation. Like the invaders throughout history, they promise to bestow on their followers plunder taken from others. "Regulation" may not sound as barbaric as "invasion," but both are force and both are used for the same purpose.

Many regulations are allegedly for protection. However, except where physical force is involved, no protection is necessary; in the absence of physical force any transaction is voluntary. Protection from anything except the physical force of other men simply violates the liberty of others in order to grant a coercive advantage to the group clamoring for "protection." One example is domestic industries which clamor for protection from foreign competition. The textile industry in the United States, for instance, has demanded protection from textile imports from Asian and Latin American countries. The situation is the international equivalent of the French tailors demanding protection from the textiles of Barthelemy Thimmonnier's sewing machines. And anything the government could do to aid the domestic industry would produce the same economic consequences as the destructive act of the French tailors. Import quotas, duties, and other restrictions on free trade can benefit any domestic industry only at the expense of the consumers, who must then buy higher-priced goods instead of lower-priced ones. The government measures do nothing to create wealth; they merely transfer it to those favored by the regulations.

Government is force, and accordingly its only proper function is defense, that is, protection from the physical force of other men. When government regulations are employed to "protect" men from anything else, government force is used *offensively* rather than defensively. It is used to *obtain* benefits at others' expense. That, of course, is what the invasions of Jericho were all about.

The principal difference among various regulations is simply which group will benefit and at whose expense. Minimum wage laws, for example, are intended to benefit the lowest wage earners—at the expense of their employers. Rent controls are intended to benefit the tenants—at the expense of their landlords. These kinds of regulations are very clearly intended to benefit one side at the expense of the other, but sometimes regulations are intended to benefit a group not a party to the exchange being regulated. For example, one of the arguments for wage-and-price controls has been to hold down the costs for the consumers. Labor and management may be forced to agree to employment contracts against the judgment of both sides in order to indirectly benefit a third party, the consumer, who is not a party to their contract. In such cases, of course, any gain to the third party will be offset by the loss to the other two. Any savings to the consumer will have come out of the pockets, so to speak, of the workers and their employers. Again, no net gain. Force will have only transferred wealth, not increased it.

REGULATORY SHOTS BACKFIRE

Because force is not the means of human advancement, attempts to *force* progress are counterproductive regardless of the good intentions behind them. Minimum wage laws, intended to advance the lowest-paid workers, increase their unemployment. The law doesn't make any employee worth more; it simply renders unemployable any worker whose services are worth less than the legal minimum. Rent controls have produced notorious housing shortages. In Sweden and France, where such controls have been in effect over extended periods, many people have had to remain on waiting lists for several years in order to rent an apartment. In proportion as governments have attempted to regulate the practice of medicine, they have succeeded only in impairing health care with red tape and producing shortages of doctors and nurses.

Whenever political leaders attempt to benefit one side in a transaction by using force against the other, the side the government intends to benefit, whether renters, employees, consumers or any other group, ends up worse off than otherwise. If this seems paradoxical, remember that any value government bestows in a forced exchange is produced not by government but by the other side in the transaction. When force aids one side, it victimizes the other and diminishes or destroys its motivation for producing values. People become less interested in being employers, landlords, doctors, or any other classification victimized by government coercion. At some point the "people of Jericho" decide it isn't worthwhile to grow any more grain.

Since in a democracy the government will grant benefits in hopes of obtaining votes, its force will usually victimize minorities for the advantage of majorities—and will end up harming the majorities as well. There are more patients than doctors, hence more votes to be gained by bestowing benefits on the patients; but when such benefits victimize the doctors, the patients ultimately suffer as well. There are more votes to be gained from renters than from landlords, from consumers than from producers, from employees than from employers; but whenever the government attempts to "buy" votes from the more numerous group by exercising coercive power against the less numerous counterpart, it ends up hurting both groups, the smaller immediately, the larger group later on. Not that it would do any good for the government to attempt to aid the minorities, which happens occasionally even in a democracy. Such efforts merely reverse the order of injury. The fundamental error in either situation is the assumption that force can produce human progress.

TWO INSTRUCTIVE EXAMPLES

After the Federal Power Commission (FPC) began to regulate the wellhead price of natural gas in 1954, the commission held the price artificially low for almost three decades to please the voting public, to benefit the more numerous gas users at the expense of the producers. Exploration for domestic gas and oil declined steadily. By 1972 no natural gas was available for new customers in nearly half the states. Meanwhile, natural gas from oil wells in the Gulf of Mexico was being burned off at a rate of 272 million cubic feet per day by oil companies which couldn't afford to transport it at the FPC price. The government, in trying to aid the consumer by force, ended up hurting both consumers and producers and precipitating the daily destruction of enough natural gas for a city of a million people.

When the Southern Railway proposed to cut rates for grain shipments by 60 percent because of the efficiencies of its new "Big John" hopper cars, the Interstate Commerce Commission (ICC) refused to approve the new rates, largely to protect barge and truck lines from the competition. Like the German boatmen who destroyed the first steamboat, the ICC prevented an improved method of transportation in order to benefit existing operators. The economic effects were the same in both cases. Wealth wasn't created; it was simply transferred. Some people gained—but at others' expense. Any gain to the barge and truck lines was a loss to the Southern Railway, its customers and, ultimately, the consumers of grain shipped at the artificially high rate (their losses being the difference between the ICC rates and those proposed by Southern Railway). The ICC regulation, therefore, produced no net gain, no progress. The only way progress can occur in transportation is when someone offers faster, cheaper or better service. Substantial improvement in any of these depends upon a new idea, not upon force. The progressive idea in the Southern Railway case was the new hopper cars. Force couldn't produce this idea, only thwart its acceptance, which is just what the ICC did.

Let's consider these last two regulatory cases further. In the case of natural gas the government held the price down, and in the case of Southern Railway it held the price up. In the one case the government attempted to benefit the consumers while in the other it attempted to benefit the industry. But in both cases the government hurt both sides. The intrusion of government force into the market "rewarded" consumers with shortages of natural gas and higher prices for grain. The effects on the industrial side were no less damaging. Domestic gas exploration practically dried up, and the transportation industry delayed adopting new equipment and more efficient techniques. The whole society was less well off than it otherwise would have been: labor and resources continued to be channeled into obsolete transportation systems, and human effort was diverted away from domestic oil-and-gas production, for which there was much demand in society.

It's important to recognize that Southern Railway attempted to lower prices in *its own interests*. It fully expected to make larger profits by increasing the volume of its business at lower prices. It was also counting on the minds of its customers to recognize the value of its service and act in *their own interests* by purchasing it. Southern Railway didn't need force because its appeal was to the minds of its customers. It was the rival transportation companies, whose services would be judged inferior by the minds of the customers, that resorted to government force to "protect" them from the market, to prevent people from using their minds. Every increment of progress is an achievement of the mind and depends on its appeal to other minds for its acceptance throughout society. It is the nonprogressive which seeks to employ force to prevent people from using their minds and to compel them to act against their own interests.

Domestic drilling for oil and gas shrank because exploration companies increasingly found it was no longer in their interests to continue. Although a higher gas price was in the interests of the industry, it also would have been in the interests of the consumer. Obviously it wasn't in the consumers' interests to have the price set so low as to endanger future supplies. The way to avoid a future shortage would have been for the price to have been high enough so producers would consider it profitable to find new supplies. (The cost of exploration would have come from the higher prices for the product.)

Just as businesses obtain sales by offering trades the consumers will consider advantageous, so also can consumers obtain products and services by agreeing to prices that producers will regard in the same manner. But instead of allowing a free price, which both sides would find to their interests, the FPC established a price to benefit one side— to the detriment of the other. A value was to be obtained by force. But although government force became an instrument in the transfer of natural gas, it failed to produce any. In fact, it proved detrimental to production.

DEREGULATION
The Natural Gas Industry

In the period 1975 to 1977 natural gas shortages became severe enough that the government finally resorted to freedom—at least enough freedom to make the system work. The Natural Gas Policy Act of 1978 started a partial, phased deregulation of the industry. Several years earlier a study by the FPC itself concluded that deregulation was "the single most effective means" for alleviating shortages of natural gas. That now proved true.

In the years 1968 to 1978 less than half the gas consumed was replaced by new reserves (46 percent). In the years 1981 to 1986 the replacement rate was 93 percent even though deregulation hadn't been fully accomplished. In 1989 approximately one-third of natural gas reserves still remained under price controls.

Furthermore, the 93 percent replacement rate occurred in the face of a developing oversupply and lower prices—thanks to Reagan's deregulation of oil prices in 1981. The new lower oil prices made fuel oil extremely competitive with natural gas.

The Oil Industry

The lesson from deregulation of natural gas was repeated even more emphatically in the oil industry, where price deregulation was complete. Despite predictions among the media and headline-seeking politicians that oil prices would skyrocket after decontrol, they actually declined gradually for two years—long before Saudi Arabia drove prices down through deliberate overproduction. There was no shortage; there was abundance. A mere four months after decontrol the number of successful oil wells drilled in the United States increased 41.2 percent. Domestic drilling reached an all-time high with 72,000 wells drilled in

1981. Oil imports, almost 50 percent of our usage in 1979, were down to
less than 30 percent by mid-1982.

The Airlines

The first chapter pointed out dramatic differences between
government-owned enterprises and their private counterparts: state-
owned farms versus private plots in the Soviet Union, the government
coal mines versus the private ones in Great Britain, public schools
versus private ones in the U.S., the U.S. Postal Service versus private
delivery, and the U.S. Social Security System versus private insurance.
There are similarly contrasting examples of government-regulated
businesses existing side by side with unregulated ones. Government has
shown no more economic wisdom in regulating business than it has in
owning and operating it. The airlines furnish one such example.

Small intrastate airlines had been operating for many years in
Texas and California. Because they were operating solely within each
state, they weren't subject to federal control by the Civil Aeronautics
Board (CAB). Thus they offered a perfect comparison between
regulated and unregulated air fares. The fares on these intrastate carriers
were about 50 percent less than on comparable regulated trips elsewhere
in the country. And for the most important intrastate run in the country,
the Los Angeles-San Francisco route, a ticket purchased in California
cost one-third less than the same ticket if purchased outside California
and subject to CAB jurisdiction. The unregulated carrier, Pacific
Southwest Airlines (PSA), used top-notch equipment and had an
excellent safety record. Consumers must have been satisfied with its
service because PSA flew about as many intrastate passengers as the
three competing regulated airlines combined, TWA, Western, and
United.

A string of studies dating at least as far back as 1951 documented
the superiority of the unregulated airlines. Some of these studies were
done by the government itself. A study by the General Accounting
Office had concluded that air fares would be 22 to 52 percent lower
without regulation. The consulting firm of Simat, Helliesen & Eichner
came to a similar conclusion in a study commissioned by the
Department of Transportation. Other studies by professors at Columbia
University and the University of Toronto all came to similar conclusions.

Finally, after *forty years* of tight controls, the airline industry in
the United States was deregulated on October 24, 1978. In the first year

alone travelers saved $2.5 billion through lower fares, yet the industry earned the highest profits in its history.

The long-term results are no less impressive. In ten years the consumers saved $100 billion in ticket prices, according to a Federal Trade Commission report. Meanwhile the airlines improved earnings an average of $2.5 billion per year. Passenger load factors improved greatly; and the more passengers, the lower the cost per seat. Millions of new customers were attracted by the lower fares. The increase in air travelers almost equaled the population of the United States as there were 447 million passengers in 1988, compared to 240 million in 1978. The productivity of airline employees jumped 29 percent. And the accident and fatality rates were down 35 to 40 percent, with improvements in every category: major airlines, charter airlines, and commuters. In all the years since the Civil Aeronautics Board came into existence in 1938 and began regulating the airlines, there have been only five years with no airline fatalities. Four of these have been since 1978, when the airlines were deregulated. Local areas are now getting better service, and smaller airlines compete with the bigger ones between major cities.

As so often happens, a progressive development in one field results in an unexpected benefit in another. An unexpected benefit of airline deregulation was a reduction in *automobile* accidents. In 1989 Prof. Richard B. McKenzie wrote:

> In an investigation last year for the Center for the Study of American Business at Washington University in St. Louis, Clemson University economist John Warner and I found that deregulation has significantly reduced air fares and increased flights. Because of cheaper, more frequent and more convenient flights, airline deregulation has led to a substitution of air travel for highway travel. Indeed, between 1978 and 1986, airline deregulation (separate from other influences) reduced passenger-car travel by an average of 4 percent a year (from what car travel would otherwise have been).
>
> That small reduction in car travel, however, has significantly reduced the number of accidents and deaths on the nation's roads. Mr. Warner and I estimate that between 1978 and 1986, deregulation has reduced, on average, highway accidents by more than 600,000 a year, highway injuries by more than 65,000 a year, and highway deaths by about 1,700 a year.... Highway travel is far less safe—approximately 100 times so—than air travel.

The authors also note that increased safety regulations for the airlines would reverse this effect and translate into more accident victims on the ground:

> If tighter safety regulations increase air fares by 10 percent, which in turn reduces air travel by only 1 percent and increases highway travel by a mere 0.4 percent (a reasonably generous set of conditions), Mr. Warner and I estimated that highway deaths would rise by about 150 a year, or by more than the annual average number of all major airline fatalities in the U.S. (140) since deregulation.[1]

By 1992, due to various mergers and bankruptcies, there were fewer major airlines. But Elizabeth Bailey, the former vice chairwoman of the CAB and currently a professor at the Wharton School of Business, asserts the industry's shakeout made economic sense. "If you look at the scope of their operations, there are economies of scale," she said. "There may be a fewer number of carriers, but each one is going to more destinations and there is actually more competition on long routes than there ever was."[2]

The Trucking Industry

A comparison of interstate and *intra*state trucking before deregulation is also illuminating. *Intra*state trucking escaped the jurisdiction of the Interstate Commerce Commission (ICC) and functioned far more efficiently. The only way these unlicensed truckers could haul interstate freight was by using the licenses of the government-approved companies, who received a fee, usually about ten percent of the trip cost. In this manner the force of government, through regulation, transferred material benefits to the favored companies at the expense of the unlicensed truckers and the consumers. Some people gained through force at others' expense. Just like the invasions of Jericho.

While the ICC transferred wealth wastefully to certain companies, it did the same thing for labor interests. Regulations forced many trucks to return empty rather than carry another load on the return trip. Some trucks were permitted to carry only certain items. Trucks carrying pizza crusts weren't allowed to carry finished pizzas. Trucks carrying unexposed film weren't allowed to carry exposed film. Trucks carrying farm implement blades painted red weren't allowed to carry the same blades if painted yellow. By forcing inefficiencies, these regulations created artificial demand for truck drivers, which the Teamsters' Union favored. But what the truck drivers gained was lost to others through artificially high prices and the absurd inefficiencies created by the regulations. In a free market people profit from improved efficiency, and society is the better for it. When some special interest group profits from the inefficiencies created by government regulation, you may be sure society is the worse for it. Society doesn't progress by means of inefficiencies.

The Motor Carrier Act of 1980 plus greater leniency by the ICC effectively eliminated all but a small residue of regulatory controls on the trucking industry. Who carried what freight and at what price on the nation's highways were now determined by the market rather than the edicts of the commission. As a result, prices for truck-load shipments dropped, and service improved. The ICC reported that shippers complaints fell sharply. The U.S. Department of Transportation estimates that American industry is saving $38 to $56 billion every year because of trucking deregulation. A survey shows the shippers who believe reliability has improved outnumber two to one those who believe it has declined. More small operators—particularly minorities—have been able to enter the business. Within four years after the decontrol began, 9000 new carriers had entered the field.

TAKING AIM AT THE MIND

Progress comes about through improved efficiency, and efficiency cannot be forced. It is inefficiency that is forced. Truckers going from St. Paul to Chicago would go through Clinton, Iowa, adding 80 unnecessary miles to their trip, only because the ICC forced them to do so.

People don't need to be forced to do what "makes sense," but remember that the intent of any regulation is to force some people to act *against* their minds, to do what doesn't "make sense" to them. As one conscientious employee of a meat company in Minneapolis remarked, "I wouldn't mind doing what they [the federal meat inspectors] tell me to do—in fact, I'd be glad to do it—if it would do any good. But everything they tell me to do just doesn't make any sense. It's all just so senseless." He was fed up, for example, with different inspectors each demanding that a certain ladder be stored in a different location in the building. The employee dutifully carried the ladder to whatever location the inspector assigned at that time demanded. The various locations included the original one, from which he had been forced to move the ladder in the first place. Finally the exasperated employee blurted out, "I've got more important things to do than carry that ladder back and forth, and I'm not moving it any more. You can go and tell Mr. Krawczyk [the owner] and get me fired if you want to, but I'm not moving that goddam ladder any more."

It's difficult to see how either the meat company or its customers benefited from government inspectors forcing a man to carry a ladder back and forth. On the other hand, in the preceding example it is easy to see how both truckers and their customers would benefit from an 80-mile-shorter route between St. Paul and Chicago. In the one case the government compelled action which benefited *neither* side while in the other case it prevented action which would have benefited *both* sides. Such examples show that where progress is concerned men's true interests were not in *opposition* but in *agreement*.

Perhaps now we can understand why a free economy, where all transactions are based upon mutual consent and mutual benefit, is progressive. Also, we can better understand the failure of force to achieve progress: if men's interests are in agreement, force is unnecessary; men will make transactions voluntarily. If transactions aren't mutually beneficial, they aren't progressive. A voluntary transaction is a demonstration of agreement. Force is a demonstration of opposition.

Every free exchange in a modern economy is the same in principle as those made by men in the dawn of civilization who traded clay pots and primitive tools. Men must use their own minds in determining whether economic exchanges are to their benefit, for there is no other basis on which trade can advance society. There is no other basis for determining that a transaction will be in the interests of both parties.

A trendy argument of the advocates of force is that individual economic choice is outmoded. We are told that it may have been workable in a simpler age but that our complex economy now requires futuristic policies of increased government regulation if we are to extend human progress. That's like arguing that to extend the height of a building we must eliminate the foundation!

If government regulation really is superior to the minds of individual citizens in making economic decisions, where is the evidence? Regulation has certainly had its chance. The ICC tried regulating interstate commerce for 108 years, until the agency was finally eliminated by legislation in December 1995. That's longer than the Soviets tried to make collectivized agriculture succeed. During that time, the ICC compiled 43 *trillion* regulatory rates. How much more time, how many more regulations does anyone need to be convinced that the method doesn't work? It would seem that if regulation were a good thing, 43 trillion of them in just the field of transportation should have been more than enough for a successful demonstration. Instead we saw absolute failure.

If our complex economy is beyond the capability of individual citizens to make correct decisions, why was it that truckers themselves could find the most efficient routes to their destinations while the ICC required routes that added senseless extra miles to their trips? When the ICC forced trucks to return empty, when it set different freight rates for the same items painted different colors, did it demonstrate in our complex age more wisdom than the common man—or less? When the ICC established those 43 trillion regulatory rates specifying the price for moving any of thousands of commodities between any two locations in the country, is there any reason to believe that those prices were more intelligent or correct than market prices would have been? The market is merely the prices agreed to by the minds of free individuals. And since deregulation, market pricing has proven indisputably superior to the previous fixed-rate system of the ICC for both the trucking industry and the railroads. Ditto for the airlines, which were regulated by a different government agency.

REGULATION FITS THE INVADER MENTALITY
The reason those seeking to gain by force can't comprehend why economic freedom leads to progress while force fails is that they believe men's interests are necessarily in opposition. Just as with the ancient invaders of Jericho, the invader mentality today can't conceive of anyone benefiting except over the opposition of others, because that's exactly what happens when values are exchanged by force. As long as men are committed to force, they will never be able to understand how they can obtain lower prices, better goods, and more abundant supplies by leaving others free to make a profit than by forcing them to sustain a loss. To the neo-invaders, it's inconceivable that, for example, men could obtain lower transportation costs without the force of the ICC or the CAB. But shipping rates on frozen vegetables dropped at least 20 percent when ICC regulations were taken off that item many years ago, and the rates on fresh-dressed poultry dropped 33 percent when the

Supreme Court ruled that the ICC had no jurisdiction over that commodity way back in the 1950s. And brokerage commissions fell after the Securities and Exchange Commission quit regulating them. In the face of countless similar examples the invader mentality still cannot accept the evidence that men can gain more from a system based on human agreement than from one based on human opposition.

A Federal Trade Commission report estimates that regulations on the advertising of prescription drugs annually cost consumers up to $1 billion more for drugs.

Professor Lee Benham of the Center for Health Administration Studies at the University of Chicago found that the prices of eye examinations and eye glasses were proportional to the degree of regulation on advertising by optometrists. In the two states with the most restrictive regulations, California and North Carolina, the average price was 66 percent higher than where regulations were least restrictive, Texas and the District of Columbia. Professor Benham estimated that consumers nationwide pay 25 to 100 percent more for these items than they would without regulation.

What the regulations demonstrate is that the progressive aims of men are in agreement, not opposition, and the intrusion of government force can only interfere with men freely offering better values to each other.

REGULATORY BENEFITS ALWAYS LESS THAN COSTS

Some people will say, "Aren't seat belts and shoulder harnesses in automobiles a good thing, which we wouldn't have without the muscle of government?" Or, "Isn't it good that we have government building codes that force certain standards for such things as insulation and electrical wiring?" Questions about other regulations may be phrased in a similar manner, but the principle is always the same. Such questions invite a comparison between something and nothing: between automobiles with and without safety features, or between buildings with and without certain construction characteristics, or between some other mandatory feature and its absence. But these are false comparisons. All mandatory "benefits" should be compared not to their absence but to what would be bought with the same money without the regulations. There is certainly nothing wrong with certain automotive safety devices *per se*—but there is also nothing inherently wrong with research on Fiji plants or Polish frogs or similar undertakings mentioned in the previous chapter. The value of all such things is comparative: they are worth either less or more than other things people could buy with the money. People voluntarily buy what they think is of greatest value. Government regulations do not produce anything out of thin air but rather out of resources which people would prefer to use in other ways. The government requirements become visible while the preferred choices of the people remain unseen because people must now do without them. Regulations haven't created any increase in value; they've simply transformed existing wealth into goods and services of lesser value while preempting purchases of greater value. The process is always an economic loss, not a gain. As with taxation, any regulatory benefit is always worth less than its cost, whereas in a free exchange any benefit is always worth more than its cost.

Not all advocates of regulation are naive enough to believe that regulatory benefits come without costs, though most fail to recognize that the costs are always greater than the benefits. This lack of economy, however, wouldn't concern these people even if they recognized it because they expect *someone else* to pay the costs. They fully intend regulations to be a means of conveying benefits to some people at others' expense. Just like the invasions of Jericho. The neo-invaders expect that the threat of government force will compel some people to *surrender* values on terms to their detriment and to the advantage of those favored by the regulations. Like any invaders, the proponents of regulation believe in using force for gain and aren't concerned about the magnitude of the losses they create for others. The politicians' only concern is that the voters who benefit—or think they do—will outnumber those who realize they suffer a loss.

In a surprising number of cases the benefits voters expect to receive at others' expense turn out to be at their own expense. For example, despite the efforts of federal officials to create the illusion that they are extracting something for the public *from* the auto industry, it is the consumers who pay for automobile safety devices. Despite the efforts of state and local officials to convince the public that such things as building and housing codes give them benefits, the costs are ultimately at the expense of the consumers. The construction industry and the landlords, just like the auto industry, have simply raised the prices of the products. Nor could anyone expect them to do otherwise. Instead of getting something for nothing, or even something for less, the consumers have found themselves getting something they didn't really want for more than they expected to pay. Professor Don A. Halperin, Chairman of the Department of Building Construction at the University of Florida has stated, "There are at least 50 regulations or requirements on any house built which probably could be omitted without any great hardship."[3]

The National Commission on Neighborhoods, in its final report to the White House stated:

> Indeed, many analysts are beginning to wonder whether the existence of the traditional code enforcement system has any net benefit in terms of protecting the public health and safety; at the same time the evidence that the code system frustrates and inflates the costs of construction and rehabilitation is extensive and convincing.

In 1989 the U.S. Department of Housing and Urban Development pressured local bureaucrats to exempt new projects in some Seattle suburbs from certain building requirements. The result was new houses selling for $20,000 to $30,000 less than similar houses in other Seattle suburbs. It is doubtful that any benefits the building codes would have provided could be worth the enormous additional cost to the home buyers. So the building codes, while providing additional features, meant a net loss for consumers.

Studies from the Center for Urban Policy Research at Rutgers University found that excessive government regulations added an average of 19.7 percent to the cost of a new home in 1980. On July 8, 1991 the federal Advisory Commission on Regulatory Barriers to Affordable Housing reported that excessive *local* regulations alone may add 35 percent to the price of a new home, with federal and state regulations imposing additional costs. So the situation has been getting worse. Remember that these are not the costs of all regulations, just the "excessive" regulations.

Why have regulations become increasingly "excessive" and costly? Because once it is conceded that a little regulation is a good thing, there is no way to defeat the argument that a little more will be even better. Thus regulations will inevitably proliferate beyond the point at which even their advocates recognize them as "excessive." The introduction of *any* regulation establishes the principle that government choices are to be preferred to the free choices of the marketplace. Once that prinicple is accepted, there is no place to draw the line against additional regulations; any line that may be drawn is entirely arbitrary and indefensible. It is only a matter of time before the line will be moved arbitrarily again and again to accommodate additional regulations accruing from the underlying principle.[5]

GREATER REGULATION, LESS BENEFIT
The Auto Industry

The waste caused by auto regulations is indicated by the cost and the use of mandatory equipment. The government required installation of seat belts even though fewer than one-third of the people would use them, thus yielding no benefit to the more than two-thirds who still had to pay for them. Then the government required shoulder harnesses, which cost more and were used by even fewer people—for years fewer than 1 in 20—thus yielding less benefit at even greater cost. Then came the seat belt interlock system, which the government finally abandoned after forcing millions of dollars to be spent on it, thus yielding no benefit at tremendous cost. Then the government required catalytic converters, which are even more costly and turned out to be downright harmful because they emitted sulfuric acid fumes. As the regulations increased, the costs escalated while the benefits diminished, then disappeared, and finally turned to harm since sulfuric acid mist is injurious to the lungs. *U.S. News & World Report* stated: "After hundreds of millions in added costs to buyers, the Agency [EPA] found the converters emit sulfuric acid fumes that injure the lungs."[4] The more the government intervened, the worse the results became.

Did the auto safety requirements have a beneficial effect on highway fatalities? Apparently not. The decade of the 1960s, during which federal auto safety regulations were introduced, became the first decade in history in which highway fatalities per 100 million miles *failed* to decrease. The decade also became the first one in which fatalities per 10,000 registered vehicles showed an *increase*. Analyzing these and other statistics, Grayson and Shepard, authors of *The Disaster Lobby*, concluded that the program of seat belts, shoulder harnesses and massive auto recalls "had no apparent effect on highway fatalities. In fact, it seemed to have a negative effect."[5]

Another man who, with more extensive and sophisticated research, came to the same conclusion is Professor Sam Peltzman of the University of Chicago. In a highly technical study published in 1975 Professor Peltzman used statistical analysis and exotic mathematical models to arrive at the conclusion: "The one result of this study that can be put forward most confidently is that auto safety regulation has not affected the death rate."[6] There is no evidence, he said, to justify "the kind of life-saving impact—indeed, any life-saving impact—of safety devices" that is claimed by their advocates.

While uncertain of why safety failed to improve, Professor Peltzman suggested that drivers may be willing to accept a certain level of risk and may compensate for safer vehicles by riskier driving. This seems plausible, and additional evidence now seems to confirm this idea. Five years after the Peltzman report, a research study by economist Mark Crain of Virginia Polytechnic Institute concluded that even mandatory auto safety inspections make drivers feel their cars are safer than they are, leading them to drive more aggressively and take greater risks.

In 1986 it was reported that in the year since seat belts became mandatory in New Jersey, traffic deaths had increased—after declining for four years prior to the law. Deaths increased specifically for drivers and front seat passengers—the very ones the law required to buckle up. And, most surprising, there was a significant increase in pedestrian deaths. Analysts speculated that an increased sense of security for drivers could lead to increased carelessness and decreased alertness.

In August 1991 the Centers for Disease Control reported that the use of automobile safety seats for children had soared for eight years— but that child fatalities had *failed* to decrease. During that period, the use of safety seats rose from 38 to 84 percent for children ages 1 to 4 and from 60 to 83 percent for children under age 1.

Economist John Semens, writing in *The Freeman*, July 1992, noted, "Hawaii, the state with the most rigorously enforced seat belt law and the highest compliance in the nation, has experienced an increase in traffic fatalities and fatality rates since its law went into effect in December 1985."

A more recent statistical study, by Professor Christopher Garbacz of the University of Missouri-Rolla, found that traffic fatalities decreased for those required to wear seat belts (typically drivers and front-seat passengers)—but increased for rear-seat passengers, cyclists and pedestrians. These results are confirmed by a study in Great Britain published in 1995.[7] Traffic fatalities did not drop in Great Britain when seat belts were made mandatory. Driver deaths dropped slightly, but pedestrian, bicycle and rear-seat deaths all rose. The same study found that helmet laws for motorcyclists haven't reduced deaths either.

We have all seen enough test dummies crashed into windshields and dashboards to realize one is more likely to survive an automobile crash if wearing a seat belt. But crash-tested dummies don't alter their driving behavior; they don't show increased aggressiveness or decreased alertness that may increase the likelihood of collisions with other vehicles or pedestrians. Though laws have increased the use of seat belts, the unavoidable conclusion is that the higher usage hasn't reduced the death toll.

While there is evidence that air bags may reduce the severity of automobile injuries, there is also evidence that air bags and even antilock braking systems alter driver behavior to offset the safety benefits, just like seat belts do. In a study published in the *Journal of Consumer Research* in March 1994, two Virginia Commonwealth University professors compared like models of automobiles with and without air bags. Economics Professors George E. Hoffer and Steven P. Peterson first analyzed insurance data from 1989 to 1991 on 20 car models equipped with air bags. For 12 of these models the relative frequency of personal-injury claims increased after air bags became standard equipment. Then the researchers looked at data for 1992 models with air bags and found that for six out of eleven models the personal-injury claim rate had also increased. Overall, the number of personal injury claims rose in 18 of 31 models with air bags from 1989 to 1992. The 1990 Honda Accord, for example, scored 91 for personal-injury claims (on a scale with 100 representing the average number of claims and zero representing no claims.) The 1992 Accords, with air bags, scored 98. The study also found that by the end of the 1990 model year every Chrysler car had a higher frequency of claims than like models before getting air bags. Yet Chrysler said the air bags were working as intended.

In January 1994 the Highway Loss Data Institute, which represents insurance companies, reported that antilock brakes aren't "reducing either the frequency or the cost of crashes that result in insurance claims for vehicle damage." The institute's study covered seven models of Chevrolet, Pontiac and Oldsmobile. These General Motors cars were selected because they had no significant design changes other than the addition of antilock brakes. The data covered 55 percent of all privately-insured cars in the institute's files. For the 1992 antilock-brake-equipped Chevy Cavalier, for example, the overall loss rate was 96 while the rate for the 1991 model—with regular brakes—

was 95 (on a scale where 100 equals the average number of insurance losses.) More significantly, however, during winter months in the northern states—precisely where antilock brakes would be expected to lower insurances losses most dramatically—the 1992 Cavaliers scored 96 while the 1991 models scored only 90. Actually, these results are not as surprising as they at first seem, because antilock brakes act differently than regular brakes only when a vehicle is skidding out of control. In most accidents that doesn't happen. So drivers, thinking they have a super braking system, drive more aggressively in common situations where antilock brakes can't help them.

These latest data have driven many analysts to the same conclusion as Professor Peltzman in his pioneering study way back in 1975. Professor Hoffer says, "If you build a safer ladder, people will climb higher."[8] He says that, just as people drive faster and follow more closely on dry, smooth roads than on wet, slippery ones, it makes sense that they drive more aggressively in cars equipped with safer technology. Similarly, Robert S. Chirinko, an assistant professor of public policy at the University of Illinois, says, "Offsetting [driver] behavior could dampen or reverse the intent of safety regulations."[9] And Professor Peltzman himself, nineteen years after his original study, in 1994 said, "I found that risk-taking behavior completely offset the lifesaving effects of mandated safety equipment." The bottom line is that safety equipment "lowers the cost of driving more aggressively."[10]

On February 1, 1996 the National Highway Traffic Safety Administration announced it would no longer push for mandatory anti-lock brakes on all new cars. It reported that anti-lock brakes reduced fatalities by 24 percent under wet driving conditions—but increased fatalities 28 percent in accidents where cars drove off the road.

Other Examples

Nor have government safety standards reduced accidents and injuries in other fields. Injuries per million bicycles in use—which had been steady to lower for several years—began to rise sharply after the Consumer Product Safety Commission issued standards for bicycle design. From 7000 injuries per million bicycles in use in 1974, the rate declined irregularly to a little over 6000 in 1978, when government standards were issued. Then the rate showed a sharp reversal, reaching almost 9000 by 1981.

When the CPSC set standards for swimming pool slides, the rise in injuries was even more dramatic: injuries more than doubled in the following year, from under 1000 in 1975 to more than 2000 in 1976.

The CPSC began requiring child safety caps for aspirin bottles in 1972. Under this requirement a slight *increase* in child poisoning from aspirin occurred. Kip Viscusi of Duke University thinks the dismal results of the safety caps may be due to a "lulling effect" of parents who feel less need to keep such bottles away from children because they are "child-proof." He also suggests that frustrated consumers may simply leave bottles open rather than struggle with the irritating child-proof caps. In April 1990 columnist John Hood concluded:

> It would be unfair and unwise to fault all government regulation of product safety because of the safety-cap debacle— if it were an isolated case. But it is not. Since the creation of the Consumer Product Safety Commission in 1972, its sweeping mandates have hurt consumers, impaired product development, and bungled the job of promoting safety....
>
> In 1985 Viscusi reviewed general accident statistics and specific cases of commission regulation for *The Journal of Law and Economics* and found "no evidence of any significant beneficial impacts on product safety."
>
> If CPSC regulations simply failed to pan out, that would be one thing. But in many cases the regulations actually make consumers less safe.[11]

The child safety cap issue is one more example of government trying to benefit some people at others' expense. The safety caps cost more than the old-fashioned kind. So everyone ended up paying more for bottles of aspirin—which they would not do voluntarily. And the loss wasn't only financial; there was also a loss of convenience, particularly severe for older, arthritic people, who experience great difficulty and considerable pain with the safety caps. The regulators decided these were small losses for people to incur in return for the benefit of reduced child poisoning. But the benefit never materialized; only the losses were real. Government couldn't create a benefit.

The example also exposes the fallacy that people are better off where government deprives them of the opportunity of making mistakes by depriving them of market choices—a regulated world where government functions to *make thinking unnecessary*. Presented with products made "safe" by government edict, people too often behave as though thinking is less necessary in the use of those products: they are less diligent in keeping medicines closed and out of the reach of children, just as they are less careful about driving cars loaded with safety features. Government cannot take aim at the exercise of the human mind in the marketplace without killing the effectiveness with which people determine a whole range of related decisions. Force is simply not an adequate substitute for the individual mind in the spectrum of decisions required for the advancement of society. Attempting to broaden regulations throughout that spectrum merely leads to totalitarian control, not progress in accident reduction or any other field.

DEFEATING PROGRESS

In a free market any new product or technique starts small, very small. It starts as an idea in the mind of one man and spreads through society only gradually as it proves its worth in the minds of others. This process, or course, is obviously the most economical way of developing any new idea. Should the idea initially prove to be a failure, the loss will be minimal by virtue of its minority position in the marketplace; and the cost will be borne only by those few who voluntarily put their money on it. Contrast this approach with that in the auto industry, where government required the entire industry to change at once. The intro-duction of auto safety devices occurred on an industry-wide scale, and the disappointing results were proportionally large. The costs were horrendous and were borne by every car buyer in the country instead of merely those willing to put their money on a new product. The colossal scale of the regulations didn't increase their chance of success. It merely increased the cost of their failure.

In the case of the auto industry the government attempted to force change. More often, however, regulations attempt to prevent it. That approach doesn't benefit humanity either. Building codes are a case in point. They have prevented or delayed the use of plastic pipe, plastic electrical cable, new adhesives, and many other new products as well as the use of labor-saving machinery and other innovative construction techniques. Each of these progressive features should have proved itself on a small scale, and if found satisfactory, would have become increasingly widespread. But building codes have prevented this process. By enforcing conformity with previous ideas they have prevented the introduction of new ones. The uniformity compelled by regulations eliminates a prerequisite of progress: the possibility of a minority diverging from the ideas and practices of the majority. Far from obtaining better products for the consumer, regulations in the construction industry have made illegal the rational economic process by which new products are introduced and steadily improved. Once again regulations intended to benefit the public have only prevented producers from offering better values to the public.

Another example of regulations delaying or preventing progress is in the drug industry. A study by Professors William Wardell and Louis Lasagna of the Department of Pharmacology and Toxicology at the University of Rochester found that since the restrictive drug amendments adopted in 1962 the United States has fallen far behind Great Britain in the introduction of new drugs. Of 82 new drugs introduced in both countries in the nine years following the legislation, 43 came first in Great Britain, only 24 in the United States. Of 98 new drugs appearing exclusively in either country, 77 were British, only 21 American.[12]

The drastic decline in pharmaceutical innovation was confirmed in a 66-page study by Professors Henry G. Grabowski, John M. Vernon and Lacy Glen Thomas. They noted, too, that the 1962 legislation doubled the cost of introducing new chemicals, increased the risks involved, and thereby reduced the number of sources for new drug discoveries and introductions, leaving only a few larger companies to do so.[13]

As a result of delays caused by drug regulation, says Dr. Murray L. Weidenbaum:

> The U.S. was the 30th country to approve the anti-asthma drug metaporotenerenol, the 32nd country to approve the anti-cancer drug adriamycin, the 51st country to approve the anti-tuberculosis drug rifampin, the 64th country to approve the anti-allergenic drug cromolyn, and the 106th country to approve the anti-bacterial drug co-trimoxazole.[14]

In still another study the number of new drugs coming on the market in the United States plummeted from 42 to 16 per year after the 1962 legislation, according to Professor Sam Peltzman. He states that consumers would be better off without the legislation, that more suffering and death are caused by precluding or delaying new beneficial drugs than by preventing drug disasters. He notes that "disasters are neither so frequent nor so severe as to begin to offset the gains from major innovations." He concludes that without the legislative deterrents to innovation "the resulting gains would have left a margin of lives saved and disability avoided that would more than have offset increased losses from unsafe drugs." Peltzman cites one drug, nitrazepam, which wasn't approved for marketing in the United States until five years after it was available abroad. Its advantage over similar drugs is its safety in overdosage. The five-year delay in marketing in this country is estimated to have cost 1200 lives. Aside from failing to achieve their medical objectives, the regulations, according to Peltzman, are costing consumers $250 to $350 million per year.[15]

The 1962 legislation was a hasty reaction to the thalidomide disaster. The toll of the drug thalidomide in the United States was exactly ten victims of birth defects. Yet we have seen that the toll was 1200 deaths from the Food and Drug Administration (FDA)'s refusal to approve just one drug, to say nothing of all the others which would have saved additional lives. Once again, what seems like a regulatory benefit if taken out of the context of its cost can be seen to bring a net loss to society if the cost is considered. Preventing dangerous drugs sounds great until one considers the cost in life-saving drugs which are also prevented. The weapon of government regulation is a loose cannon that produces more casualties, kills more people, and forces Americans to endure more pain and suffering than the unsafe drugs it is supposed to prevent.

Dale H. Gieringer, a policy consultant affiliated with the Decisions and Ethics Center of the Department of Engineering-Economic Systems at Stanford University, notes that the tragic cost of the thalidomide birth defects was

> probably far exceeded by the harm caused by subsequent over-regulation…. In fact, economic studies have been virtually unanimous in concluding that FDA regulatory stringency has hurt more people than it has helped. The bottom line is that FDA regulation certainly cannot be proved "safe and effective"—thereby flunking its own criterion.[16]

Actually, the FDA doesn't even deserve the credit it has been accorded for keeping thalidomide off the market. The agency was, in fact, moving toward approval of the drug when the company itself reported the horrible news. It was simply bureaucratic sloth, not discerning scientific judgment, that had delayed the approval of thalidomide. Even then, it took more than four months for the FDA to realize that many people were still at risk—and even that realization came from outside the FDA, by Dr. Helen Taussig of Johns Hopkins University. Still more months elapsed before the FDA took purposeful action. Robert Goldberg, a senior research fellow at Brandeis University's Gordon Public Policy Center, has written:

> Months after the entire matter had been reported, Senator Estes Kefauver and his staff, along with the FDA, contrived to dramatize the catastrophe through the medium of the press as a means of securing passage of legislation giving the FDA more power over the industry. The tactic worked. The world was at last shocked into action, the legislation passed, new heroes were manufactured....
>
> [S]ince that time, the FDA has undermined the public health with capricious decisions and arbitrary delays without any offsetting safety benefits. For 30 years, by invoking the legendary defense of public safety in the thalidomide case, the FDA has sat on or rejected drugs for depression, schizophrenia, kidney cancer and epilepsy—not because they were unsafe, but because...the agency didn't think the drug was so important or effective.[17]

The unseen victims who die because *new* drugs are delayed or prevented from coming on the market aren't the only losses from drug regulation. There is another class of victims: those who would benefit from the *same* drug that is banned because of its demonstrated harm to others. Thalidomide is usually cited as the premier example of the benefits of drug regulation. Yet even in the case of thalidomide there were far more people whose lives could have been saved by that drug than the ten people in the United States who were harmed by it. Biochemist Sandy Shaw writes:

> Actually even the thalidomide case was not a clear example of proper action by the FDA. For most people, thalidomide is an effective sleeping aid that is far safer than barbiturates which are widely abused, addictive, and hazardous. The exception, of course, is in the case of unborn children during a short critical period of development. Over 1000 people die each year from barbiturate-alcohol interactions who might have been alive if they had used thalidomide instead.[18]

Now it turns out that thalidomide has great potential for treating a wide variety of diseases, including AIDS, leukemia, multiple sclerosis, lupus, rheumatoid arthritis, diabetes, leprosy, prostate cancer and breast cancer. The government of Brazil has been supplying thalidomide to leprosy victims for twenty years. In 1996 it was supplying the drug to 30,000 leprosy patients. Meanwhile, tens of thousands of people dying from AIDS in the U.S.—to say nothing of the other diseases just mentioned—were denied the benefits of that drug by the FDA's prohibition.

In 1992 the average time required for testing and approving a drug in the United States was ten years. In 1996 Robert M. Goldberg, now an adjunct scholar at the American Enterprise Institute, wrote:

> Under [FDA Commissioner] Dr. Kessler, the average amount of time it takes to develop a new drug has climbed to an all-time high of 15 years. He cites a General Accounting Office study showing that review times have fallen to 19 months from 33 months, but that report looks only at the FDA's review of final drug application. Since Dr. Kessler became commissioner in 1990, other phases of the FDA's review have gotten longer, driving up development time overall.
>
> The reason? The number of people used in clinical trials has increased, the number of clinical procedures per patient has doubled, and the amount of information the FDA demands before accepting a new drug application has skyrocketed. In particular, the number of clinical procedures required in testing cancer drugs increased 153% since Dr. Kessler took office....
>
> Carl Peck, former director of the FDA's own Center for Drug Evaluation and Research, believes the FDA's approach to drug review is outdated and needlessly involves more than 25,000 people each year in drug trials. These are people who, instead of being exposed unknowingly to inactive placebos, could be receiving care or obtaining new medicines in the real world.
>
> Rather than extending faster drug review and a more liberal definition of "benefit" to all drugs in development, Dr. Kessler has turned accelerated approval into political patronage. AIDS groups lobbied for faster approval and, lo and behold, the need for two trials disappeared. Republicans swept into office demanding FDA reform and—presto!—cancer drugs were placed on the fast track.... [W]hy leave drugs that might help patients with other serious diseases and conditions on the slow track? Where is the public health benefit of giving faster access to one group of Americans while denying access to others?...
>
> The sudden reversal in the FDA's policy on cancer drugs reflects two sides of the same coin: A desire to hold on to power and a deep disdain for the notion that people can make important medical decisions for themselves. Dr. Kessler once wrote that:

"If members of our society were empowered to make their own decisions about the entire range of products for which the FDA has responsibility...then the whole rationale for the agency would cease to exist."[19]

In the same manner that government regulation has prevented beneficial pharmaceuticals from coming on the market, it has closed the door to many other beneficial products and services. By requiring occupational licenses, business permits, and other certifications, federal, state and local governments restrict entry into the market. Of course, the argument for these restrictions is that the public needs to be protected from unscrupulous operators and inferior products, which the government in its wisdom is supposed to weed out.

In practice, however, the government has not been effective in weeding out inferior quality. For example, Professor George Stigler of the University of Chicago made detailed statistical comparisons for new stock issues over many years both before and after the advent of the Securities and Exchange Commission. He concluded that the SEC has had virtually no effect on the quality of new securities.

A Federal Trade Commission study reveals that the incidence of fraud among television repairmen in Louisiana, which has a state licensing requirement, is about the same as in states where repairmen are not licensed—and TV repairs cost more in Louisiana.

A U.S. Department of Labor study says that state licensing boards are "riddled with faults...fraught with chaotic and inequitable rules, regulations and requirements and prone to restrictive and exclusionary practices as a result of pressures exerted by special interest groups"— which seek to obtain benefits by force.

When the Civil Aeronautics Board came into existence in 1938, it immediately certified the nineteen airlines then operating across state lines—and would not certify a single new trunk carrier over the next 40 years! Not one single new company was allowed to compete in spite of the enormous growth of air traffic during this period. Entry into this field of transportation was foreclosed just as effectively as in the case of the river boatmen in Germany who prevented the lonely steamboat inventor from offering his services to the public. Had there been a "Civil Nautical Board" in Germany in the 1700s, the same effect could have been achieved politically rather than physically.

Since the demise of the CAB following airline deregulation, the airlines are free from this kind of certification or licensing; and the industry and the public are better served without it. But government still licenses or certifies people in a great many other fields, from beauticians and plumbers to day care operators and real estate agents; and the public is worse off for it. For example, a Federal Trade Commission report says that state licensing of dentists adds $700 million every year to dental care costs in the United States.

The advocates of licensing argue that it eliminates unqualified practitioners, but there is no evidence that it upgrades the overall quality of any occupation or profession. True, some unqualified people are weeded out; but, as in previous examples, the costs are once again greater than the benefits. These costs are not only financial, for licensing also eliminates some people who would make valuable contributions. As one writer on this subject put it: "Under today's licensing requirements, Thomas Edison could not have been certified as an engineer, Abraham Lincoln would have been barred from the practice of law, and Albert Einstein could not have been even a high school science teacher."[20] Yet all did more for human progress than this type of government regulation.

THE REAL TARGET: INDIVIDUALISM

It is not upon the dismal record of government regulation as an instrument of economic or social progress that its advocates base their reliance on force. Rather it is upon the tacit recognition that only through force can the individual be prevented from acting for himself.

To act for oneself means to act by one's own mind and for one's own interests. So the battle for regulation becomes an assault against both. It attacks the competence of the mind (the ability of free men to choose for themselves) and the worthiness of self-interest.

The argument that regulations are needed to protect people from their own bad decisions is an argument for protecting them from their own minds. It assumes not only that free men will too often make wrong decisions but—even more preposterously—that government will some-how make the right ones! The exact opposite is true. In industry after industry, country after country, the free market consistently outperforms government regulation—which would not happen if free men were less able than government officials to decide what is good for them. Far from proving their wisdom, the regulatory agencies have proven themselves capable of such stupidity that the argument of their superiority over the minds of free men is not only untenable but laughable. If the earlier examples in this chapter are not sufficient evidence of such stupidity, consider these: the Office of Safety and Health Administration ordered a man with only one employee, his wife, to build separate rest-rooms in his business even though they use the same bathroom at home. The same agency ordered another employer to provide ear protection for a deaf employee because "even though he can't hear the noise, it might cause some other kind of damage that we don't know about."

A variant of the free-minds-are-inadequate argument attempts to justify government regulation on the grounds of the incompetence of even a portion of society. It goes like this: granted a free market works better overall, for most people, but we need government regulations for the minority that is less able to make economic decisions, who would be "victims" of the unrestrained greed in a free economy. First of all, the less competent in society are not victims in a free economy; they are beneficiaries. When airline deregulation lowered the price of air travel, it lowered the price for everyone, rich or poor, smart or stupid. Everyone benefited from the airline's greed in desiring to sell more plane tickets. When oil prices were deregulated, the same thing happened; prices at the gas pumps were lower for everyone, whether genius or fool. Gas station operators, like the airlines, were interested in selling their product to anyone. A customer is a customer; one man's money is as good as the next man's. The same is true when people buy bread and milk at the supermarket. The store offers the same items at the same price to everyone, even the less competent. That's the equality of the marketplace. Thus the less able members of society benefit just as everyone else does from the lower prices throughout a free economy.

In the same manner that the free market lowers prices for everyone, government regulations raise them for everyone. Under regulation, air fares were higher for everybody. Building codes raise the cost of all homes to which they apply. When regulations raise the costs of eye glasses, television repairs and dental care, they raise them for rich and poor, wise men and fools.

When an individual makes an unwise decision in the market, few people suffer, usually just the individual himself and perhaps those closely associated with him. But when government makes an unwise regulatory decision, everyone suffers. Only the government could force the whole nation to pay too much for air travel, freight transportation and prescription drugs. And when the government fails to approve a life-saving drug such as nitrazepam, it deprives the whole society of its benefits, the poor and the less competent as well as the wise and the wealthy. That's the equality of government regulation.

Those in society who are less able don't need government regulation any more than anyone else. They need, and are entitled to, protection from force and fraud, the same as every other person in society. Beyond that, what they need is not government regulations but free markets—the more so because they can least afford the added costs such regulations silently impose on the consumer. Nor can they afford to circumvent the regulations, as the rich sometimes can do. For example, the wealthy can afford to travel to foreign countries to obtain drugs and medical treatments not available in this country because of regulations.

It isn't enough, however, to point out that regulations are detrimental to the very persons who supposedly make them necessary, that is, the minority who allegedly are too inept to make economic decisions without governmental intervention. Certainly these detrimental consequences aren't what the advocates of regulation expect, but it's not only their false expectations of beneficial con-sequences which must be challenged but the fundamental premise of their argument. It is this: that because *some* people are less adept at serving their interests in a free market, *other* people should be restricted in serving theirs; that because of how *some* people might exercise their rights, *other* people should be deprived of some of their rights, by force, in the form of governmental regulation. Thus some people are to benefit by force at other people's expense. Just like the invasions of Jericho.

It is the individual pursuit of self-interest which results in all of the economic benefits to the whole society in a free economy. The lower prices, abundant supplies, and new and better products are consequences others enjoy from people's selfish pursuit of their own profit. These desirable consequences are the effects of which individual self-interest is the cause, and this cause-and-effect relationship cannot be reversed. Limit the individual's right to pursue his self-interest and you limit the beneficial consequences to the rest of society.

Once other people's interests begin to be placed ahead of those of the individual, there is no natural line of defense to halt further incursion. The invaders are within the walls. More and more causes will be deemed "superior" to the individual; more and more regulations will result, further restricting the individual's right to use his own mind and act for his own interests. And the negative effects will be felt through-out society.

Behind the proclivity to regulate human affairs lies a basic anti-individualism, a belief that man must be prevented from being selfish, that he must be forced to serve some "higher purpose" than his own life, whether it be the needs of others, the good intentions of the politicians, or the wishes of the majority. Free men will act for their own interests. If men are not to act for their own interests, then they must not be left free; they must be regulated.

A free market is an economic expression of the moral principle that every individual has a right to live for his own sake. It is the system of exchange where every man may exercise his right to the pursuit of happiness, where anyone may enter a transaction for no other purpose than the satisfaction of his own life and where no one can be forced to serve another's interests. A regulated economy is a system of economic coercion established on the principle that the economic interests of some people, like those of Jericho, must be subjugated to those of others.

Chapter Six
THE SECRET WEAPON: INFLATION

One of the most important inventions in human history, one which we use every day and yet usually take for granted, is money. Like other human advancements, it was a product of human thinking, not human force. Government didn't invent money, and all government monetary policies throughout history have only demonstrated that force can't create values, only take them away. Governments can issue money, but they can't give it value. In fact, the more money they issue, the less value it has. When this happens, inflation is occurring.

THE EVOLUTION OF MONEY
In order to fully understand inflation, one must understand the nature and development of money. Before money—and in periods following its destruction by governments—men bartered. A man with some surplus wheat, for example, might make a *direct exchange* with another man for a goat, a tool, or something else. Or another man might be willing to work a certain length of time for the man with the wheat in order to earn it. So services as well as goods could be traded in this manner. Government neither taught nor forced people to make such exchanges. People decided for themselves when and what to trade and were willing to do so when they thought they could gain by the process. When two people voluntarily agreed to an exchange, they would both benefit.

The reason both sides could benefit, the reason they could *agree* to a trade, was the fact they *disagreed* on the relative values of whatever was to be exchanged. If, let us say, two fish were to be exchanged for one basket of wheat, it might at first appear that two fish were equal to one basket of wheat. But if that were the case, there would have been no reason to trade. A trade would occur only if the person offering the fish considered the wheat more valuable while the other person had the opposite opinion. Each person entered the transaction to obtain a *greater* value. Because of their differing viewpoints, one man's gain was not another's loss but his gain as well.

If one side, let's say the man with the fish, were to agree to the exchange and then run off with the other man's wheat without giving him the fish, he would have been guilty of fraud. He would have obtained the other man's wheat by deception—rather than approval—of his mind. He would have the wheat not by right but by the physical force of possession. He would be forcibly retaining another's property simply by physically controlling it. In such an instance one man's gain would be another's loss.

Under a system of direct exchange people could make mutually beneficial transactions, but there were many limitations. For one thing, it was difficult to match wants with offerings. If a man wanted to trade his wheat for a goat, he had to find someone with such an animal who also happened to want wheat. Well, what if the only person willing to part with a goat wanted some chickens instead? If these two men could find a third who wanted wheat and had chickens to trade, they all could do business, assuming they could agree on the ratios of the commodities. *Indirect exchange* would make it possible for all three to be satisfied. The man with the goat could trade for the wheat, which he didn't want, and use it as a *medium of exchange* to buy the chickens. This type of exchange made possible a broader range of trading and greater human satisfaction than were possible through direct exchange. In this simple example three people were satisfied instead of two, as would have been the case if the man with the wheat had found the direct exchange he was looking for initially. The introduction of a medium of exchange didn't result in a loss to anyone. It simply made it possible for more people to benefit by facilitating trades that otherwise wouldn't have been made. One man's gain was still another man's gain.

Once the mechanism of indirect exchange was understood, it became the base for further advancement. Men extended the range of their thinking and saw how they could extend the use of indirect exchange beyond the range of goods and services immediately available. To illustrate this development, let's return to the previous example, where the men with the wheat and the goat needed the third man, the one with the chickens, to bridge their differences. Now let's assume this third man was absent from the scene. But let's also assume that the man with the goat had progressed somewhat in his thinking. He might then have been willing to trade for the wheat if he thought it might improve his chances of trading for chickens at some future date. Why might he have thought so? Well, perhaps he knew that there were usually many people looking for wheat but few who were looking for goats. The greater demand for wheat in his society would in itself give wheat greater *acceptability*, or *marketability*, in future transactions. But there were other reasons, too, why wheat might have been more acceptable for future trades. One was its *divisibility*. Let's assume the man was offered eight baskets of wheat for his goat, but he really wanted six chickens for it. Maybe someone would come along with only three chickens to offer. The man couldn't very well trade only half of a goat unless he wished to kill it. But if he had the eight baskets of wheat instead, he could easily part with four of them to obtain the three chickens and buy three more chickens later from someone else. The wheat was divisible; the goat was not. Even though he didn't care for the wheat itself, the man with the goat may have improved his economic position by trading for it. If so, he would still have been acting for greater value and for his own interests.

If the man were to trade his goat for wheat in the expectation of later trading the wheat for chickens or anything else, he would have been dividing his trading in two and spreading it across time. He would have made only half of his intended exchange. He would have given up his goat and not yet received the chickens he wanted, which he expected later. These two trading halves are described by the terms *sale* and *purchase,* terms which are not applicable to a direct exchange.

Every voluntary exchange is made for greater value, but one made for a medium of exchange is always an intermediate transaction. *Anyone making a sale acquires a medium of exchange in order to purchase something of greater value in the future.* In order for this to be possible, the medium of exchange must retain its value over a period of time. It is the ability of a commodity to serve as a *store of value* which makes it possible for it to serve as a medium of exchange over time. The longer a money can retain its value, the more possibilities it opens up for exchanges between men. Just as indirect exchange at any given time multiplies the range of trade far beyond anything possible through direct exchange, so, too, is the range further multiplied by extending it through time.

Extending the time frame of trading doesn't necessitate a loss for anyone. In the preceding example the man with the goat was able to make a better deal for himself by spreading his trading across time. But in doing so, he provided a sale to the man who wanted a goat earlier and a purchase to someone who wanted to sell his chickens later. All three people were acting for their own interests, but they benefited themselves and each other in ways that wouldn't have been possible without a medium of exchange functioning as a store of value over time. One man's gain was still another man's gain.

The concept of a medium of exchange was devised and disseminated by the human mind. It owes nothing to force. People weren't forced to abandon the barter system; they did so voluntarily because they found a better method of trading. They accepted the new method only as they realized its advantages, either by thinking out the process independently or, more often, by learning from others; but only as each man grasped the process of indirect exchange in his own mind could he accept it and utilize it for himself. The new method of exchange increased the possibilities of trade for everyone, but it forced no one to utilize them. In fact, only a man's own mind could determine the possibilities because they were dependent upon the range of his thinking: the more far-sighted his thinking, the more possibilities he discovered for trading.

No other species is capable of thinking ahead and planning for its future the way man can. The most striking difference in the human brain compared to those of lower animals is the development of the frontal and prefrontal lobes. These are the portions of the brain which enable man to think long range, to act for distant goals, to forego immediate benefits in favor of greater ones in the future. This is the mental capability that was required for the development of money.

When a medium of exchange became generally accepted throughout a society, it was *money*. But this didn't happen overnight. Just as people weren't forced to accept the idea of indirect exchange, neither were they forced to accept any particular commodity as a medium of exchange. They could use any commodity they wished, and, indeed, a great variety of commodities were so used. But every commodity is different from every other, and consequently some worked better than others as media of exchange.

First of all, the more valuable commodities were preferred as trading media. Since the purpose of an exchange is to gain value, a man would be reluctant to trade something he valued for a medium of exchange not considered valuable in itself, nor could he expect someone else to give something of substantial value in return for it later. Every commodity used as money was valuable as a commodity before it became money, or it wouldn't have become money. But among the commodities with sufficient value to serve as money, there were other characteristics which made some more suitable than others. For example, as we have already noted, some commodities, such as wheat, had greater divisibility than others, such as animals. Things such as houses and boats, though valuable, likewise couldn't be divided without a severe loss of value. Tobacco was an easily divisible commodity and convenient to handle and transport while lumber was not. Some commodities, such as fresh fish and fruit, were too perishable to serve as a store of value. Some commodities were not sufficiently uniform: diamonds, for example, though exceedingly valuable, had such wide variations in quality and size that they wouldn't serve well as money. Eventually some commodity in every society was found to work better as a medium of exchange than any other. This selection didn't occur by coercion but by countless individuals using their minds to obtain better values in their trading.

At first only a few people in a society used a particular medium of exchange. Gradually, however, more and more people saw the advantages of trading in that commodity, usually by seeing how well it worked for those more astute than themselves, and that commodity would become generally accepted as money.

At various times in various places many things have been used as money: wheat, tobacco, cocoa, pepper, salt, whiskey, furs, copper, gold, silver, nails, fishhooks, iron hoes, beads, and many other things. Each of these was the most marketable item in the society. In addition to the fact that it was *valuable,* each had at least some measure of *divisibility, durability, uniformity and rarity* which gave it advantages over other commodities as money. But these moneys were themselves unequal in the very characteristics which made them preferable to other commodities as media of exchange in the first place. Beads, for example, were a commodity with greater divisibility than iron hoes. Furs, which could rot or burn, were less durable then metals. Whiskey was not as uniform as pepper. Salt was too common to have sufficient value in convenient quantities compared to other monetary commodities which were rarer. Silver was more valuable than iron because it was rarer, and it was a better store of value because it didn't rust. Whenever two societies began commerce with each other, traders discovered such differences. The money of one society would be found superior and would come to be used by both—voluntarily. People would discontinue their old money for the same reasons they discontinued using other commodities as media of exchange within their own society: they found something better. They didn't have to be forced. They saw the change was to their advantage.

As any given money achieved wider circulation, it further increased trading possibilities. Whereas bartering was limited to one's own circle of acquaintances, a common money made it possible to carry on trade in distant lands with people one didn't know or ever need to meet, people who didn't even speak the same language.[1]

The expansion of trade furthered progress in another way, too. The ability to trade with others was what made possible the division of labor. And as the ever-greater use of a common money expanded the scope of trade, it permitted an ever-greater specialization of labor. New occupations, new services, new industries developed which couldn't possibly have been supported by local trade.

As trade grew among different parts of the world, the number of media of exchange diminished. People were constantly discarding the less satisfactory ones until they arrived at the metals. These simply had greater divisibility, uniformity, and durability than other moneys. A metal could be divided and remelted any number of times without any loss of value, and it could be cast in coins and bars of such uniform size and purity as to be indistinguishable from each other. Over the centuries gold and silver, which are rarer and more resistant to chemical action than copper and iron, came to be preferred. And by the end of the nineteenth century gold edged out its ancient rival and became the preferred medium for international trade, although silver continued to be important in the Orient and still was often used for smaller trans-actions within countries elsewhere.

Gold did a better job of meeting all the requirements of money than any other commodity. It has always been rare; men have never been able to get enough of it, and there is still no prospect of it becoming abundant, even in our age of affluence. It's rarer than silver and doesn't tarnish as silver does. It's the most malleable metal known and has always been considered useful and beautiful. Gold is the most durable substance man has ever found. In fact, it's virtually indestructible. It has been buried with the dead for thousands of years, has lain in sunken ships for centuries, and yet it hasn't decayed or corroded. Because of its rarity, gold can provide great value in small quantities, which are convenient to handle and transport. Because of its rarity and durability, it can serve as a store of value longer than any other commodity. In addition, its durability and unbelievable heaviness (it's half again as heavy as lead) make it difficult to counterfeit.

The worldwide use of gold as money was the result of countless centuries of monetary evolution. It was the result of the choices—not the coercion—of millions of people over thousands of years. It came about in the same way as every other invention or scientific advance: by men using their minds to identify the characteristics of nature and to find ways to use them for their own satisfaction. In the case of money, men learned the different characteristics of various commodities, determined which would be most useful to them in trading, and proceeded to trade accordingly. This is how money came into being and how it evolved toward gold. The use of gold as world money represented the thinking behind billions of exchanges in hundreds of media.

> This process: the cumulative development of a medium of exchange on the free market—is the only way money can become established. Money cannot originate in any other way: neither by everyone suddenly deciding to create money out of useless material, nor by government calling bits of paper "money." For embedded in the demand for money is the knowledge of the money-prices of the immediate past; in contrast to directly-used consumers' or producers' goods, money must have pre-existing prices on which to ground a demand. But the only way this can happen is by beginning with a useful commodity under barter, and then adding demand for a medium to the previous demand for direct use (e.g., for ornaments, in the case of gold). Thus government is powerless to create money for the economy; it can only be developed by the processes of the free market.[2]

Notice that gold became world money because of the thoughts and actions of hundreds of millions of people who never set out to create a world money. Their only intent was to obtain greater values for themselves. The progression toward a world money and the benefits it brought to others were incidental. In the same way that the men with the goat, wheat, and chickens incidentally benefited each other when they acted only for their own interests, so, too, were more extensive commerce and better money of benefit to others even though people adopted them for their own selfish gain. One man's gain was still another man's gain, not his loss.

How could a world of money evolve from millions of individuals acting for themselves, without centralized planning, without any regulation, without any government authority? Because where monetary progress was concerned, men's interests weren't in opposition but in agreement—something that is incredible to those who believe in the necessity of human conflict. Everyone engaged in production or trade had an interest in sound money. It was a tool for mutual cooperation to mutual advantage. It took nothing away from anyone but increased the possibilities for everyone by facilitating greater trade. It forced no one to utilize those possibilities. Sound money didn't compel people to think, but those who chose to do so found it an aid in economic calculation, efficient trading, and long-range planning.

Like other monetary advances, paper money came into being because it was advantageous for all concerned. Under a division of labor, specialists arose who could perform various services for others better than most people could for themselves. Among the various specialists were those who would provide security for the wealth of others. Banks of deposit existed at least as far back as Ancient Greece and Egypt. Before the advent of paper, depositaries occasionally used parchment, leather, and even clay tablets in ways which foreshadowed the use of paper for financial transactions. After paper came into use in Europe, it was sometimes employed as a substitute for coin, most notably in Venice in the sixteenth century. The bank of Venice, which was founded as a safe-deposit institution, issued paper receipts in return for deposits of coin or bullion, and these receipts were used by financiers as paper money. But the modern usage of paper for currency, as well as the emergence of central banking, grew out of the practices of the goldsmiths in England in the seventeenth century.

English merchants customarily deposited their money for safe-keeping in the Tower of London—until 1640, when the king seized 120,000 pounds, which he repaid "only after long delay and much protest."[3] Thereafter, people began to store their coins with the gold-smiths, who had facilities for safe storage.

Then people discovered that if they wanted to make a purchase, they didn't have to re-claim their gold to do so. Instead they could authorize their goldsmith to pay it to those from whom they made purchases. It was simply more convenient that way. It was even more convenient when, as often happened, the people receiving the gold would simply deposit it again with a goldsmith for safe-keeping anyway. Soon the paper receipts were circulating just like money, and the gold rarely left the goldsmiths' vaults.

The goldsmiths became the bankers, and the paper receipts were the origin of both bank notes and checks. Receipts made out by the goldsmiths in round sums and payable to the bearer were bank notes. Receipts made out in any amount by the owners of the gold and payable only to specified persons were checks.

People weren't forced to deposit their gold with goldsmiths. Indeed, many people did not. But those who did thought they had something to gain, namely, greater security. Furthermore, the use of paper receipts as money represented an improvement over the direct use of gold for some of the same reasons that gold itself had come to be preferred as a medium of exchange. Gold could be divided far more easily, finely, and uniformly on paper than the metal itself. Because of its light weight, paper was more convenient, especially for large purchases and those made over great distances. And gold coins which remained in the goldsmiths' vaults had greater uniformity than those which circulated, for the latter were subject to wear and to such despicable practices as clipping, filing, and sweating, by which criminals removed small amounts of gold from coins. Paper money backed by gold combined all the advantages of both materials. It had the conveniences of one and the value of the other, and the goldsmiths' vaults provided the additional benefit of a more secure storage of value. Thus even the development of paper money was the result of men acting for better value.

But notice that the value of paper money depended upon the gold behind it. Paper money merely represented gold. And if a goldsmith failed to honor a paper receipt, he would have been guilty of fraud just as much as the man in our earlier example who obtained another's wheat without giving him the fish he was led to expect in return. The goldsmith would have acquired someone's gold by deception and would have been using the vault as force against another's property, forcibly retaining it against the wishes of the owner. In the barter example the victim was defrauded immediately whereas in the paper-receipt example the fraud was perpetrated over a period of time, but the principle is obviously the same in both cases. The one example is no less fraudulent nor less criminal than the other.

The fact that paper money was "as good as gold" because it actually represented gold was what gave that money the stability needed for long-range economic calculation. Sound money, itself a creation of the human mind, became, in turn, the means for realizing the full potential of the human mind to plan for the future. People would spread their transactions over extended periods of time only if they could calculate how they could obtain greater benefits by doing so. Men would invest in factories, for instance, which would take many years even to return their cost, only if over a longer term they could be expected to bring a greater return than short-term investments.

But although sound money facilitated the long-range thinking of some men, it took nothing away from others. The men who financed factories did so for their own gain, but in doing so they provided some people with employment and others with manufactured goods. The factory owners, the workers, and the consumers who bought the factory products were like the men who traded their wheat, goat, and chickens: each acted only for his own gain and yet benefited the other two. The benefits each man received were greater in his own mind than what he gave in return and greater than he could obtain elsewhere, or he wouldn't have participated. The factory owners wouldn't have built a factory unless they expected it to be more profitable than anything else they could do with their money. The workers would accept employment at the factory only if it offered them more than other jobs or being self-employed. And the consumers would buy the products of the factory only if in their judgment they were of greater value than the money to buy them or anything else the money would buy. One man's gain was still another man's gain.

In the above example the long-range thinking of one group, the factory owners, provided quicker benefits to the other two. The group which made it possible for the others to benefit received its reward last. The extended range of thinking by the factory owners increased their investment possibilities, but it gave the workers and consumers additional choices in the present, without them having to stretch their minds into the future. These people weren't forced to utilize the new options others created for them. They voluntarily acted upon them when doing so was to their own advantage; otherwise they ignored them. Every successful long-term investment creates near-term opportunities for others, which they consider worth accepting. Every investor, every saver who deposits his money in an institution which invests it, is helping to create jobs, products and opportunities for others. Every lender allows other people to use his money in the present, when it is of greater value to them, in return for which he expects greater value in the future. In every case the long-range gains of some people, who act only for their own interests, first create incidental benefits for others. And anything that impairs long-range economic calculation is detrimental not only to those with economic foresight but, indirectly, to others as well.

INFLATION

Money is a creation of the mind, and sound money is an aid to the process of thought. But money which loses its value through inflation thwarts the mind by destroying the means of economic calculation and future planning. It defeats the very purpose of dealing in money. Remember the only reason for acquiring money is to exchange it for something of greater value in the future. How can this be done with money which itself is losing value? In a free trade a man consents to part with a value in return for one he regards as greater, but inflation takes value from him and leaves nothing in return—just as in our earlier example where the man with the fish ran off with another man's wheat and left him nothing in return. In that example of fraud the wheat was obtained by deception. Inflation, too, takes values from men by deception; it steals value even when men do not realize it is being taken from them, much less with their consent. Inflation is a fraud perpetrated over time rather than immediately as in the example of the man with the fish who defrauded the other man of his wheat.

In the example of the men with the wheat and the fish, we earlier assumed the agreed terms of exchange to be one basket of wheat for two fish. In a direct exchange, where there is no money, the "price" of one commodity is given in another commodity. Now if twice as much wheat were to become available in that society, fish would become twice as expensive; one basket of wheat would buy only one fish. There would simply be more wheat with which to bid up the "price" of fish. Observe that increasing the amount of wheat, however this might happen, would do nothing to increase the *amount* of fish—it would only increase their *price*. Even if ten or twenty times as much wheat were available, that in itself would do nothing to increase the supply of fish; it would merely raise their price to ten or twenty times its previous level.

Now if the "price" in a direct exchange is determined by the ratio of the supplies of the two commodities, then we can see that when all exchanges in society are made in one commodity, a common medium of exchange, the general price level will be determined by the supply of that commodity in relation to the total supply of goods and services. If the money supply is doubled, then, other things being equal, the cost of everything will double. Increasing the amount of money in society will do *nothing* to increase the amount of goods or services which money is used to purchase; it will simply increase their prices. Even increasing the money supply by ten or twenty times will do nothing but raise prices by that amount.[4]

The only instance in which increasing the money supply will increase the goods in society is when money itself is a commodity. If something such as wheat, tobacco, or gold is money, then an increase in its supply, though it still will not increase the goods which it will purchase, will in itself constitute an increase in material wealth. There will be more food, cigarettes, or metal for artistic or industrial use.

But these material values cannot be produced by force. Being force, government cannot create wealth in any form, neither in money itself—real money—nor in the things money can buy. Though force cannot create values, it can take them away—and that is exactly what happens when the force of government is employed in regard to money. We have seen that every step in the development of money and economic progress was the result of people acting for *greater* value, which they did voluntarily. The only reason for applying government force in the realm of money is to compel people to accept *lesser* values in their economic exchanges, which they won't do unless forced.

By depreciating money, government steals some of its value, which it spends, like taxes, at a loss. The loss of value in the money is used to pay for the loss incurred in government spending. Monetary debasement, like taxation, is a way of using the force of government to seize wealth from some people and spend it, against their judgment, for things of less value to them. It is to conceal the fact that its spending always results in a net loss that governments extract costs from the money itself rather than from the people in the form of taxes. Many instances of government spending would be recognized as such obvious and colossal losses if paid for through taxation that the people would refuse to tolerate them.

Some of the methods which for centuries have been used by governments to subtract value from money are the same as those which criminals have used for just as long, namely, removing some of the metal from coins by clipping, filing, and sweating.

> The right to clip, degrade, or debase the coinage, or to change the standard, was looked upon complacently as the prerogative of sovereignty. To debase the currency became, as it were, a crown right.[5]

Clipping and filing the edges of coins were crude means of stealing value from them. Sweating was a little more subtle. In this process a bag of gold coins was shaken, causing the coins to wear against each other. When a small percentage of the gold had worn away, it was collected from the bag in the form of a fine gold dust. Which was then minted into new coins. The amount of gold remained the same—but the money supply increased!

Increasing the money supply in such a manner obviously added nothing to the wealth of society. It certainly didn't increase the amount of goods and services any more than it increased the amount of gold. But it did increase the amount of goods and services the king could purchase. The king had more money than before, so he could buy more of whatever was for sale in his kingdom. But since there were no more goods and services than before, there were less left for the people to purchase. The king ended up with more; the people, less. It happened in the following manner.

The increase in the money supply led inevitably to higher prices, but this didn't happen instantly. When the king spent the new "money," he was able to do so before prices went up. Then as the "money" circulated throughout the kingdom, prices rose because there were more coins with which to bid for the *fewer* goods and services which remained. Because of the higher prices, other people couldn't buy as much with their money. Though the king benefited the most by being the first one to get his hands on the additional money, he wasn't the only one to benefit. But all those who benefited necessarily did so at the expense of others whose money lost corresponding value. One man's gain was another's loss.

Prominent among the losers were all those people who previously sold goods and services in order to make purchases in the future. These were the people with savings. They found that spreading their transactions across time resulted in a loss because the medium of exchange lost value in the interval. Their planning for the future was made to work to their detriment instead of to their benefit, as they expected. Their minds were turned against them.

Inflation is an increase in the supply of money without a corresponding increase in the supply of goods and services. Higher prices are the unavoidable consequence. The example given, of degrading coins in order to increase their number, is only one method of inflation, an easy one to understand. Some methods are more complicated, but all are the same in principle. Every inflation creates "money" without creating value—a practice which necessarily removes value from the extant money, not always physically as in our example, but always by reducing its purchasing power, which is the real measure of value in money. As we pointed out earlier, the general level of prices is determined by the ratio of total money to total goods and services. More money, therefore, means higher prices unless goods and services are also increased, something force—and hence governments—cannot accomplish.

The "usefulness" of force in regard to increasing the money supply is not in creating value—which it can't do—but in compelling people to accept money of less value. The only purpose of legal tender laws, for example, is to force people to act against their judgment and accept debased money, money they wouldn't accept voluntarily. Such laws have great utility for inflation, as we shall see.

One ancient method of inflation somewhat similar to that already described is the minting of debased coins. Instead of removing precious metal from previously minted coins, as mentioned above, governments would mint coins with less precious metal in the first place. By substituting some percentage of a less valuable metal (such as copper) for a more valuable one (such as gold or silver) in minting coins, governments were able to stretch the supply of the more valuable metal to a greater number of coins. Once again the money supply was artificially increased, with the same consequences as before. History has endless examples of this inflationary technique. Consider the Roman *denarius.* It began as a coin of 99 percent silver, but step by step the emperors reduced its silver content until it was nothing but copper. Legal tender laws forced people to accept the debased coinage at the same value as the previous coins. Finally, when the *denarius* became so shrunken in value that even the imperial government couldn't enforce its official worth, the emperor introduced a new silver coin, the *antoninianus,* which quickly began the same downward course as its predecessor and ended up with only two percent silver. In that state it became the world's first "sandwich" coin, a copper coin with a thin coating of silver. Soon the Roman government could no longer force the people to accept this either.

> Commodities began replacing money as the chief instruments of commerce.... Few people were willing to exchange valuable goods for the worthless Roman coinage, and the old power of the legions to compel its acceptance declined with each passing day. The soldiers themselves were angry and rebellious at being continually defrauded of their wages through the issuance of debased or worthless coin.[6]

Minting debased coins is an ancient method of stealing value from money, but we have seen it in recent times in our own country as the percentage of silver in American coins dropped from 90 percent to 40 percent to zero. The silver-like surface of our present sandwich coins is nickel, not silver.

Debasing the currency in the manner just described permitted a far greater theft of value than coin clipping or sweating. In the latter methods only very small amounts of precious metal could be removed; larger amounts would make the coins unusable, even unrecognizable. But the substitution of base metal for gold or silver in the coinage permitted the coins to retain their shape, size, and appearance while any amount of their value was taken away. The scale of this reduction in value might be compared to what would have occurred had the coin clippers kept the coins and circulated the clippings, if that were possible. Yet even coinage debasement of this magnitude was dwarfed by the possibilities for increasing the supply of money and reducing its value through the use of paper.

Just as governments can increase the money supply by reducing the amount of gold or silver in coins, they can accomplish the same thing by reducing the amount of gold or silver which paper money represents. This is called *devaluation*. If the devaluation is 100 percent, then the currency no longer represents any gold or silver. Obviously the money supply can then be increased by any amount. A 100 percent devaluation is seldom acknowledged to be just that; government leaders find it less disgraceful to refer to it by a phrase such as "going off the gold standard." For the same reason, they often refer to any devaluation as a "currency adjustment," or "monetary reform," or some other euphemism. Whatever they call it, governments have been removing value from money in this fashion for as long as they have been using paper currency.

The last pieces of United States paper which Americans could redeem for precious metal were the silver certificates, which the government ceased to honor in the 1960's and completely replaced with bank notes. The one dollar bill, for example, formerly bore the words "Silver Certificate" where the words "Federal Reserve Note" now appear, and beneath Washington's picture were the words "One dollar in silver payable to the bearer on demand." By the use of its legal tender power, the government compelled people to accept the Federal Reserve notes on par with silver certificates until the latter could be withdrawn from circulation.

The fact that paper currency is not money itself but merely represents the value in which it is redeemable was stated succinctly and brilliantly by Mr. C. V. Myers in a letter to the Secretary of the Treasury, which was published in *Myers Finance Review:*

April 14, 1970

Mr. David Kennedy,
Secretary of the Treasury
U.S. Treasury Department Washington, D. C. USA

Dear Sir:

I am enclosing two $100 Federal Reserve notes inscribed... "Redeemable in lawful money at the United States Treasury, or at any Federal Reserve Bank," one signed by Henry Morgenthau, Jr. (1934); and one signed by Henry H. Fowler (1950), both Secretaries of the Treasury.

Webster defines redeemable "to pay off (mortgage or note)..." "to convert (paper money) into coin"—"to fulfill as a promise."

That is what I ask for here.

The reason I approach you directly is that Federal Reserve branches have in the past failed to make good on this pledge of the U.S. Treasury. Instead they have claimed that the note is in itself lawful money. This is unacceptable: For to make a promise and in the next breath to say that the promise is its own fulfillment is patently absurd.

To maintain that the promise can be fulfilled by repetition of the promise (another Federal Reserve note) is likewise patently absurd. To point to subsequent legislation nullifying the promise (as Fed branches have done) is patently a repudiation of the promise.

I do not think that you will repudiate on the written pledge of a U.S. Secretary of the Treasury.

I confront you here with the solemn guarantee of the richest nation in the world, and I am asking that the promise be fulfilled. I do not know what you will send me as lawful money but you must know what the U.S. Treasurers called lawful money in 1934 and in 1950, when they wrote these promises. I do know you have silver dollars in the Treasury and I will be satisfied with them.

Thanking you in advance.

Yours very truly,

MYERS' FINANCE REVIEW
C.V. Myers.

P.S. Since I have several thousand dollars in these pledges, this is no academic exercise, but a matter of considerable material importance.[7]

Mr. Myers argued further, in the same publication:

If I give you a written pledge which I promise to redeem with 10 bushels of wheat at any time, I am certainly obliged to give you the wheat on demand. To claim that the promise is the same as the wheat is utter nonsense. If it was the wheat I would not have had to write a promise. *If the note was lawful money, Morgenthau and Fowler obviously wouldn't have written the promise.* This is just elemental common sense.[8]

Earlier we pointed out that if a goldsmith failed to deliver gold as promised on his paper receipts, he would be guilty of criminal fraud. The same standard, however, is rarely applied to governments.

The fact that paper is not, and cannot, be the same as that which is written upon it is dramatically illustrated by the following excerpt from Hilaire Belloc's classic, "The Mercy of Allah":

The enemy was repelled, but victory was not won. The war dragged on for a year and there was no decision. Gold was scarce and the government was in despair.

I easily relieved them. "Write," said I, "promises to be repaid in gold." (They did as I advised, paying me a trifle of half a million for the advice.)

I punctually met for another year every note that was paid in. But too many notes were presented for the war seemed unending and entered a third year. Then did I conceive yet another stupendous thing. "Bid them," said I to the Sultan, "take the notes as *money.* Cease to repay in gold. Write not 'I will on delivery of this paper pay a piece of gold,' but '*this is* a piece of gold.'" He did as I told him.

The next day the Vizier came to me with the story of an insolent fellow to whom fifty such notes had been offered for a camel for the war and who had sent back not a camel but another piece of paper on which was written, "This is a camel."

"Cut off his head," said I. It was done and the warning sufficed. The paper was taken and the war proceeded.[9]

This little story contains all the essential ingredients of any government's monetary debasement. The government is conducting its operations at a *loss,* in this case because of a war. It attempts to cover its losses by inflicting losses upon others, in this case through the exchange of goods for paper. It attempts to do this first by *deception,* by saying the paper is gold. When the deception fails, the government resorts to *force* to make it work: the camel owner having shown too much "elemental common sense," the government acts against his mind—by severing his head.

Not every government enforces its monetary policies in such brutal fashion, but every government's enforcement depends upon the power of physical force, however applied. No less than in the case of the Sultan, the U.S. government's power to enforce acceptance of its Federal Reserve notes rests upon its power of physical coercion. And though it may not be employed in decapitation, it is nevertheless employed *against men's minds,* to compel them to act against their judgment, to accept a money of *less* value to them.

Every government which replaces a redeemable paper currency with an irredeemable one attempts to deceive its people by assuring them, as the Sultan did, that there is no difference.[10] But the deception is carried beyond mere false statement; the unbacked currency is made to resemble its predecessor as much as possible. In the United States, for example, the irredeemable bills differed only very slightly from their antecedents. The words "Federal Reserve Note" were added, of course, but the significant difference was the subtle deletion of the phrase "Redeemable in lawful money..." or, in the case of silver certificates, "...payable to the bearer on demand." But despite the government's attempts to deny and disguise the difference, the redeemable currency acquired its value from representing a material asset; the irredeemable one, from imitating the former. One had real value; the other, false value. But a "maker of false money" is a counterfeiter!—unless it happens to be the government. In that case the money supply is merely being increased.

When a counterfeiter spends his bogus bills, he obtains goods at other people's expense. His gain is always their loss. The merchants from whom he bought the goods are the losers if the counterfeits are discovered and can't be passed on. And if they aren't discovered—let's assume perfect counterfeiting—then the loss is spread among a great many people in the form of higher prices, just as in our earlier example where the king increased the money supply by increasing the number of coins without creating any real wealth. The same result is produced by government increasing the amount of paper money without a corresponding increase in material value.

Notice that in paper inflations, as in coin inflations, governments employ the same tactics as criminals, force and fraud. The methods of the counterfeiter, the failure to honor written promises, the attempts to foist less valuable money upon the people, the use of force to retain values acquired by deception or to compel people to part with wealth without their consent, all these are characteristic of government monetary policies which always take away value. The eminent economist Henry Hazlitt put it well:

> This is what "monetary management" really means. In practice it is merely a high-sounding euphemism for continuous currency debasement. It consists of constant lying in order to support constant swindling. Instead of automatic currencies based on gold, people are forced to take managed currencies based on guile. Instead of precious metals they hold paper promises whose value falls with every bureaucratic whim. And they are suavely assured that only hopelessly antiquated minds dream of returning to truth and honesty and solvency and gold.[11]

A man who forces another to surrender his money, or any material value, under the threat of physical violence is a criminal. The same action by our government was merely termed "calling in the gold." On April 5, 1933 President Franklin Roosevelt, brandishing the threat of ten years imprisonment or a $10,000 fine or both, demanded the surrender of all gold. After paying the people $20.67 per ounce for it, he raised its price to $35.00, thus cheapening the value of the paper with which he had just paid them. On August 9, 1934 the same president "called in the silver," demanding the surrender of all silver bullion within ninety days. Although the U.S. government valued the addition of silver to its reserves at $1.29 per ounce, the government paid the victims of its nationalization only fifty cents per ounce—and then subjected them to a special tax of fifty percent on any profits even at that price! Once again "monetary management" didn't create value; it took it away. Unlike the history of monetary progress, where men adopted a new money voluntarily because of its greater value, Roosevelt inflicted staggering losses upon people in forcing them to accept a less valuable money.

Issuing irredeemable paper currency isn't the only way of using paper to create inflation. There is more subtle machinery than the printing press. To understand this method of inflation, the most important one for us, let us return to the early development of paper money, the goldsmiths' receipts.[12] Remember that, as a convenience to the depositors, the goldsmiths would transfer gold among accounts according to the depositors' instructions, so that their accounts would reflect their sales and purchases. If two men had deposits with the same goldsmith and one made a purchase from the other, the goldsmith could adjust his ledger accordingly, subtracting the amount of the purchase from one account and adding it to the other. No wealth was created; it simply changed ownership. But *what if the goldsmith entered a credit in one man's account without a corresponding debit in another?* Obviously no real wealth would be created, but the money supply would be increased because the new credit entry could be spent like any other money: if the man with the inflated account made a purchase, the goldsmith would deduct that amount from his account and credit it to someone else. As in our previous inflationary examples, the increase in the money supply merely enabled someone to purchase some of the existing goods without offering anything of material value in return and left fewer goods—and higher prices—for others. The goldsmith was creating more "money" than he had gold, but in this case he created it on his own books rather than by issuing an excessive number of circulating receipts, the other method which he could have used.

What if, when the goldsmith created the artificial credit in one man's account, that man withdrew gold for the full amount of his account? If all the other depositors then did likewise, the goldsmith wouldn't have enough gold to meet his obligations. But it was unlikely that all the depositors would demand their money at the same time, and the goldsmith knew it. As long as he had enough gold to meet any likely demand, he wasn't worried. Meanwhile, what would the man who benefited from the artificial credit entry do with the gold he withdrew? If he spent it, the merchants he patronized would probably deposit it with the goldsmith in their accounts. The gold would make a round trip, returning to the goldsmith, where it would replenish his supply of gold on hand for meeting withdrawal demands. So who was hurt? Same answer as before: everyone who had to pay the resulting higher prices.

Modern banks handle credit in the same manner as our goldsmith. When a bank makes a loan to someone, it simply enters a credit in his checking account. This addition represents no addition of material wealth, but it does increase the money supply; it's just as spendable as checks written against deposits of coins or paper currency. The previous money supply *plus* the new addition of checking-account money will then bid for the *same amount* of goods and services previously available. Result: higher prices.

But there is more to this story. The checks written by the man who received the loan will turn up as deposits in the accounts of those who sold goods or services to him, and these deposits permit *more* loans. Like the goldsmith, the bankers know that it's unlikely all depositors will demand their money at once and hence only a small percentage of cash is kept in reserve. The size of this reserve is regulated by the Federal Reserve Board. If the reserve is 16½ percent, the banks can create new purchasing power, in the form of loans, equal to the remaining 83½ percent—and this process can be repeated with the deposits those loans generate. For example: if a man borrows $1,000 from a bank on his signature and buys something with it, and if the person from whom he makes the purchase deposits the $1,000 in his own account, his bank can then lend out 83½ percent, or $835. If this amount is lent, spent, and deposited in someone else's account(s), then another 16½ percent must be kept in reserve and the remainder, about $700, can be lent out again. The next time roughly $580 can be lent, etc. The completion of this exercise will reveal that every dollar held by the bank as reserve generates five dollars in loans. This five-fold increase in the purchasing medium, the money supply, occurs without any increase in the amount of goods and services which the money is used to purchase. Because of its "multiplier" effect, bank credit is an extremely potent form of inflation.

It's also an extremely deceptive method. The people don't see any physical increase in the quantity of currency in circulation. And while the substitution of debased coins for those of genuine worth, or of irredeemable paper for redeemable currency, produces noticeable differences in the money despite government attempts at deception, such differences don't appear in money created by bank credit. Checkbook money is all the same, whether created by a physical deposit of material value or a stroke of the pen at the bank.

Since upwards of 95 percent of all business in our country is transacted by check, "demand deposits," as checkbook money is called, are a far larger and more important component of the money supply than is actual currency. And the creation of demand deposits by bank credit is by far the most important method of inflation in America today.

Now, who has the greatest need for credit? Whose operations always produce a loss, cannot create wealth, and require the constant influx of new money from outside sources? Who is it that can borrow billions of dollars on nothing but a signature? That's right, the federal government.

Thanks to its own creation, the Federal Reserve System, which Congress created by the Federal Reserve Act of 1913, the federal government can easily satisfy its gluttonous appetite for loans. When the federal government wishes to borrow money from the Federal Reserve System, a member bank, in return for the government's signature in the form of U.S. government securities, creates a corresponding deposit in the checking account of the U.S. Treasury, its tax-and-loan account. The Treasury then spends its checking account money as in our previous example, with the same multiplier effect.[13]

Just as credit expansion adds to the money supply, the repayment of loans causes the money supply to contract. But who is it that always borrows and never pays off its debt? That's right, the biggest borrower of all, the federal government. To quote Mr. Hazlitt again:

> Our politicians, and most of our commentators, seem to be engaged in an open conspiracy not to pay the national debt— certainly not in dollars of the same purchasing power that were borrowed, and apparently not even in dollars of the present purchasing power....
> On the debt we contracted twenty years ago we are paying interest and principal in 48-cent dollars. Are our politicians hoping to swindle government creditors by paying them off in dollars twenty years from now at less than half the purchasing power of the dollar today?[14]

Of course, if government creditors receive 48-cent dollars, they aren't the only ones to lose. Everyone else's dollars are worth only 48 cents, too. One man's loss is another man's loss as inflation takes value from everyone's money.

Throughout history money has meant wealth because it was, or represented, material value. The evolution of money has been the process of searching for an item of value which would best facilitate the exchange of other material values. Money is synonymous with wealth because of its relationship to material goods, to commodities which exist, are possessed by someone, and are valuable in the lives of human beings. Now, however, our money supply is based on the opposite of wealth, on debt, on material values which do not yet exist, which are not possessed but owed. Debt is *negative* wealth.

Banks extend credit to private borrowers on the assumption of future production. It is by adding to the amount of goods and services in society that an individual or corporation expects to be able to repay a loan with interest. Governments, on the other hand, cannot expect to produce material wealth in the future any more than in the past because force cannot produce wealth. Government borrowing is predicated not upon productive power but confiscatory power, not upon the ability to create wealth but the force to seize it. Except for foreign invasion, the only ways any government can ever pay its creditors are by taking money away from the people (taxes) or by taking value away from their money (inflation). In any case government can gain wealth only by inflicting losses upon others. Private borrowing is predicated on the creation of future wealth; public borrowing, on the creation of future losses.

Because of inflation, Americans have lost $10,068,390,000,000 in purchasing power from savings in the half century since World War II. This is the money of people who tried to utilize that distinctive capability of the human mind for long-range planning by providing for their own financial future. But these people are not the only ones to suffer from their loss. Savings institutions and life insurance companies seek to invest money productively. When they are able to do so, more goods and services are produced for other people to enjoy. When inflation destroys investment funds, it takes wealth away from the owners of those funds, but it also deprives other people of the additional goods and services which would have been produced. One man's loss is another man's loss.

Inflation also deprives people of a corollary benefit of increased production: lower prices. Remember that the general price level is determined by the ratio of total money to total goods and services. If the money supply increases while the amount of goods and services remains unchanged, prices will rise. But if the amount of goods and services increases and the money supply does not, or at least does not increase as rapidly, then prices will fall. Inflation is thus doubly destructive: pumping up the money supply leads to higher prices, and it adversely affects the production of goods and services by destroying investment capital and people's willingness to save and invest.

Where there is rampant inflation, as in some of the South American countries, life insurance annuities, pension plans, bonds, and mortgages are either non-existent or nearly so. And without the accumulation of capital, little progress is made in improving productivity, upon which a rise in the standard of living depends. Unable to make long-range economic calculations, unable to retain financial value through their money, people live from day to day. The time-span of their economic thinking is foreshortened. Immediate benefits are preferred to future ones; people will not forego what money will buy today when it will buy less tomorrow. Here, for example, is a description of economic conditions in Brazil by noted investment advisor Harry D. Schultz:

> Long-term financing as we know it does not exist. Investors prefer physical rather than financial assets, which might just disappear tomorrow.
> The net result of this is that many excellent investment opportunities in Brazil are never filled. There is also a tendency for inventory investment and/or direct investment to be for relatively short periods. The type of industry that is likely to make a profit five years from now is of little interest.
> There is a lack of interest in services such as power, transport, communications, etc., where there is a price-rigid economic overhead; and so the arteries of Brazil constantly break down and thwart business.
> The incentive is to invest in flexible-price quick-yielding sectors. Industry is completely at the mercy of inflation, and industries which require long maturation periods are sacrificed in favor of light industry. This of course slows down growth rate and is the main reason why we all run out of ideas after we have thought of coffee, when talking about what Brazil produces.[15]

The time frame of financial thought and action was even shorter in the great inflation in Germany after World War I. Workers had to be paid daily and, near the climax in 1923, *hourly.* Wives would meet their husbands at the factories to get their pay and spend it before it lost further value. No one could count on the money as a store of value for even an hour, prices often doubling in that time. Inflation eliminated the future from economic consideration and virtually reduced people to the level of animals that are incapable of acting beyond the range of the moment. No one could think in terms of savings, mortgages, long-term leases, or other financial arrangements common in a civilized, industrial society. Despite all the money the people were not richer but poorer. The mark in late 1923 was worth one-trillionth of its 1913 value. Imagine what it would be like to have a trillion dollars and ten years later find all that money was worth only one dollar. That was the scale of the German inflation. German money became so worthless that Franz Joseph Strauss, later Finance Minister of West Germany, relates that in 1921 he and his brother took a wicker basket full of money to a butcher shop to buy some meat. They set the basket down on the sidewalk while they looked at meat and prices, and the basket was quickly stolen. Not the money, just the basket. The money had been dumped on the sidewalk.[16]

In China after World War II inflation was so rapid that restaurants would give customers *estimates,* not prices, for items on the menus since the prices would be higher by the time people finished eating. When prices are so uncertain that people will not dare to print them on menus, who will dare to build restaurants? Or factories? Or anything else?

Inflation in Hungary and Rumania after World War II was even worse than the hyperinflation in Germany after World War I. Other twentieth century lessons in severe inflation occurred in Greece, Poland, Russia, Austria, Finland, France and Bulgaria. The Marxist Allende government in Chile managed to reach a quadruple-digit annual inflation rate in the 1970's before being overthrown. Argentina's inflation rate was 1010 percent in 1985, and supermarket prices were increased twice daily; in 1989 the inflation rate was 4200 percent. In 1986 the government of Brazil was devaluing its currency *daily.* Prices in Brazil at the end of 1988 were 14,000 times higher than in 1980. 1994 marked the ninth consecutive year that Brazil had an annual inflation rate of greater than 1000 percent.

Dr. Gerald Swanson, Associate Professor of Economics at the University of Arizona, who has extensively studied inflation in South America, says:

> It isn't unusual for South American shoppers to see the price of bread increase between the time they enter a grocery store and the time they leave it. Savings lose their value. The only incentive is to spend.[17]

In Bolivia in 1983 the annual inflation rate was 11,749 percent, and in 1985 it reached 25,000 percent. But the worst inflation of the 1980s was in Nicaragua in 1988 when the annual rate was 36,000 percent.

Every instance of hyperinflation has been preceded by the demonetization of gold. The essence of this act is that it replaces a money backed by material value with one backed by nothing but government force. The tragic history of inflations amply demonstrates that force is as impotent for creating wealth through a nation's money as it is in any other application. Forcing people to accept more and more worthless money can bring them only poverty, not prosperity.

In the United States the demonetization of gold was accomplished not by a single step but by a series of steps over many decades. For this reason the deterioration of the dollar has not been as rapid as that of many other currencies. Nevertheless, every step away from gold has been a step toward inflation. Our government has been no more able to create wealth than any other, but it could and did increase the supply of dollars. The first step in this inflationary process was the Federal Reserve Act.

This act *lowered* the reserve requirements of banks, thus increasing the multiplier by which banks could expand the money supply through loans. Although this legislation was a direct result of a short but rather sharp banking panic in 1907, such was the confidence in the power of coercion that Americans accepted the idea that a new banking system backed by government could be made sound with lower reserves than before. In other words, force was accepted as a substitute for material wealth in the banking system.

Much of the appeal of the Federal Reserve System lay in the argument that a central banking system would permit a pooling of funds for emergencies. In case of a run on a bank, reserve funds could be supplied from other banks to meet withdrawal demands. But such a rescue operation would function exactly like the goldsmith "borrowing" from one of his accounts to meet a withdrawal demand from another. The central banking system would simply juggle funds between banks in the same way that certain goldsmiths juggled funds between accounts. No wealth would be created in either case. The system didn't eliminate bank failures, as it intended; it encouraged banks to overextend themselves and led to the closing of every bank in the nation in 1933.

The Federal Reserve Act reduced not only the necessary legal reserves held at the Federal Reserve Banks but also the vault cash requirements. According to monetary historian Dr. Elgin Groseclose:

> If the vault cash requirements of national banks prior to 1914 had been retained in the Federal Reserve Act, member banks would have been required to hold about $4.4 billion instead of $2.9 billion (in 1931). This means that, in the

aggregate, total reserve requirements were about 34 percent less in proportion to their deposits than they were before the Federal Reserve Act was passed.[18]

In 1917 the reserve requirements were lowered further in order to assist in floating government war loans.

Then in the 1920s the banking system stretched its reserves still further by the "wholesale reclassification of demand deposits into time deposits in order to take advantage of lower reserve requirements."[19] In addition the Federal Reserve aggressively expanded the money supply through its credit operation in the belief that "easy" money could contribute to prosperity in this country and support the British pound in foreign exchange markets. From 1923 through 1927, $548 million in Federal Reserve credit was forced into the banking system, an amount which the system itself multiplied many times.[20]

In 1928 the Federal Reserve realized its mistake and began to contract credit, triggering the crash of 1929 and the ensuing depression, which inflation by then had made inevitable anyway. The prosperity of the 1920's, like the money upon which it was based, turned out to be only the appearance of wealth, an image unbacked by material value. Many years earlier, in arguing against the Federal Reserve Act in the final days before its passage, Senator Elihu Root had warned that it "provides a currency which may be increased, always increased" but provided no protection "against the occurrence of one of those periods of false and delusive prosperity which inevitably end in ruin and suffering."[21] His warning, of course, went unheeded and was forgotten by the time the "ruin and suffering" of the Great Depression arrived. The Federal Reserve System, established for the expressed purpose of preventing another depression like the one in 1907, was the direct cause of a much worse one!

As long as there was even a partial link between the dollar and gold, there was at least a partial restraint on the government's power to inflate. Although Roosevelt in 1933 destroyed gold convertibility for Americans, the dollar remained convertible for foreigners until 1968. In between, the gold backing of the dollar was reduced several times. In 1945 the requirement that Federal Reserve Banks maintain a gold reserve of 35 percent for notes and 40 percent for member bank deposits was reduced to only 25 percent for notes and deposits combined. The gold reserve requirement against deposits was eliminated in 1964, and the one for notes was dropped in 1968. Finally, in 1971 the last tenuous link between gold and the dollar was severed when the dollar became inconvertible even for foreign central banks. With silver certificates already removed from circulation, the dollar became a pure fiat currency. In the words of monetary analyst Donald Hoppe:

> There is, in fact, no difference whatever between the Federal Reserve currency of today and the German Reichsbank currency of 1914-23. Both currencies were deprived of any legitimate identity as bank notes when their redeemability was denied; they then became *de facto* pure fiat currencies, because their value depended *solely* upon a government-decreed "legal tender" status.[22]

By increasing the money supply without a corresponding increase in real wealth, the Federal Reserve System produced exactly the same results as every other inflation by any other government. It robbed the existing money of purchasing power through higher prices. Since the advent of the Federal Reserve System, the American dollar has lost more than 99 percent of its value.

Americans accustomed to constantly rising prices are usually startled to learn that before the Federal Reserve System the general price level had dropped for most of forty years. People with savings could look forward to a rising standard of living, to their money buying *more* as the years passed—a condition which obviously encouraged savings and, indirectly, investments. There were no wage-and-price controls or government commissions to force price rollbacks, and prices had been dropping for many years before the first antitrust law was enacted. Lower prices were due to nothing but increased productivity. This was the age of the classical gold standard. It was also the age which saw the rise of giant corporations and the so-called robber barons of industry. Though it has been painted as a sordid period in our history, it was actually the time of greatest improvement in per capita *real* income. From 1874 to 1913 the average gain was 4.7 percent, more than double the rate since 1947,[23] when we have had the "benefit" of extensive monetary management, gigantic public spending, and abundant government regulation. Apparently all our federal budget deficits, our subsidies, our "fine tuning" of the economy, our give-away programs, and the rest of our social legislation did less for per capita income than stable money and self-interest before such government intervention.[24] When one considers the enormous number of scientific and technological advances since 1947, the economic gains of the earlier period are even more impressive.

Beginning in 1933, in the crisis atmosphere of the depression, Congress attempted to solve with a string of new legislative measures the problems it had created in money and banking with the passage of the Federal Reserve Act. More laws didn't solve the problems; they merely increased political control over the banking system. "The Banking Act of 1935," writes Elgin Groseclose in his history of the Federal Reserve System, "practically turned the Federal Reserve System over to Franklin D. Roosevelt and New Deal influences."[25]

As monetary policy came increasingly under political influence, short-term considerations became increasingly dominant. The politicians' range of thinking invariably extends no further than the next election, and their primary concern is the immediate satisfaction of the mass of voters by any means expedient.

To justify their short-range policies, the New Deal politicians found an economic theoretician with a range of thinking that matched their own, John Maynard Keynes. Once, when someone criticized an inflationary policy of Keynes as being shortsighted and incapable of producing any benefit in the long run, Keynes resorted to one of his favorite phrases, "In the long run we are all dead."[26] He didn't refute the criticism. He simply didn't concern himself with long-range consequences. No wonder politicians for decades regarded him as the high priest of economics.

The New Deal transformed the nation's monetary system into a powerful machine by which long-term economic gains could be sacrificed for short-term political advantages, a machine through which the force of government could be both extensively employed and effectively disguised in economic affairs.

> One point may be made clear at once: without the Federal Reserve the New Deal would not have been possible. Monetary management was the core and the motor of the New Deal. The Federal Reserve provided the mechanism by which money was managed. It also was the veil by which these manipulations were concealed and given the illusion of normal fiscal operation in the traditional convention. It permitted the Administration to avoid the naked seizure and exercise of power. By filtering its activities through the monetary fabric, government retained the appearance of functioning within the historic private enterprise system. Thus, government was never compelled to requisition or sequester property for its needs; it could always acquire it by purchase, since its means were unlimited.[27]

The above comments on the New Deal are even more applicable to succeeding administrations, for they have used monetary management in exactly the same way but even more extensively. The belief in force as the means of human advancement, popularized by Roosevelt, has only grown since then. There are far more government agencies, programs, and controls over our lives now. And now, even more so than in the 1930s, the monetary system is the "core and motor" of this government expansion.

Contrary to popular belief and the intent of the politicians, the machinery of government has only consumed wealth, not created it. Enlarging the "core and motor" of ever-greater government has generated ever-greater losses through inflation, nor could it be otherwise when employing means which are in every respect counter to the history of monetary and economic progress.

Every advance in the history of money has come about from men acting through choice rather than coercion, to gain material value rather than lose it, by extending rather than reducing the range of their thinking. Government, on the other hand, obtains value through coercion, at a loss to the people, and spends it more flagrantly than ever before for *immediate* satisfaction of the voters who demand benefits NOW, with no thought to the future costs. By saving, people forego immediate satisfactions in favor of greater rewards in the future, a value increase that is furthered by the utilization of savings to improve productivity. Government monetary management works in reverse. It buys immediate benefits at the expense of greater future rewards and in the process retards improvements in productivity by its assault on savings. This assault is a double-barreled one because inflation both destroys purchasing power and encourages short-range thinking, even in non-governmental expenditures. Moreover, by postponing payment for the benefits it buys, by forever postponing payment of the debt through which it acquires them, the government hides the true costs of its purchases and the fact they are worth less than their costs. Sound money permits people to plan economic gains over time, but inflation permits politicians to obscure losses over time.

INFLATION AS INVASION

Planning ahead, the farmers of Jericho set aside stores of grain—savings—for the future. The invaders were the opportunists who seized other people's savings, who wanted to enjoy benefits NOW which they had done nothing to produce. Today, as in the days of ancient Jericho, the people who control the power of organized force employ that power to confiscate other people's savings. They dispense unearned rewards to some through government benefits programs that are paid for by seizing other people's savings through inflationary monetary policy.

Now, as at Jericho, the issue of whether or not people are allowed to use their own savings is the issue of whether they are free to live for themselves or forced to serve others by surrendering the harvest of their labor. Inflation, by redistributing men's earnings, turns some men into the unwilling servants of others, particularly those in government.

Inflation is a means of transferring wealth from the creditors to the debtors. And who is the biggest debtor of all? The federal government, of course. By acquiring anything it wants through its own debts, government transfers purchasing power to itself from the people, whose money depreciates proportionally.

The reason men of force loathe gold is that it is the perfect defense against inflation. It is the bastion which must be overcome if the invasion of monetary value is to succeed. But there is more at stake in the battle than material wealth. Gold represents value uncontrolled by government; it permits men to achieve economic self-determination, to live freely and independently, to work and save and use their wealth for themselves. Gold is the economic fortress defending every man's right to live his life for its own sake. It is this fortress which must be annihilated if men are to be forced to serve the government and made dependent upon it.

PART II
FRIENDS OR ENEMIES

Chapter Seven
IS CAPITALISM INJURIOUS TO YOUR HEALTH?

As long as the people of Jericho were left alone, they had no reason to regard their neighbors as enemies. It was through invasion, by seeking to gain value through force, that the latter made enemies of themselves. In the same way, all those who produce any other material values are not the enemies of those who have less—unless the latter seek to seize their wealth. The production of wealth doesn't require human conflict; its seizure does.

UNDERSTANDING THE INVADER MENTALITY

Unlike the producers, the invaders find hostility necessary to their way of life. They thrive on it. It is their means of bettering themselves. To them, other people are the enemy from whom wealth must be wrested. And the invaders' cause is advanced by stirring up animosity toward the victims, by convincing their own people that the people of Jericho are somehow their enemies. An invasion requires a hostile attitude, both for its attempt to justify its violence and for executing it effectively. Who ever heard of a friendly invasion?

It is the use of force to gain value which necessitates conflict; and in proportion as men accept force as the means of human advancement, they become convinced of the inevitability of human conflict, which, in fact, they cause. Whether it be the argument "The *only* way for us to get that grain is through invasion" or "The *only* way for us to obtain a particular economic or social objective is through government intervention," force is the means of gaining something for some people at others' expense. And since people will not voluntarily agree to a loss, the opposition of the victims reinforces the invaders' belief that force is necessary and that conflict is the natural and unavoidable condition of human existence.

The invaders interpret the world only in terms of their own methods and experience. Since they don't create wealth, they don't think about its being produced; they assume that the quantity of material values is static and that one man's gain is another's loss, just as in an invasion. Believing men's interests are in opposition, the invaders cannot see how an economic exchange can be in the interests of both sides.

The limitations of the invader mentality militate in favor of the invaders' methods. Because they view all wealth in their own terms, the invaders are quick to regard themselves as the victims of other people's gains. They view the acquisition of wealth as a battle against other men and those with greater wealth than themselves as somehow having triumphed over them, which they resent. The more wealth other people produce, the more aggrieved the men of force feel. Resentment builds up. The animosity needed to support violent action begins to mount.

What the invaders do not understand—and cannot so long as they regard force as the means to wealth—is that values need not be static. Production and trade increase values: production, by creating goods and services; trade, by upgrading their worth by moving them to destinations where they are of greatest value, as evidenced by what they will bring in return. The fact that production and trade increase values makes it possible for men to gain wealth by dealing with others to *their* gain.

The trader and the invader deal with others in totally different ways and with opposite effects. The trader enriches himself by enriching others, the invader by impoverishing them. The one deals in terms of values, the other in terms of violence.

Every society functions on the basis of either the trader or the invader. Men deal with others either by their agreement or over their opposition. Agreement characterizes men's attitude toward transactions from which they expect to gain; opposition, those from which they expect to lose. A society in which all transactions are based on the agreement of the participants would logically be characterized by both agreement and gains. But since everyone can't possibly agree on everything, the only way such a society can exist is if everyone is free to deal with others when he thinks he will gain and to abstain when he thinks he won't—if the only transactions are those based on *mutual* agreement. Voluntary agreement is the basis of harmony among men and the reason why a free society can be both harmonious and diverse, as well as prosperous. The name of this social system is *laissez faire* capitalism.

The invaders view the diversity of a free society as evidence that men's interests conflict. They interpret any disparity of wealth as "injustice"—in accordance with their belief that anyone who has more has caused someone else to have less. In their view the basis of human harmony is not agreement but uniformity. For if no one has more than they do, then they will not feel anyone has bettered himself at their expense. They will feel no resentment. And they believe the way to obtain uniformity is the same as the way they obtain anything else—by force.

Of course, the idea of every government scheme for economic uniformity ("equality") is to bestow wealth on some people by taking it away from others. By force. Just like the invasions of Jericho. When the "liberals" propose more government programs, they are simply proposing more invasions. And they are just as convinced of the righteousness of their cause and method as those ancient invaders.

When today's invaders challenge their political opponents with the statement, "What government programs have you proposed for benefiting the needy, the unemployed, or any other group in society?" they are really asking, "What invasions have you proposed for benefiting this or that group?" The question itself indicates that they, like the invaders of Jericho, have never grasped the alternative, never understood the role of the mind in human advancement, never realized the significance between choice and force in human interaction. They don't know the difference between the trader and the invader, between dealing with others to their gain and dealing with them to their loss.

The more government intervenes in the economy, the more society functions on the basis of the invader. In a completely government-run economy, a true socialist state, everyone is both invader and victim. Everything government gives, it must take from others, and when it gives all, it must take proportionately. But the advocates of such a society hope that they will gain more by the government invasions of other people's wealth than they will lose by surrendering their own.

The "liberals" commonly boast of their compassionate concern for their fellow man and believe that the redistribution of wealth will lead to a society of human harmony and brotherly love. But their means defeat their aims. Neither harmony nor love can result from the invader-victim relationships inherent in coercive economic and social programs. The more the exchange of values is determined by force, by government, rather than by the choices of the participants, the more the process makes men enemies of each other.

Because every material benefit government confers upon anyone is someone else's loss, more government intervention means more losses, more victims, and more opposition. The governments which have made greatest effort to manage their economies have been characterized by staggering economic losses and a level of internal opposition that could be quelled only by escalating brutality against their own people, such as in the Soviet Union, communist China, Castro's

Cuba, and Idi Amin's Uganda. All have been scenes of atrocities committed by governments in the name of managing the national economy.

The goal of a uniform, national economic policy is a logical result of an invaders' concern with the military effects of size and the single-minded purpose necessary for a successful attack. The strength of an invasion comes from many people pursuing the same end, but the strength of an economy comes from many people pursuing different ends. Uniformity is a military advantage; diversity, an economic one. The massing of physical power is important for overcoming opposition, but it is irrelevant to men who deal by agreement. Men who deal by choice don't depend on the power of size and numbers. They deal in terms of value, not physical strength.

A "mixed" economy is a semi-civilized state of both traders and invaders. It is a society where men have begun to grasp the significance of productivity but don't understand it fully and aren't yet sufficiently civilized to give up the invaders' methods entirely. The prevailing view is that although production and trade are desirable, society can't exist without at least an occasional invasion against at least some of its members. The idea of using force for gain isn't rejected on principle; it's accepted for "good" causes or whenever it meets the approval of a sufficient number of voters.

All the arguments for a mixed economy are based on viewing the exchange of values as an invader would. If, for example, other men are enemies, as they are to an invader, then it can be argued that they must be restricted, regulated, controlled; one's enemies must be restrained as much as possible. But if everyone participated only in transactions which he regarded to his advantage, as in a free market, he would have no reason to regard other people as enemies. They would be his unintentional benefactors, and he would have no reason to want to restrict them.

It is sometimes argued that a more complex economy requires government intervention. It is said that an increasing number of transactions by millions of people for their own benefit will somehow add up to injury for others. But this argument is simply an extension of the invaders' beliefs that men's interests conflict and that men gain by injuring others. If, on the contrary, men gain by benefiting others, if their transactions are based on their interests coinciding rather than con-flicting, then the overall effect of such transactions should be beneficial rather than harmful. Yet because they don't understand the difference between the trader and the invader, the mixed-economy theorists propose coercive transactions—every one of which is injurious to someone—as a means of remedying the "harmful" effects of free trade. Somehow, they believe, aggregating profitable transactions will result in harm while aggregating coercive (harmful) ones will produce a beneficial effect. Such are the consequences of the belief that benefits result from harming others, as in an invasion.

Governments which propose to distribute benefits to their people—whether directly or through intervention in the economy—must generate hostility for the same reasons as the invaders of Jericho. Sometimes, as at Jericho, the victims are foreigners. Sometimes they are countrymen, hated and plundered by their own government.

When the victims are foreigners, the invasions in modern times have typically taken the form of nationalizing foreign properties. Such seizures are always preceded by campaigns of hatred of outsiders and attempts to portray foreign corporations in the only terms the invaders understand: as invaders themselves, as though foreign investment constituted an invasion, as though it resulted in the loss of wealth rather than the production of it. Armed with an ignorance of production and a self-righteous belief in their use of force, foreign governments, like the invaders of Jericho, have seized oil, copper, bauxite, potash and other industrial properties. For example, Argentina nationalized the oil industry in the 1920s. Mexico did the same thing in 1938. Bolivia nationalized the mining industry in 1952. Zaire expropriated the copper industry in 1967. Peru and Zambia took over copper and other metal mines in 1970. Chile seized Anaconda, Kennecott and other properties in 1971. Guyana nationalized its bauxite mines in 1971, and various other bauxite-producing countries followed suit. Jamaica raised its taxes on bauxite 687 percent—a tax rate tantamount to expropriation. Over several years various governments in the Middle East took over the foreign oil companies in that part of the world. In 1974 Venezuela nationalized the oil industry and also the iron-mining properties of US Steel and Bethlehem Steel. In 1975 Peru expropriated the properties of Marcona. In 1976 India took over Caltex Petroleum, a subsidiary of Texaco and Standard Oil of California.

The invaders cultivate the same kind of animosity toward the wealthy within their own country as they do toward foreigners, and for the same reasons. Whether it be the small merchants or the large corporations, whether it be the bourgeoisie or the big bankers, the invaders always feel other people's wealth is at their expense. And their hostility sparks their invasionary operations. Whether these take the form of unusually high taxes against wealthy nationals or the butchering of millions of countrymen, as in Stalinist Russia, the seizure of wealth by government is based upon and preceded by a campaign of hatred of the victims as "enemies of the people." And the subsequent assault is invariably carried out under slogans of brotherhood or concern for the public welfare.

CORRECTING MISUNDERSTANDINGS ABOUT THE INDUSTRIAL REVOLUTION

The early days of the Industrial Revolution are frequently cited as evidence that under *laissez faire* capitalism the wealthy are indeed "enemies of the people." The harsh conditions of the early factories, the low level of wages, the child labor are all cited as evidence that those who accumulated wealth did so at other people's expense. But this is merely the invader mentality once again attempting to explain the production of wealth in its own terms and to stir up animosity for its own initiatives. Like other invaders, Karl Marx had no understanding of production and trade and sought to explain some people's wealth by other people's losses. Furthermore, he and other socialist philosophers could gain support for their massive government invasions of other people's lives only by preaching human conflict—"class warfare"—and by convincing people that they were being victimized, rather than benefited, by the economic gains of other men.

Knowing the invader mentality, we should not be surprised by its interpretation of economic history. As the Nobel prize-winning economist F. A. Hayek pointed out many years ago, "Because the theoretical preconceptions which guided them [the socialist philosophers] postulated that the rise of capitalism must have been detrimental to the working class, it is not surprising that they found what they were looking for."[1] What is surprising is that their interpretation was accepted so widely and for so long when it is so contrary to historical fact. This popular fallacy is responsible for much of the animosity toward capitalism, as Hayek explains:

> There is, however, one supreme myth which more than any other has served to discredit the economic system to which we owe our present-day civilization.... It is the legend of the

deterioration of the working classes in consequence of the rise of "capitalism."…Who has not heard of the "horrors of early capitalism" and gained the impression that the advent of this system brought untold new suffering to large classes who before were tolerably comfortable?…The widespread emotional aversion to "capitalism" is closely connected with this belief that the undeniable growth of wealth which the competitive order has produced was purchased at the price of depressing the standard of life of the weakest elements of society.

That this was the case was at one time indeed widely taught by economic historians. A more careful examination of the facts has, however, led to a thorough refutation of this belief.[2]

Hayek points out that the growth of population itself "largely contradicts the common belief about the harmful effects of the rise of the factory system."[3]

Numbers which had been practically stationary for many centuries began to increase rapidly. The proletariat which capitalism can be said to have "created" was thus not a proportion of the population which would have existed without it and which it had degraded to a lower level; it was an additional population which was enabled to grow up by the opportunities which capitalism provided. In so far as it is true that the growth of capital made the appearance of the proletariat possible, it was in the sense that it raised the productivity of labor so that much larger numbers of those who had not been equipped by their parents with the necessary tools were enabled to maintain themselves by their labor alone; but the capital had to be supplied first before those were enabled to survive who afterward claimed as a right a share in its ownership. Although it was certainly not from charitable motives, it still was the first time in history that one group of people found it in their interest to use their earnings on a large scale to provide new instruments of production to be operated by those who without them could not have produced their own sustenance.[4]

Or consider this passage by the eminent economist Ludwig von Mises:

The factory owners did not have the power to compel anybody to take a factory job. They could only hire people who were ready to work for the wages offered to them. Low as these wage rates were, they were nonetheless much more than these paupers could earn in any other field open to them. It is a

distortion of facts to say that the factories carried off the housewives from the nurseries and the kitchen and the children from
their play. These women had nothing to cook with and to feed
their children. These children were destitute and starving. Their
only refuge was the factory. It saved them, in the strict sense of
the term, from death by starvation.[5]

Quite clearly, then, the factory system was to the benefit of the
workers, not to their detriment. Though life was harsh by our standards,
the advent of capitalism allowed millions of people to live who would
have perished otherwise. Hayek also notes that

> so long as this increase of the numbers of those whose output
> reached a certain level brought forward a fully corresponding
> increase in population, the level of the poorest fringe could not
> be substantially improved, however much the average might
> rise.[6]

Hayek also makes the penetrating observation that the pessimism
about the effects of industrialization apparently began, not in the
manufacturing districts themselves, but in "the political discussion of
the English metropolis which was somewhat removed from, and had
little part in, the new development."[7] It was from this source that the
radical intelligensia, themselves "with little firsthand knowledge of the
industrial districts,"[8] developed their political propaganda. But when a
London lady, Mrs. Cooke Taylor visited some of the industrial districts
for the first time in the 1840's, she wrote:

> Now that I have seen the factory people at their work, in
> their cottages and in their schools, I am totally at a loss to
> account for the outcry that has been made against them. They are
> better clothed, better fed, and better conducted than many other
> classes of working people.[9]

Even the children who worked in the factories were better off than
their counterparts—those who survived—outside the factory system.
According to economist W. H. Hutt, "Compared to the factory workers,
the agricultural laborers lived in abject poverty, and the work to which
country children were put was far more exhausting than factory labor."[10]
Robert Hessen notes, "The [factory] children's hours of labor were very
long, but the work was often quite easy—usually just attending a
spinning or weaving machine and retying threads when they broke."[11]

If the factory system actually benefited the workers, then government restraints upon it, whatever the good intentions of the reformers, must have been detrimental to the workers. This certainly seems to have been the case. For example, Philip Gaskell, an avowed antagonist of the factory system, upon seeing the plight of large numbers of children deprived of their work by the Factories Regulation Act, admitted it only "increased the evils it was intended to remedy, and must, of necessity, be repealed."[12]

According to Hutt:

> The salient fact, and one which most writers fail to stress, is that, in so far as the work people then had a "choice of benefits," they chose the conditions which the reformers condemned. Not only did higher wages cause them to prefer factory work to other occupations, but, as some of the reformers admitted, when one factory reduced its hours, it would tend to lose its operatives as they would transfer their services to establishments where they could earn more.[13]

The demand for shorter hours, Hutt points out, was a demand for leisure—which is "only demanded after the more primary of human wants are amply satisfied." Furthermore, he continues, "Until man has something to do in leisure, or until the commodities for use in leisure are sufficiently cheap and plentiful, what is the use of it to him."[14] It was the increased productivity of the factory system—not political action—which made shorter work hours both feasible and valuable.

Similarly, it was factory productivity, not government edict, which put an end to child labor. When the system enabled adults to be sufficiently productive to support their children, it was no longer necessary to send the children out to earn their own living. The factory system itself, by evolving greater productivity, was doing more to ameliorate the harsh conditions of the times than government did, or could do, in this regard. By interfering with the productivity of the factories, the political reformers retarded the industrial progress upon which the workers' welfare depended.

> That the apparent benefits wrought by the early Factory Acts are largely illusory is suggested by the steady improvement which was undoubtedly taking place before 1833, partly as a result of the development of the factory system itself. All authorities, it is believed, admit that conditions were at

their worst where domestic work prevailed and in the smaller
factories and workshops, and there was a constant tendency for
these to be eliminated through the competition of larger and
more up-to-date establishments. The effect of the Act of 1833
was actually to set up a countertendency, for work was inclined
to drift to workshops and the smaller factories which were more
easily able to evade its provisions.[15]

HISTORY REPEATS ITSELF

What happened in England in the early years of the Industrial
Revolution has occurred, in essence, over and over again. Throughout
the advance of industry, the invaders have consistently viewed material
values in their own familiar terms rather than in terms of production and
trade. They have argued that industrial wealth was acquired by harming
people rather than benefiting them. They have exhorted men to turn to
force rather than to industry to satisfy their wants, and they have stirred
up hostility among the people to gain support for their assaults. They
have preached the conflict of human interests, portraying human life as
an invader would: as a struggle against other men. They have pictured
the producer as an enemy of the consumer, the employer as an enemy of
the employee, the "haves" as enemies of the "have-nots." But a free man,
of whatever group, deals with other men only when his interests
harmonize, rather than conflict, with theirs. And just as production and
trade are of mutual benefit to the participants, laws inimical to
production and trade are ultimately to mutual detriment, as were the
early Factory Acts in England.

The same invader arguments, the same shortsighted vision and
fallacious charges which led to the Factory Acts in England, were still
being used a century and a half later in our own country for similar so-
called health and safety acts. A few examples are the Occupational
Safety and Health Act of 1970 (OSHA), the Federal Coal Mine Health
and Safety Act of 1969, the National Motor Vehicle Safety Act of 1966
and subsequent laws regulating the manufacture of automobiles.

The proponents of these and other regulatory measures never
understood the difference between the trader and the invader. Their
arguments all implied that the marketplace rewarded injuring others,
either through dangerous automobiles or other hazardous products or
through unsafe working conditions in mines and factories. Government
intervention, they claimed, was needed to stop the carnage, to protect
people from their "enemies" in the marketplace. Representative

Dominick V. Daniels, for example, arguing for the OSHA bill in the House, said, "Every day we postpone passage means 55 more American workers will die; 8,500 will be disabled, and 27,200 will be injured."

The legislative assault against the auto industry was preceded by stirring up hostility against the auto makers with the charge that they were selling increasingly dangerous automobiles to the public. The man who popularized this preposterous notion was Ralph Nader, through his book *Unsafe at Any Speed.* In the preface to this book he claimed not only that "the automobile has brought death, injury, and the most inestimable sorrow and deprivation to millions of people," but also that "this mass trauma began *rising sharply* four years ago, reflecting *new* and unexpected ravages by the motor vehicle." (Italics added)

What neither Congressman Daniels, nor Ralph Nader, nor those deceived by their rhetoric understood was that the basis of market transactions is benefits, not injuries, that neither consumers nor employees will voluntarily trade on any other basis—and companies that do not deal on that basis do not stay in business. If factory workers in the harsh conditions of the early 19th century would accept employment only to their benefit, why would the workers and consumers of today be willing to trade on any other basis? Are we to believe that people today, far better educated than their forebears, far more affluent, and with far more options available to them, would accept economic transactions to their detriment, which even the paupers of the 19th century would not do?

Just as the early socialist philosophers postulated that the rise of capitalism must have been detrimental to the working class, the modern critics of capitalism postulate that it must be detrimental to today's workers and consumers. Now, as then, the economic primitives seek to explain market gains as an invader would, in terms of injuries and losses to others.

In the same way that the critics of early capitalism ignored evidence contrary to their preconceptions, evidence that the early factory system benefited the workers and continually improved their condition, the modern critics have likewise ignored facts which do not fit their assumptions. The truth is that capitalism today, as in the past, has constantly upgraded working conditions and products, and such improvements are not surprising or mysterious but logical, inevitable consequences of freedom in the marketplace.

For example, in the half century *before* OSHA, accidental worker deaths per 100,000 population dropped 67 percent. According to the National Safety Council's *Accident Facts,* fewer workers lost their lives in 1971 than in 1912 even though there were twice as many workers in 1971 and they were producing seven times as much.

And automobiles, along with other products, were becoming progressively safer, not more dangerous. For example, as Grayson and Shepard have pointed out, there were actually fewer total highway deaths in 1960 than in 1939 even though in 1960 there were three times as many vehicles traveling three times the mileage and at much higher speeds. The National Safety Council recorded a steady year-by-year decrease in highway deaths per 10,000 registered vehicles from 1913, when it began keeping track, until 1960. "Actually," say Grayson and Shepard,

> the very first American automobiles were remarkably safer than the horse-drawn vehicles they replaced, and the automobiles of the early 1960's, when Nader prepared his book, were about five times as safe, in terms of highway fatalities, as the earliest models.
>
> In other words, contrary to the Nader indictment, the manufacturers of American cars had been making their products safer and safer and safer, year after year after year.[16]

When Congressman Daniels said, "Every day we postpone passage means 55 more American workers will die; 8,500 will be disabled; and 27,200 will be injured," he seems to have been implicitly promising that the passage of the OSHA bill would put an end to these accidents and injuries. But government could no more cure the problems of production in America in the 20th century than it could in England in the 19th. In fact, like the early Factory Acts, modern health and safety legislation has proven ineffectual, costly, and often hurt the people it was intended to benefit. For example, the Kingsport Foundry in Tennessee, after spending several hundred thousand dollars to comply with safety and environmental standards, noted with concern that its accident rate actually increased since 1970.[17] And an operations chief for a coal mining company was quoted in *U.S. News & World Report,* June 14, 1976 as saying, "Our safety record is worse now than it was prior to the act [the Federal Coal Mine Health and Safety Act of 1969]."

The same article gives an example of how the federal mine safety rules add to injuries, by requiring metal-roofed canopies in many mines.

> The canopies, which cover the continuous-mining machines and the shuttles that transport the men, are supposed to protect miners from cave-ins. However, the height of many shafts is less than three feet, and the men sometimes strike their

heads on the canopies as they ride along the bumpy mine floor or, in trying to avoid that, they will move their heads to the side of the car and be injured by mine walls.

Because of the federal regulations, hundreds of coal mines were forced to close, thousands of workers lost their jobs, and coal was much more expensive for the consumer. And coal mining wasn't any safer. In 1980 there were 32 percent more accidents in coal mining than in 1970 even though less than half as much coal per worker was being produced, due to the regulations.

Nor are other jobs safer because of OSHA. In fact, the industrial accident rate, which had been dropping steadily since 1912, when records were first kept, began to rise after the passage of OSHA. After two full years of these regulations, the number of job-related injuries and illnesses *increased* from 5.6 million in 1972 to 5.9 million in 1973, and lost workdays in manufacturing increased 7.1 percent.[18] After five years of OSHA, *Factory* magazine reported: "Almost one percent of the nation's work force has been killed by their jobs since OSHA came into existence." More than 300 workers were dying every day from work-related injury or illness.

Speaking of the OSHA regulations, Paul Mueller, health and safety manager for Green Giant, observed, "The adoption of a mass of standards without consideration of their effectiveness led to more problems and confusion than it did good." Coercion does not create safety, but it may reduce it, as another safety director explained: "Most of our accidents are not equipment-oriented. Our records show this. The human factor is the thing we should be concentrating on, and *OSHA tends to pull you away from this,*" says Robert Vandenburg, director of industrial safety at General Mills. The irrelevance of the OSHA regulations is also cited by Mr. Mueller: "So few of the injuries in our industry involve a violation of standards as we know them."[19]

In a five-part series for the Associated Press in 1976 Brooks Jackson and Evans Witt concluded:

> In the five years since the Occupational Safety and Health Administration was formed, the highly controversial agency has produced no reliable indication that it has saved many workmen's lives or prevented any significant number of serious job injuries.[20]

On November 22, 1978 *The Wall Street Journal* published the latest Labor Department statistics on work-related deaths. For places with eleven or more employees there were 4,760 fatalities—21 percent more than the previous year. (The department didn't have reliable figures for places with fewer employees.)

In 1992 the U.S. Department of Labor reported a 14 percent increase in the injury and illness rates in U.S. workplaces from 1975 to 1988. We should compare this increase not only to the consistent decrease before OSHA but to the rates in Japan. Japan does not have a system of punitive and intrusive government regulations, as we do. If an unregulated industrial environment is detrimental to the worker, and a regulated one beneficial, the injury and illness rates in the two countries should reflect this. Yet the figures show the exact opposite; Japan's rates declined during the same period ours increased. In Japan the rate plummeted 81 percent in the period 1968 to 1988. For the period 1983 to 1987, the overall U.S. rate was seven times higher than the Japanese rate; and for manufacturing, the U.S. rate was eleven times higher, according to analysts Richard Wokuta and Josetta McLaughlin, writing in the Bureau of Labor Statistics *Monthly Labor Review,* April 1992.

In Chapter Five we noted that federal regulations have not made automobiles any safer. We should also remember that these regulations were costly not only to the auto companies and consumers but to the many workers who lost their jobs when the Corvair was discontinued as a result of Nader's attack. The fact that a senate investigation later denied the validity of his charges, even though the investigation was chaired by a senator from Nader's home state who was himself a well-known critic of big business, did not correct the damage that had been done. No one was ever compensated for the "new and unexpected ravages" of Nader's attack, and the laws he fomented are still on the books, compelling economic waste and restricting the freedom under which continuous progress had occurred in the auto industry for half a century.

The method used to precipitate such legislative assaults is the familiar one. Like ancient invaders, those who advocate the aggressive use of force—"progressive" legislation—whip up hostility among the populace to gain support for such action. They tell people they are being victimized by others, that force can conquer these enemies. It's an old tactic, but it works again and again.

INCITING FEAR AND HOSTILITY ABOUT FOODS

The tactic which was so successful in the issues of auto safety and job safety was also employed in regard to the safety and wholesomeness of the food Americans eat. Through a whole string of scares the public was frightened into believing their health was being victimized by the food industry's quest for profits. Here, we were told, was a "problem" created by free men in the market, one which free minds allegedly could not solve but which government would remedy through force.

The "Filthy Meat" Scare

Prior to the passage of The Wholesome Meat Act of 1967, much hostility was stirred up against the meat industry by vivid descriptions visiting inspectors gave of unsanitary conditions in meat plants where federal inspection was not mandatory. But "the law was enacted on the basis of half-truths, partial facts and some outright lies," according to Oscar Sussman, a health expert with impressive credentials: former vice president of the Veterinary Medical Association of New Jersey, former president of the National Conference of Public Health Veterinarians, first vice president of the New Jersey Public Health Association, senior instructor in meat inspection at Rutgers University, senior Fulbright professor, and consultant to the World Health organization.

Sussman explained that "many false horror stories were exploited" to convince the public of the need for the legislation. For example:

> During the debate on the Wholesome Meat Act of 1967, its proponents, with great success, tossed out the names of a variety of diseases, such as tuberculosis, leptospirosis and brucellosis for public horrification.
> The proponents did this in spite of the fact that no one has ever demonstrated that even one case has been spread to man in the United States by consumption of meat.
> Despite this, one federal official described them as diseases "which can be transmitted through meat and constitute a direct potential threat to human health."[21]

Sussman noted that the carcass-by-carcass method of meat inspection which was being made mandatory was incapable of detecting diseases which people were being frightened into believing they needed the Meat Act to protect them against:

> Public Health workers know of not one case of tuberculosis, brucellosis, salmonellosis or trichinosis that could have been prevented by looking at the carcass of an animal. Their views were not asked for, nor—in the few instances when made available to Congress—were they heeded.[22]

The American public was given a false impression that a problem existed—and then offered a false remedy! Further illustrating the ineffectiveness of government inspection, Sussman cited an instance in New York City where

> seven federal inspectors were present when ton after ton of tainted horse meat was utilized and sold for human consumption. This, under the very noses of a highly touted U.S. inspectors group and with the "U.S. Inspected" stamp applied.[23]

Sussman also cited the work for Dr. Arthur Wilder, who, in the *New England Journal of Medicine,* reported a higher percentage of salmonellae contamination in U.S. inspected poultry than in uninspected poultry. And in 1976 *Consumer Reports* found that canned chili with meat, which had 750 times as much federal inspection as canned vegetables, was the dirtiest product in the study.

On July 24, 1992 the Associated Press carried the following news item:

> Federal inspections are so sloppy that top-of-the-line "USDA Prime" and "USDA Choice" labels turn up in grocery meat cases on everything from cheaper cuts of beef to pig ears, feet and tails, investigators said....
>
> A U.S. Department of Agriculture investigators' report obtained under the Freedom of Information Act found that shoppers may be paying for what appears to be the tastiest and most tender grade of beef, but taking home a cheaper cut, or something that isn't beef at all.
>
> Inspectors from the USDA's Agricultural Marketing Service are supposed to make sure that the meat for sale is properly labeled.... But, according to the March 1992 report, the marketing service "could not provide adequate assurances that meat products are being properly labeled and advertised."
>
> Other violations include improperly applying beef grade labels to pork or other "non-beef" products, including ox tails, pork ribs, pig feet, tails and ears.

So government inspection has, over a quarter of a century, been a false remedy. The "problem," too, was false. Sussman wrote:

> The real truth is that, prior to the new law, the American meat industry furnished consumers with an abundance of nutritious, inexpensive meat and poultry.... [The industry] should be commended for having produced a product excelled

nowhere in the world. It would continue to produce it, without federal inspection.[24]

Interestingly, there is no government inspection program for fish and seafood comparable to that for meat and poultry, but statistically you are less likely to get sick from fish or seafood than from government-inspected poultry.

A remarkable technology for reducing food spoilage and improving safety for the consumer has been known for over forty years, but its use has been prevented in the United States by our own federal government. Here is one more example of government preventing progress. Irradiation of foods has long been approved by the World Health Organization and other international health agencies. It has been subjected to hundreds of tests and has been used in thirty-seven countries with no evidence of any adverse effects. Irradiated food has been available for more than thirty years in France, Japan and Israel, and NASA has supplied it to U.S. astronauts for twenty years.

In 1992 the U.S. Dept. of Agriculture estimated that 35 percent of chicken carcasses sold to consumers were contaminated with salmonella bacteria—yes, even with federal inspection! Lawrence Glickman, head of pathobiology at Purdue University, puts the figure at over 50 percent. The Centers for Disease Control in Atlanta receive reports of 45,000 cases of salmonella poisoning a year but say the true figure may be as high as 4 million because most cases go unreported. By any standard, federal inspection has failed miserably to protect the consumer from salmonella. Yet a method, irradiation, has been available which is far more effective than federal inspection, *which would make federal meat and poultry inspection obsolete*—and the government prevents it from being used for 40 years, until 1992, when it was approved only for poultry.

In 1993 four children died and several hundred people became sick from eating hamburgers from Jack in the Box restaurants in the Pacific Northwest. All our laws and government inspections didn't prevent this tragedy. The restaurant chain and its suppliers had complied with all government regulations. Despite the clamor for even more government inspection, that wouldn't solve the problem because the bacteria responsible can't be detected by inspection. Is there a way to ensure bacteria-free meat that would have prevented such a tragedy from occurring? Sure, not by government inspection, of course, but by the process that the government—under the guise of "protecting" the consumer—for decades wouldn't allow for poultry and still wouldn't allow for beef: irradiation. The process is so effective in destroying bacteria in foods that otherwise-perishable foods will keep for months, in some cases years, without refrigeration.

On February 9, 1994 the CBS television program *48 Hours* aired an investigative program illustrating how federal meat and poultry inspections fail to protect the public. It showed film of unsanitary practices in a South Dakota meat-processing plant with four federal inspectors on duty at the time. Members of the CBS staff also purchased 30 packages of government-inspected ground beef from stores in Boston, Atlanta and San Antonio and found ten to be contaminated. They also purchased thirty government-inspected (non-irradiated) chickens from various stores, had them tested, and found only five with a clean bill of health.

In March 1996 the Russian government banned all imports of U.S. poultry, saying the birds didn't measure up to Russian sanitary conditions. It cited the U.S. Department of Agriculture's own figures of 3,000 deaths and millions of cases of food poisoning in the U.S. from federally-inspected meat and poultry.

On May 23, 1996 *The Wall Street Journal,* in an article about USDA meat inspection, stated:

> It has become increasingly routine for them [the inspectors] to pop into a plant for 15 minutes or so, conduct a cursory look around, then rush off to the next plant, according to food-inspection union leaders.
>
> Some inspectors are too busy to collect food samples for bacteriological testing. Meanwhile, it isn't uncommon for plants to operate for days without seeing an inspector, despite a federal law requiring daily inspections.... The Agriculture Department has stopped keeping track of such "nonvisits," rather than documenting how routinely it fails to abide by the 1906 meat-inspection law that requires continuous inspection of processing plants.

The American public has long believed that federal meat inspection came about and is necessary because of industry selling filthy meat in the first place. The 1906 Meat Inspection Act, the basis of federal meat inspection for more than half a century, until the 1967 Act, was the result of unsanitary slaughterhouse practices portrayed in Upton

Sinclair's novel, *The Jungle,* which told of such things as men falling into tanks, being ground up with animal parts and processed into lard. But that book was "not a well-researched and dispassionate documentary," says Dr. Lawrence W. Reed, President of the Mackinac Center for Public Policy. He writes:

> Sinclair relied heavily on both his own imagination and on the hearsay of others. He did not even pretend to have actually witnessed the horrendous conditions he ascribed to Chicago packinghouses, nor to have verified them, nor to have derived them from any official records.
>
> Sinclair hoped the book would ignite a powerful socialist movement on behalf of America's workers. The public's attention was directed instead to his fewer than a dozen pages of supposed descriptions of unsanitary conditions in the meatpacking plants. "I aimed at the public's head," he later wrote, "and by accident I hit it in the stomach."
>
> Though his novelized and sensational accusations prompted later congressional investigations of the industry, the investigators themselves expressed skepticism of Sinclair's integrity and credibility....
>
> [The] authoritative 1906 report of the Department of Agriculture's Bureau of Animal Husbandry...provided a point-by-point refutation of the worst of Sinclair's allegations, some of which they [the investigators] labeled as "willful and deliberate misrepresentations of fact," "atrocious exaggeration," and "not at all characteristic."[25]

President Theodore Roosevelt said of Sinclair:

> I have utter contempt for him. He is hysterical, unbalanced, and untruthful. Three-fourths of the things he said were absolute falsehoods. For some of the remainder there was only a basis of truth.[26]

Surprisingly, there were already hundreds of local, state and even *federal* meat inspectors operating before the 1906 Meat Inspection Act. But in the House Agriculture Committee investigation following the publication of Sinclair's book, it was noted that not even one of those officials "ever registered any complaint or [gave] any public information with respect to the manner of the slaughtering or preparation of meat or food products."[27] Furthermore, more than two million visitors toured the Chicago stockyards and packinghouses annually, and thousands of people worked there. Yet none of them reported the atrocious conditions Sinclair described.

Dr. Reed also makes the point that Chicago packers accounted for less than 50 percent of the nation's meat products and that "few if any charges were ever made against the sanitary conditions of the packinghouses in other cities."[28] So consumers had plenty of other options. The Chicago meat producers would have faced the prospect of a tremendous loss of business if conditions in their plants were anywhere near as unsanitary as Sinclair alleged. It was to their self-interest to maintain sanitary operations.

The Meat Inspection Act of 1906, like the Wholesome Meat Act of 1967, was the result of false charges portraying the meat industry as an "enemy of the people." The phony propaganda of a book that was intended to "open countless ears that have been deaf to Socialism"[29] led the public to accept a government service that was not only unneeded but ineffective, even counterproductive. Although that service has had decades to improve its effectiveness, our earlier examples and the *48 Hours* program in 1994 demonstrate what a failure it has been. Nevertheless, *48 Hours* offered a rerun of 1906 and 1967, advocating even greater government intervention on the assumption profits in a free market are made at the expense of human health. Just like with "unsafe" automobiles, coal mines and factories.

The DES Scare

DES (diethylstilbestrol), a synthetic form of estrogen which had been used in prescription medicine since the 1940s, had been used as a growth stimulant in cattle since 1954. Eighteen years later it was being fed to 75 percent of the 30 million cattle slaughtered annually in the United States. There is no evidence that even a single individual ever suffered harm from DES in the tens of millions of cattle that scores of millions of Americans devoured during all those years.

DES enabled a 500-pound animal to attain a marketable 1000-pound weight in 34 fewer days and with 500 pounds less feed than otherwise. It also increased by 7 percent the amount of protein and moisture in the meat and reduced the percentage of fat. A reduction in dietary fat is widely promoted as a health measure.

Since 1940 it has been known that all types of estrogen can produce cancer in test animals, so no evidence of DES in the meat was to be allowed. As late as 1968, testing techniques were unable to identify traces of DES below ten parts per billion (about five drops per 25,000 gallons). By 1972 a highly sensitive radioactive tracer technique was able to detect extremely small (hundredths of a part per billion) DES residues in about 2.5 percent of animals sampled. Importantly, the DES was found only in the livers.

Meanwhile, Dr. Arthur L. Herbst, a Boston gynecologist, reported on an extremely rare form of vaginal cancer among young women who had one factor in common: during pregnancy their mothers had received massive doses of DES medicine to reduce the risk of miscarriage.

The stage was now set for branding the "greedy cattle raisers" as *enemies of the people* for "poisoning" the nation's meat supply. People were panicked into thinking they were being exposed to the risk of cancer through the beef supply. In a subcommittee hearing on DES Senator Edward Kennedy set the tone with the alarmist statement that "we are here today because DES, a known cancer-causing agent, is appearing on thousands of American dinner tables." Fears were raised about that most popular of beef products, hamburger, even though no DES was ever found in it or any other form of beef except liver—and even there it was found in only a very small percentage of the animals tested. The issue was portrayed as one of cattle industry profits versus public health. Doctors Elizabeth Whelan and Frederick Stare state:

> The *"us vs. them" attitude* surfaced…. DES was described by critics as a means of "saving cattlemen some $90 billion yearly." Of course, no link was made between the savings of cattlemen and the cost of ground chuck at the local market.[30] (Italics added)

Come April 1973 the FDA banned all uses of DES as a cattle growth stimulant, citing the evidence of 0.04 to 0.12 parts per billion of DES in beef liver. Just how "dangerous" DES was to Americans in their meat supply is indicated by another action the FDA subsequently took on DES in the same week—it approved its use as a "morning after" birth control pill in ENORMOUSLY larger doses!

Those two FDA actions are in themselves marvelously inconsistent, but there are further inconsistencies, too, in the banning of DES as a cattle growth stimulant, as Drs. Whelan and Stare point out:

> First, DES is an estrogen—but it is not the only source of estrogen to which American eaters are exposed. Milk, eggs, and honey have estrogen. It has been estimated that there is 1000

times the amount of estrogen in an egg than there is in a serving
of affected liver from an animal treated with DES. Additionally,
the popular oral contraceptive has *far* more synthetic estrogen
than would a serving of liver with DES traces....

Second, and even more fundamentally, a woman's body
regularly produces estrogen. *Nature* [a British scientific journal]
estimated that it would take 500 pounds of liver containing 2
parts per billion of DES to be equivalent (in terms of DES
quantity) to the daily production of estrogen by a reproductive-
age woman. Men, too, have their own share of natural estrogen.

Third, women who were formerly treated with estrogen to
prevent miscarriage received up to 125 mg. a day during pregnancy. To ingest a dose equivalent to just 50 mg. of DES, you
would have to, at one sitting, eat 25 tons of beef liver containing
2 parts per billion of DES.[31]

Of course, the highest DES content cited by the FDA in the 1973
banning was not 2 parts per billion but 0.12. To get the equivalent dose
of DES from that concentration, one would have to eat not 25 tons but
more than 416 tons. But not all beef liver showed evidence of DES. If
liver with DES concentrations of up to 0.12 parts per billion occurred in
only 2.5 percent of the animals, one would have to eat 16,666 tons of
liver to get 50 mg. of DES.

Estrogen is found not only in milk, eggs, and honey, as mentioned
above, but in various plant foods. Biochemist James Miller noted,
"Every day we eat far more estrogenic substances from plant foods than
...DES contaminants in meat."[32]

Whelan and Stare point out that there was no evidence that the
minute traces of DES found in the livers were harmful to man or
animals. On the contrary, they say, all evidence points to the fact that
DES and other estrogens produce "no effect" at low levels. And the
levels of DES in the liver certainly were low:

> One would have to eat 1,000,000 pounds of liver from
> beef treated with DES to take in the amount of synthetic
> estrogen contained in just one morning-after pill.[33]

The Nitrite Scare

Sodium nitrate is a chemical which occurs naturally in air, water,
soil and plants, including vegetables. It has been used for thousands of
years in curing and preserving meat. When nitrate is used in curing
meats, it automatically changes to nitrite, which is currently added

during the curing process. In addition to giving cured meats their distinctive flavor and appearance nitrite retards spoilage by slowing oxidation and prevents botulism, a painful bacterial toxin that causes paralysis and death in human victims. There is no known substitute for nitrite in preventing botulism.

On the basis of one study in which rats were fed huge doses of nitrite the FDA in 1978 announced that it was planning to ban nitrite from meats because it caused cancer in rats. Later the FDA softened its stand because of doubts about the validity of the original study and because of fears that banning nitrite would cause far more deaths from botulism than would occur from cancer because of the nitrite. Instead of an outright ban the FDA then advocated a reduction in the use of nitrite and said it planned to phase it out as better alternatives became available. Though this revised policy was a concession to nitrite's indispensability, it clearly implied that nitrite still posed a danger to human health. To this day many people still think they might get cancer from eating bacon, ham, luncheon meat, wieners and other meat products containing nitrite.

According to a report by the Comptroller General of the United States in 1980:

> The primary sources of nitrate and nitrite ingested in the average diet are vegetables and cured meat; 95 percent of nitrate (nitrate converts to nitrite) comes from vegetables and about 5 percent of nitrite comes from meats.[34]

Thus even if we totally eliminated all bacon, ham and other cured meats, 95 percent of the "danger" would still exist—but we are expected to believe that the 5 percent added by industry is the "problem." The recommended nitrite level for curing bacon is 120 parts per million (ppm). By contrast, lettuce naturally contains 600 to 1700 ppm of nitrate; spinach, 500 to 1900 ppm; beets, 1200 to 1300; radishes, 1500 to 1800 ppm. Celery, eggplant, turnip greens, leeks, onions, asparagus, cabbage, broccoli and corn also contain nitrate. Some individual samples of vegetables have shown concentrations as high as 3000 ppm.

When people eat these vegetables, human saliva converts the nitrate to nitrite through bacterial action. The same process also takes place in the stomach and in the intestines. In fact, Steven Tannenbaum, Professor of Food Chemistry at Massachusetts Institute of Technology says that "probably thousands of times more nitrite is formed in the intestine than is contributed to the intestine from preformed nitrite in the diet."[35]

Along with consuming nitrite, and producing it himself, man ingests many plant and animal foods with amines (such as amino acids from protein) which combine with the nitrite in his stomach to produce N-nitroso compounds (nitrosamines and nitrosamides) in far larger quantities than he could ever ingest from bacon or ham. Yet N-nitroso compounds "cause cancer in virtually every organ, and in every species tested," says Edith Efron in her exhaustive study of cancer research, *The Apocalyptics: Cancer and the Big Lie.* "The human body," says Efron, "is a natural nitrite and nitrosamine factory."[36] Even without food in one's mouth a person's saliva naturally contains about 6 ppm nitrite. Thus everybody is carrying a "known cancer-causing agent" in his mouth 24 hours a day.

The reason we are not all dead already from our own body chemistry is that these carcinogens are simply not dangerous at certain concentrations. The human body itself makes a mockery of the idea that any amount of a carcinogen, however small—even one molecule—may cause cancer. It is impossible to eliminate carcinogens from the human body or human food or the environment. Time and again, however, the government announces the result of some study where rats or mice got cancer from some laughably huge quantities of some chemical— quantities that could never occur outside the artificial environment of the laboratory. The government then bans the chemical in even the most minuscule concentrations. Industry becomes the villain, the public sees itself as the victim, and the government poses as the hero for "protecting" human health.

The Cyclamate Scare

By 1969 Cyclamate, an artificial sweetener, had been on the market for over twenty years. Americans were consuming 15 to 20 million pounds of it per year. Three out of every four people in the United States were ingesting cyclamate in 172 brand-name products from low-calorie soft drinks to puddings, fruit juices, salad dressings, candy, jams and jellies, ice cream and chewing gum. This widespread consumption plus eighteen years of intensive research had shown no connection between cyclamate and cancer or any other health problem.

Then in October 1969 cyclamate was banned on the basis of one study of 240 rats in which 8 at the highest dosage developed bladder tumors. The study itself was flawed and ambiguous. All the rats received at least two chemicals and some received three. So which chemical actually caused the tumors? There was no proof it was the cyclamate.

In 1973 the German Cancer Research Center in Heidelberg reported that a whole series of studies failed to establish a link between cyclamate and tumors. That same year Abbott Laboratories submitted a sixteen-volume petition to the FDA covering 22 long-term studies in rats, mice, and hamsters which showed no connection between cyclamates and cancer. These studies, together with those of other researchers all over the world, made cyclamates "the most thoroughly tested potential component of the human diet" in history. The FDA told Abbott to go home and do more tests. Abbott petitioned again in 1982 on the basis of 59 new studies and other data. Still the FDA refused to rescind its ban.

To ingest the amount of cyclamate the 8 rats received in the study on which the FDA based its ban, you would have to drink 24 gallons (about 350 bottles of diet soda) *every day over a lifetime.* Actually, you couldn't drink that much of anything in one day (who would try?) without fatal consequences. It would take only about half that much *distilled water* in a single day to kill you; death would not come from cancer—you would die much faster from upsetting the electrolyte balance in your brain, as proven a by well-documented examples in medical history.

By 1985 cyclamate products were being sold in more than forty countries, with no evidence of any adverse health effects.

A Few Other Scares

When cyclamates were banned, saccharin was the only sugar substitute for diabetics and weight-conscious consumers. On April 15, 1977, the FDA proposed to ban saccharin on the basis of a study where rats developed tumors after being fed saccharin equivalent to 800 cans of diet soda per day. The public clamor and ridicule that erupted over that announcement led Congress to prevent the ban: it passed the Saccharin Study and Labeling Act, which imposed a moratorium on any ban against saccharin, ordered further study, and mandated warning labels on the product.

Other substances with even much smaller risks than saccharin have not escaped a ban the way saccharin did. Just how small these risks can be is indicated by the example of the banned Trichloroethylene (TCE), as described by Prof. Murray Weidenbaum:

I had a discussion with HEW when they were saying that trichloroethylene, an additive that used to be used in decaffeinated coffee was carcinogenic. But the dosage needed to induce cancer was equivalent to a human being drinking 50 million cups of decaffeinated coffee, every day, for a lifetime.

I put it to the people at HEW, "If every man, woman and child in America drank 10 cups of decaffeinated coffee daily, how many cases of cancer would result in this country? Ten a year?"

"Oh no, not that many."

"Five a year?"

"No."

"One?"

The poor fellow had to tell me he didn't think there would be even one additional cancer a year but that he couldn't be quite sure.[37]

EDB (ethylene dibromide) had been used for 30 years to fumigate grain and other crops against insect infestation and mold contamination. No health problems developed from this long period of use. Then came a study in which rats developed cancer after being fed 12,000 times the legally approved dose five times a week for thirty weeks. Yet workers who had sprayed crops with EDB had inhaled regularly, for decades, even greater doses than that which gave the rats cancer; and these workers still showed no increase in cancer! Even the man responsible for the rat study downplayed the risk, saying, "We've had 30 years exposure to EDB. So why alarm the public with one more cancer scare, especially when it's not a very likely cancer risk?"[38] The risk was 10 to 100 times less than the risk of cancer from the black pepper on your dinner table— and 1000 times less than from aflatoxin, a natural mold carcinogen common in peanut butter. Says Dr. Bruce Ames, Chairman of the Department of Biochemistry at the University of California at Berkeley and one of the foremost authorities on carcinogens:

Aflatoxin is about 1000 times more potent as a carcinogen in rats than EDB. Why make a big fuss about tiny traces of EDB, when the risk from eating the average peanut butter sandwich comes out as more…. (The risk from eating a peanut butter sandwich is so low I don't think twice about eating one.)[39]

Yet in the wave of hysteria over EDB housewives around the country were throwing out perfectly good Duncan Hines cake mix—as publicly urged by the governor of New Jersey. Dr. Keith C. Barrons noted that not only were the levels of EDB in the samples extremely low but, "Add to this margin of safety the fact that grain-derived foods are only a portion of the human diet, and further, that much of any EDB present would be reduced by cooking or baking, and the risk fades into insignificance."[40]

The apple scare is still fresh in our memories. In 1989 an organization calling itself the National Resources Defense Council claimed that it sampled 32 apples and found 23 of them to contain residue of the pesticide Alar. It did not say the amount was one-fortieth of the EPA allowable limit. The FDA then tested 3801 apples and found one apple—that's right, ONE apple—with Alar (at one-twentieth of the EPA limit)—"Implying that the NRDC sample was doctored, if the report was not fraudulent."[41] No matter. Another panic was on its way. According to biochemistry professor Thomas Jukes, an award-winning cancer researcher at Berkeley, the carcinogenic risk from Alar is 30 times less than one slice of bread, 2800 times less than one 12-ounce bottle of beer, and about equal to one quart of the chlorinated tap water that tens of millions of Americans drink every day. But the facts never had a chance. CBS, more interested in anti-industrial sensationalism than responsible journalism, made Alar "the most potent cancer causing agent in our food supply." Its popular program *60 Minutes* asked, "And who is most at risk? Children who may develop cancer from this one chemical." Some 20 school boards destroyed completely safe apples rather than feed them to students. A public opinion poll showed 60 percent of Americans thought apples were a serious health risk. EPA announced it would ban Alar.[42]

THE REAL WORLD

Poisons

Philip J. Wingate, a retired research chemist and DuPont executive, writes:

> What would be the likely reaction of the public if a manufacturer of breakfast foods proposed to improve the taste of his products by adding small amounts of the following chemicals to them: acetone, acetaldehyde, methyl butyrate, ethyl caproate, hexyl acetate, methanol, acrolein, and crotonaldehyde?
> No doubt the air would be full of flying injunctions and sticky lawsuits because every one of these chemicals is a poison....

> Nevertheless, all eight of the chemicals listed above are found, along with many others, in ripe strawberries....
>
> Not only is a ripe strawberry loaded with chemicals, but it acts as a chemical reactor right while it sits on the breakfast table waiting to be eaten. The acetaldehyde is being oxidized to acetic acid, the crotonaldehyde to crotonic acid, and the methanol to formaldehyde.[43]

Formaldehyde is both toxic and carcinogenic. It is found not only in strawberries but in bread, cola and beer.

Give a substance a technical name, and the layman assumes it is a product of science and industry, rather than nature. Tell him it is a poison, and he is sure it is! The public tends to think of "chemical" as meaning synthetic compounds invented by the chemical industry, but the natural world is made up of chemicals. The air, the oceans, and the continents are seething masses of chemical reactions. So are our own bodies. The myth has been created that nature is benevolent and that most poisons in our world are man-made—the awful products of the highest form of Man the Maker: Industrial Man. In reality the opposite is closer to the truth. Nature is full of poisons. Dr. Barrons again:

> The world around us abounds in nature's toxic substances, and our food is no exception.... In tests with laboratory animals some of nature's toxic substances have proven more poisonous than any man-made chemical, and their concentrations in food are generally much greater than the synthetic impurities that have generated so much fear.[44]

A potato contains about 150 different chemical substances, including solanine, the highly poisonous component of deadly nightshade. In a year the average American eats 119 pounds of potatoes, which contain 9,700 milligrams of solanine—enough to kill a horse. Potatoes also contain fat-soluble neurotoxins that are detectable in the blood of all potato eaters. High levels of these neurotoxins cause birth defects in rodents.

Lima beans contain hydrogen cyanide. So do cherries, plums, apricots, peaches, pears and peas. Even cabbage, broccoli and cauliflower contain cyanide compounds. Nutmeg, parsley and dill contain highly toxic myristicin and apiole. Myristicin is also found in carrots, parsnips and bananas. There is enough caffeine in 100 cups of coffee to produce convulsions and possible death in humans if ingested in a single dose.

The poisons just mentioned are not dangerous to us in small amounts. No one is going to eat 119 pounds of potatoes at one sitting. So no one—except rats in the artificial environment of a laboratory—is going to get 9,700 milligrams of solanine or toxic doses of any of the other food chemicals cited. Long ago the Swiss physician and chemist Paracelsus observed, *"Everything is poisonous. The dose alone determines the poison."* Even plain water can be poisonous in large enough doses, as mentioned earlier. Suicide by drinking large quantities of water was known in Ancient China.

Of course, people can live without potatoes or any of the other foods we've named. No single food is necessary to human health. But if you start to eliminate every food that contains a poisonous substance in any amount you would starve. Many fruits, vegetables, cereals, meats, and dairy products have traces of arsenic. If you turn from these foods, which are produced on land, to those which we harvest from the sea, you do not escape the problem. Shrimp, oysters, mussels, prawns and other marine foods have even more arsenic—up to 174 ppm. (This arsenic is due to the natural environment, not pollution. The oceans contain more than 3 billion pounds of arsenic—enough to kill the human race several times over.) Dozens of foods contain this one poison, and there are many others in the foods we eat every day. Even alfalfa sprouts and yogurt—darlings of the health-food faddists—contain dangerous substances. The alfalfa contains highly toxic canavanine, which attacks the immune system. And cataracts developed in 100 percent of the rats fed yogurt exclusively in a study at Johns Hopkins Hospital in Baltimore.

Not only are small amounts of poisonous substances unavoidable in our diet, they are necessary to human health. Take vitamin A, for example. It is essential in amounts we normally ingest, but at highly excessive levels it can cause liver damage, cancer, birth defects including brain deformities, and even death. Man can also be poisoned by the salts of copper, tin, cobalt, and even iron; yet every one of these minerals is essential to human health. Even arsenic has been found to be essential. It would be foolish for us to ban vitamins and minerals from our diet because they are poisonous in large doses when they are necessary to us in small doses.

Carcinogens

In the same way that the world is full of natural poisons, it is also full of natural carcinogens. They are inescapable. They are in the food we eat, the soil we walk on, the air we breathe. They are produced by plants, trees, bacteria, viruses, fungi, and our own bodies.

We have already mentioned nitrates, which are produced in many vegetables and in man's own body. The artificial sugar substitutes cyclamate and saccharin were reported to be cancer risks, but the same is true of natural sugars. Sucrose, the best known sugar (from sugar cane and sugar beets) is reported to be a potential carcinogen. Fructose, found in all fruits, is a reported carcinogen.

Orange, lime, lemon, and grapefruit oils are reported to be carcinogens or carcinogen promoters. Dates, strawberries, blackberries, apricots and cherries contain coumarin, a reported carcinogen. Corn oil, cottonseed oil, and sunflower oil are reported to be carcinogens. Raisins and chopped walnuts contain malonaldehyde, which is reported to be a carcinogen. American cheese, Swiss cheese, mozzarella and ricotta cheeses also contain malonaldehyde. "Plant estrogens, such as those in carrots, are said to be comparable to the proved (carcinogenic) synthetic estrogen DES."[45]

Black pepper, cinnamon, ginger, nutmeg and mace contain safrole, a reported carcinogen. Mustard and horseradish contain carcinogenic allyl isothiocyanate, which is also found in lesser amounts in broccoli and cabbage. Salt is reported to be a carcinogen. Coffee, tea, and cocoa contain several carcinogens. So do soybeans.

All fruits, vegetables and animal feed contain terpenes, which are reported carcinogens. Ethyl carbamate, found in bread, yogurt, soy sauce, olives, beer and wine, "produces tumors in a wide variety of tissues in rats and mice, whether administered orally, by inhalation or by injection."[46]

Fungi produce carcinogenic mycotoxins. The aflatoxin mentioned in regard to peanut butter is one of these. There are many others, and they are everywhere. The French-based International Agency for Research on Cancer reports that "virtually every food stuff or food product is potentially susceptible to contamination (by aflatoxin) which may occur at any stage of food production or subsequent processing. Samples of nearly every dietary staple have been found to contain some aflatoxin at one time or another."[47] These staples include, among others, coconuts, sunflower seeds, hazelnuts, Brazil nuts, walnuts, pecans, corn, wheat, oats, barley, rye, sorghum, rice, black pepper, chili pepper, cocoa, wine, peas and sweet potatoes. Aflatoxin is about one thousand times more carcinogenic than EDB and one million times more carcinogenic than saccharin, which the government has made such a fuss about protecting us against. Another fungal carcinogen, patulin, is common in apple juice—and is both far more carcinogenic and far more prevalent than Alar. One FDA study of apple juice in the United States found 37 percent of the samples contained patulin.

Raw beef, pork, turkey and chicken contain malonaldehyde. Cooking makes things worse. Broiling, roasting, baking, braising, boiling, frying and smoking foods produce a variety of carcinogens, including the polycyclic aromatic hydrocarbons benzo(a)pyrene and benz(a)anthracene. Benzo(a)pyrene—usually linked to the energy and automobile industries—is also produced by bacteria and growing plants; sizable quantities are found in cabbage, lettuce, spinach, leeks and tea. As early as 1973 the Panel on Chemicals and Health of the President's Science Advisory Committee stated, "Evidence is now conclusive for the presence in vegetables of the potent carcinogens 3,4 benzo(a)pyrene and 1,2 benzanthracene and other polynuclear aromatic hydrocarbons (PAH), as normal products of plant biosynthesis, rather than from contamination." At least seven types of PAH are produced by phytoplankton, algae, various vegetables and other plants. PAHs were also found in 1996 in the meteorite from Mars that contained the remains of bacteria indicating that primitive life once existed on that planet. PAHs can also be formed during star formations and in other ways that don't involve life. Vinyl chloride, which Efron calls "the very symbol of synthetic evil," is also found naturally in tobacco, the most notorious carcinogenic plant.

Of the elements considered essential to life at least ten are reported carcinogens: chromium, cobalt, copper, iron, manganese, nickel, selenium, zinc, arsenic and even *oxygen.* Vitamin A is reported to be a carcinogen and vitamin B_{12}, a carcinogen promoter.

Carbon tetrachloride, which is produced by natural atmospheric processes, is reported to be a carcinogen. Ozone and the oxides of nitrogen, which are reported to be carcinogens, are produced by lightning on a scale that dwarfs the manmade output of these gases. Various bacteria and fungi oxidize organic nitrogen and ammonia into the oxides of nitrogen and N-nitroso compounds.

We have already mentioned human saliva, estrogen and intestinal bacteria as carcinogens, but our bodies produce many more. Other natural sex hormones—estradiol, estrone, estriol, progesterone, testosterone—are reported carcinogens. Our bodies produce insulin, without which we could not live; it is a reported carcinogen. "Cholesterol, found in the human brain, spinal cord, and fat, is reported to be both carcinogenic and a carcinogen promoter."[48] Human blood contains many carcinogens; if it were an industrial product, it would be classed as a "toxic substance." Mother's milk contains lactose, which is a reported carcinogen.

Furthermore, radiation is carcinogenic, and our bodies are radioactive. They could not be otherwise, for everything on earth, the oceans, the atmosphere, water, rocks, soil, the tissues of all plants, animals and man contain traces of entirely natural radioactivity. Dr. Petr Beckmann, Professor Emeritus of Electrical Engineering at the University of Colorado, has stated:

> The Capitol in Washington, due to the uranium and thorium content of its granite, is so radioactive that the NRC [Nuclear Regulatory Commission] could not license it as a reactor.... Members of Congress who meet in it have enough carbon 14 and potassium 40 in their bodies to qualify as LLW (low level wastes), or as some of them like to call it, as radioactive garbage.[49]

Based on Senator Edward Kennedy's estimated weight, Dr. Beckmann calculated the radiation the senator's body produces. According to this calculation, the senator is contaminating himself, the people around him, and the environment with a "known cancer-causing agent" at the rate of 15,665 radioactive disintegrations per second.

The carcinogenicity of substances in our food, our environment, and our bodies is reported by researchers from animal tests at very high dosages—at or near the highest doses that the animals can tolerate without dying prematurely. Such studies prove that what Paracelsus said of poisons is also true of carcinogens: Everything is a carcinogen; the dose alone determines the carcinogen. At high enough doses everything in the world is indeed carcinogenic. Conversely, at low enough doses the same substances are not dangerous—which obviously must be true, or we would have perished long ago from constant exposure to the huge number of natural carcinogens. Yet on the basis of animal tests at very high dosages the government declares various substances to be carcinogenic at ANY dosage. Even one molecule!

THE FICTIONAL WORLD OF THE ANTI-INDUSTRIALISTS

The "one-molecule" theory of cancer, also called the "no threshold" theory, first came to public attention in the 1970s during congressional hearings on DES. In 1975 Jacqueline Verrett of the FDA, explaining the DES controversy, said, "Researchers from the National Cancer Institute assured Congressmen that it might be possible for only one molecule of DES in the 340 trillion present in a quarter pound of beef liver to trigger human cancer, as far as they know."[50]

Let's try to put this in perspective. A linear comparison may be helpful. A sixteenth of an inch is about one trillionth of the distance to the moon. If there are 340 trillion molecules in a quarter pound of meat, then one molecule would be in the same proportion to it as a sixteenth of an inch is to 170 round-trips to the moon. It is absolutely ridiculous to be concerned about a hazard that small when man faces incomparably greater risks every day from natural sources. If just one molecule of a carcinogen could trigger cancer, then man would be facing this danger *hundreds of millions of times more often* just from his own saliva than from DES, to say nothing of all the other carcinogens in his own body, his food and the environment.

If the public had known the truth about carcinogens, the government would never have been able to generate the fear and hostility that was necessary for a successful assault against the food and chemical industries. But—just as with the "Filthy Meat" Scare—the public was not told the truth; it was told "half-truths, partial facts and some outright lies." In her monumental work on cancer research, which is the source of most of the natural carcinogens cited above, Edith Efron writes on government withholding this information and misleading the public in many other ways:

> Serious falsehoods have been disseminated. Information on crucial issues has been deliberately withheld by government agencies, resulting in false implications. Misinformation has poured through the nation because premature studies were deliberately released. Finally, actual myths and distortions of scientific history have been systematically pumped into this culture. In each of these cases, government agencies and high officials in the scientific bureaucracies are implicated. They are not alone in misinforming the country, but they are the most significant sources.[51]

Efron began by investigating synthetic carcinogens because that was where she, like everyone else, was led to believe the problem lay. But her research raised questions:

What if I had not been guided by *government theory?*...
What if I had hunted for natural carcinogens as diligently as I
had hunted for synthetic carcinogens?... So I decided to look
with equal diligence for natural carcinogens. And I found them.
Somehow, the theoreticians, the regulators, and the apocalyptic
movement itself had misplaced them. The natural carcinogens
were sitting there quietly in the literature on carcinogenesis,
along with the synthetics. The only difference was that they had
not been publicized. In fact, in the national uproar over
"chemicals," and the *presentation to the public of the concepts
that science, technology, industry, profits, and capitalism were
the causes of as much as 90 percent of human cancer,* they had
hardly been noticed....

[E]ven when a veritable torrent of data on the
carcinogenicity and mutagenicity of natural foods and on every
process of cooking had finally emerged, the FDA's lips were
apparently glued together: Government science was silent on the
subject....

[T]he Biologist State was concocting a pseudo-science
and regulating industry on the basis of a fairy tale, while it was
manipulating theory and data the way a cardsharp shuffles
cards.[52](Italics added)

At the heart of the matter were the concepts that "science,
technology, industry, profits, and capitalism were the cause of as much
as 90 percent of human cancer." Man the Maker, Industrial Man, HAD
to be the *enemy of the people*—because that was the theoretical preconception which fit the invader mentality, the mind-set of those who see
human existence as a battle against other men and force as the weapon
for solving human problems. It was the very process of producing
material values, of reshaping the world through the capability of the
human mind, that the anti-mind crusaders wanted to wage war against
and defeat by force: government action. Since the facts could not
possibly justify their aims or method, it was necessary to "manipulate
theory and data the way a cardsharp shuffles cards" in order to obtain
popular support for the attack.

Earlier we noted Friedrich Hayek's observation regarding the
critics of early capitalism: "Because the theoretical preconceptions
which guided them [the socialist philosophers] postulated that the rise of
capitalism must have been detrimental...it is not surprising that they
found what they were looking for." The same is true of the modern
critics of capitalism—which also explains why they were all looking for

carcinogens only among synthetic chemicals in the first place, while ignoring the more numerous and more potent natural ones.

And just as in the early days of capitalism, it was the "radical intelligensia," themselves with little firsthand knowledge of industry or science, which originated the anticapitalist ideas—ideas which had no basis in fact but which fit the preconceptions of the invader mentality. Now it was the intelligensia of the New Left and the counterculture of the 1960s.

The politicians, as might be expected, were receptive to identi-fication of the new enemy and the underlying assumptions of the invader mentality. Government, after all, is force; and that force can only be applied against other men. Laws control men, not nature. A human enemy was needed. Efron observes perceptively:

> There are no Senators seeking to enhance their careers by subjecting nature to grillings under hot television lights. There is no ardent political constituency demanding that nature's chemical innovations be arrested. There are no dramatic legal contests in which nature is the defendant. And thus, there are no Xerox machines endlessly churning out government bulletins about nature's latest toxic, carcinogenic, and mutagenic derelictions and mailing them to the press.[53]

It quickly became conventional wisdom in Congress that Industrial Man was imperiling not only the rest of the nation but the entire world, the global ecosystem. Laws proliferated accordingly. Efron cites 33 federal laws passed between 1969 and 1977 to deal with the new "peril." These laws specifically identify the sources of global peril as "technological advances," "new processes in American industry," "industrial development," "new materials and processes," etc.

Congress itself, of course, had little firsthand knowledge of industry and science. It wouldn't have mattered. In the same way that the critics of early capitalism ignored evidence contrary to their preconception, the modern critics—and Congress—likewise ignored facts which did not fit the assumption that there was no safe dose, no "threshold," for any carcinogen, not even one molecule. For example, toxicologist W. J. Hayes explains that threshold levels are "biological facts," and the *absence* of a threshold has never been demonstrated; quite the contrary: even compounds with the highest biological activity, such as botulinum toxin and "dioxin" (tetrachlorodibenzodioxin), are known to be inactive below certain concentrations.[54] Other experts explain that the one-molecule theory ignores "all the fundamental principles of cell biology."[55] The American Council on Science and Health states flatly, "This 'no threshold' proposition cannot withstand scientific scrutiny."[56] But just as in the case of the "Filthy Meat" Scare in 1967, such views, which opposed the "official" one, were not given even a hearing while the "official" theory was widely publicized. Efron says that the one-molecule theory is a "fairy tale" and "a moral fiction devised to permit regulatory action in the absence of epidemiological knowledge."[57]

Toxicologist M. A. Ottoboni states that no animal on earth could survive "if it were not capable of handling small amounts of a wide variety of chemicals. It is only when we overwhelm the natural defense mechanisms of our bodies, by taking too much at one time, or too much too often, that we get into trouble."[58] So here we are back again to the Paracelsus idea that "the dose makes the poison." In her 1978 presidential address to the American Association of Cancer Research, Elizabeth Miller said, "Much data have clearly established that chemical carcinogenesis is a strongly dose-dependent phenomenon.... The strong dose dependence is too often slighted in public discussions of possible human hazards."[59] Such views were ignored, if they were heard at all, by members of Congress and the activists spouting the one-molecule theory. Even Herman Kraybill of the National Cancer Institute noted that dose dependency was never brought up in the public argument over carcinogens.

To cling to the one-molecule theory, its advocates had to ignore or side-step still other facts. How, for example, could they reconcile their theory with the reality that at least ten elements proven to be carcinogens in large doses were essential to human life in small doses? Were such universally recognized essentials as oxygen and iron to be regarded as potentially dangerous in even a single molecule? Yes, said one faction within the National Cancer Institute, arguing that there was no threshold, no safe dose for even these vital elements. No, said another faction, arguing that the fact that human life required certain carcinogens was major evidence that they did not cause cancer at low levels. The first faction was represented at OSHA hearings; the second was not.

Even more devastating to the theory that carcinogens were potentially dangerous in *any* amount was the fact that some carcinogens turned out to be *anti*carcinogens at low levels. In small amounts these substances actually inhibit or prevent the formation of cancer, even though in large doses they are known to cause cancer. Selenium and vitamin A are prime examples.

That some carcinogens turn out to be anticarcinogens at low dosages should not be as surprising as it may first seem. It has long been known that small, nontoxic amounts of chemical poisons stimulate the body's resistance to larger doses of the poisons in the future. It was later discovered that the same principle applies at the biological level to viruses and bacteria. This is the basis of vaccines by which people can be inoculated against a variety of diseases. When a person is injected with a small amount of a weakened form of a disease-bearing germ or virus, the body's natural defense mechanisms are provoked into building up an immunity to the disease.

This same phenomenon can be seen in the way insects develop resistance or immunity to various pesticides and in the way bacteria develop immunity to antibiotics. Conversely, the reason the American Indians were so vulnerable to the white man's diseases is that, having had no exposure to them, they never had a chance to develop any natural immunity. Thus they succumbed quickly when smallpox, influenza and measles were brought to their shores. For example, 90 percent of the entire tribe of Blackfoot Indians died in just two years from smallpox.

According to the one-molecule theory, constant exposure to carcinogens increases one's risk of cancer so that the day may come "when that extra molecule of a carcinogen may overload the system and cancer begins to grow."[60] Thus increased exposure to even low-level carcinogens should produce an increased number of cancers—but there is evidence that exactly the opposite happens. For example, people with a higher level of nitrates in their saliva have lower—not higher—rates of cancer. Rather than increasing susceptibility, the slightly higher level of these carcinogens evidently provokes natural defense mechanisms to create greater resistance to cancer.

In line with the "fairy tale" underlying its regulations, the government engaged in another fiction: pretending as a matter of *official policy* that contrary evidence did not exist. A 1980 OSHA policy document states:

> If the available evidence indicates that the chemical is not positive for carcinogenicity, OSHA's position on that particular chemical is the same as if the chemical had never been tested for carcinogenicity.[61]

Thus no amount of scientific testing would satisfy the government that cyclamate or any other substance did not cause cancer. The government would simply regard such tests "the same as if the chemical had never been tested." Efron writes:

> In the realm of cancer prevention, the manufacturer may wish to, or be obligated to, demonstrate that a substance is noncarcinogenic. But once he steps into OSHA's world, he has no means of doing so, for OSHA has declared that no negative finding will be acknowledged. *In OSHA's universe there is no "innocence" among American industrialists—there is only the "guilt" that has been proved and the "guilt" that has not yet been proved.* Kafka could not improve on this situation.[62] (Italics added)

Of course, the whole purpose of the animal tests was to discriminate between carcinogens and noncarcinogens. By a policy that has "outlawed the very capacity for discrimination which makes the animal test practically applicable," says Efron,

> OSHA has declared that there is no rational basis for OSHA's own regulation on the basis of those tests. OSHA has victimized industry, the public, and the geneticists—and has finally jammed a knife into its own brain.
>
> If OSHA were an individual scientist, one would unhesitatingly pronounce that scientist a lunatic. But OSHA is a bureaucracy, and bureaucracies cannot be so diagnosed....
>
> The first conclusion we can reach is that "regulatory science" is devoid of elementary logic. The second conclusion we can reach is that "regulatory science" and its defenders will take any position that comes to hand *to maintain political power over industry,* whether those positions are rationally coherent or not.[63] (Italics added)

RESULTS

Less Risk—or More?

Once again the government offered both a false impression of a problem and a false solution. Industry was not the problem, and regulating industry was not the solution. Cancer prevention through government regulation is a public illusion through which the government has systematically, though unintentionally, subjected the public to *greater* health hazards, usually small but sometimes significant—in any case larger than the dangers it protects against.

Remember how Chapter Four showed that government spending bought various benefits only at the expense of things more valuable? Government regulation of the food industry operates in the same way in regard to human health. Any benefit is generally less than its cost in terms of the health risks to people.

For example, the banning of cyclamates may appear to be a positive, if small, benefit if taken out of the context of its cost. Eliminating even a remote cancer risk seems like a good thing—until we consider the cost in terms of *greater* health risks elsewhere as a result, which are the "price" of this benefit. When cyclamates were banned, saccharin was the only other artificial sweetener available. And while the carcinogenic risk from saccharin is extremely small, it is nevertheless larger than from cyclamates. No one doubts that 800 bottles per day of diet soda containing saccharin will produce cancer, at least in rats, but there is considerable doubt that cyclamates will produce cancer at *any* dosage. The results of the single flawed study on which the government based its ban of cyclamates could not be repeated, and dozens of other studies have found no link whatever between cancer and cyclamates at any dosage. Furthermore, in the study that led to the ban on cyclamates, all the rats had received at least two chemicals, some three, as noted earlier. One of those chemicals was saccharin. So it may well have been saccharin that caused the rat cancers that led to the ban on cyclamates in the first place.

In addition, when the artificial sweetener aspartame was approved by the FDA for carbonated beverages in 1983, many people flocked to it because of the prior government scares about cyclamates and saccharin. But the FDA noted "an increasing number of complaints from consumers about headaches, dizziness and a wide variety of other symptoms they attributed to consuming aspartame-containing products."[64] The Centers for Disease Control acknowledged that "some segments of the population might be sensitive to the sweetener." So the government's "benefit" of eliminating theoretical cancer risks that were extremely small—or perhaps nonexistent in the case of cyclamates—led some people instead to a product that produced real—not theoretical—headaches, dizziness and other symptoms for some of them.

Substituting sugar for the artificial sweeteners also carried risks. For diabetics, who were important users of cyclamate, sugar would be extremely dangerous. For others, the additional calories were a concern. A 12-ounce can of diet soda usually contains one calorie or less versus about 150 calories for the sugared variety. Obesity is a widely recognized health risk. For many people already overweight, a few additional pounds would almost certainly be a greater health risk than the puny risks from cyclamate or saccharin.

In the case of EDB the alternatives were to use substitutes or not to spray the crops at all. Both choices are riskier than EDB. The American Council on Science and Health states:

> Substitutes for EDB fumigants are phosphine, methyl bromide and a 4:1 mixture of carbon tetrachloride and carbon disulfide. Each of these alternatives is more hazardous to pesticide applicators during fumigation than EDB. Carbon tetrachloride and methyl bromide are animal carcinogens, and phosphine and carbon disulfide are flammable (EDB is a flame retardant).... As is all too typical, the known benefits of EDB and *the potential hazards of its alternatives* were largely ignored in the "hysteria" to ban the pesticide.[65] (Italics added) [Phosphine has since been linked to genetic damage in workers.[66]]

As for the other possibility, not spraying crops, Dr. Bruce Ames says:

> If we do not use fumigants on grain, there will be much more insect infestation and mold contamination, and the cancer risk from the powerful mold carcinogens may be much greater than the risk from EDB residues.[67]

Because of the greater dangers without EDB, Dr. Ames said that "the public health could be endangered by banning the use of ethylene dibromide as a fumigant."[68] He also points out:

> There are other risks arising as a consequence of scaring the public unnecessarily. There is roughly a one-in-a-million risk of death from a car accident in driving a distance of 60 miles. I suspect that the risks to the public are greater if everyone starts driving to the supermarket to return [EDB contaminated products].[69]

In the same way that spraying grains with EDB was less risky than not spraying them, spraying apples with Alar was less risky than not spraying them. Fourteen years before the "Apple Scare" Drs. Whelan and Stare wrote:

Refreshing apple cider. Enjoy it? If it's derived from organically grown apples, perhaps you ought to decline. Patulin, a toxic metabolite of several fungi and a substance known to be cancer causing, has recently been identified in certain types of unfermented apple juice. According to *Nutrition Reviews,* "Juice derived from apples grown on organic farms where trees have not been sprayed is likely to contain considerable quantities of fungus-rotten apple extract."[70]

The relatively greater risk of not spraying, and not using preservatives, is also emphasized by Dr. Robert White-Stevens, professor of biology and chairman of the Bureau of Conservation and Environmental Science at Rutgers University, who said that

there are no medically annotated records of any consumer becoming sick, developing cancer or dying from the direct consumption of any food stuff that has been treated with any registered pesticide, preservative or food additive used in accordance with...label recommendations.

Yet there are numerous instances, medically recorded every year, of consumers becoming sick and of fatalities from consumption of foods contaminated with natural toxins, most of which could have been prevented by the correct use of...pesticides and preservatives.[71]

U.S. Surgeon General C. Everett Koop told Congress in June 1991:

While approximately 9,000 people die from bacteria-caused food poisoning each year, there is no scientific evidence showing that residues from the lawful application of pesticides to food have ever caused illness or death.

If the government had gone ahead with its original plan to ban nitrite in meat, it would have substituted a far greater health hazard, botulism, for a trivial carcinogenic risk. The government's own estimate was 22 deaths from botulism in the first year after banning nitrite. There have been no known cases of botulism in nitrite-cured meat.

In the case of selenium the FDA's conclusion that it was carcinogenic at high levels led the government to delay 15 years before approving low levels of it as an animal feed additive. According to Berkeley's Dr. Jukes, there are areas of the United States where soils and crops are deficient in selenium, and some parts of the world are so deficient that crops are sprayed with a sodium selenite solution as a public health measure. The "price" for the government "benefit" of eliminating a virtually—if not totally—insignificant risk of cancer from selenium was that for 15 years people in selenium-deficient areas were prevented from receiving indirectly (via farm animals) a valuable *anti*-carcinogen. Once again, the cost was greater than the benefit.

Another way in which the phony warnings about pesticides have had the opposite effect from that intended and actually *increased* exposure to carcinogens is described by Dr. Ames:

> One consequence of disproportionate concern about synthetic pesticide residues is that some plant breeders are currently developing plants to be more insect-resistant and inadvertently are selecting plants higher in natural toxins. A major grower recently introduced a new variety of highly insect-resistant celery into commerce. The pest-resistant celery contains 6,200 parts per billion (ppb) of carcinogenic (and mutagenic) psoralens instead of the 800 ppb normally present in celery. The celery is still on the market.[72]

More Cancers—or Fewer? Or, Who is Lying—
The Facts or the Politicians and the Media?

In October 1975 Dan Rather of CBS-TV News announced:

> The news tonight is that the United States is number one in cancer. The National Cancer Institute estimates that if you are living in America your chances of getting cancer are higher than anywhere in the world.

That same month Senator John Tunney opened a hearing on the Toxic Substances Control Act by saying:

> Americans are getting cancer at an ever-increasing rate. In fact, the rate of cancer mortality in this country has increased over 20 percent in the past 25 years. It is clear from the National Cancer Institute studies that cancer is, indeed, a by-product of an industrialized society. Up to 90 percent are caused by contaminants placed in the environment by man.

Well, you can believe those gentlemen, or you can look at the numbers. The only type of cancer which increased in the last twenty-five years—or 40 years—is lung cancer. All other types (stomach, colon and rectal, prostate, esophagus, etc.) have either declined or stabilized in their rates, according to statistics of the American Cancer Society. And lung cancer is universally recognized as being caused by tobacco smoking, not by industrialization or food additives.

Over the 25 years that Senator Tunney was talking about, lung cancer increased 300 percent. If this enormous increase is lumped together with the flat or declining rates for other types of cancer, one arrives at an "overall" increase of around 20 percent—a figure that is utterly misleading, if not completely dishonest. It is absolutely unjustifiable to try to give the false impression that there is a general increase in cancer when only one type is increasing and all others are not. During that same period, for example, stomach cancer plummeted by 50 percent. And it is inexcusably deceptive to try to infer that an "overall" increase is due to an "industrialized society" when the only category of increase results from smoking.

As to the CBS claim that the United States was number one in cancer, Efron shows this to be "nonsense." According to the best figures available at the time, cancer mortality for U.S whites ranked in the *lowest third* of the industrialized nations, with 23 nations rated higher. For U.S. blacks the rate was higher, but there were still eight nations, including such industrial "giants" as Uruguay, with higher cancer mortality. The United States was definitely not number one. It wasn't even close.

Who is the Enemy? Who is the Friend?

Industry was being vilified for increasing cancer, but cancer was not increasing (except for lung cancer). Regulations were not lowering cancer rates, for they dealt with manmade chemicals, which, in the words of Dr. Ames, are "just a drop in the bucket" compared to nature's carcinogens. Moreover, as shown with the examples of cyclamates, saccharin, EDB and Alar, any positive effect from government regulations tends to be more than offset by negative ones if the full context of secondary consequences is considered. If food additives, preservatives, and agricultural chemicals really were dangerous, one would expect that statistics on stomach cancer would prominently reveal this. Yet stomach cancer has shown a consistent and dramatic decline for decades—during the very time industrial growth was being blamed for "poisoning" the planet. So who was responsible for this decrease in cancer?

That's right. That "enemy of the people," Industrial Man. A report by the American Council on Science and Health states that "the best way

to minimize the potential hazard posed by naturally occurring carcinogens would be to eat a wide variety of foods, since this would minimize
the chance that any single carcinogen would...overwhelm the body's
natural ability to handle low amounts of hazardous substances."[73] Thanks
to industry, Americans today have a *far* more varied diet than their
grandparents. It is *industrial progress* in food handling, storage,
preservation and transportation that has made it possible for inland areas
to have abundant supplies of fresh and frozen seafood, for the snow-belt
states to have strawberries in the winter, for the entire country to enjoy
citrus fruits produced in Florida and California or imported from tropical
countries, and for all Americans to enjoy a wide variety of vegetables and
fruits when they are out of season. This great variety of foods—the "best
way to minimize" natural carcinogenic risks—is not the product of any
law, regulation or other government action. It is the product of the very
industrial progress that is blamed for an "increase" in cancer.

The wide variety of foods in ample supply is not the only way in
which industrial progress has helped to reduce cancer. BHT (butylated
hydroxytoluene) and BHA (butylated hydroxyanisole) are widely used
preservatives that have been widely attacked as "health hazards" by the
anti-industrialists. Lurid but unsupported reports of carcinogenic,
mutagenic, and other adverse effects from them have circulated for
many years by those whose mentality predisposes them to regard such
products as harmful. But studies have shown that, when added to the
diets of mice, these chemicals produce a marked *reduction* in stomach
cancer. Analysis of dietary changes in human populations in various
countries supports the conclusion that these anticarcinogenic benefits
occur in humans as well. Sharp declines in death rates from stomach
cancer in various countries coincide with the introduction of BHA and
BHT in those countries. Also, Drs. Whelan and Stare state:

> The United States currently has one of the lowest death
> rates from stomach cancer, followed by Australia, Canada, and
> New Zealand. The eating habits and methods of food
> preservation in these countries parallel ours. European countries
> such as Finland, Hungary, Italy, Poland, and West Germany,
> where there is no widespread use of antioxidants (BHT and
> BHA) in food preservation, have the highest death rates from
> stomach cancer.[74]

Of course, when industry was making available the great variety
of foods which we enjoy, no one had any idea that this diversity itself

would minimize the risk of cancer. The companies involved were simply trying to produce more food for their own profit. Once again, however, just as with the early food producers at Jericho, this production created an incidental and unforeseen benefit for others. Similarly, BHT and BHA were introduced into food solely because of their value as preservatives. No one had any idea that they would be anticarcinogenic. But here, too, other people received this valuable and unexpected benefit as a byproduct—just like the valuable and unexpected consequences from the invention of agriculture. Just as at Jericho, the actions of the producers were no threat to others; there was no basis for conflict. Nevertheless, the "invader mentality" viewed these progressive innovations in precisely that way. And in order to support this view government agencies, high officials, and others favoring government activism had to resort to "a moral fiction," "serious falsehoods," "misinformation," and "actual myths and distortions of scientific history," in Efron's words.

The modern advocates of force have claimed that the role of government must be expanded to deal with the new "threats" of modern society. They claim that government must be expanded beyond the classic functions of protecting life, liberty and property in order to deal with the "threats" of scientific and technological advances. But the coercion they put forth as the "modern" method for dealing with these trumped-up threats is in principle the same one employed by the invaders of Jericho. The entire situation is just like that of 10,000 years ago. Now, as then, some men were advancing the human conditions by applying their minds to nature while others sought to advance their society by force against other men. The first group was reshaping the material world to produce more and better food; the second group sought to "reshape" the first group, through armed conflict at Jericho, through the force of law by the neo-invaders of our own time. And now, as then, force against other man was powerless to create human progress. Food preservatives, such as BHT and BHA, and the wide variety of foods available at supermarkets were not products of laws or regulations any more than agriculture was invented by the spears and clubs used at Jericho. Nor were human beings better off because of laws or regulations regarding meat inspection, cyclamates, saccharin, nitrites, EDB or Alar.

Eventually, after years of manipulating data, concealing the truth, and spreading misinformation, the government had to abandon the fiction that industrial progress was responsible for up to ninety percent of human cancers. Contrary evidence was too overwhelming. On February 19, 1990 Robert Scheuplein, director of the office of toxicological sciences at the FDA, said that *natural* carcinogens account for more than 98 percent of the cancer risk in the human diet. At an address to the annual meeting of the American Association for the Advancement of Science, Scheuplein said the average consumer takes in at least a gram of natural carcinogens in food daily, compared to about 200 millionths of a gram of man-made chemicals.

The October 9, 1992 issue of *Science* reported on a federally-funded study at the University of California at Berkeley. The lead authors of the study were Dr. Lois Swirsky Gold, director of the carcinogenic potency project at the government's Lawrence Berkeley Laboratory and Dr. Bruce Ames, biochemistry professor at Berkeley. The study concluded that 99.9 percent of the carcinogens in food are natural chemicals that develop from cooking or are secreted by plants in self-defense—"natural pesticides."

On February 15, 1996 a 20-member panel of the National Research Council, an arm of the National Academy of Sciences, reported: "The great majority of individual naturally occurring and synthetic food chemicals are present in the human diet at levels so low that they are unlikely to pose an appreciable cancer risk." The report also concluded that if there were any such risk the greatest contributors were probably natural chemicals, which far outnumber synthetic ones.

CULTIVATING DISCONTENT

It has been reported that both Ester Peterson and Betty Furness, consumer advisors to Presidents Kennedy and Johnson, often complained that consumers weren't complaining enough. Both advisors organized gripe sessions, where, in the words of Grayson and Shepard, "shoppers were exhorted to find something, *anything,* wrong with the business establishment and to register an indignant beef." The authors continue:

> Where in 1960 there were so few consumer complaints that the opinion polls didn't even take notice of them, by 1967 an Opinion Research Corporation study revealed that 55 percent of all Americans felt the need for new consumer protection laws. By 1969, the figure had increased to 68 percent, and by 1971, it had topped 70 percent.
>
> From the evidence, it would appear the consumers of America had been talked into feeling persecuted.[75]

Automobiles, jobs, food were all becoming safer. Yet by being told the exact opposite, the public was being whipped into a frenzy of hostility toward the industries which were providing things. Only by portraying these industries as "enemies of the people" could the neo-invaders incite the populace to support legislative assaults against them.

Chapter Eight
WHAT ABOUT THE ENVIRONMENT?

Those who attack the makers of wealth and progress continually seek victims of industrial growth. They need such victims not only to justify their own hostility and to recruit supporters to their militant ranks; they need them to reconcile the evidence of others' economic advancement with their own conviction that one man's gain necessitates another's loss, as in an invasion. And if victims cannot be found among those who are involved in production and trade, then they must be "found" elsewhere. If employees as well as employers, or consumers as well as producers, *both* benefit, then according to the invader mentality, they must have done so at the expense of others in society. So much the better for those with this mentality, for the "victims" will be all the more aggrieved for having had no responsibility for their plight. All the more cause for hostility!

How are innocent bystanders supposedly victimized by others' prosperity? Allegedly by depletion of the earth's resources, which subjects them to scarcity; by pollution of the environment, which injures their health; or by "raping" the landscape through mining, forestry, cultivation, or urban development, which threatens their future survival or that of their children. If people are led to believe that greater productivity by others means scarcity for themselves, or that every industrial advance by others is at the expense of increasingly poisoning their own air and water and making the earth less valuable and usable for themselves, then it is easy to understand their hostility not only toward the producers but toward the factory, the automobile, and the very system which produced these things. But if men turn against the system which creates material values, the only method open to them is the one for which their hostility has prepared them: force.

Of course, progress does not need victims. Adam Smith observed in *The Wealth of Nations* that when men pursued their own self-interest in the market, they were led as if by an "invisible hand" to promote the interests of society in ways which they did not intend. Today we know this is true in a way which never occurred to Adam Smith: the environment has gotten better, not worse, through a free economic system. But once again those of the invader mentality, who regard other men as enemies, have been "manipulating theory and data the way a cardsharp shuffles cards" to show that free men, particularly productive men, have been making things worse; this time it's the environment. Once again, just as with carcinogens, the neo-invaders have ignored the fact that nature is the biggest problem, not other men. And once again their efforts to solve the problem with force against other men have only made matters worse.

AIR POLLUTION
Industry Clears the Air

At the time of the Clean Air Act (1970) an orchestrated propaganda campaign had convinced the public that the air in our cities was steadily worsening, due to industrial progress. But our air was getting progressively cleaner, not dirtier, and had been doing so for a long time precisely because of industrial progress. According to Professor Matthew Crenson of Johns Hopkins University, sulfur dioxide pollution had been declining for thirty or forty years. In 1971 he wrote, "In some cities the sulfur dioxide content of the air today is only one-third or one-fourth of what it was before World War II."[1]

In 1931 and 1932 measurements in fourteen cities by the United States Public Health Service showed an average particulate concentration of 510 micrograms per cubic meter. But measurements in 1957 by the Department of Health, Education and Welfare showed an average of only 120 micrograms per cubic meter, and the average continued to drop. In 1969—the year before passage of the Clean Air Act—it had already dropped to 92 micrograms per cubic meter.[2]

In cities across the country, in New York, Chicago, Philadelphia, even Los Angeles, the air had been getting better and better before the politicians tried to help. The annual number of days of eye irritation in the Los Angeles Basin had dropped steadily since 1960, as had the number of days for equalling or exceeding state standards for total oxidants, carbon monoxide, and sulfur dioxide. In New York, the city conducting the most thorough air-pollution monitoring in the nation, the maximum concentrations of sulfur dioxide, carbon monoxide, nitric oxide, aldehydes, and suspended particulates had each declined steadily since measurements began in 1966. This trend toward improved air quality was a consequence of neither intervention by the government nor altruism by the industrialists but of the fact that constant upgrading in human conditions occurs when everyone is free to choose what he thinks is best for himself. The "invisible hand" is at work with respect to natural, environmental factors because men's interests are not naturally in opposition.

In 1973 Grayson and Shepard observed, "The long-term trend toward cleaner air is corroborated by scientific study after scientific study. It is totally irrefutable."[3]

In 1994 Dr. Hugh Ellsaesser published data on major airborne pollutants that were *available at the time of the Clean Air Act in 1970.* These graphs of particulates, settleable dust, sulfur dioxide, oxidants and carbon monoxide in major cities clearly show that air pollution was decreasing, not increasing.[4] Yet in contradistinction to the facts, Senator Edmund Muskie, champion of that legislation, claimed, "In 1970, it was clear that our efforts were failing. The air was getting dirtier rapidly."[5]

A major reason for the upward trend in air quality was the conversion to cleaner fuels for heating, such as oil and gas, from coal or wood; as recently as 1950, 45 percent of America's homes were still heated with coal or wood. But auto emissions also became cleaner, and here again the trend started before government intervention or agitation by consumerists. The auto industry had been working for years on the problem. By 1968 cars with significantly improved emission characteristics were already being produced, and newer anti-pollution equipment was being tested. By 1970, when the Clean Air Act was passed, auto emissions had already been reduced 70 to 80 percent from the level of two decades earlier. But the Clean Air Act required 90 percent of the remaining 20 to 30 percent be eliminated by the time the 1976 models rolled off the production lines—a requirement so unrealistic that Congress had to postpone the deadline three times in the next six years. Professor Haagen-Smit, the man who discovered the photochemical reactions that produce smog and knew more about the subject than anyone, labeled these air quality standards as "absurd." But he was a scientist, not a politician.

Government Makes Matters Worse

The advocates of the stringent requirements of the Clean Air Act clamored about how the auto industry was degrading the air, but they never seem to have considered the fact that coercion might make the problem worse. They never learned from—indeed, they preferred to hush up—the nation's first experience with governing auto emissions. Legislators in California, concerned about smog over Los Angeles, enacted a law in 1965 requiring a reduction in the carbon monoxide content of auto exhausts. The result was automobiles which emitted lower levels of carbon monoxide—but which emitted more oxides of nitrogen instead, which generated more smog than carbon monoxide. The result of the federal standard for 1976 was equally counter-productive: the sulfuric acid-producing catalytic converter.

On March 15, 1977, the *Journal of Commerce* reported that "several EPA officials agree with the statement last year by the then-administrator, Russell Train, that 'anticipated emission reductions (from controls on cars) are not being achieved.'" EPA official Norman Shutler admitted, "In actual use, the controls aren't working well."

On June 27, 1977 the EPA released the results of a two-year study showing that since 1974 a drop in carbon monoxide emissions of about 25 percent, due to catalytic converters, was accompanied by an increase of about 50 percent in emissions of the oxides of nitrogen.

An article in *The Wall Street Journal* of November 20, 1979 noted that smog in Los Angeles, which was decreasing before the introduction of the federally-required catalytic converter, had "significantly worsened" since 1977. In 1978 the number of days when the air was rated "very unhealthful" had increased 23 percent from the average for the preceding five years, and ozone readings averaged 14 percent higher than in the preceding six years. "The only reasonable explanation is that vehicle (emission) controls aren't performing as well as they were projected to perform," asserted J.A. Stuart, executive director of the Air Quality Management District.

Meanwhile, acid rain became a problem of increasing concern. Was there a connection? In 1975 Chrysler Corporation revealed a study indicating that in the absence of the catalyst practically no oxidation of sulfur dioxide to sulfur trioxide occurs; hence no related acid deposition. A 1975 EPA study noted that the sulfuric acid emissions from catalytic converters "represent a very real health hazard that would come about over a period of time." In 1978 an EPA internal report stated: "A hard acceleration with a hot catalyst…will probably produce large amounts of sulfuric acid due to the storage/release mechanism." More on acid rain later.

By 1990 the auto industry was producing cars with 96 percent cleaner exhausts than two decades earlier. Nevertheless, Congress that year passed another Clean Air Act, which would require auto emissions to be 97.5 percent cleaner than two decades ago. Keep in mind that emissions in 1970 were 70 to 80 percent lower than twenty years before. So 96 percent of the remaining 20 to 30 percent, which was already eliminated before the new legislation, meant that about 99 percent of auto pollution had already been eliminated, compared to 40 years earlier. The 1990 legislation, by requiring cars to be 97.5 percent cleaner (instead of the 96 percent already achieved) would make tailpipe emissions 99.375 percent cleaner than 40 years earlier, compared to 99 percent without the legislation. At a cost of additional tens of billions of dollars annually the Clean Air Act of 1990 promised to eliminate an additional—trivial—0.375 percent of pollution. Once again the cost of a government program is far greater than any possible benefit.

Setting the stage for the 1990 legislation, EPA declared that 81 areas containing 100 million people didn't comply with federal emission standards regarding ozone. Sounds like a terrible problem doesn't it?—one that calls for another law to keep those "enemies of the people" the auto makers from fouling our environment so horribly! Well, it doesn't seem like such a problem, nor a cause for much hostility against the industry, if we see how EPA arrived at that figure. If the ozone level exceeded federal standards for any three separate days over a three-year period and for only *one hour* during each of those three days—and for just one monitoring site in an entire region—then the whole *region* was deemed out of compliance. Furthermore, the EPA made no allowance for unusually hot weather, which increases ozone concentrations. With the unusually hot summers of 1987 and 1988 many cities that normally have no problem were cited for non-attainment of the federal standard. Actually, even Los Angeles was in compliance 95 percent of the time; the rest of the "non-attainment" cities were in compliance 99.47 percent of the time.

The 1990 Clean Air Act will add 15 to 25 cents per gallon to the price of gasoline and as much as $1000 to the price of an automobile over the next several years, as various requirements are phased in. But will the air actually be any cleaner?

In December 1990 preliminary results were released from a $16 million study of "reformulated" gasolines, which the 1990 Clean Air Act required by 1995 in the nine U.S. cities that most often exceed ozone standards. The study was funded by 14 oil companies and the 3 American auto makers. Co-chairman of the study John J. Wise noted that the "oxygenates" added to promote cleaner burning can produce some compounds that are more likely to cause smog. Furthermore, while reformulated gasolines make some cars run cleaner, they make others run dirtier. The newer cars achieved hydrocarbon reductions of about 6 percent, but in 1983-1986 models the hydrocarbons rose

9 percent. For nitrogen oxide emissions the results were reversed: these emissions were reduced in the older cars but increased slightly in the new ones.

A study by Tom Austin, a former executive officer of the California Air Resources Board, concluded that the reformulated gasolines would be 15 percent less fuel efficient and would increase nitrogen oxide emissions. Motorists, he said, will "end up paying more for dirtier air."[6]

The 1990 Clean Air Act required 39 cities in the fall of 1992 to begin using gasoline with higher oxygen levels, allegedly to reduce carbon monoxide levels. The two "oxygenates" available in 1992 were MTBE (methyl tertiary butyl ether) and ethanol. But EPA received complaints of headaches and nausea from users of MTBE in Alaska, Colorado, Montana and New Jersey. Alaska's governor banned further sale of MTBE after 120 health complaints in the first four weeks of its use in that state. EPA officials admitted they were surprised to find MTBE in blood samples from people in Alaska. The other additive, ethanol,

> makes gasoline evaporate quicker, which the EPA says releases volatile organic compounds into the atmosphere. These compounds can potentially react with sunlight in the summer to make ozone.[7]

At high levels above the earth, ozone is considered beneficial because it deflects ultraviolet radiation. At low levels, however, it is considered a pollutant. Even the EPA admits that ethanol produces more nitrogen oxides and hydrocarbons than regular gas. In 1995 the Congressional Budget Office stated that ethanol's rapid evaporation contributes to ozone pollution, particularly in hot weather. Wisconsin officials have stated that requiring ethanol makes it difficult for Milwaukee to meet federal ozone standards to reduce smog.

The benefit most often claimed by the champions of ethanol is a reduction in carbon monoxide emissions. Carbon monoxide is a non-problem (as explained in the following section), but ethanol's effectiveness even here is questionable. According to the late Dr. Petr Beckmann, publisher of *Access to Energy,* "ethanol does *not* decrease carbon mono-xide or nitrogen oxides emissions (except possibly at high altitudes), and it may *increase* ozone emissions."[8] (Italics Dr. Beckmann's)

A test on state-owned vehicles by the Arizona Department of Transportation showed that oxygenated fuels did not reduce carbon monoxide emissions *under regular driving conditions,* regardless of the results claimed in EPA laboratory experiments. *The Arizona Daily Star* carried the following news item on November 26, 1989:

> PHOENIX (AP)—Oxygenated fuels did not improve vehicle emissions during 1 million miles of testing on the road, according to a study by the Arizona Department of Transportation.
>
> ADOT began testing oxygenated fuels in February 1987, including gasolines blended with ethanol and MTBE—the two types of oxygenated fuels currently being sold in the Phoenix area. State law requires that Phoenix-area service stations sell only oxygenated fuels from October through March in an effort to reduce carbon monoxide pollution....
>
> But an ADOT study released Friday said the oxygenated fuels did not reduce emissions. In fact, carbon monoxide levels occasionally increased when state-owned vehicles ran on oxygenated fuels, said ADOT....
>
> "It should be clearly understood that the experiment was a field test and differs greatly from laboratory experiments within a totally controlled environment," said the ADOT report.
>
> ADOT's testing, started in 1987, involved five types of alternate fuels: gasolines blended with ethanol, MTBE, and methanol; as well as compressed natural gas and propane.
>
> ADOT released its first report in October 1988, concluding that oxygenated fuels showed no significant improvement over plain unleaded gasoline. State officials then extended the study another year to double-check ADOT's findings. The second test ended Oct. 1, 1989, although the results were not released until Friday.

A report by the National Academy of Sciences in December 1991 states that "using ethanol as a blending agent in gasoline would not achieve significant air-quality benefits, and in fact would likely be detrimental."[9] And an article in *Science* in 1993 by J.G. Calvert of the National Center for Atmospheric Research *et al.* states: "No convincing argument based on combustion or atmospheric chemistry can be made for the addition of ethanol to gasoline."[10]

Ethanol is also a *net energy loser.* The energy needed for growing the corn (for farm machinery, fertilizers, pesticides) and distilling the alcohol is more than you can get from burning the ethanol that is produced.[11] Ethanol is not a conservation measure that will stretch out our petroleum reserves; Americans will burn *more* gasoline, not less, because of ethanol.

It takes much less energy to produce ethanol from sugar cane than from corn. Brazil has had such an ethanol program for many years. Yet Brazil has found that producing ethanol even from sugar cane is twice as expensive as producing gasoline. Eli Pelin, a leading energy economist at Sao Paulo University says that all the spending and good intentions "have left us with the worst of all possible situations. There is no plausible economic explanation for the alcohol program."[12] A World Bank study says Brazil's ethanol program generates a $2.7 billion annual deficit. Even Werther Annicchino, president of Brazil's largest ethanol-producing conglomerate, admits that ethanol is uneconomic. Without government support, he says, "ethanol couldn't compete with gasoline."[13]

In December 1987 the U.S. Department of Agriculture reported that the costs of ethanol from corn "are so large that ethanol production cannot be justified on economic grounds even if existing producers could get by with present subsidies." On February 3, 1993 a spokesman for Ashland Oil stated on a Twin Cities newscast that the government subsidy his company receives of 74 cents per gallon is not enough to make ethanol economic.

Ethanol results in financial loss, a net energy loss, a loss of fuel efficiency (fewer miles per gallon), and destroys carburetors in older automobiles. Usually the people who drive older cars do so because they can't afford newer ones. They are the people who are least able to afford the hefty repair bills for replacing carburetors.

But there are even further losses. Many small engines aren't designed to run on ethanol mixtures and are, in fact, destroyed by them. Owners of brand new outboard motors, lawn mowers, chainsaws, and snow blowers have had the engines burn out because of ethanol. It doesn't make sense to put ethanol in machines that are harmed or even destroyed by it—but, remember, the purpose of any regulation is to force people to do what does not make sense to them, to force them to act *against* their minds rather than by them. By depriving people of the choice of a non-ethanol gasoline, government requires them to act against their own interests by damaging their own equipment.

The advocates of government programs always view the losses some people suffer, such as from ethanol, as a trade-off for benefits others allegedly receive, in this case cleaner air. Once again, the policy is a manifestation of the invader mentality that attempts to benefit some people *at others' expense.* It assumes that the "greatest good for the greatest number" can be achieved by sacrificing the interests of various individuals. As always, the sacrifices turn out to be greater than the benefits, a net loss to society. Society advances only through the *fulfill-ment* of individual interests, not at their expense. The entire ethanol program is simply one more method of transferring a benefit to some people at other people's expense and at an overall loss. In this case the corn growers and the ethanol producers and lobbyists benefit at the expense of the consumers and taxpayers (who pay for the subsidies) and the owners of those older automobiles and certain small engines which are damaged by ethanol.

On July 8, 1996 reporter Roger O'Neil on NBC's Nightly News stated: "Last week a federal study concluded there is no evidence that special fuels do anything." The study he was referring to was a report on oxygenated fuels, such as ethanol, by the National Research Council, the investigative arm of the National Academy of Sciences. Colorado was selected for the study because it was the first state to require oxygenated fuels and hence had the longest record of data, eight years. The study was only of carbon monoxide emissions, not of other pollutants, some of which the oxygenates themselves produce. But even at Colorado's high altitude—where oxygenates would be most likely to be effective in reducing carbon monoxide—there was no evidence of such benefit. On the July 8th program, Professor Douglas Lawson from Colorado State University at Ft. Collins, Colorado, said, "We are not getting the effects that models had predicted. We need to re-examine the problem and decide how to better spend our dollars to improve air quality." In 1996, in addition to the federal requirement for oxygenated fuels in selected cities, thirteen states required these special fuels, thus forcing millions of Americans to spend millions of dollars ineffectively. Because of government requirements, Americans burned 1.4 billion gallons of ethanol in 1996.

The 1990 Clean Air Act also required "alternative fuels" for auto-mobiles for 1996 and an even cleaner-burning version for 2001. Methanol is often cited by government officials as most promising. But the promotion of methanol has been singularly quiet about its potential problems, says John E. Kinney, an environmental consultant and Diplomate, American Academy of Environmental Engineers:

> For example, one ounce may be fatal; it is not only acutely toxic to humans—it affects the central nervous system and the optic nerve—but it is also a cumulative poison, for it takes a long time for removal from the body. Methanol is highly soluble in water…. So if there is a spill to stream, lake or under-

ground aquifer, damage will be great and long term. Oil and gasoline spills, regardless of their magnitude and the attention they receive, have a limited time of damage. Neither has much solubility in water.

Also, methanol cannot be blended alone directly with gasoline.... So expensive co-solvents have to be added. Questions remain on combustion controls to prevent unacceptable discharges of harmful products such as aldehydes, which have very high smog forming potential.

Moreover, since the fuel value is less, it will take 1.8 gallons of methanol to equal the effectiveness of 1.0 gallons of gasoline.[14]

How could such a costly and foolish monstrosity as the Clean Air Act of 1990 have been foisted on the American people? The United States in 1990 was already spending $115 billion a year on pollution controls, more than two and one-half times the amount of the entire 12-nation European Community, which has a far greater population density. The 1990 Clean Air Act is adding another $40 billion per year—with some estimates running as high as $100 billion annually. *The Wall Street Journal* notes, "Members of Congress tell us privately that the Clean Air Act was rushed to passage because no one wanted to publicly oppose any bill with the words 'clean air' in it."[15]

California is again in the forefront of regulating auto emissions, just as it was in the 1960s. It now mandates that zero-emission vehicles must be 2 percent of all new automobiles sold in 1998, 5 percent of those sold in 2001 and 10 percent of those sold in the year 2010. The only remotely plausible way of meeting this requirement is with electric cars. But a 1995 Carnegie-Mellon research report by a team of experts concludes that electric cars would be *worse* for the environment. Writing in *Science,* the authors state that such cars would have to rely on lead batteries—which would release 60 times more lead per kilometer than comparable cars burning *leaded* gasoline. They note that the two best alternative batteries available—nickel-cadmium and metal hydride—are highly toxic to both man and environment, as well as incredibly expensive.

Biggest Polluter: Mother Nature

While it's important to recognize that industrial progress, unfettered by government control, has improved air quality, not degraded it, it's perhaps even more important to maintain perspective on man's activities in relation to those of nature. There is a popular belief that the air was significantly purer before there were any automobiles or factories. But nature has long been polluting the air with the very substances for which modern man is criticized, and it has been doing so on a scale that dwarfs human activity.

Take carbon monoxide, for example. According to Dr. John J. McKetta, former Chairman of the National Air Quality Commission and Vice President of the National Council for Environmental Balance, ninety-three percent of the carbon monoxide in the atmosphere is produced by nature. This poisonous gas is produced by the trees and other foliage which the eco-worshippers adore. But doesn't the remaining seven percent, which is man-made, represent an increase over what existed before the automobile, and won't it get worse if we just add more cars? Curiously enough, the answer is no. Carbon monoxide concentrations are actually slightly higher over the oceans than they are over the land, where all the automobiles are. The reason is that carbon monoxide is removed from the air by soil fungi (aspergillus), which enrich the land and use up all of the carbon monoxide that man produces. It's significant that nine-tenths of the automobiles in the world are in the northern hemisphere, yet there is no hemispheric difference at all in the carbon monoxide content of the atmosphere. Nor is the carbon monoxide content increasing on a worldwide basis. So there never was any threat from carbon monoxide in the environment. The more we produce it, the more soil fungi flourish and gobble it up. Once again the public was panicked by a scare that had no realistic basis but which led to more laws, government control over industry, and increased costs for consumers.

Carbon monoxide is definitely toxic, but the dangers from it in our environment have been exaggerated. In Los Angeles it may reach concentrations of 35 parts per million. In parking garages and tunnels it may reach 50 parts per million. But the carbon monoxide content of cigarette smoke is 42,000 parts per million!

The oxides of nitrogen are also produced abundantly by nature. More than 99 percent of these present in the atmosphere result from such natural processes as biologic action, organic decomposition, lightning, and ultraviolet light acting upon the oxygen and nitrogen which are always present in the air. So even if we were able to remove all of the man-made portion of these oxides, more than 99 percent would still remain.[16]

Or consider methane. Harold J. Paulus, Professor of Environmental Health at the University of Minnesota and a nationally recognized air pollution expert, says, "The greatest source of methane pollution in this country isn't industry at all, but our swamplands. Swamps put out 1.6 billion tons of methane per year, while people create, at best, only 70 million tons."[17] In other words, the swamps, which so many anti-industrialists want to preserve, are polluting the air with methane almost twenty-three times faster than industry, which they denounce as a source of pollution.

An official publication of Oregon's Environmental Protection Agency, *Public Works,* says that burping cows "must rank as the number one source of pollution in the U.S." They disgorge 50 million tons of hydrocarbons into the atmosphere each year and "there presently exists no available technology for controlling these hydrocarbon emissions."[18]

Sheep are even more efficient producers of methane than cows. Each sheep produces about five gallons of methane per day. According to David Lowe, a New Zealand geophysicist, "If you could hook up a sheep to the carburetor of your car, you could run it several kilometers a day. To power the same vehicle by people, you'd need a whole football team and a couple of kegs of beer."[19]

Another natural pollutant of the air is terpenes, which are emitted by pine trees. These hydrocarbons react with oxygen, the oxides of nitrogen, and ozone to produce the same effect over the Great Smokey Mountains, the Blue Ridge Mountains, and many other heavily wooded areas, that man has created over Los Angeles. In the words of Professor Paulus:

> Pine forests exude particulate hydrocarbons that react photo-chemically with light to produce haze. The Blue Ridge Mountains in Appalachia are topped by this haze. It looks very beautiful over the trees, but if it were anywhere else, it would look like car exhaust.[20]

Forests alone produce 175 million tons of hydrocarbons annually—more than six times the total from all man-made sources. And by the way, if you have an average-sized suburban lawn, the grass in your yard emits more hydrocarbons every year than your automobile.

In July 1995 some 200 scientists completed a month-long field study of how ozone forms over a typical city with smog. The study involved six laboratory-equipped airplanes, weather balloons, 100 air-sampling ground stations, and wind-measuring radar. Flying over the Nashville area, researchers noticed a big difference in flying over green fields and in flying over thick oak forests around the city. "Over the forests, there are markedly higher levels of isoprene, a highly reactive gas given off by trees. Isoprene causes ozone just like the evaporation of gasoline."[21]

Although ozone levels in the lower atmosphere are widely blamed on automobiles, three scientists at Michigan State University reported in 1989 that ozone measurements taken at twenty stations in Michigan between 1871 and 1903—when there were no automobiles—reveal ozone patterns and levels that are the same as today.[22] Furthermore, EPA's own five-volume study of ozone could find no adverse effects of ozone on human health.[23]

In 1978 the EPA suppressed a scientific study showing that up to 80 percent of air pollution was caused by plants and trees rather than cars and smokestacks. Following a suit filed under the Freedom of Information Act to pry out the report, EPA officials told John Holusha of the *Washington Star* that the report was suppressed because it "possibly would confuse hydrocarbon control strategy." Associated Press International charged that EPA officials pressured the scientist involved to "put the data in perspective that could be defended by EPA."[24]

We have not yet even mentioned the greatest sources of air pollution, volcanoes and wind. According to the late Dr. William Pecora, former Director of the United States Geological Survey, just three volcanic eruptions in the last century (Krakatoa, Indonesia, 1883; Katmai, Alaska, 1912; and Hekla, Iceland, 1947) produced more particulate and gaseous pollution of the atmosphere than the combined activities of all the men who ever lived! And the modern era has been one in which volcanic activity has been relatively quiet. There have been eras in which it has been at least ten times greater. The spectacular explosion of Krakatoa is often thought to be an exception, perhaps the worst natural disaster in the earth's history. However, there have been at least 18 volcanic explosions as large or larger than Krakatoa just since the year 1500. When Mt. Pinatubo in the Philippines erupted in 1991, it blasted 30 million tons of sulfur dioxide into the stratosphere. Pinatubo was the largest volcanic eruption in at least half a century. Even so, it was dwarfed by the Laki volcanic eruptions in Iceland in 1783-84, which emitted 147 million tons of sulfur dioxide, according to the estimates of Thorvaldur Thordarson of the University of Hawaii.

As for wind, although it ranks with volcanoes as one of the two largest sources of pollution today, there have been times when its effects have been far greater. Analysis of the Greenland ice sheet shows that when some of its layers were formed thousands of years ago, the atmosphere contained *forty times* as much dust as it does today. What all the world's industries emit is truly trivial by comparison.

"Man is an insignificant agent in the total air quality picture," says Dr. Pecora. "Those individuals who speak about restoring our inherited environment of pure air, pure rain, pure rivers, pure coastlines and pure lakes never had a course in geology. Natural processes are by far the principal agents in modifying our environment."[25]

Human efforts are so puny compared to those of nature that man has a difficult time doing serious environmental damage even when he tries. The gigantic fires from the more than 700 Kuwaiti oil wells deliberately torched by Iraq produced "insignificant" damage to the global environment, according to a study completed in 1992 by Peter Hobbs, professor of atmospheric science at the University of Washington, Seattle, and Lawrence Radke of the National Center for Atmospheric Research in Boulder Colorado. The study concluded that the oil fires had marked effects on air quality and some aspects of the weather in the Gulf, but only small effects beyond the Gulf and *insignificant* effects globally. Yet those fires produced 3,400 metric tons of soot per day— about 13 times the soot emitted daily from all combustion sources in the U.S. And those fires in that small area emitted sulfur dioxide at a rate equal to 57 percent of emissions from all electric utilities in the United States, an area nearly 600 times larger than Kuwait.

Nature pollutes the air not only from below but from above. Ten thousand tons of meteors drop into our atmosphere every day, from eternity to eternity. Of course, most of these are very small, but small particles stay suspended longer in the air and distribute the pollution over a wider area.

Man may be an "insignificant agent" in the total air quality picture, as Dr. Pecora said. But here, again, just as with carcinogens, the overwhelming factor of nature's activity is ignored while Man the Maker is vilified as the enemy through a series of unfounded scares in order to panic the public into backing the next legislative attack. This is exactly what happened with the issues of carbon monoxide and hydrocarbons in auto exhausts. Here are a few other scares.

The Oxygen Depletion Scare

The prophets of doom argue that man is using increasing quantities of oxygen because of the growth of population and industry while at the same time he is draining swamps, cutting forests, and destroying other oxygen-producing vegetation in order to build more parking lots, freeways and factories. Mankind is using roughly twenty billion tons of oxygen annually. The figure is impressive. Yet even at this rate, it would take about six thousand years to use even one-fifth of the total oxygen in the atmosphere. That's if no more were being produced. But the facts about oxygen production are even more surprising than those about its consumption. Every school child learns that green plants, in the presence of sunlight, take in carbon dioxide and give off oxygen; but few know that phytoplankton in the oceans produces more oxygen than all the trees and green plants in the world. The real surprise, however, is that the net gain from the photosynthetic process is extremely small since the oxygen produced is exactly enough to convert plant tissue back again to carbon dioxide and water. "The evidence is now overwhelming," says Dr. McKetta,

> that photosynthesis is inadequate to have produced the amount of oxygen present in the atmosphere…. The oxygen in the atmosphere had to come from another source. The most likely possibility involves the photodissociation of water vapor in the upper atmosphere by high energy rays from the sun and by cosmic rays. This process alone could have produced (over the history of the earth 4.5×10^9 years) about seven times the present mass of oxygen in the atmosphere.
>
> The significance of this information is that the supply of oxygen in the atmosphere is virtually unlimited. It is not threatened by man's activities in any significant way. If all the organic material on earth were oxidized, it would reduce the atmospheric concentration of oxygen by less than one percent. We can forget the depletion of oxygen in the atmosphere and get on with the solution of more serious problems.[26]

While we still have much to learn about the effects of high energy radiation upon the stratosphere, we do know that the world's oxygen supply hasn't been diminishing because of the activities of modern man. In 1970—the year of the Clean Air Act —Dr. Lester Machta of the Environmental Science Services Administration and Ernest Hughes of the National Science Foundation reported that the percentage of oxygen in the air—to one-thousandth of one percent—was exactly the same as in 1910. This conclusion was the product of three years of study at seventy-eight points on the globe.

The Acid Rain Scare

It is widely believed that acid rain (1) is the product of industrialization, (2) has been increasing along with industrial growth, (3) is harming the environment, and (4) is caused mainly by coal-fired boilers, particularly in the power industry, which burns three-fourths of the coal mined in the United States. These points are widely accepted by the public because that is all the public has been told—over and over again. There is ample evidence that none of the above is true, but this evidence has been systematically withheld. Some of the contrary evidence has been available for many years, but it has been conveniently ignored by those intent on convincing the public that Man the Maker is the "enemy of the people" and that force is the answer to the problem: more laws. In 1989, for example, public television carried a one-hour special on acid rain featuring all of the above points, offering none of the contrary evidence, and concluding with righteous indignation that the only solution was to get the politicians to act NOW. The cause of acid rain was presumed to be obvious, and further studies were derided as a delaying tactic of obstructionists. The cause of the problem is not so obvious to those whose minds are not closed because they already "know" the solution.

Northeastern United States has an acid rain problem. It has been widely trumpeted that this results from pollution in the heavily industrialized Great Lakes states, which is carried northeast by normal weather patterns. But this cannot explain how acid rain from hurricanes in the *opposite* direction is even more acid. Dr. McKetta says:

> Most hurricanes come to the U.S. from the Atlantic Ocean. The acid rain that falls from hurricanes is…more acid than the acidity that the Northeastern United States is complaining about. This is mostly *natural* acid rain, because there are no industries out in the Atlantic Ocean.[27]

Dr. McKetta should know what he is talking about. He has been appointed by three United States presidents to various positions, including membership in the National Acid Rain Task Force. He has been National President of the American Institute of Chemical Engineers and has been named one of thirty Eminent Chemical Engineers in the United States. He has received many other honors and awards.

Acidity is measured on a pH scale from 1 to 14. A pH value of 7 is neutral. Lower numbers are acid; higher ones are alkaline (the opposite of acid). The scale is logarithmic. This means that 5 is ten times more acid than 6; 4 is ten times more acid than 5, or 100 times more acid than 6.

Distilled water has a pH of 7. Rain is naturally acid because of carbon dioxide in the air (which forms carbonic acid), and the *natural* amounts of sulfur dioxide and the oxides of nitrogen (which form sulfuric and nitric acids). According to Dr. McKetta, the pH of natural rain—unpolluted by man—is probably 4.4 to 4.6 in most cases, and acid rain of pH 4.0 has been found in Samoa in the South Pacific, the jungles of South America, the arctic coast of Alaska, Hawaii, and islands in the middle of the Indian Ocean. This rainfall is more acid than tomatoes, yet in such remote locations it is difficult to put the blame on industry.

It is even more difficult to blame industry for comparable acid rain hundreds and even thousands of years ago. Ice-pack analysis in the Antarctic, the Himalayas, and Greenland shows consistent pH values of 4.4 to 4.8 over thousands of years in those pristine environments, with some measurements as low as 4.2. These are comparable to the 4.0 to 4.5 range common in the northeastern states and in Scandinavia today.

California has an acid rain problem. But California has no coal-fired utility plants, and there are no industries upwind in the Pacific Ocean.

Also, if the burning of coal is the main cause of acid rain, how could acid rain have gotten worse in recent decades when we were burning *less* coal? Remember government regulation of natural gas, which was discussed in Chapter 5? Well, when government held the price of natural gas artificially low in order to please the voters, it undercut the market for coal, which was higher priced. So the use of coal plummeted. In 1954, when the government began regulating natural gas, the nation burned only 390 million tons of coal, compared to 630 million tons in 1947. It took more than thirty years for coal consumption to reach the 1947 level again. Meanwhile, 22 percent of the nation's coal mines closed in 1970 because they couldn't meet the standards of the Federal Coal Mine Health and Safety Act of 1969. In 1970 over 700 coal-burning foundries closed because they couldn't meet the requirements of the Clean Air Act. The same act forced 235 coal-fired electric generating plants to switch from coal to natural gas or oil. It took the Arab oil embargo in 1973 to stimulate renewed interest in coal and raise its consumption back to the levels of the 1940s.

The alleged culprit in the burning of coal is sulfur dioxide. If the charge is true, how could acid rain have increased when sulfur dioxide emissions were dropping rapidly for a half-century? We already noted that sulfur dioxide emissions at the time of the Clean Air Act were only one-third or one-fourth of pre-World War II levels. Between 1970 and 1987 they dropped another 40 percent even though coal consumption was now increasing. In some cities, then, sulfur dioxide emissions had declined about 85 percent in a half-century. According to EPA data, between 1973 and 1986 total sulfur dioxide emissions in the United States decreased 8.5 million tons, or 26.6 percent, while coal use by electric utilities increased 76 percent.

There is a great deal of other evidence that controlling sulfur dioxide emission will not alleviate the problem of acid rain. For example, in 1984 Alan W. Katzenstein, a private consultant on acid rain, wrote:

> From 1965 to 1978, sulfur dioxide emissions were reduced 38 percent in the EPA's New England region and 40 percent in the New York and New Jersey region. These emissions changes are reflected in the parallel drop in sulfate concentrations in the rain, which fell 33 percent...and about 30 percent.... But the acidity of rain showed no long-term changes in either place, suggesting that sulfate does not determine the acidity of rain...
>
> [T]he acidity of rain...increased from the mid-1950s to the mid-1970s in Virginia and Pennsylvania. But in Virginia, the acidity increased 74 percent while sulfate fell 3 percent, and in Pennsylvania the acidity increased 216 percent while the sulfate dropped 23 percent. Clearly, sulfate did not determine the acidity of rain there....
>
> [T]he hard evidence that is available in the literature convincingly shows that our experience in reducing sulfur-dioxide emissions has not reduced the acidity of rain so far. Nor is there a theoretical basis for expecting that further reductions will produce results that are any different from what has actually happened over the past two decades.[28]

Europe offers more of the same evidence. From 1965 to 1980 sulfur dioxide levels increased 35 percent, but there was no increase in the acidity of rainfall.

When trees were dying in the Black Forest in Germany and in the Alps, these events were widely publicized as effects of acid rain. But sulfur dioxide levels were very low in both places. The true cause of the dead trees had nothing to do with acid rain, as explained by London's *Daily Telegraph* on August 9, 1985:

We may have heard the last of the "acid rain" scare. The culprit, apparently, is not power station exhausts, but a virus; and a senior biologist at Stuttgart University, Prof. Burkhard Frenzel, has succeeded in isolating it. Huge parts of the Black Forest in West Germany, he says, have been destroyed by this virus, which is being spread by an "avalanche of forest insects" migrating from Czechoslovakia.

Let us be thankful we paid no attention to those unthinking environmentalists who long demanded that we spend an estimated £1,800 million ($2.7 billion) on removing sulphur particles from power station chimneys. It is now clear that this reckless measure would have greatly increased the price of electricity to no avail.

After the collapse of the acid rain and aerosol-ozone theories, is it asking too much that the next environmentalists' "scare story" be treated with proper skepticism?

In Austria trees were dying for a different reason, though once again acid rain was blamed. Then in 1981 a road through the sick forest was resurfaced, and an adjacent area became heavily coated with gravel dust. Within a few months that part of the forest recovered, with the trees nearest the road clearly recovering better and quicker. The forest wasn't dying from acid rain; it was dying from *too much clean air!* The trees needed the minerals supplied by the dust, a type of gneiss. The effect proved repeatable on a special test area of some 12 acres. Not only did the trees there improve, but so did the grass, blackberries and raspberries.

In the same way that the forests benefited from the dust, many living things benefit from the sulfur dioxide in the atmosphere. Here, again, it is to no one's benefit to get the air too clean, according to Dr. I.W. Tucker, Professor of Environmental Engineering at the University of Louisville:

> It is difficult to understand the tremendous public and political pressures to control all manner of pollution and to a degree far beyond what man or nature at any stage of civilization could possibly realize and from which no significant benefit can be expected....
>
> In particular, I deplore the efforts of the EPA (and others) on a continuing and massive basis to release statements suggesting dire consequences to human health from any and all levels of pollutants, however minuscule. Examples of this are legion, but perhaps are most clearly seen in the case of sulfur dioxide.

Sulfur dioxide is a material that has been around since the beginning of time on this planet, and is a natural constituent of pristine air. It is unavoidably injected into our air mass from episodes such as the...eruption of Mt. St. Helens. Sulfur happens to be one of the essential nutrients for life—human, animal and plant—and its presence in the atmosphere is an essential part of maintaining what we call the biosphere.

As industry takes coal from the ground, it includes an amount of sulfur that represents the biomaterial from which the coal is derived. It will only be recycled profitably as someone specifically removes it from the coal and replaces it in the forests; or it is taken from the stack gases in a form suitable for redistribution to our productive land; or it is allowed to be discharged into the air and widely distributed as natural fallout. The last thing one should do is to bury it in a dump where it will do no earthly good—but that is exactly what EPA has been mandating....

The current processes being promoted for flue gas desulfurization are those which simply collect the removed sulfur in the form of a waste of no earthly value to be placed in some kind of pit at considerable expense and of no benefit to anyone....

[A]llowing sulfur to be discharged from the stack actually provides a most efficient means of distributing it to farm land in an economical manner.[29]

Why, then, did we become so concerned about sulfur dioxide in the first place? Because of a certain Dr. John J. Finklea, a former research official in the Environmental Protection Agency.

The Finklea story began in 1971, when Kennecott Copper Corp. went into federal court to challenge the standards for sulfur dioxide emissions set by the EPA. The court ordered EPA to justify the standards.

EPA couldn't. It had set the standards by guess and by God and without a real study of how sulfur dioxide actually affects public health or plant life.

Dr. Finklea then was director of the agency's Community Health and Environmental Surveillance System. EPA ordered him to conduct the research as quickly as possible.

Dr. Finklea went to work like a man obsessed, driving his staff to complete about 20 complex scientific papers in six weeks....

The reports didn't satisfy Dr. Finklea. *They didn't prove what he wanted to prove.* He rewrote some; he deleted material that did not show a connection between sulfur pollution and health; he threw out statistics that weakened or contradicted the case against sulfur dioxide; he wrote in estimates of the health impact of sulfur dioxide that were either dubious or unsupportable.

This became the basis on which EPA was able to order coal-fired electric utility plants, among others, to install scrubbers at a cost of billions.

A year ago, a group of scientist at such prestigious universities as Harvard, Columbia and MIT joined in a report, which said that many EPA regulations are not only costly but unrealistic, as well, and that *many will do more harm than good.*[30] (Italics added)

The report of those scientists was, of course, ignored by the regulators and Congress. Like Dr. Finklea, they weren't interested in reports that didn't say what they wanted to hear. Nearly twenty years later, when Congress passed the 1990 Clean Air Act, it ignored a far more extensive and important report—the results of a 10-year study on which it had just spent $537 million of the taxpayers' money. That report didn't say what Congress wanted to hear either. The 1990 legislation bore no relation to the findings of the National Acid Precipitation Assessment Project (NAPAP) and instead mandated a costly crash program for the removal of more sulfur dioxide. It required a cut of 5 million tons in sulfur dioxide emissions by 1995 and an additional 10 million tons by the year 2000. One of the scientists who participated in the NAPAP study was Dr. Edward C. Krug of the atmospheric chemistry section of the Illinois State Water Survey. On April 23, 1990 before the National Press Club in Washington, D.C. he stated:

> The nation is already sold on acid rain theory. A consensus was established before anyone knew anything. Consequently, the idea of throwing billions of dollars into reducing acid rain has all the political support it needs *without any proof as to the theory's validity.*

Dr. Lawrence Kulp, who was NAPAP Director of Research, is critical of the 1990 Clean Air Act and says it will have the perverse effect of delaying or precluding the use of advanced clean-coal technologies now being developed. Over the longer term, then, we will be worse off than we would have been without the law. A byproduct of the 1990 law will be countless tons of limestone sludge, which EPA will require be buried somewhere.

Similarly, we are worse off now because of the 1970 Clean Air Act than we would have been without it. That act not only wasted billions of dollars on unnecessary expenditures; there is strong evidence it has actually made rain more acid. Dr. McKetta writes:

> There is some scientific evidence that increased acidity in rainwater may be the result of a decrease in the concentration of alkaline particles in the atmosphere rather than an increase in acidity. The Clean Air Act (1970) required the removal of many particles from the air. Many of these were alkaline particles. So now we have an ironic situation. The attempt to remove the particulates may have caused an increased acidity in the rain.[31]

Mr. Katzenstein on the importance of these acid-neutralizing particles:

> In fact, the best information at the moment points to the acid-neutralizing calcium, magnesium and ammonium in rain as having stronger influence on the final acid levels than do the acid-promoting sulfate and nitrate components[32]

Dr. Beckmann on the same subject:

> The acid-forming sulfur dioxide and nitrous oxides used to be partly neutralized by the compounds of calcium, magnesium, potassium and sodium in the fly-ash, but particulate emissions have been restricted much more severely than gaseous pollutants. By whom? By the friends of clean air and a healthy environment....
>
> The effect was actually observed in Tennessee, where the acidity was caused by increased use of electrostatic precipitators to remove (neutralizing) particulates from coal smoke.
>
> The same effect was noted in Illinois, though here the neutralizing particles came from windblown soil. The acidifying constituents were found fairly constant, but the acidity changed with fluctuations of the neutralizing particulates (more windblown soil in dry years)....
>
> One of the measures taken by utilities in southern California after being ordered to eliminate acid fallout altogether was to add neutralizing agents such as magnesium oxide to their fuel oil—in other words, supply what fly-ash does in a coal-fired plant.[33]

The National Research Council lends further support to the idea that controls adopted to reduce fly ash pollution may have eliminated necessary neutralizing agents and unwittingly promoted acid formation. Furthermore, the council said, tall power plant stacks, previously favored by the government to reduce low-level pollution, may have stimulated chemical problems in the upper atmosphere. The counterpart of Adam Smith's "invisible hand," which had been improving the environment in incidental and unexpected ways, is the "heavy hand of government," which was now making the environment worse in unexpected ways.

Government has made the acid-rain problem worse in both directions. While it has reduced the alkaline particles, which neutralize the acid, it has also increased the acid components. A study for the Dept. of Energy back in 1981 found that the biggest culprits may not be coal-fired boilers after all but commercial and residential *oil*-fired boilers *and catalytic converters on motor vehicles*. Dr. McKetta also speaks of the effect of catalytic converters:

> There is also a great deal of scientific evidence that rain's acidity may be increased by the use of catalytic mufflers on automobiles. The minute particles of material that pass the catalyst are more reactive to form acids.[34]

Dr. McKetta says that acid rain is mostly a local problem: each region is its own largest source of pollution. The idea that the acid rain in the northeastern states is due to Midwestern coal-fired plants is not supported by scientific evidence. Lakes in the Adirondacks aren't acid because of the rain. They are acid because of soils that are the most acidic in the world. Water that flows through even one foot of this soil is so acid that fish cannot grow in it.

> These lakes have been formed by the glaciers as they receded North many, many years ago, and if the glaciers cut out dirt over basaltic rock, which is highly acidic, those lakes are acid and will be acid forever. If those glaciers cut out the earth over calcitic rock, you will find that those lakes are alkaline and do propagate fish. In fact, in many areas in the Adirondacks, some of these lakes, the highly acid lakes, and the alkaline lakes, may be only four or five miles apart.[35]

Here, again, the role of nature is far larger than that of man.

Another aspect of nature is extremely important in the formation of acid rain. R. J. Murris of the Netherlands points out that global forest damage reported in 1982-83 corresponds to the 1982 eruption of the exceptionally acid Mexican volcano *El Chicon*. He continues:

There is a convincing correlation between the acidity of
the Greenland ice sheet layers and major volcanic eruptions in
the past, such as Krakatoa and Katmai, Alaska. Especially
remarkable is the period of low acidity of the ice lasting from
1920 to 1960, when no major eruptions occurred—but industrial
pollution did continue![36]

Five scientists, using carbon dating, have established correlations
between historic eruptions of the *El Chicon* volcano and the deposition
of acidity in the Greenland ice sheet. The two peaked together in 1300
AD and 623 AD, when there were no coal-fired plants or other industrial
sources of pollution.

There are numerous examples of dying forests, acid lakes, failed
crops, etc. which are blamed on acid rain but which in fact have other
causes. In many cases trees have been found to be simply dying of old
age, blight, pathogens or various pests, such as the gypsy moth, pine
bark beetle, tussock moth, and so forth. There are other explanations for
lakes. In Wisconsin certain lakes are acid because of adjacent bogs.
Other examples are given in a Hudson Institute report by Dr. William M.
Brown. He points out that historic data on many lakes is severely biased
by a 1955-56 drought, which resulted in wind-borne deposits of dust
rich in calcium and magnesium—acid neutralizers. The alleged
acidification of these lakes in later years from industrial pollution was
merely a return to normal. Adjusting for that drought, Dr. Brown found
little change in lake acidity between the 1950s and 1970s—and that
change was a *decrease*.

Of course, those who believe in getting what they want through
force against other men weren't looking to nature for causes of acid rain.
They were looking to industry, for the same reasons they were looking
there for causes of cancer while ignoring all the natural carcinogens. To
their mentality, industry *had* to be guilty before they even understood
the problem. And they certainly weren't about to focus on the catalytic
converters. That would be an admission of the folly of requiring them in
the first place. In view of the large number of voters who had been
forced to purchase these devices and hence would react negatively, such
a revelation was politically unacceptable. So it was inevitable that
warnings of the acid emissions from these devices, even within the
government itself as far back as 1975, would be ignored. The only
politically and ideologically acceptable way to obtain clean air was by
attacking the "enemy of the people," industry, and subduing it through

regulatory laws—and the more (financial) losses that could be inflicted in the process, the better. In an invasion the victims' losses are the invaders' gain. So the more losses for industry, the more clean air the victors would feel they were winning, and the more "trophies" the politicians could hold up to their army of supporters.

The Chlorofluorocarbon Scare

The current scare, that CFCs (chlorofluorocarbons) are destroying the ozone layer in the upper atmosphere, isn't the first such scare. There have been a couple of others. When they were debunked, those who *want* to believe industrial progress produces this kind of damage had to come up with still another "explanation." Here, just as with the cancer scares, the advocates of regulatory "science" proved they "will take any position that comes to hand to maintain political power over industry, whether those positions are rationally coherent or not."

The first ozone scare began in 1971 with Dr. James McDonald of the University of Arizona at Tucson. He argued that water vapor left by supersonic transports would diminish the ozone in the stratosphere and thus increase the ultraviolet rays reaching the surface of the earth. Dr. Barry Commoner echoed this idea in *The Closing Circle* and warned that "terrestrial life would be seriously threatened by solar ultraviolet radiation."[37] McDonald claimed that the additional radiation would produce 7,000 to 40,000 more cases of skin cancer annually in the United States. The argument was ridiculous, but it produced enough fear to lead Congress to cancel a supersonic transport prototype.

John Maddox, the distinguished British scientist and editor of the highly-respected *Nature* magazine, put this first ozone scare in perspective. He pointed out that "water vapor turns out to be much less destructive of ozone than he [McDonald] had assumed and the link between ultraviolet light and cancer is much less strong than he supposed."[38] Yet even with McDonald's generous assumptions, Maddox pointed out that the "danger" was of such magnitude that the predicted amounts of additional radiation would have been avoided if everyone wore a hat or carried an umbrella one day of his life! Incidentally, natural meteorological processes leave far more water vapor in the stratosphere than aircraft ever could.

The fear mongers next focused on the oxides of nitrogen, which also were products of fuel combustion in the supersonic transports. These exhaust emissions were said to be much more potent ozone destroyers than water vapor. It turned out, however, that a small decrease in ozone in the upper stratosphere was more than offset by an increase in the lower stratosphere. The net effect was an actual *increase.* So the purveyors of ozone doom had to come up with something else.

Now it was the CFCs. Here was an even more attractive target—a product widely believed to be produced only by industry, whereas water vapor and nitrogen oxides were also produced by nature. Since not much was known about CFCs, exaggerated claims of their damaging nature couldn't be quickly debunked. Within six years, however, enough evidence had accumulated to show that the original claims of danger had been exaggerated at least 100 fold, according to Dr. McKetta. Though the prophets of doom claimed the situation was getting *more* perilous and something had to be done "before it's too late," every report by the National Academy of Sciences (NAS), based on better and better data, showed that the danger was less than previously thought. In fact, each subsequent projection was less than *half* the previous one. Reports issued in 1979, 1982, and 1984 projected ozone losses after the year 2000 of 18.6 percent, 7 percent, and about 3 percent. The more we knew about the problem, the less there was to worry about. But that didn't stop the media, the politicians, or the rest of the industry-is-the-enemy crowd from playing on people's fears and clamoring for greater regulation. Their agitation led in 1989 to a multi-government treaty to halt the production of CFCs—"ignorance raised to the level of an international treaty," as Dr. Beckmann put it.

The ozone layer is by no means uniform. Its thickness varies with latitude and shifts with the seasons. Both of these entirely natural variations are far greater than the 3 percent projected by NAS for beyond the year 2000.

Because of the latitudinal variation, the shielding effect of ozone decreases toward the equator. In our latitude this leads to a doubling of skin cancer for every 250 miles toward the equator. According to Dr. Beckmann:

> If, for example, the NAS report were wrong by a factor of 3, and the ozone layer were to be depleted by 10 percent, the increase in skin cancer risk would be the same as moving 4 degrees south—less than moving from Niagara Falls to New York City or from San Francisco to Los Angeles.[39]

Osmond Holm-Hansen, head of polar research at the Scripps Institute of Oceanography reported in 1989 that ultraviolet radiation through the much-publicized antarctic "hole" in the ozone layer was similar to that on a summer day in Virginia Beach.

There is a 25 percent difference in the ozone layer between Miami and Vancouver because of their different latitudes. And the thickness of the ozone layer above New York or Denver (same latitude) changes 25 percent between April and September every year. Weather conditions in the northern latitudes have been known to vary the ozone concentration as much as 40 percent within a few days. So even if CFCs turned out to be destroying the ozone, it wouldn't be a calamity of the proportions claimed. Or even a calamity at all. The world's population has already adapted to far greater ozone changes than the 3 percent increase projected by NAS, and it has done so with no discomfort and without even realizing it.

But even such a small "danger" is unlikely. There are sound, proven theoretical reasons "why the destruction of the ozone layer will almost certainly turn out to be a lot of baloney,"[40] in the words of Dr. Beckmann.

Normal oxygen consists of a molecule of two atoms (O_2). Solar radiation splits this molecule into single atoms, each of which then combines with an unsplit molecule to form ozone (O_3). Dr. Beckmann explains how this process achieves an equilibrium density and is self-healing:

> As radiation loses its energy to the molecules of the atmosphere (in this case short ultraviolet radiation to the dissociation of oxygen molecules), the concentration of the product (ozone) at first increases with the distance penetrated by the radiation; but since the atmosphere becomes denser and the radiation weaker, the ozone concentration will decrease again. A maximum concentration is therefore formed at a certain altitude. If this mechanism is upset—for example, by chemical reactions that deprive the ultraviolet radiation of its energy sink—the radiation will merely penetrate deeper into the atmosphere and will lose its energy where it is denser. That is, the maximum of the layer will simply be formed at a somewhat lower altitude. The principles of this stability were derived by Sir Edward Appleton in the 1920s and confirmed by his experimental demonstration of ionized layers in the atmosphere, and they were one of the reasons why he was awarded a Physics Nobel Prize in 1947. His equations are valid for *any* atmospheric layer formed by the absorption of *any* radiation, and the doomsdayers have not breathed one word of explanation why this self-healing stability would not hold for the ozone layer.[41]

Dr. Beckmann explains the shielding effect of ozone and how ozone is returned to oxygen:

> The ozone strongly absorbs *long-wave* ultraviolet radiation, turning most of its energy into heat. This radiation would kill plant life if it reached the earth's surface. If the oxygen-splitting process went on forever, there would be no normal oxygen (O_2) left to turn into ozone (O_3). What returns the ozone back to oxygen consists of two categories. The first is undisputed: ultraviolet (and other) solar radiation, which tears off the extra ozone atom to leave a normal oxygen molecule, and in the process loses some of its deadly energy (the rest is lost as heat to the ozone molecules). This is the effect that shields us.
>
> But there is another category of effects that could change the ozone back to oxygen: chemicals that stray into the stratosphere. And now the fun starts. There are no less than 150 simultaneous chemical reactions that could do the trick *if* the culprit is the chlorine, though not necessarily that from CFCs (there is plenty of chlorine from natural sources). But there are other possibilities. Nitrogen oxides from both natural sources and fertilizers could do it. Methane could do it. Carbon dioxide could do it. There is not a soul on earth that knows which of these have what effect (if any) in removing ozone compared with orthodox dissociation by solar radiation. But there is no shortage of souls who have a pet theory and want more taxpayers' money to prove it, and there is an oversupply of souls who already have the precise answer and puke it all over the Sunday supplements.[42]

In 1989 Robert W. Pease, Professor Emeritus of Physical Climatology at the University of California, Riverside, noted that the "questionable theory" that CFCs cause depletion of the ozone layer had gained so much momentum "not because of scientific proof, but [as] the result of constant reiteration of disaster scenarios." He pointed out that numerous public pronouncements giving the impression of universal scientific acceptability of the theory are "far from true." Many scientists, he said, are still skeptical because of "incompatibility between the theory and what we know about the ozone layer." He said the theory ignores the equilibrium nature of ozone and its rapid self-healing capability—and pointed out that the ozone layer was *increasing* rather than being depleted:

> At very high altitudes a disrupted equilibrium is restored in a matter of minutes; at lower levels of the stratosphere, in a matter of weeks or months. In any event, repair takes place rather

quickly. Depletion of ozone can occur only by reducing the equilibrium density of ozone molecules. This makes for relatively insignificant depletions. No doubt many CFC molecules have reached the ozone layer, but it is unlikely both that they are depleting the ozone to the extent the activists say, and that such damage, even if it existed, would take centuries to repair.

Since the same narrow band of ultraviolet light breaks down both CFCs, releasing their ozone-destroying chlorine, as well as oxygen, creating ozone, there is a "competition" between the two processes for this necessary solar energy. The probability that an oxygen molecule will be broken apart, rather than a CFC molecule, depends upon the relative abundance of the two gases in the ozone layer. Calculations based on high-altitude CFC samplings and data supplied by the National Oceanic and Atmospheric Administration show 60,000 ozone molecules are created for every chlorine atom released from a CFC molecule.

With this probability, how can the equilibrium density of the ozone layer be materially reduced? In other words, the paucity of measurable proof of depletion may be because depletion is not actually occurring. It is of interest to note that surface measurements by the National Oceanic and Atmospheric Administration indicate that the total amount of ozone above the U.S. is actually increasing.[43]

There is more stratospheric ozone today than there was 35 years ago, but the pattern doesn't show a steady trend. There are significant ups and down throughout this period. (Global ozone measurements began only in the 1950s.) From a low in 1961, there was a general uptrend in ozone to 1979, then a decline to 1985, then an uptrend to 1991, followed by a decline of two or three years, which now seems to have ended. While the latest decline may have been related to the eruption of Mount Pinatubo in 1991, the most striking correlation with variations in global ozone levels can be found in a comparison to sunspot activity. A paper presented by Dr. Hugh Ellsaesser at a symposium in Vienna on May 10, 1994 includes a graph comparing the two. The patterns are amazingly similar. No similar correlation can be found in comparing ozone levels to CFC discharges.

Furthermore, discharges of additional man-made pollutants are likely to make the ozone situation better, not worse. Professor S. Fred Singer, an atmospheric physicist at the University of Virginia and director of the Science and Environmental Policy Project, says, "Human activity will continue to generate pollutants such as carbon dioxide, methane and nitrogen oxides, which will *counteract* the destruction of ozone by CFCs."[44] A 1984 report by the National Aeronautics and Space Administration, *Present State of Knowledge of the Upper Atmosphere,* predicted that with realistic increases in CFCs and other chemicals there will be ozone *increases* over the next few decades; and "if atmospheric methane continues to increase at a substantial rate, the combined effects of methane and fluorocarbons may never result in a decrease in column ozone."

Unable to come up with any hard evidence for their claim, the ozone-depletion theorists have taken the "hole" in the ozone layer over Antarctica as indirect evidence. This so-called "hole" is not an actual hole; it's a 50 percent reduction in ozone that occurs for about four to six weeks annually. But the hole comes and goes every year with *no net loss of ozone.* In fact, even when the hole is present, there is no net loss of ozone: ozone decreases in the hole are more than made up for by increases in the donut-shaped ring of ozone surrounding the hole. The bigger the hole, the fatter the surrounding ozone "donut" becomes. So how can CFCs be destroying ozone over Antarctica when no ozone is disappearing? That the ozone hole represents ozone that is temporarily displaced rather than destroyed has been known since 1986,[45] but to my knowledge this fact has never been reported in the hundreds of articles carried in the news media on the "destruction" of ozone over Antarctica. Nor has it ever been admitted by the environmentalists.

But there is an even more important fact that has never been admitted by the environmentalists or the media. It is that the existence of the hole was documented almost thirty years before they claim it was discovered. The ozone depletionists claim this Antarctic phenomenon was discovered in 1985. In fact, it was first observed in 1956 by Gordon Dobson of Oxford University, who was the founder of research on stratospheric ozone, and for whom the standard ozone-measuring unit is named. Dobson documented the phenomenon again in 1957. Two French scientists, P. Rigaud and B. Leroy, confirmed the findings in 1958 and related their observations to solar activity. And several Japanese scientists also reported the existence of the Antarctic ozone hole before 1985. The significance of this information is that it totally destroys the theory that CFCs are responsible for the ozone hole. If that hole existed as far back as the 1950s, then it couldn't possibly have been caused by CFCs because there weren't yet any significant discharges of CFCs into the atmosphere. *If this one statement were all you knew about this issue, it is all you would need to realize that CFCs can't be responsible for the ozone hole.* The anti-CFC crowd *requires* that the ozone hole didn't exist until much later. So that's the way it has been reported to the public.

The theory that CFCs are destroying the ozone layer presents several other questions for which there are no satisfactory answers. For example, as Dr. Dixy Lee Ray has asked, if CFCs break down and release chlorine in the stratosphere, "what happens to the rest of the molecule? At least 192 chemical reactions and another 48 photochemical reactions have been identified in the stratosphere, but none involves CFCs."[46] No breakdown products of CFCs have ever been found in the stratosphere.

Another question: how do CFC molecules, which are four to eight times heavier than air, reach the stratosphere in significant numbers?

> All experience with freon and related CFCs shows that they are non-volatile and so heavy that you can pour CFCs from a container and if some of them spill, they will collect at the lowest point on the ground, where soil bacteria will decompose them. Of course, some molecules will be caught in upward air eddies or otherwise carried upwards, but this is a very small fraction of the total.[47]

An even more difficult question is why there is an ozone hole over the *South* Pole when most CFCs are used in industrialized countries in the *northern* hemisphere. There is no similar "hole" over the North Pole. Those who believe industry must be "the enemy" are somehow willing to blame Antarctic ozone depletion on CFCs discharged thousands of miles away. Meanwhile, they ignore any connection to an active volcano just 15 kilometers upwind from the observation station at McMurdo Sound. This is the station which measures the chlorine concentration in the Antarctic atmosphere that supposedly "proves" the link to CFCs. Mt. Erebus, on Ross Island in Antarctica's Ross Sea, erupts *continuously,* unlike most volcanoes, which are intermittent, often with long dormant periods. This conveniently-overlooked volcano belches 1000 tons of chlorine per day into the stratosphere. Furthermore, Mt. Erebus is a small volcano. When Mt. Pinatubo erupted in 1991, it blew two million tons of chlorine into the stratosphere in a single day. At that rate, it put the chlorine equivalent of all the CFCs produced in the entire world in 24 hours into the stratosphere in less than one minute. And most man-made CFCs never reach the stratosphere.

Here's another item you won't read about in all the reams of articles about how CFCs are destroying the ozone layer. *Van Nostrand's Scientific Encyclopedia,* 1989 edition, page 2973, under the heading *Volcano* and the subheading "Volcanic Introduction of Chlorine into the Stratosphere," states:

> Researchers have observed, for example, that the Augustine Volcano (Alaska) which erupted in 1976, may have injected 289 billion kilograms of HCL (hydrochloric acid) into the stratosphere. That is about 570 times the 1975 world industrial production of chlorine and fluorocarbons.

Another example is the eruption of Mount Tambora in Indonesia in 1815. According to Dr. D. L. Ray, this volcanic outburst "ejected 211 million tons of chloride. At the highest rate of worldwide CFC production, it would have taken 282 years to produce as much chloride-yielding CFCs as this one eruption."[48]

While volcanoes are a far larger source of stratospheric chlorine than CFCs, there is another, even larger source: ocean salt lofted into the atmosphere by vast ocean storms. UV radiation releases chlorine from this source in the same way as from CFCs. A single hurricane—with the energy of 10,000 hydrogen bombs—puts so much ocean chlorine skyward that it is absurd to be concerned about spray cans of CFCs. It shows how irrationally and desperately the ozone Chicken Littles want to believe in their theory.

> Where the chlorine really comes from, if you want to talk business, is primarily volcanoes and sea spray.... Maduro and Schauerhammer...give the amounts of chlorine emitted into the atmosphere in million tons/per year as seawater, 600; volcanoes 36; other natural sources, 13.4 resulting in a total of 649.4 million tons of chlorine per year from natural sources. Compare this with CFCs with 0.75 megatons per year, of which 7.5 (16.5 lbs.) are released by photo-disassociation in the stratosphere.
>
> Thus while the ozone produced in recombination is doubtlessly reduced somewhat by chlorine and other trace elements, this has been going on by natural causes for hundreds of millions of years without any evidence of damage to living matter. The alleged man-made increase amounts to 0.75/650 = 0.0000115 percent and provides a living for...media monkeys but is of no consequence for ozone depletion.[49]

Scientist Linwood Callis of NASA's Atmospheric Sciences Division has studied how atmospheric ozone is destroyed by a variety of factors, such as the sunspot cycle, volcanic eruptions, highly energetic electrons, and changing tropical wind patterns. He concludes: "CFCs come in a very poor last as the cause for lower levels of global ozone."[50]

The theory that CFCs destroy the ozone layer has always assumed: 1) that CFCs were indestructible outside the stratosphere, and 2) that CFCs were all man-made. Both these assumptions have been proved wrong. In 1989 scientists reported the rapid breakdown of CFCs by soil bacteria in Australia and in China's rice fields, as well as in laboratory experiments;[51] these studies showed that CFCs are destroyed within a few days or weeks. And as far back as 1983, it was shown that macroalgae and invertebrates in the oceans produce CFCs.[52]

Dean Hegg *et al.* in 1990 reported that CFCs in smoke from forest fires may equal 50 percent of all freon discharged into the atmosphere.[53] It has been assumed that the fires release CFCs that have been sequestered in the soil and plants. But if soil bacteria destroy CFCs within a few days or weeks, and if most CFCs fall quickly to the ground because of their heavy weight, it seems unlikely that large quantities of CFCs could accumulate over time until released by a forest fire. It may be that the fires themselves produce CFCs. It may also be that CFCs produced in the ocean are carried skyward by the same process which lofts ocean chlorine, only to be deposited later over forests through precipitation or simply by gravity. These latter points, of course, are speculative. What we do know is that Mother Nature is fully capable of creating CFCs and destroying them rather quickly right here on earth.

The Global Warming Scare

Many people have been scared by the claim that the so-called greenhouse effect is heating up the earth's climate. Allegedly this is due mainly to carbon dioxide (CO_2) from the burning of fossil fuels. The earth, which is heated during the day by the sun, re-radiates some of this heat in the form of infrared radiation. Nitrogen and oxygen are transparent to this radiation, but carbon dioxide absorbs it, preventing the escape of this heat from the atmosphere. Thus the climate warms as carbon dioxide increases, according to greenhouse theory. The theory is unproven. Various computer models based on the theory predict future warming, but none has shown a satisfactory correlation with historical data. The inability of such computer models to correlate with the past casts grave doubts upon their accuracy in predicting the future.

Dr. Hugh Elsaesser, who is retired from the Lawrence Livermore National Laboratory and the U.S. Air Force Weather Service, says climatologists are hung up on *radiative* transfer while ignoring strong evidence of *convective* heat transfer. The latter, he says, strongly overshadows any greenhouse effect and works toward climate stability.

Way back in 1910 a physicist named R. W. Wood built two greenhouses. One had a glass roof, which traps infrared radiation; the other, a quartz roof, which is transparent to infrared rays. Surprisingly, the temperature in both greenhouses was the same. There was no "greenhouse effect." The greenhouses were both warm because of a simple lack of convection—just the way your car heats up when you park it in the sun with the windows closed.

The work of physicist Sherwood Idso of the Department of Agriculture's Research Service in Phoenix also counters the greenhouse-theory assumptions about carbon dioxide. As explained by Dr. Beckmann:

> [T]he old theory was pretty shaky as it stood, and now Idso has taken a kick at its very foundations: CO_2 has several absorption bands besides the infrared one, as does water vapor (and all gases), and while the long-wave thermal radiation may be kept in by one (infrared) CO_2 band, the shorter wavelengths of the incoming solar radiation will be kept out, apparently by the combined effects of both CO_2 and water vapor, so that less heat becomes available to be trapped in the first place. Once again, nature appears to be self-healing.[54]

There are many factors in global climate which correlate with temperature changes better than the greenhouse theory. One is the varied way in which the earth's surface reflects or absorbs incoming radiation. Light areas, such as clouds or snow, reflect more than dark areas. According to James Coakley of the National Center for Atmospheric Research, an increase of 4 to 7 percent in certain types of cloud cover could offset a doubling of carbon dioxide. Some of the other factors influencing global temperature include atmospheric particle scattering, humidity, biochemical processes of phytoplankton in the oceans, and variations in solar activity. Some of these, and still others, work against the greenhouse effect, some in favor of it, and others independent of it. So the process is very complicated and by no means fully understood.

Historical records of carbon dioxide in the atmosphere can be found in the remains of organisms buried in marine sediments. These findings are confirmed by analysis of the ice sheets of Greenland, the Himalayas and the Antarctic. Without doubt the carbon dioxide in the atmosphere has varied widely for tens of thousands of years. However, there is no evidence that the ups and downs of carbon dioxide concentration have caused the ups and downs of global temperature over all these millennia.

The concentration of carbon dioxide was higher 130,000 years ago than it is today, having risen almost without interruption for 15,000 years. Then it declined most of the next 20,000 years in an irregular pattern that brought it back to about where it was before the rise. All this happened without the burning of fossil fuels and without any environmental protection laws.

In the last 10 million years there have been 17 ice ages, which alternately formed and melted ice sheets hundreds of feet thick and covering much of the continents. The scale of those temperature changes renders insignificant the tiny temperature changes the public has been panicked into worrying about today.

At the end of the last Ice Age, about 10,000 B.C., the carbon dioxide content was at the highest level of the past 100,000 years. This is exactly the opposite of what the greenhouse theory would have predicted. The earth then entered a warming period for the next six thousand years—during which the CO_2 content of the atmosphere steadily decreased. Again, this is exactly opposite to the greenhouse theory; a decrease in CO_2 should have brought cooling, not warming. And, obviously, the burning of fossil fuels was not a factor in such climate changes thousands of years before the Industrial Revolution.

There is no question that the carbon dioxide content of the atmosphere is now increasing. There is no evidence, however, that this is connected with either global warming or the burning of fossil fuels. In 1981 the National Atmospheric Laboratories reported that although the carbon dioxide content of the atmosphere had increased to 320 ppm from 288 ninety years earlier, the earth had been gradually getting *cooler* over that period. They predicted this cooling trend would continue for 7000 years.

When temperatures in the 1980s were warmer, the warming theorists shouted, "I told you so." The "trend" of a decade was flaunted as "proof" while 9 decades of contrary evidence that preceded it were conveniently ignored. In the matter of carbon dioxide levels, where trends are in thousands of years and a century is a mere blip, the greenhouse theorists were claiming that three warm years in the decade of the 1980s settled the issue. One prominent scientist, Dr. James Hansen of NASA's Goddard Institute, testified before a Senate committee in June of 1988 that he was "99 percent sure" the greenhouse effect was already under way.

He was a very small minority *in the scientific community,* but that's not the impression the media gave. The same media which scarcely a decade earlier were publicizing warnings of a coming ice age[55] pounced on Hansen's statement and were now filling the public with warnings of the opposite threat and familiar claims that something had to be done "before it's too late." As with the ozone scare, a questionable theory gained acceptance "not because of scientific proof, but as the result of constant reiteration of disaster scenarios."

The scientific community was less impressionable than the public to media hype. At the fall meeting of the American Geophysical Union in 1988, amid the torrent of publicity that followed Hansen's testimony a few months earlier, only a single scientist could be found who thought the greenhouse effect had begun. Jerome Namias, who headed the extended forecast division of the National Weather Service for 30 years before moving to the Scripps Institution of Oceanography, said that other factors explain recent weather "quite adequately without the greenhouse effect."[56] William Sprigg, Director of the National Oceanic and Atmospheric Administration's climate office in Rockville, Maryland, said, "The case has not been made that greenhouse gases explain what we see."[57] Yet the media in general continued to discuss the greenhouse effect as though it represented a widely-held scientific opinion, if not an incontrovertible fact.

In 1989 a team of scientists from the National Oceanic and Atmospheric Administration reported on a new study that concluded there had been no warming in the previous century. The report said that "there is no statistically significant evidence of an overall increase in annual temperature or change in annual precipitation for the contiguous U.S. [between] 1895 and 1987."

Patrick Michaels, the Virginia State Climatologist and Associate Professor of Environmental Sciences at the University of Virginia, wrote:

> [D]espite all the carbon dioxide, methane and chloro-
> fluourocarbons we've pumped into the atmosphere since the

Industrial Revolution, U.S. and northern latitude temperatures
have actually declined over the last half-century....

From reading the newspaper accounts, one gets the
impression that disaster has already begun....

In spite of the current increase in CO_2, and despite the
headlines, there's precious little evidence that the Northern
Hemisphere has warmed up significantly over the last 50 years.
Moreover, when we look to the medium-high latitudes of our
hemisphere, generally conceded to be most prone to climatic
change, the warming simply isn't there.

A look at the temperature curves from the National
Research Council's 1983 report "Changing Climate" sums up
the problem. The northern latitudes, from 24 to 90 degrees north,
have actually cooled off since 1930. The tropics warmed up
slowly from 1880 to 1920, and then stopped. The Southern
Hemisphere has warmed steadily throughout the period.

There is not one graphic in the entire 496-page report that
indicates a statistically significant warming of the northern
latitudes of our hemisphere since 1930.

The real bad actors in the warming scenario have been the
Northern Hemisphere oceans. They simply refuse to go along
with the program, showing nothing but slow cooling since World
War II.[58]

Even scientists willing to concede there may have been a slight
warming have been generally skeptical about attributing it to the
greenhouse effect. For example, Andrew R. Solow of the Woods Hole
Oceanographic Institution wrote in December 1988:

There are indications that current warming is unrelated to
the greenhouse effect. The warming is far below that predicted
under the greenhouse effect....

The conclusion is that we cannot yet make useful
predictions about climate, and that *existing data show no
evidence of the greenhouse effect.* Many people will be surprised
to hear that this is more or less the view expressed in scientific
journals, where articles are subject to peer review. Unsubstantiated or misleading statements only appear in such journals
when the review process fails. *Congressional testimony and
interviews in the press are not subject to peer review, and that is
how unsubstantiated and misleading statements come to
dominate public discussion.*

Some will say that the scientific establishment demands
an unreasonable degree of certainty before accepting a new idea.
But in the case of climate change, and particularly with regard to

detecting change with existing data, *it is not a question of evidence being tenuous. It is a question of there being no evidence at all.*[59] (Italics added)

In 1992 the George C. Marshall Institute issued a report on global warming. The institute's board is practically a *Who's Who* of science. It includes such names as Frederick Seitz, a past president of both the American Physical Society and the National Academy of Science and a recipient of the National Medal of Science, and Robert Jastrow, who headed NASA's Goddard Institute of Space Science for 20 years. The report states:

> The predictions of the greenhouse theory are contradicted by the temperature record to such a degree as to indicate that the...greenhouse effect has not had any significant impact on global climate in the last 100 years....
>
> Nearly the entire observed rise of 0.5 degrees Centigrade occurred before 1940. However, most of the manmade carbon dioxide entered the atmosphere after 1940. The greenhouse gases cannot explain a temperature rise that occurred before these gases existed. Furthermore, from 1940 to 1970, carbon dioxide built up rapidly in the atmosphere. According to the greenhouse calculation, the temperature of the earth should have risen rapidly. Instead...the temperature actually *dropped.*[60]

On May 21, 1993, the Associated Press reported that a scientific study of tree rings from some of the world's oldest trees reveals that there has been no global warming from human activity. Ricardo Villalba, of the University of Colorado at Boulder, and Antonio Lara, of the University of Arizona, analyzed the annual rings of alerce trees in Chile and Argentina. Some of their samples were more than 3600 years old. The seasonal record of growth in the width of tree rings is a record of past climate. Professor Villalba said, "During the past 100 years, the temperatures were not higher than they were in previous times. We can say that there was no indication of global warming."

Raphael G. Kazman, Professor Emeritus of Civil Engineering at Louisiana State University, offers this interesting explanation of global warming:

> It might be fair to classify the current panic on global weather trends as a modern form of idolatry. The idol in question, to which we are to sacrifice our money and labor, is

some computer program that allegedly foretells an ominous future. But this future, if enough is sacrificed, can be modified—and the priesthood of the idol will then tell us whether our sacrifices will change the outcome or whether further sacrifice is needed.[61]

There is no evidence at all that the current increase in carbon dioxide is due to the burning of fossil fuels. Marine sediments show centuries ages ago where carbon dioxide increased almost three times faster than the rate of the past century. Besides, all the burning and every other activity of all the people on earth account for only a small fraction of the world's carbon dioxide production. According to a publication of the International Atomic Energy Agency in Vienna,[62] natural sources account for approximately 96 percent of the earth's carbon dioxide. Dr. McKetta puts the figure at 99 percent. Of the 1 to 4 percent that is due to man, only a small fraction is due to the 6 percent of the world's population living in the United States. China burns 936,000,000 metric tons of coal annually—and burns them *its* way, not ours—regardless of any EPA rules coming out of Washington. How could U.S. policy possibly have a significant effect on CO_2 levels worldwide even if the earth's temperature were being raised by the greenhouse effect?—which it is not! Natural production of CO_2 is so overwhelming that it's unlikely man's minute contributions could affect global trends in any significant way even with a united global effort. Termites alone produce 50 *billion* tons of carbon dioxide annually.[63] This is ten times the amount from all the fossil fuels burned in the whole world in a year. (Termites also produce 20 to 50 percent of the world's methane.)

Professor L. L. Van Zandt of the physics department at Purdue University puts the issue of carbon dioxide emissions in perspective with some simple arithmetic. From the dimensions of the earth and known atmospheric pressure (both of which are indisputable) he calculates the weight of the atmosphere to be 11.9 billion billion pounds. Using a figure of 0.04 percent for atmospheric CO_2 in 1950 and 0.06 percent in 1992, he calculates that the atmosphere contained 2,400 billion tons of CO_2 in 1950 and 3,600 tons in 1992. With human activity releasing 6 billion tons of CO_2 per year and natural phenomena releasing 200 billion tons per year (97 percent of total), Professor Van Zandt states:

> Simple division tells you that if every molecule of
> human-released CO_2 at the current rate of production *stayed in*

the atmosphere, it would take another 200 years for the post-1950 change to be matched. Or looking backward, since minus 200 years takes us back to before the Industrial Revolution, *it means that if every CO_2 molecule from every factory, car, steam engine, barbecue, campfire, and weenie roast that ever was since the first liberal climbed down out of a tree right up until today was still in the atmosphere, it still wouldn't account for the change in CO_2 since 1950.*[64] (Italics added.)

Note that the above conclusion assumes that every human-released CO_2 molecule stays in the atmosphere. In fact, that's not the case. Carbon dioxide is constantly being recycled back out of the atmosphere as well as being added to it; therefore, human CO_2 emissions are of even less consequence than the above quotation would indicate. Professor Van Zandt calculates that the average CO_2 molecule is recycled back out of the atmosphere in about 12 years. He then draws these two conclusions:

> Human activity, carried out at the present rate indefinitely (more than 12 years) cannot possibly account for more than 6 percent of the observed change in CO_2 levels.
> Entirely shutting off civilization—or even killing everybody—could only have a tiny effect on global warming, if there is any such thing.[65]

Thus, even *if* global warming were being caused by an increase in CO_2, it should be quite clear that mankind can't be responsible for this increase in any meaningful degree. But wait! Carbon dioxide isn't the only greenhouse gas. There are others, such as methane, other hydrocarbons and aerosols—but by far the most important one is water vapor. Indeed, water vapor accounts for 98 percent of any warming that may be due to the greenhouse effect. Carbon dioxide and all other greenhouse gases account for less than 2 percent. In other words, if mankind could eliminate all of the increase in CO_2—including the 96 to 99 percent produced by nature as well as the small remaining percentage that is produced by human activity—98 percent of the greenhouse warming would remain unaffected!

A major voice in sounding alarms about global warming has been the United Nations-sponsored Intergovernmental Panel on Climate Change (IPCC), but its credibility has come under serious attack. Charles L. Harper, a planetary scientist at Harvard University has said that the latest IPCC report "may have more to do with the politics of fear than with objective science."[66] The most important attack, however, has come from the distinguished Dr. Frederick Seitz. In a June 1996 article entitled "A Major Deception on 'Global Warming,'" he wrote:

> This IPCC report, like all others, is held in such high regard largely because it has been peer-reviewed. That is, it has been read, discussed, modified and approved by an international body of experts. These scientists have laid their reputations on the line. But this report is not what it appears to be—it is not the version that was approved by the contributing scientists listed on the title page. In my more than 60 years as a member of the scientific community...I have never witnessed a more disturbing corruption of the peer-review process than the events that let to this IPCC report.
>
> A comparison between the report approved by the contributing scientists and the published version reveals that key changes were made after the scientists had met and accepted what they thought was the final peer-reviewed version.... Nothing in the IPCC Rules permits anyone to change a scientific report after it has been accepted by the panel of scientific contributors and the full IPCC.... Few of these changes were merely cosmetic; nearly all worked to remove hints of the skepticism with which many scientists regard claims that human activities are having a major impact on climate in general and on global warming in particular.[67]

The IPCC report was attacked on different grounds by Dr. S. Fred Singer, director of the Science and Environmental Policy Project, who attended the IPCC meetings in Madrid and Rome that preceded the report. In January 1996 he wrote that he would not consider the IPCC summary report as either "well-balanced" or "accurate."

> It does not tell untruths; it misleads by presenting only selected facts and omitting important information: When it points to the climate warming in the past 100 years, it doesn't reveal that the major temperature increase occurred around 1920, well before most of the carbon dioxide accumulated in the atmosphere. Nor does it mention the absence of any warming in the satellite data of the past 16 years. Most important, the IPCC never disavows its claim of only three years ago that climate data and model-derived temperature increases are "broadly consistent." They clearly are not —making any predictions of future warming suspect.

The summary doesn't make it explicit that the IPCC time scale for warming has now been stretched out—doubled, in fact, from 2050 to 2100, making any possible impact less dramatic;...it quotes a global warming as low as 0.5 Celsius by 2100—only half of the IPCC lowest 1995 prediction.

Such an ultra-low value, while barely compatible with current observations, would be inconsequential, and even difficult to detect in view of the large natural fluctuations of the climate. Global warming would become a nonproblem. The mystery is why some insist in making it a problem, a crisis, or a catastrophe—"the greatest global challenge facing mankind."[68]

The proponents of global warming theory have tried to scare the public with the specter of polar icecaps melting and raising the level of the oceans. Not only has there been no global temperature increase, as evidenced by satellite data, but the world's two great ice sheets, in Antarctica and Greenland, have been growing. The Greenland ice sheet has thickened by two meters since it was first measured by laser altimetry in 1980. "Imagine the press hue and cry if it had thinned so much," said Professor Michaels, "and try to imagine why 'evenhanded' environmental reporting has so far ignored this report, published in *Geophysical Research Letters* nearly a year ago."[69]

According to Dr. Robert E. Stevenson, secretary general of the International Association for Physical Sciences in the Ocean:

Mean sea level has not changed in the past century (which puts the lie to the ecologists' argument that global warming is melting the polar icecaps); atmosphere temperatures, though having up-and-down cycles, have not established a trend in either direction...and *the gases in the stratosphere caused by humans' activities are insignificant.*[70] (Italics added)

Haroun Tazieff is a world-renowned volcanologist who has held many prestigious positions at universities and research institutes. Most recently he was France's secretary of state for the prevention of major natural and technological disasters. In response to an interviewer's question, he replied:

Global warming is an outright invention. It is absolutely unproven and in my view it is a lie. A lie that will cost billions of dollars annually.... There is no danger from the CFCs to the ozone layer, nor is there any danger from CO_2, no greenhouse effect, nor any risk of any kind of global warming. It is, to me, a pure falsehood.[71]

Here is just one more issue through which those holding the primitive conviction that men are natural enemies seek to prove it. Their arguments of global disasters from industrial progress are an attempt to prove that human interests *must* conflict when some men alter the world in some small way for their own advancement, as the people of Jericho did. Of course, the predicted disasters never materialize because men's interests are not naturally in conflict. But by establishing laws on the basis of phony scenarios, the advocates of force establish control over the lives of other men, just as an invader would.

Dr. Hugh Ellsaesser has studied global warming since 1972. In 1989 he wrote:

> [T]he trends in airborne pollutants were down and not up before the Environmental Protection Agency was formed, and the Draconian and expensive program to clean our air has not achieved the targeted air-quality standards.... What more do we need to realize that those who are trying to sell us clean air either don't know what they are talking about or have objectives quite different from those claimed?[72]

CHEMICAL POLLUTION

In the same manner that industrial progress in a free economy steadily improved rather than degraded air quality, it has brought other environmental benefits. For example, though it is popularly believed that we are increasingly poisoning our environment with modern chemicals—DDT being a prime example—the exact opposite is true. We are poisoning it less. What is overlooked or ignored is the fact that chemicals such as DDT replaced others which were far more dangerous. John Maddox writes:

> Especially because pesticides now epitomize the supposed assault on the environment, it is significant that since the early part of the nineteenth century, all kinds of noxious chemicals have been used as insecticides. In the twentieth century, hydrogen cyanide, the most poisonous of gases, was widely used in fumigating against bedbugs and also for ridding ancient buildings of deathwatch beetles.[73]

The same deadly gas was also used against insects on citrus trees in California.

The use of arsenic in insecticides, which dates from the nineteenth century, has diminished significantly since World War II, when DDT became popular. In 1939, when a Swiss scientist named Paul Mueller discovered that DDT was lethal to insects, almost 30,000 tons of the pesticide lead arsenate were produced in the United States; but production of this substance dropped by eighty percent in the two decades following World War II as DDT and other chlorinated hydrocarbons came to be preferred. The opponents of DDT should remember that while arsenic is much less effective against insects, it is far more indiscriminate than DDT in its lethal effects upon other organisms.

Several fluorine compounds were also used in insecticides prior to World War II, but none are used now. They're too hazardous and have been replaced by the newer, safer chemicals. Insecticides, like automobiles, food and air quality, have gotten continually safer and better under the capitalistic system. Lethal pesticide accidents have declined sharply and continuously for decades; by 1989 they were only one-fifth as numerous as forty years earlier. Here, again, the improvement came from extending industrial progress, not restricting it.

DDT wasn't banned because it was dangerous. The World Health Organization said that DDT "has had an exceptionally good safety record with no indication of teratogenic or mutagenic effects or of carcinogenicity in man." The same organization estimated that over 100 million people were alive who would have died without DDT. Dr. Robert White-Stevens said DDT was banned because "superstition and political caprice triumphed over science and human decency."[74]

In EPA hearings on DDT some 300 technical documents were introduced and 150 scientists testified before Edmond Sweeney, purposely selected as a judge totally unfamiliar with either pest control or agricultural chemicals and, therefore, completely unbiased. Over 9000 pages of testimony and argument were accumulated over 9 months of hearings. The world's major scientific organizations testified on behalf of DDT. Nobel-Prize winner Dr. Norman Borlaug testified that if DDT is banned "I have wasted my life's work." No proof was presented that DDT was harmful to man. No evidence was ever introduced of even a single person dying from it. In his final decision, April 26, 1972, Judge Sweeney said not only that DDT presented no hazard to man; he went further. He said, "The uses of DDT under the regulations involved here do not have a deleterious effect on freshwater fish, estuarine organisms, wild birds, or other wildlife." The outcome was described by Dr. White-Stevens:

>   When all the testimony was completed, Sweeney wrote his "Conclusions and Points of Law" and decided that there was insufficient evidence...to justify a ban on DDT, and that all those registrations of use which had been rescinded, should be promptly restored.
>   It is said, Ruckelshaus, who had initially stated, "We will settle this question on DDT in these hearings once and for all," and who never attended a single session, did not even bother to read Sweeney's decision, let alone the 9000 pages of testimony. Instead he ignored all the evidence presented and had a minor official in EPA, who clearly had no knowledge of elementary chemistry let alone of agricultural pesticide chemistry, write an injunction that was published.[75]

After the hearing an official from the National Audubon Society—which previously declared DDT harmless to birds for the spraying of gypsy moths in Pennsylvania—called the distinguished Dr. Borlaug a paid liar (See *New York Times,* Aug. 14, 1972). Ruckelshaus later admitted he made a political—rather than a scientific—decision.

While progress in insecticides had brought enormous benefits to mankind, those who sought to make the world better by restrictions only made it worse. Banning DDT condemned millions of people to death, millions more to disease, and precipitated environmental disasters such as the destruction of millions of acres of forests and, as a consequence, the organisms which depended upon them. The tussock moth defoliated thousands of acres of forests in Washington and Oregon. The gypsy moth—which by the late 1950s was confined to less than 200 acres—by 1978 infested nearly ten million acres in a dozen eastern states and had wiped out over 75 percent of the oaks in some areas.

Third World countries simply follow the lead of the United States in environmental matters. Not only do these poor countries lack the resources to conduct their own investigations, but, according to John E. Kinney, an environmental engineer with personal experience in the matter, they are financially pressured by our government to obey our EPA policies. He writes:

>   A number of sub-Saharan African countries that had nearly eradicated malaria were informed by the U. S. Agency for International Development (AID) after the Ruckelshaus

decision that if they were to continue receiving U.S. funding they had to ban use of DDT. AID requires nations to obey all our EPA dictates, even when the dictate amounts to an opinion that has not been reduced to regulation in this country.[76]

The results have been disastrous for them—and not just because of DDT and malaria. Here's another example:

> About 300,000 Peruvians suffered from cholera (and 3,516 died) when government authorities decided to stop chlorinating the water supply. U.S. Environmental Protection Agency studies showed that chlorine might cause a slight increase in cancer.[77]

Death has come not only from disease but from the substitution of far more hazardous chemicals. Once again, those who favored banning a substance failed to consider the fact that alternatives were more dangerous. Kenneth Mellanby, a British entomologist, states, "The first result [of banning DDT] was that extremely poisonous insecticides such as parathion were used, and these caused hundreds of human deaths."[78]

The same effect was evident even in the United States. Dr. John L. Wong notes that the bans on DDT and other organochlorine pesticides

> give the public immediate satisfaction, but this is little consolation for farm workers who are forced to use *more toxic substitutes*. In 1985, California reported that accidental poisoning incidents involving pesticides have gone *up* 14 percent a year since 1973.[79] (Italics added)

In Ceylon (now Sri Lanka), thanks to DDT, there were only seventeen cases of malaria in 1963. Then the use of DDT was discontinued—and in 1968 more than 10,000 people there died from the disease. More than a hundred times that many became infected with it before spraying with DDT was resumed in Ceylon that year. In India two years after DDT was taken off the market the annual death toll from malaria alone rose from 200,000 to over 3 million.

In Colorado that medieval pestilence once known as the Black Death, bubonic plague, appeared, spread by fleas from prairie dogs, whose population exploded after "environmentalists protested their extermination and carried them in cages to the wilderness to restore the delicate checks and balances of nature."[80] Several people became infected with the plague before the Environmental Protection Agency finally permitted local use of DDT.

Thus those who sought a better world through government coercion, who so often claim that production and trade necessitate victims, themselves created victims: victims of disease. It is the anti-industrialists, who clamor about the horrors of early capitalism and the victims of modern wealth, whose own goals are at the expense of the lives and health of other men. It is not industrial progress but rather a world free of industrial effects that requires human suffering. The forests and the prairie dogs are merely additional innocent victims. Dr. J. Gordon Edwards, Professor of Entomology at San Jose University, describes the human toll:

> Numbers of people have needlessly died of insect-transmitted diseases, starvation, malnutrition and associated maladies. These human beings would and should have lived longer had they not been unnecessarily deprived of the benefits of chemicals such as insecticides, herbicides, fungicides, nematocides, rodenticides and bacteriacides....
>
> Right now 15 to 20 million people are dying of direct starvation each year, while at least that many more are succumbing to the indirect effects associated with malnutrition and protein-calorie deficiency. The knowledge and ability to reduce those figures is available now...but not without pesticides and other agrichemicals.... At least 10 million people die annually from malaria, alone. Millions more perish from the side-effects of malaria and other diseases, and additional millions are killed by various other preventable and treatable maladies.
>
> It would appear reasonable to conclude that, directly or indirectly, between 60 and 100 million people are dying every year as a result of the anti-pesticide campaigns which have resulted in restrictions or bans on the pesticides that could prevent such deaths.[81]

So several times as many human beings die *every year* because of bans on DDT and other pesticides as were killed by Hitler's holocaust, by both sides in all the years of the Viet Nam War, and by the atomic bombs of Hiroshima and Nagasaki combined. Thus have those who with righteous zeal sought to gain their ends through government force employed that force like the ruthless invading armies throughout history, with no regard for the human beings slaughtered to achieve their "noble" aims. Dr. Robert White-Stevens calls it "Authorized Genocide."

While the federal government was sanctimoniously banning perfectly safe chemicals such as DDT and EDB with great fanfare, it was itself quietly producing toxic materials on a far larger scale. The Department of Defense alone generates 400,000 tons of hazardous wastes a year, more than the five largest chemical companies combined. These wastes are not only the special products of chemical and atomic weapons but common industrial items such as waste oil, fuels, and solvents. The government is far less careful than industry about disposing of such items. The Department of Defense has frequently been cited for violating EPA regulations and even been fined for doing so. (One public agency paying a fine with taxpayers' money to another!)

The federal government also owns many power plants that do not meet the same emission standards as private and local governmental power plants. For example, the federal government's Tennessee Valley Authority has 59 coal-fired plants and has fought court battles for years (and won) to have them exempt from state clean air standards, with which everyone else has to comply.

On May 22, 1990 the American Broadcasting Company reported that the nation's largest polluter was the federal government. ABC news commentator Peter Jennings stated that putting the federal government in charge of environmental protection was like putting the fox in charge of the chicken coop. He noted that federal agencies do not comply with either state or federal environmental standards. Polluters, he said, include military bases, federal prisons—and even the EPA itself!

THERMAL POLLUTION

Another argument against industrial progress is that the increased amounts of waste heat which are generated are detrimental to the environment. But the diatribes against thermal pollution ignore the fact that once again Mother Nature is by far the biggest polluter. As an illustration of this, Dr. McKetta made some interesting calculations following an announcement by the Governor of Ohio in support of legislation making it illegal to raise the temperature of Lake Erie by more than one degree Fahrenheit. According to Dr. McKetta, if all the electricity produced in Ohio in a year were devoted exclusively to heating Lake Erie, it would raise its temperature less than three-tenths of one degree. Yet nature changes the temperature of the lake by more than 40 degrees between winter and summer. Then remember that nature has made far greater climatic changes with the Ice Ages.

Dr. Beckmann puts man's thermal pollution in perspective as follows:

> To reach even one percent of the energy incident on the globe from the sun, we would have to convert energy on a mind-boggling scale; every American man, woman, child and infant on the breast would have to consume, from midnight to midnight, no less than 2 MW of power, which he could do by running 600 clothes dryers all day and all night, or by cleaning his teeth twice a day with 15 million electric toothbrushes. *And the rest of the world would still have to consume twice as much.*[82] (Italics added)

WATER POLLUTION

Remember some years back the clamor that was raised about detergent suds in American rivers and streams? Photos of foam heading downstream dramatically publicized the problem. But the solution did not come from any federal laws. It came from the industry itself. The suds were caused by alkyl benzene sulfonate, a wetting and sudsing agent that was not broken down by sewage treatment. When something better was developed, linear alkylate sulfonate, the entire industry adopted it, ending the controversy.[83] The progressive solution came, as it always does, by men applying their minds to nature, not by applying force to other men.

With other environmental problems, too, more is being accomplished by scientific advance than by political restrictions. Dr. Dickson Liu, a Canadian scientist, has shown that polychlorinated biphenyls (PCBs), another pollutant of our waterways, can be reduced from concentrations of 300,000 parts per billion to less than 20 parts per billion in about a week by means of a common sewage bacteria which breaks the PCBs down into carbon dioxide and harmless light-weight organic acids.[84]

A General Electric biologist, A. M. Chakrabarty, has engineered a strain of bacteria that eats oil. Though there are now dozens of ways to clean up oil spills, the new microbe holds promise of being the most efficient of all. It releases a soap-like surfactant to emulsify the oil into tiny droplets. It then digests these droplets, breaking them down into carbon dioxide and water.

Of course, man is not the only one polluting the waters. Mother Nature's contributions are awesome. According to Dr. W. H. Gross, "Products of natural weathering have made over 99 percent of the earth's water unfit to drink."[85] The Lemonade Springs in New Mexico discharge sulfuric acid in concentrations ten times greater than coal mine discharges. The Mississippi River dumps two million tons of natural sediment daily into the Gulf of Mexico. Worldwide, an estimated two billion tons of sediment are deposited *daily* on deltas and continental shelves.

The levels of mercury in our waters are due almost entirely to nature. Although industry was initially blamed when fish were discovered with small but significant amounts of this poisonous substance, fish similarly "contaminated" were soon discovered in waters with no industrial effluent. Then fish caught a century ago and preserved at the Smithsonian Institution were found to have comparable concentrations of mercury. And if further evidence was needed that nature was the culprit, it came with the discovery of high levels of mercury in the buried remains of fish up to two thousand years old found in Peru and in the United States. "There is no hope," says Dr. W. H. Gross, "of clearing up nature's distribution of mercury in seals, whales, tuna and many other aquatic animals, because mercury plays a fundamental part in their bodily function. These animals are naturally at a level of about 0.5 ppm mercury.... As a reasonable precaution, therefore, one should not eat more than four tins of tuna every day for a year. Vary your diet a little."[86]

Nature even creates oil spills. Far more oil is dumped into the oceans every year from seabed fissures than from all the drilling accidents and leaky tankers combined. Great public furor was created over the oil-well blowout in the Santa Barbara Channel in January 1969, but nature has been leaking up to 160 barrels of crude oil per day into the channel for countless centuries. At that rate, in the last century alone nature would have put twenty-five times as much oil into the channel as the notorious oil-well blowout. And that's just for one century and in that one location. Worldwide, Mother Nature leaks 70,000,000 gallons out onto the land surface every year and far more into the oceans. No accurate scientific estimates exist for natural oil seepage into the oceans, but it is clearly immense. In the 1970s a layer of oil accidentally found in the Atlantic, from a natural underwater seep, was 800 nautical miles long, one nautical mile wide, and 100 meters thick. Those dimensions made it 117,500 times larger than the man-made oil spill of the Exxon-Valdez off the coast of Alaska in 1989, about which there was so much furor.

Because of the natural leakage of oil in the Santa Barbara Channel, a presidential task force reported in June of 1969 that there was only one way of preventing future leaks there: pump the field dry.

Accordingly, Secretary of the Interior Walter Hickel authorized the companies with leases there to resume unlimited drilling. That certainly was not what the anti-industrialists wanted. They didn't want to stop oil leaks; they wanted to stop oil drilling. It was obviously to the oil companies' advantage to resume drilling, and those convinced of the opposition of human interests could not conceive of how the oil companies' interests could agree with their own. They could not grasp the idea that industrial activity might improve rather than degrade the environment. They had the old invaders' view of values as static: if someone gained, someone else *had* to lose, by way of the environment if nothing else—almost as though the oil companies profited from the spills. Yet it is the companies' concern for profit which motivates them to guard against spills; they can make a profit only on the oil they sell, not on that which they spill. A company with a greater waste factor would be at a competitive disadvantage to one with an equal investment bringing more product to market. Man-made oil spills should therefore be quite rare, and in fact they are. Only four major spills have resulted from the 18,000 offshore wells that have been drilled in United States waters since 1894,[87] and the frequency of all types of spills is declining. The platform spill rate plummeted by a factor of 22 from 1964 to 1979, with a decrease every year and the largest decreases *before* passage of the Environmental Protection Act.

Reports of catastrophic environmental damage from the Santa Barbara blowout were gross exaggerations. A 900-page report by a team of forty scientists, who investigated the blowout for over a year, disclosed that surprisingly little damage had actually occurred, that there was no permanent damage to the environment, and that nature was healing with remarkable swiftness the little damage that could be documented. That was all forgotten, of course, by the time of the Exxon-Valdez spill.

After the supertanker Amoco Cadiz split in two on rocks off the coast of France in 1978, the French government declared that "severe, irreparable and permanent damage" had been done to "the coast waters of Britanny, its shoreline, marine life and environment." At that time, the Amoco Cadiz was by far the worse man-made oil spill in history— 6 times larger than Exxon-Valdez—but by 1981 the area was virtually back to normal. Similarly, after an oil spill in the inland sea of Japan, even the oyster, pearl and edible seaweed industries soon were back in business there.

Pollution control authorities seem to have learned little from these earlier spills; the media, nothing. Following the Exxon-Valdez spill in 1989, the public was inundated with stories of how Alaska's beaches were ruined for decades. The eco-system had been destroyed, we were told. Fishermen had lost their livelihood, their families were now economically deprived, their future perilous. Yet in the summer of 1990 there was a record harvest of 40 million pink salmon, far surpassing the previous record of 29 million. And the herring harvest reported the highest rate of catch ever, 8,300 tons in only 20 minutes.

Some may argue that the exaggerated reports by media and environmental authorities aroused public consciousness and led Exxon to spend $2 billion on cleanup that otherwise wouldn't have occurred. So wasn't some good achieved by advocacy journalism and the result better than it otherwise would have been? Just the opposite. *Science,* April 19, 1991, reported that the treated beaches were now in worse shape than the untreated ones. A report by the National Oceanic and Atmospheric Association said natural recovery would not have cooked lower members of the food chain or caused other hot-water damage.

The cleanup job could have been done more effectively by oil-eating bacteria (bioremediation), according to researchers from the biotechnical division of the U.S. Army Chemical Research and the University of Illinois. The Chakrabarty bacterium was not used largely because of fears over the introduction of a foreign bacterium. "It raises questions about what impact it will have on the environment," said Robert Mastracchio, technical manager at Exxon Alaska Operations.[88] General Electric's biological services laboratory had even suspended further work on Chakrabarty's engineered bacterium because of the public's unfounded concern.[89]

Nevertheless, a strain of *natural* oil-eating bacteria (forced through a natural-selection process to subsist on hydrocarbons) was introduced in an Exxon-Valdez experiment and worked very effectively. This experiment showed that "the microbial surfactant can remove three times as much oil as water can."[90] Admiral D. W. Ciancaglini, the U.S. Coast Guard's on-scene coordinator said, "Data have clearly demonstrated the effectiveness of bioremediation technology in removing not only surface oil, but also oil buried deeply within the shoreline."[91] But by the time the experiment was finished, Exxon was already far into its cleaning program of hot water jet sprays

and an army of scrubbers. The unfounded fears of so-called environmentalists had prevented a superior cleanup method and resulted in a
very costly method that was less effective than if the job had simply
been left to nature.

WHY THE FUSS?

An example of the magnitude of the exaggerations surrounding
the Santa Barbara incident, as well as an indication of why they
occurred, is given in this explanation by Dan Smoot:

> The Santa Barbara Channel oil spill was not an ecological
> disaster. However, organized environmental groups wanted the
> nation to think it was; and that is the way the mass media
> reported it—as if with the purpose of *working the public into a
> frenzy of hatred* for the oil industry....(Italics added) Commen-
> tators on the national networks routinely referred to the
> "hundreds of thousands" of birds that were killed. More than
> four years later, they were still using that round figure. In mid-
> June 1973, when there were oil slicks in the Santa Barbara
> Channel from natural seepage having nothing to do with drilling
> activities...network commentators reminded the public of the
> "hundreds of thousands of birds" killed there by the oil well
> blowout in January 1969. But what was the truth? On page 86 of
> a special study entitled *Energy Crisis in America,* published in
> 1973, the tediously factual *Congressional Quarterly* says that
> "an estimated 600 birds were affected by the oil" from the 1969
> spill in the Santa Barbara Channel.[92]

For years those seeking environmental gains through force—
certain environmental groups, members of the news media, and
politicians—had been unable to effect passage of national
environmental legislation. To gain the public support they needed, it was
necessary to *stir up hostility,* to provoke the anger of the American
people and show them an enemy to attack. Since the facts of the Santa
Barbara incident themselves were insufficient for this purpose, it was
only through orchestrated exaggeration that the public could be worked
"into a frenzy of hatred" that would lead them to resort to force.

It worked. Though similar bills had failed in previous years, the
National Environmental Policy Act of 1969 passed quickly and
unanimously in both the House and Senate. The only disagreement in
the Senate seemed to be not over the assault itself but over who was
leading the charge, Senators Jackson and Muskie both claiming

sponsorship of the bill. But President Nixon, too, wanted to lead the offensive. Without waiting for the bill Congress was sure to pass, he established an Environmental Quality Council by executive order.

The issue of pollution has become a major argument by which the neo-invaders attempt to gain converts to their conviction that men are natural enemies, that human conflict is inevitable in the very conditions of man's existence, particularly a civilized existence. In the same way that Karl Marx argued that progress was at the economic expense of other people, today the argument is that it is at the environmental expense of others. And just as Marx persuaded people to employ force—government—against others for economic gains, the neo-invaders turn to government for environmental gains. Of course, as already noted, capitalism was improving rather than degrading men's general economic conditions, and the same progress was occurring in environmental conditions. It might be added that government has demonstrated no more competence in dealing with environmental matters than with economic ones, and for the same reason.

Chapter Nine
WHY WE ARE NOT EXHAUSTING THE WORLD'S RESOURCES

Along with the pollution issue, the neo-invaders employ another major men-are-enemies argument: that industrial development is exhausting the earth's resources and thereby impoverishing others. This argument, which appears over and over again in the writings of men such as Barry Commoner, Paul Ehrlich and D. Van Sickle is simply a modern restatement of the invaders' belief that the producers' gains are other people's losses. In reality, greater productivity means more—not less—for others.

When the people of Jericho began to grow grain, they no longer needed to depend on the surrounding countryside for hunting and gathering. Consequently, the food supply was improved not only for themselves but for the neighboring people who still relied on these traditional methods. The land devoted to cultivation may have reduced the area for other food sources by the same amount, but this area was less than the people of Jericho would have required if they had continued their previous method of survival since agriculture produced far more food per unit of land. The introduction of agriculture meant more food, not less, for the surrounding people as well as the farmers.

The same process of indirect benefit is evident in every other human advancement. When some men began to use copper or bronze tools, they left more stones for those who were still making their tools from stones. When some men began to use iron, the world's "supply" of metal increased. It increased again when others took to using aluminum. When the Suez Canal was built, it left the traditional route around the Cape less crowded for others. As men adopted the automobile, they no longer drew upon the world's supply of horses, upon which others still relied. In proportion as men have turned to synthetic fabrics, they have left more of the world's cotton, silk and wool to others. When men started to burn coal, they didn't diminish the supply of fuel for others; they expanded it. When men learned to utilize oil and gas, they expanded it again.

The invader mentality simply doesn't grasp the significance of production. It can't understand the fact that material values can be increased because it doesn't understand that materials acquire economic value as a consequence of man's productive capability. That capability alone is what gives value to things which have had no value to anyone for many millennia. The quantity of materials on earth is not nearly as relevant as the quantity which is usable by man, and the latter has been *increasing*. Though man can't increase the former, there seems to be, as John Maddox put it, "no easily foreseeable limit to the ways in which even the most unlikely substances may be put to useful ends."[1]

Nor is there any reason to fear we will run out of "substances." Finite though the earth may be, it is still vastly larger than most people realize. There are a million tons of air for every person in the world, and we are making no dent at all in the supply, as shown by exploding the myth about oxygen depletion. There are 300 million tons of water on the earth's surface for every human being, and we are not consuming this resource either; there is as much water on the planet as there ever was. There are 50 tons of iron in the oceans for every person, but it will be a very long time, if ever, before man will even bother with this supply because the continents are so much more richly endowed. Iron comprises five percent of the earth's crust, and some of the metal is present in practically every cubic foot of it. While we aren't likely to run out of iron, aluminum, which is an excellent substitute for it in many applications, is even more abundant. It is the most plentiful metal on earth.

The abundance of these and other elements only emphasizes that the important figures are the amounts which are usable by man, not the absolute totals. The only practical limits we face are economic, not physical. We are clearly not going to use up, say, all the iron or aluminum on the planet; the relevant question is how much can be produced at a given price with a given technology. The answer changes as the technology changes. Projections of resource scarcity are inherently inaccurate because of the impossibility of projecting advances in technology. Projections are always said to be based on observable trends, but one trend which is clearly observable yet conveniently ignored is that in economic terms the world's resources are becoming more abundant. Most projections of scarcity don't even mention the factors of production, yet no discussion of resources can be meaningful without them.

In the same way that Marx couldn't understand how the factory system benefited one class without leaving another less well off, those today who don't understand the factors of production can't grasp how industrial progress can leave anything but less for others. For example, Barry Commoner, noted for his Marxian economics, concludes that "the *availability* of the (metallic) resource tends constantly downward."[2] It's no coincidence that the most vocal critics of resource consumption also preach human conflict and advocate force—socialistic programs—as much as they criticize the capitalistic system. Here is an illustration of the alleged conflict of men's interests from *The Ecological Citizen* by D. Van Sickle:

> [I]ndustrialization will be impossible for underdeveloped nations, even if they overcome food and population problems, without metal.... It is criminal to continue life styles and consumption patterns which will not only leave future generations destitute but will create emergencies before the century ends.[3]

THE METALS

First of all, there is no danger that we are going to use up the earth's metals any more than we are going to use up its air or water. Except for the absolutely insignificant amounts of metal launched into space and not recovered and the still smaller amounts of heavy metals converted to energy through nuclear fission, the amount of metal on the planet is exactly the same as it has always been. Rather than "consuming" metal, production simply converts it from ore into forms that are usable by man. The amount of metal in the world remains the same, but a larger percentage is available for human use.

As ore is converted into finished goods, goods no longer considered usable are consigned to scrap—which becomes a resource, for the future if not the present. As one resource (ore) is drawn down, the other (scrap) builds up. The only reason that more metal is not presently recycled is that in most cases it is cheaper to produce metal from ore than from scrap. Instead of being concerned about this cost relationship, we should view it as evidence that exploration and extraction alone are doing a magnificent job of staying ahead of scarcity. Should they be unable to do so in the future, we shall simply draw more heavily upon our increasing reserves of scrap and less upon our reserves of ore. Regarding iron ore, for example, Maddox writes:

> Each year, a large quantity of steel scrap accumulates in the United States, and indeed large quantities are exported for use elsewhere. Steelworks in advanced societies continue to manufacture and use pig iron in making steel only because this is economically advantageous. If there were to develop even a

modest shortage of iron ore, it would be entirely possible for steelmakers to reduce drastically their consumption of iron ore, relying instead on the vast quantities of scrap which have accumulated.[4]

So we are not running out of iron. And our usage of the metal is increasing the usable supply for others, not diminishing it. For as we in "advanced societies" do not use all our scrap, "large quantities are exported" to other countries. Far from preventing their industrialization, we appear to be aiding it. Nor is this the only incidental benefit other nations receive or the only way in which their supplies of metal are increased as a consequence of the productive achievements of other men.

It is through the utilization of existing resources that productive men develop new ones. By availing themselves of the ores which they knew how to use, men built the tools and developed the technology for using others. In employing steel for their own use—instead of saving the known deposits of iron ore for future generations—men made all sorts of tools, instruments, and machinery for exploring, extracting and fabricating other metals. They learned much about metallurgy and mining techniques which has been of incidental benefit to the rest of the world and to future generations. And though they intended to serve only their own interests, they gave the human race a host of new metals, from aluminum to uranium, which previous generations had never enjoyed. Magnesium, a lightweight metal that can be substituted for aluminum, and is sometimes preferred to it, is being commercially extracted from the practically inexhaustible supply in the oceans. Wilfred Beckerman, who served on the British Royal Commission on Environmental Pollution, writes:

> It has been estimated that sea water contains about a billion years' supply of…magnesium, 100 million years' supply of sulfur, borax and potassium chloride; more than one million years' supply of molybdenum, uranium, tin, cobalt; and so on. Yet who would have thought of including sea water in the list of resources available to us thirty or more years ago? This sort of process of adding to the resources available to society has been going on throughout history. There could hardly be more conflict between the lip-service paid by many eco-doomsters to the need for imaginative, forward-looking vision and the static, unimaginative nature of their concept of resources, with its failure to take account of the vast increases in resources over the past.[5]

Titanium, the fourth most abundant structural metal and the ninth most abundant element in the earth's crust, is virtually non-corrosive, offers the strength of steel with forty percent less weight, and has some interesting electrical properties. Today it is a familiar material, especially in the aerospace and chemical industries. A single Boeing 747 uses at least 8000 pounds of titanium. In 1945 world production of the metal was only about ten pounds a year.

By 1975 there were twenty-five companies in America fabricating titanium mill products, and well over eight million pounds of the metal were *exported* from the United States. In addition, the United States' annual exports of titanium dioxide and pigments had reached 30,379 tons and titanium ores and concentrates, 3,264 tons.[6]

In the same manner that utilizing the familiar metals has enabled man to develop the means for exploiting new ones, it is by using high grade ores that he has developed the means for exploiting lower grade deposits. It was the mining of high grade iron ore that made it possible to develop a commercial taconite industry. It was the mining of high grade bauxite which led to the technology for producing aluminum from lower grade material.

Now, the lower the grade, the more abundant are the deposits. So as we are able to utilize lower grades, our supplies of ore keep increasing, not diminishing. The amount of taconite available is far greater than all the quantities of high grade iron ore that were ever mined. Aluminum ore reserves, too, have been increasing, as described by John Maddox:

> Over the years, techniques have been developed for purifying aluminum even in the presence of iron and silica, with the result that it is now possible to extract aluminum from ores that would have been quite useless in the 1930s. As long ago as the early 1960s, the monumental study by Landsberg, Fischman and Fisher, *Resources in America's Future,* estimated that proven world reserves of aluminum ore had doubled from 1,600 million tons to 3,600 million tons between 1950 and 1958, and that the chemical techniques available at the end of the 1950s made a further 5,000 million tons of aluminum ore accessible to the metallurgists. With the development of extraction plants capable of producing large quantities of aluminum metal at great speed, price has become much less dependent than it used to be on the quality of the ore. And now it is likely that the costs of extracting aluminum from ores of all kinds will be reduced by the development of a direct extraction process which avoids one of the

expensive intermediate steps in the process. This is why it is no surprise that the price of aluminum metal has fallen gradually for the best part of two decades. Given inflation, this is tantamount to a substantial reduction of real cost, and there is no sign that this trend will be halted.[7]

Not only have the reserves of ore been increasing, the costs of the metal have been *dropping* despite the lower grade ores being used. And this process has been going on longer than the two decades covered in Maddox's description. A century ago, when high grade ores still remained virtually intact, aluminum was prohibitively expensive. Though the metal had been known since 1825, in 1886 the price was $11.13 a pound—and those were uninflated dollars. In that year Charles Martin Hall made his famous discovery—an inexpensive process for producing aluminum—and within two years the price had plummeted to only two dollars. Today the price is 76 cents a pound. (No adjustment is made for inflation, or the present price would seem much lower.)

Of what use would aluminum be to the people of underdeveloped nations at eleven dollars a pound? At that price they could neither afford finished products nor find much of a market for selling even high grade ore, if they were lucky enough to have any. Yet Mr. Van Sickle condemns as "criminal" the very "life styles and consumption patterns" which resulted in making aluminum an affordable material for hundreds of millions of people.

What has happened with aluminum has also happened, though not always as dramatically, with steel, lead, copper, and many other metals. The real economic costs of metal production have continued to drop even though in some cases the ores mined decades ago were several times richer than those now being processed.

In 1980 Paul Ehrlich bet economist Julian Simon on the difference between $1000 worth of each of five commodities then and the worth of the same amount ten years hence. Ehrlich, a prophet of shortages, bet the prices would be higher in ten years. The choice of commodities was his, and he chose five metals, copper, chrome, nickel, tin, and tungsten. He lost on all five and in 1990 paid up by mailing a check to Professor Simon.

In addition to bringing various metals within the price range of more people, the mining industry, by switching to lower grade ores, has made vast quantities of previously worthless material in other countries a valuable resource for them. The industry then provides a market for the resources it has "created," giving people in those countries the means by which they can purchase things of *greater* value to them, such as food, finished goods and Western technology. All of which would seem to indicate that the advanced nations are accelerating rather than impeding the development of other countries and that human interests, even between developed and undeveloped parts of the world, are not inherently in opposition.

While more efficient production has increased the supplies of metals, technological innovations have also resulted in using those supplies more efficiently. For example, the development of carbides in the early 1950s resulted in factory production tools which outlasted the toughest high-speed steel tools by 100 to 1. In a Pennsylvania coal mine a carbide bit, drilling side by side with a conventional steel bit, continued in service while 284 steel bits were blunted and discarded. Incidentally, the development of tungsten carbide bits capable of drilling 400 times the footage of steel bits was one of the factors which led to the economic development of taconite. It was too expensive to drill blast holes in low-grade rock with diamond drills, or with steel ones, which had to be replaced frequently.

More recently, improved steel alloys and better designs have made possible substantial savings in the use of structural steel. There are a host of other ways in which economies have occurred, and are continuing to occur, in the use of metals. Here are just a few pertaining to copper, a metal for which shortages are frequently forecast.

The use of better steel in armatures reduces the amount of copper needed in armature windings. The transistor and the integrated circuit have drastically reduced the amount of copper used in certain applications and provide energy savings as a bonus. And the products are better, not worse, for these economies.

Cryogenic technology, still in its infancy, is also reducing copper requirements in certain usages because super-cooling enhances the flow of electricity in conductors. Superconductors do not use copper at all; they utilize ceramic compounds and transmit electricity even more efficiently, with no resistance. In recent years the development of several new superconducting materials has raised the temperature required for superconductivity from near absolute zero (minus 452 degrees F.) to temperatures where practical applications are possible (currently minus 253 degrees F.) In 1995 Dr. Arthur Robinson explained why the new "warm" superconductors had become practical and the importance of new ones that perform well even in strong magnetic fields:

> Liquid nitrogen currently costs about 25 cents per gallon and is moderately long-lived in properly insulated containers. It is manufactured from air, so it could even be made at the point of use in large scale applications.
>
> Many of the anticipated first uses for "warm" superconductors involve production of magnetic fields such as in electric motors, electromagnets for medical imaging, and frictionless levitated passenger and freight trains. These new superconductors are especially important because, unlike earlier versions, they retain most of their superconductivity even in significant magnetic fields.[8]

By 1991 American Superconductor had already made a finger-sized wire that could carry more electricity than copper cables as thick as a man's arm. In that same year, Reliance Electric built the first practical power application of a superconductor, an electric motor utilizing superconducting wire. A Reliance spokesman said efficiency gains of 60 percent might be possible in large industrial motors using high-temperature superconductors.

In March 1992 Sanyo, the Japanese electronics manufacturer, announced it had developed the world's first superconducting transistor. It had a theoretical speed ten times that of existing semi-conducting transistors and required only a hundredth as much electricity.

Glass fibers are already replacing copper in telephone and television cables. By 1990 more than 4 million miles of such fiber optic cable was already in use in the United States. The fiber, thin as a human hair, can carry up to 167 television channels. A bundle of six fibers can carry more than 1,000 channels. By contrast, the coaxial cable it replaced, which was 3 to 4-inches in diameter, could transmit no more than 40 channels, and most such cable could transmit only 20. A single fiber strand can transmit 16,000 phone conversations at once, compared to 24 for the copper wire it replaces. The new light-wave communications fiber can also carry a signal twice as far as coaxial cable without the need for repeater amplifiers to regenerate the signal. Being non-metallic, the fiber is immune to electrical interference. In addition to its use in the telephone and television industry, the new technological marvel holds great promise for the computer and aircraft industries. It also promises to make the prospect that we will run out of copper, never a serious threat, even more remote. The raw material for the new glass fibers is "plentiful and cheap. A thimbleful of purified silicon oxide, derived from sand, can produce a mile-long optical strand."[9]

We are not, however, likely to run out of copper. As with aluminum, we have been increasing our reserves despite our greater usage. Beckerman writes:

> Copper consumption rose about fortyfold during the nineteenth century, and demand for copper was accelerating.... Annual consumption had been about 16,000 tons in the first decade of the nineteenth century, and was over 700,000 tons in the first decade of the twentieth century. Given the rapid growth of consumption, the "known" reserves of copper at almost any time in the nineteenth century would have been exhausted many times over by subsequent consumption if there had been no new discoveries. But at the end of the nineteenth century known reserves were bigger than at the beginning....
>
> From the supply point of view, faster rates of growth have taken place precisely because of faster rates of growth of technical progress of all kinds, and faster development of the basic resources required. Resources have still increased to match demand. For example, in 1945 estimated known copper reserves were 100 million metric tons. During the following twenty-five years 93 million metric tons were mined; so if we were to accept the eco-doomsters' sort of analysis, there should be almost no copper left by now. But no, present known reserves are over 300 million tons.... In fact, copper consumption has trebled during the last twenty years, and we still have more copper left in the "known" reserves than we had at the outset.[10]

One of the world's leading geologists, David Lowell, has estimated that the top mile of the earth's crust contains 3000 trillion tons of copper.[11] Other metals are similarly abundant, according to Beckerman:

> Given the natural concentrations of the key metals in the earth's crust, as indicated by a large number of random samples, the total natural occurrence of most metals in the top mile of the earth's crust has been estimated to be about a million times as great as present known reserves.[12] Since the latter amount to about a hundred years' supplies this means we have enough to last about one hundred million years. Even though it may be impossible to mine to a depth of one mile at every point in the earth's crust, by the time we reach the year A.D. 100,000,000 I am sure we will think up something.[13]

Of course, the majority of such deposits are of too low a grade to be economic at present; but it was not many years ago that vast deposits of taconite and bauxite, which we are presently using, were considered too low grade to be economic. Furthermore, if copper came into short supply, aluminum, which is a good electrical conductor, would be a frequent substitute.

There are many instances where one metal can be substituted for another. More impressive—and more disruptive of predicted metal shortages—is the substitution of a non-metal for a metal, as in the case of glass fibers for copper cables. Yet this kind of substitution has been occurring all around us for many years as plastics have been replacing metal in ways beyond counting.

MINERAL EXTRACTION: AT OTHER PEOPLE'S EXPENSE— OR TO THEIR BENEFIT?

One way in which the arguments about resource scarcity carry the men-are-enemies message is by the inference that the mineral wealth of people today is *at the expense* of the people of tomorrow. A basic opposition is assumed between their interests and ours, which results in regarding men as "generational enemies." Yet we are obviously better off than preceding generations—and better off in large measure because of the progress they made in using the earth's resources for themselves. Those places on earth where preceding generations were less successful in doing so are the underdeveloped countries of today, where human life is characterized by grinding poverty, not unspoiled riches. In the same manner that we have benefited incidentally from the progress of our forebears, future generations will benefit from ours. The more successful we are in advancing ourselves, the more they will benefit, the less successful we are, the less they will receive, just as with the under-developed countries today. How, then, can it be said the interests of future generations clash with our own or that our gains are at their expense?

The idea that men are "generational enemies" is also expressed in the assertion that mining mutilates the earth and renders vast areas unusable, or at least less valuable, for future generations. But compare the enormous benefits we have received, directly and indirectly, from the extraction of minerals with the fact that the land surface disturbed by all mining in the United States since 1776 is less than three-tenths of one percent of our total area.[14] This figure includes metallic and non-metallic ores, coal and other fuels, stone, cement, and even sand and gravel operations. If the tiny area disfigured by mining is the price of our magnificent standard of living, it is difficult to avoid the conclusion that we have gotten a terrific bargain rather than suffered a loss.

But there is more to this issue. Although the amount of land disturbed by two centuries of mining is small to begin with, one-third of that has already been reclaimed by man or nature. And the situation is getting better, not worse. Since 1930, according to the United States Bureau of Mines, only sixteen-hundredths of one percent of the country's land has been disturbed, and forty percent has been reclaimed. Since there was less time for the natural healing process, the proportion reclaimed by man must have been larger as well as the total. In any case the reclamation rate since 1930 has been more than half again as great as in the preceding 154 years. By 1971 the annual reclamation rate had reached 80 percent—without all the environmental laws which have restricted mining since.

Those who view as a loss the holes left in the ground by mining neglect to consider that what was taken out of them was exchanged for things of *greater* value. And because men's interests are not naturally in opposition, what one generation regards as of greater value than its minerals will generally prove of greater value to succeeding generations as well. By selling their minerals, people are able to gain such things as roads, bridges, buildings, power plants, sewer and water systems, and communication networks, much of which will be beneficial to the next generation and beyond. Without inheriting these things, which are invariably taken for granted, people would find it in their interests to trade their minerals to get them, just as their predecessors did.

Another thing which people may acquire in exchange for minerals, particularly in underdeveloped countries, is food. Since food is consumed while minerals left in the ground are not, it may be asked how such a trade could be of benefit to future generations. But if people trade for food, they have more time to be productive in other respects in the same way that the people of Jericho, by discovering agriculture, then had time for other civilized achievements, from which we have all benefited.

Another benefit acquired from the exchange of minerals is the opportunity for development of local skills and industries. Between 1860 and 1880, for example, copper was Detroit's largest export. When the ores were exhausted, about 1880, Detroit did not disappear. "By 1880," writes Jane Jacobs,

> Detroit had produced so many exports—paints, varnishes, steam generators, pumps, lubricating systems, tools, store fixtures, medicines, furniture, leather for upholstery, sporting goods—that they soon more than compensated for the loss of the refineries.[15]

With such industries, with such skilled labor on hand, is it surprising that the automobile industry sprouted in Detroit two decades later? The city had exactly what the automobile industry required. In the same way that some men use metals productively, to create additional wealth, other men, like those in Detroit, productively employ what they receive in exchange for metal ores. Those who sell minerals acquire the means to create additional wealth just as do those who buy them.

Great Britain is another example. For generations the British exported coal to the incidental benefit of their successors, who inherited an increasingly advanced and diversified industrial economy. Though they had less coal than their predecessors, they had instead the skilled labor and mechanical means for creating additional wealth. When Britain began to import coal after World War II, her economy began to falter not from the exhaustion of coal, which was still plentiful, but from the failure to sustain the productive system which its people had inherited.

As with Great Britain and Detroit, there is no reason the export of mineral wealth from the Middle East cannot lead to still greater prosperity for succeeding generations in those countries. People there can inherit things, knowledge and opportunities of greater value than oil in the ground. But whether or not they will employ them productively remains to be seen.

Still, fuels are actually consumed, and the belief persists that such consumption means less fuel for future generations. If we look no further, it is easy to conclude that men must indeed be "generational enemies" insofar as energy is concerned. But the fallacy here is that only consumption is considered; once again there is no inclusion or understanding of the role of production. Despite all the fuels which have been consumed, energy, like metals, is *more abundant and cheaper than ever before* and for the same reason: productivity. Although metals are not actually consumed and fuels are, there are many similarities between the two in regard to the production of increased supplies.

ENERGY RESOURCES

There is energy all around us, but as with the iron and aluminum common in soils and waste rock, we don't think of it as a resource if we are unable to utilize it. There is energy not only in the familiar fuels but in every bit of matter, in the rays of the sun, the force of the wind, the tides of the ocean. We can never run out of energy. But neither can we utilize all the energy available in nature. The supplies we can utilize are determined by our technology and change with it. Crude oil has been oozing out of the ground in places around the globe for thousands of years, but for most of that time no one knew how to utilize it. With advancing technology, the amount of energy to which man has access has been *increasing* despite the fuels that have been consumed. Those who forecast the exhaustion of energy resources do not consider this trend. Nor do they consider the fact that without earlier advances, the fuel supplies they lament about consuming would not even be regarded as energy sources today.

A case in point is natural gas. It used to be regarded as a nuisance rather than a resource. For many years the oil producers simply "flared" (burned) it at the wellhead just to get rid of it because there was no technology for utilizing it.

It is by using existing sources of energy that men learn to develop new ones, in much the same way that men learned how to produce new metals by using the old ones. In the same way that steel has been used to develop aluminum, magnesium, titanium and other metals, coal and oil have fueled the development of new energy sources.

Every new metal which came into common use no doubt seemed to the men of its time as though it must surely have been the last one. And from the time men first learned to use wood as a fuel, every new fuel, coal, peat, oil, natural gas, must also have been thought of as the last. Yet now, when it might seem that our knowledge is so pervasive that still another new fuel is less likely than ever, there is the prospect of another previously useless material, shale oil, becoming a resource on a scale that will dwarf previous fuel supplies. It has been estimated that at the present consumption rate world petroleum reserves will last about 250-300 years (double the estimates of 20 years ago) while natural gas could provide the world's energy needs, at the current rate, for 600 years and coal, 2500 years. But there is enough shale oil to last 40,000 years at the same rate of consumption.

Just as, for both economic and technological reasons, it was through the use of high grade iron ore and bauxite that it became feasible to utilize taconite and low grade aluminum ores, so, too, it is through utilizing petroleum reserves that shale oil is becoming feasible. It can't yet compete with petroleum, largely because the latter is still so plentiful; but the utilization of petroleum reserves is providing vital knowledge of chemistry and extraction processes for making shale oil an economic resource. And as with taconite and aluminum reserves, the new energy reserves will be far more abundant than the higher grade resources previously consumed.

Even more impressive is the development of more revolutionary sources of energy. If shale oil may be thought of as a new type of fuel in the same general class as others—in the same way that magnesium and titanium represent new types in the previously familiar class of metals— then nuclear energy represents a whole new class of energy analogous to the development of non-metals that take the place of metals. And just as such developments as plastics and light-wave transmission fibers demonstrate that future shortages are not inevitable just because the metals are finite, so, too, does nuclear energy demonstrate that no energy shortage is inevitable just because the fossil fuels are finite.

Because of advances in nuclear power, the supply of energy to which man has access is thousands of times greater than just a few decades ago. In the early 1970s one ton of uranium was yielding as much energy as 20-30,000 tons of coal, more than double the yield of a few years earlier. Now one ton of uranium yields as much energy as 3.5 million tons of coal. With current efficiency, the supply of nuclear fuel is practically inexhaustible, but the yield is still increasing. And then there is the matter of "breeder" reactors, which create more fuel than they consume and can manufacture a truly endless supply of energy.

Even that will not be the last word in energy development. Once again the utilization of existing energy sources is leading to new ones. In the future other materials, such as thorium, will probably be used in nuclear reactors. Of greater importance, however, will be the advent of commercial power from hydrogen fusion, which is expected in 10 to 20 years. This process will provide much larger energy yields than are now possible with fission reactors and may make a bucket of water yield as much energy as one hundred tons of coal. And our fuel supply will be as abundant as the water on earth.

Until an adequate number of nuclear plants come on-stream, we have more than ample coal to meet our energy needs. According to government geologists, the United States has enough coal for 1500 years.

Though scientists and power companies have pursued their own selfish interests, they have made such vast reserves of energy available that the human race need never fear exhausting them. Once again, as if led by the "invisible hand" of Adam Smith, free men advancing their own welfare have concomitantly advanced society.

But in the same way that progressive action causes beneficial, if unintended, consequences for others, coercive action, however well intended, produces detrimental secondary effects in addition to the original injury. The "heavy hand of government" performs exactly the opposite of Smith's "invisible hand" and inflicts damage in unexpected ways.

THE HEAVY HAND CREATES THE ENERGY CRISIS

Because of the government's strict regulation of atomic energy, the development of nuclear power for peaceful purposes took far longer than almost everyone expected. Though well meant, the government's action prevented the public from receiving a safer and cleaner fuel sooner and extended the period of dependence upon coal. Since the 1950s, however, the Atomic Energy Commission had been routinely advising electric utilities that nuclear energy was "just around the corner," thus discouraging them from long-term coal contracts, with debilitating effects upon the coal industry.[16]

In 1954, when the Federal Power Commission began to regulate the price of natural gas, the initial injury was to the oil and gas industry. But a secondary effect of the artificially-low gas price was to damage the other fuel producers by destroying their markets. Coal couldn't compete at the government-decreed rates for gas, and the coal industry nose-dived, as mentioned in the previous chapter.

With the passage of the Federal Coal Mine Health and Safety Act of 1969 and the Clean Air Act of 1970, coal production dropped 30 percent in 1970. In the next two years nearly 850 underground coal mines closed. Mines that were unable to afford either the capital outlay needed to meet government requirements or the loss in worker productivity under the new rules had no choice but to close. According to the Bureau of Labor Statistics, coal mine worker productivity, which had been steady and even increased slightly in the late 1960s, declined drastically and continuously after the passage of the Health and Safety Act in 1969. From an index of 142.4 in 1969, worker productivity dropped to 130.1 in 1971. By the end of 1979 the index was down to 101.3. In 1969 the coal mines were producing 16.8

tons of coal per man per day; in 1979 only 7.8 tons per man per day.

What the Health and Safety Act did to the production of coal, the Clean Air Act did to its market. By authorizing standards for sulfur dioxide emissions, the act forced a great many electric power plants which had been burning high-sulfur coal to convert to low-sulfur oil, a switch from an abundant domestic fuel to one in short supply and increasingly imported. "Between 1967 and 1972," says Dr. Petr Beckmann, "the utilities alone (mainly by abandoning coal under the Clean Air Act) increased their oil consumption *twenty-three* times."[17] By 1971, says Eugene Guccione, the editor of *Mining Engineering,* the East Coast of the United States "became dependent on the Arab countries for more than 94 percent of the residual oil needed for heating and power generation."[18]

In order to produce low-sulfur coal and raise productivity, the industry turned more heavily to strip mining, which is more efficient. It also obviates the need to comply with the onerous underground regulations. It also happens that most of the low-sulfur coal lies near the surface. In 1971, coal from strip mining exceeded underground production for the first time. Interestingly, however, especially in view of the absence of federal strip mining legislation—which members of Congress were still trying to make law in 1976—the industry actually reclaimed 30 percent more land in 1971 than it used.

Nevertheless, the federal government did provide the mechanism, through the National Environmental Policy Act of 1969, for delaying extensive strip mining in the Western states for several years. The politicians who professed such concern about the environment thereby prevented the mining of Western coal with one-half to one-tenth the sulfur content of Eastern coal. And because Western coal occurs in thick seams, strip mining in Western states would disturb at least 90 percent less land than in the Eastern states, according to Guccione. He calculated, for example, that 30 million tons of coal could be mined from 300 acres in the Powder River Basin in Wyoming but would require 4,500 to 7,500 acres in a state such as Illinois.[19]

In 1971 militant environmental groups also seized upon the National Environmental Policy Act of 1969 as a way of halting the construction of nuclear power plants. Injunctions were obtained even against 13 previously-licensed plants on the grounds that adequate environmental impact statements had not been filed.

Nuclear energy was being delayed. The use of coal was in a severe government-induced decline. Add to all this the several years delay in the Alaskan oil pipeline due to a string of lawsuits, appeals and other delays—chiefly relating again to the National Environmental Policy Act—and it is hard to conceive of how the American people could have been made more vulnerable to the forthcoming Arab oil boycott if anyone had tried.

In the same way that any attempt to use government force in an economic role always results in unforeseen secondary economic losses, the failure to use government force in the one role in which it is justified—defense—also results in unexpected secondary losses beyond the original capitulation. For many years the United States government, while being willing even to go to war to bring *democracy* to *other* people, had been increasingly reluctant to defend the property rights of its own citizens. This reluctance, first evident abroad, was apparent even within the United States by the 1960s as riots and vast increases in all types of crime swept the country. The banditry first tolerated abroad became accepted even at home. From 1960 to 1975 crimes against property in the United States increased 178 percent while the population grew approximately 15 percent.

During this period the Arabs nationalized American oil properties in piecemeal fashion. They could do so with impunity. When previously our government made it plain that it would do nothing at all to defend a billion dollars worth of American property from Castro's nationalization in Cuba, 90 miles from our shores—at a time when our military superiority was overwhelming and unquestioned worldwide—the Arab governments could be reasonably confident that Washington would take no action to protect American property in the Middle East. Furthermore, just a few years earlier the United States government had condemned the British and French governments for asserting their property rights by recapturing the Suez Canal—in a virtual rout—from the bandit Egyptian government. After pressuring the British and French to withdraw and relinquish their rights to the invaders who had seized their property, the United States was in no position to assert the sanctity of American property rights in that part of the world.

Thus did the laws, regulations and even foreign policy of our federal government combine to bring about an energy shortage in the United States in 1973. To deal with the shortage, the government established the Federal Energy Administration, expanded it to 20,000 employees, and came to the conclusion that coal production should be doubled by 1985!

For a quarter of a century the federal government had been working, usually unwittingly, to create a market scarcity in our most abundant fossil fuel, coal. On the other hand, industry had been achieving great progress for an even longer period in making scarcer fuels, such as oil, increasingly abundant.

THE ELUSIVE BOTTOM OF THE BARREL

American men, machinery and money contributed greatly to the development of the Middle East oil industry, but look at the productive gains made here in our own country. In 1920 experts predicted that only seven billion barrels of oil remained in the United States. By 1943 four times that amount had been consumed, and there were 20 billion barrels of proven reserves. Since then, reserves have grown in spite of increasing consumption and predictions of future shortages. Now we have almost 30 billion barrels of proven reserves, and our Outer Continental shelves have been estimated to contain 100 billion barrels.

Worldwide the outlook is even rosier. In the decade of the 1980s the world consumed 200 billion barrels of oil, but by the end of the decade world reserves were 50 percent greater than at the beginning. From 1970 to 1991 the world's *proven* oil reserves—i.e., known to be in the ground, not just estimated—nearly doubled, from 523.5 billion barrels to 1,003.3 billion barrels. And estimates beyond the proven reserves tripled, from 1 trillion barrels to 3 trillion.

Oil companies are searching for oil in more remote places and developing the means to drill deeper wells. They have also developed the technology for drilling in deeper waters. In 1947 the first offshore well out of sight of land was completed. In 1964 a diver for an oil company set a record by diving 525 feet to work on a drilling rig. In 1976 the same diver plunged 905 feet to perform similar work 50 miles from the North Pole.

In 1985 the world's deepest oil-drilling platform, which belonged to Shell, sat in 1,025 feet of water. In 1996 the same company was installing a drilling tower in water more than twice that depth—which will tap oil deposits as much as 14,000 feet beneath the water. The 320-story structure will be the tallest in the world, more than twice the size of the Sears Tower. Yet even before installation of that structure was completed, Shell and a consortium of three other oil companies in 1996 announced plans to drill a well at a world-record water depth of 7,625 feet—three times deeper! "Anything's possible," said Jack Little, chief executive of Shell Exploration & Production. "Even we don't know how deep we can go."[20]

In addition to finding new sources of oil, industry has developed ways of extracting more oil from deposits. Pumps are employed where there is insufficient pressure (from natural gas) to cause the oil to gush to the surface. But pumps can withdraw only the pools of free-flowing oil, a small fraction of the deposit. To force oil out of the sand and rock, water is injected to displace it to the pools where it can be pumped. This process, called secondary recovery, still leaves more than half of the oil. Then there is tertiary recovery, which may be accomplished in several ways, such as injecting steam or chemicals to reduce the viscosity of the remaining oil or by "fireflooding," a very slow-moving burn which pushes the volatile crude in advance.

Another technique for extracting more oil is horizontal drilling. It begins with a conventional vertical well, but at an appropriate depth the drill bit is directed to take a 90 degree turn. It's an idea that has been around for decades but only recently perfected. Though not applicable everywhere, it can be spectacular where oil reservoirs lie between vertical geologic fractures. In 1989 Oryx Energy Co. drilled a horizontal well in south Texas that tested 3,262 barrels of oil per day. You can appreciate the significance of this if you realize that Texas has 200,000 producing oil wells and their average production is only about 10 barrels per day. Between 1989 and 1991 two spectacular horizontal wells in Texas tested 12,254 and 19,568 barrels per day. The first 32 commercial horizontal wells in Texas' Pearsall Field averaged 700 barrels per day.

New technology of a different sort has breathed new life into the oil industry at Alaska's Prudhoe Bay. Here natural gas injected into the frozen earth is allowing far more oil to be pumped than was originally thought possible. "If we hadn't gone ahead with these technological investments, we'd be just about finished,"[21] said Ronald Chapman of Atlantic Richfield Co., one of the three companies that co-own the Prudhoe field. Instead, an additional 7.075 billion barrels of oil—the equivalent of discovering another large field in the North Sea—is expected to keep the field producing until the year 2030. Moreover, the technological success at Prudhoe has led to the development of at least six satellite fields.

Petroleum products can also be manufactured from coal. The Republic of South Africa, which has no known deposits of oil but enormous reserves of coal, has been producing gasoline from coal since

1955. As a by-product of this endeavor, the South Africans have a substantial and profitable plastics industry.

It is also possible to make that clean and most popular of fuels, natural gas, from coal. Conversion of coal to gaseous fuels is almost twice as efficient as conversion of coal to electricity, says Eric H. Reichl, president of Conoco Coal Development Company. But, according to this 30-year veteran of the industry, gas plants were not built because of the unrealistic levels to which government controls held the price of natural gas.[22] *In situ* coal gasification, which gasifies the coal without removing it from the ground, also enlarges our usable coal resources by enabling us to utilize coal that isn't economical to mine.

In the same way that utilization of petroleum resources has contributed to the technology for commercial development of shale oil, the gasification of coal, along with petroleum technology, will extend man's knowledge for developing *gas shale.* With present technology about 285 trillion cubic feet of gas are already recoverable from a shale deposit that may hold the largest reserves of natural gas in the world. No, not in the Middle East—in eastern United States! Dr. Douglas 0. Patchen, a geologist at West Virginia University says the deposit may contain as much as 460 quadrillion cubic feet of natural gas.[23]

A source of natural gas with far greater economic potential is the "geopressurized" zones underlying the Gulf coast region, both on and offshore. Limited investigations have disclosed there may be 60,000 to 80,000 trillion cubic feet of gas dissolved in water and as free gas above the water zone. "This is an almost incomprehensibly large number," said Dr. V. E. McKelvey, Director of the U.S. Geological Survey. He noted that even the lower figure "represents about ten times the energy value of all oil, gas and coal reserves of the United States combined."[24] Exxon recently began production from the largest commercial gas field in history, in Indonesia. It contains a mere 45 trillion cubic feet of gas.

Coal and nuclear power alone, however, can meet our needs—something which solar and other "glamour" energy sources cannot do. According to Dr. Petr Beckmann, "Solar can supplement, but cannot substitute; wind, tidal and geothermal cannot contribute more than two percent of total consumption."[25] Any development of these resources will merely add to our abundance, not avert scarcity. Even without them there is every reason to think that energy will continue to be more abundant and cheaper in the future than ever in the past.

As man has progressed in the production of energy, he has also learned to utilize that energy more efficiently. James Watt's steam engine of two centuries ago had an efficiency of only about five percent. Today's internal combustion engine typically has an efficiency of 20 to 25 percent while modern turbines are usually above 30 percent. Combined cycle steam-gas plants operate at about 55 percent efficiency. But on May 16, 1995, General Electric Company announced development of a new generator with 60 percent efficiency. The new product is the result of a "unique integration" of science from GE's jet aircraft division with other elements of GE research and production.

The key to the new advance is the way the whirling blades of the gas turbines, which are similar to jet engines, are cooled. Instead of using air from the turbine's compressor—the conventional method—GE's new system cools the blades with steam from the steam turbine. Recycling the steam back into the steam turbine eliminates inefficiencies of the older system. And the better cooling permits higher firing temperatures in the utility plants, which further increases efficiency.

> A single percentage point increase in efficiency can reduce power-plant operating costs by $15 million to $20 million over the life of a typical plant with a capacity of 400 to 500 megawatts of power. That means GE's five-point jump in efficiency over the best plants operating today could save a utility up to $100 million in fuel bills.[26]

While industry has been making energy more abundant, producing it more efficiently, and making it cheaper for the consumer, what has the federal government been doing? Here's an answer given in 1995 by John A. Hill, former deputy administrator of the Federal Energy Administration, the predecessor of the U.S. Department of Energy:

> The government has spent more than $100 billion over the past 35 years for clean coal technologies, solar energy, conservation and synthetic fuels; none of these programs added one viable technology to the commercial marketplace.[27]

ENVIRONMENTAL CONSEQUENCES OF ENERGY DEVELOPMENT

The more efficient use of energy has brought with it incidental environmental benefits. For example, steam locomotives, which were severe polluters, were replaced by diesel and electric ones because they were more efficient; but they also happened to be much cleaner. The automobile, which provided more efficient—and safer—transportation than the horse, also made our cities cleaner and more sanitary by putting an end to the vast quantities of horse manure and urine in our city streets. And, despite the uproar of so-called environmentalists who protest the construction of power plants, the efficiencies of mass-produced power from central utilities have also led to a cleaner environment. "Ten thousand small fires," explains Dr. Beckmann, "create more pollution than one big one, because a much larger fraction of the total energy goes out of the chimney of a home than out of the stack of a power station."[28]

Similarly, *in situ* coal gasification is a more efficient way to utilize coal because it obviates the need for mining it. But it is also an environmentally cleaner method because it doesn't disturb the land surface and keeps most of the ash underground along with most of the other by-products that would otherwise be vented through smokestacks.

Even the efficiencies of nuclear power are accompanied by environmental cleanliness. Nuclear plants do not emit the sulfur dioxide, fly ash, carbon dioxide and nitric oxide discharged by coal-burning plants. A 1000 megawatt nuclear power plant uses about seven *pounds* of fuel per day, compared to 11,000 tons of coal for a 1000 megawatt coal-burning plant. That coal plant every day produces 42,000 tons of waste gases and as much ash as the spent fuel that all 108 nuclear electric plants in the U.S. in 1995 produce in a year. Much has been made of the safety of nuclear wastes, but not a single person has ever been killed by the handling or storage of nuclear power plant wastes in the forty-year history of U.S. nuclear power generation. The same cannot be said for coal.

The nuclear plants also emit *less* radiation, not more, than coal-burning plants. This paradox arises from the fact that coal contains traces of radium and thorium. "In fact," says Dr. Beckmann, "for the same energy produced, a coal-fired plant usually has higher emissions, and there are coal-fired plants that would violate NRC *radiation* standards for nuclear plants."[29] He quickly adds that "this is an amusing sidelight rather than a real threat" because the amounts of radiation are so low. But it does point out once again that progress does not require victims, that it brings unexpected benefits rather than incidental injuries to others.

There are other incidental benefits that accrue from nuclear power which are far more significant to human health than the reduced radiation. Nuclear energy is safer to produce and safer to the public than the fossil fuels. It is the *absence* of nuclear progress, not its presence, which requires victims. For example, a study by Professor B. L. Cohen of the University of Pittsburgh concludes that the coal equivalent of the *present* nuclear power production in the United States would require an annual list of victims as follows: 2 million cases of chronic respiratory diseases, 16 million man-days of aggravated heart-lung disease problems, 750 dead miners, and 500 deaths from transportation of the additional coal.

R. G. Hart, vice president of Whiteshell Nuclear Research Establishment, states:

> The critics would like you to believe that the mining and refining of uranium, the fabrication of nuclear fuels, the transport of uranium fuels, and the operation of nuclear power stations are all very hazardous operations. The record shows that all of these steps lead to a fatality rate of about 0.3 people per 1,000 megawatts of electrical capacity per year. The comparable figure for coal-fired units is about three people per 1,000 megawatts per year. I don't want to leave you with the impression that coal-fired generation is an unacceptably hazardous operation. It isn't. Its accident rate is comparable to that of many industrial activities. However, the nuclear accident rate is considerably better.[30]

A study by R. Wilson of Harvard and W. J. Jones of the Massachusetts Institute of Technology, relating deaths to power consumption, confirms the figures cited by Mr. Hart. The Wilson-Jones study concluded that coal and oil-fired plants produce three excess deaths per billion kilowatt-hours, which means 50,000 deaths per year. Dr. Beckmann notes that these are "not potential deaths in hypothetical accidents, but 50,000 people who were buried or cremated..."[31]

In the light of such figures the government's delays in the construction of nuclear power plants, no matter how motivated by concern for public safety, are revealed as definitely adverse to public health. Government restrictions on nuclear development have caused death and injury to people by preventing them from obtaining safer power in the same way that government restrictions on new drugs have resulted in deaths by preventing people from obtaining safer ones, such as nitrazepam.

The safety of nuclear power is emphasized by the report of the Rasmussen Commission, a team of 60 experts headed by Professor

Norman Rasmussen of the Massachusetts Institute of Technology. Among the findings of its exhaustive 3-year study, the commission reported: fatal accidents are 10,000 times less likely from nuclear power plants than from many non-nuclear events, such as fires, explosions, toxic chemical releases, dam failures, airplane crashes, earthquakes, etc.; for a person living near a nuclear plant the chance of being killed or injured by a reactor accident is one in five billion or one in 75 million per reactor year respectively (compared to one in 4,000 for a motor vehicle fatality); and large dollar-value damage is 1,000 times more likely from a non-nuclear accident than from a nuclear one.

Despite the furor about storing radioactive wastes, safe disposal can be accomplished in a number of ways. Disposal is a nonproblem scientifically and technically; the only actual problem is political acceptance.

We should remember, too, that what is useless or even nuisance material today may become a resource tomorrow. It's happened before. Already scientists wish they could retrieve and utilize some of the early radioactive wastes that were disposed of at the bottom of the ocean. In any case, the production of nuclear wastes involves relatively small quantities and will not take place for long. As fusion reactors replace the fission ones, they will put an end to the production of such wastes in the same way that fission reactors put an end to the sulfur dioxide, fly ash and nitric oxide from coal-fired plants. Once again a more efficient method of utilizing energy will also be an environmentally cleaner one. Once again it will be seen that men's interests are not naturally in opposition, that industrial progress by some men is not a threat to other men or their environment but of incidental benefit to both.

Due to their productivity, the countries which have consumed the most energy are those where today it is most abundant. The countries most in danger of exhausting their fuel supplies are those where people have always lived very simply and stringently. Their meager way of life hasn't conserved their fuel supplies or the ecology of their lands; it has destroyed both. Lack of progress—stagnation—can be far more destructive of the environment than progress.

In the poor countries of the world nine-tenths of the people— one-third of the world's population—depend on wood for fuel. In these countries, according to the United Nations Food and Agriculture Organization, the annual consumption of wood exceeds one ton per person. The demand for firewood is causing widespread deforestation and subsequent erosion of topsoil. Treeless circles are widening around towns. In Upper Volta the denuded landscape extends for a radius of 43 miles around Ougadougou. In many other parts of Saharan Africa, tree removal is advancing the Sahara Desert. A quarter of a million acres in North Africa are said to be lost each year to the desert through deforestation.

In the African nations of Sierra Leone, Guinea, the Ivory Coast and Ghana, primary rain forest and secondary bush has been disappearing at an alarming rate. When Sierra Leone became independent in 1961, about 60 percent of the country was primary rain forest. By 1994 the figure was 6 percent. During the same period, rain forest in the Ivory Coast dropped from 38 percent to 8 percent. The deforestation has resulted in soil erosion, more flooding, more mosquitoes and more malaria.

U.S. News & World Report, September 12, 1994 noted:

> A free market would discourage inefficient food production on farmland hacked out of tropical rain forests. Yet policies of "self-sufficiency" and protectionism encourage just such environmentally unsound and unsustainable policies. Indonesia, for example, is clearing 1.5 million acres of tropical forest to grow soybeans for chicken feed at a cost above the world price; India produces milk at two to three times the world price....
>
> Advanced intensive methods of cultivation have dramatically reduced the amount of land, water, soil and energy required to produce a ton of grain.... While poverty and a lack of intensive production methods have forced millions of Third World farmers to overgraze marginal range land or plow up steep hillsides with primitive methods, modern techniques such as "no-till" farming that have been widely adopted in developed countries have cut soil erosion rates dramatically—often virtually to zero—while boosting yields significantly.

In South Asia the loss of fertility through erosion is threatening food production. Flooding, caused by increased runoff, is a growing threat to human life and agriculture as well as to the environment. Rapid siltation is slashing the useful life of dams for irrigation and electricity. Sri Lanka has lost half of its forests in twenty years. In Nepal wood is being consumed 7 times faster than it is being regrown. With wood scarce, many people burn dried manure, thus depriving the soil of needed fertility. In India, a country with a history of food shortages and a need for fertilizers, the people burn more than 300 million tons of manure each year. And manure could hardly be considered an environmentally clean fuel.

Chapter Ten
THE TRUTH ABOUT OVERPOPULATION
AND FOOD SHORTAGES

PEOPLE AND SPACE

A variation of the resource-exhaustion argument is that of over-population. Ominous forecasts are made of men becoming so numerous that they will run out of not only resources but eventually even room on which to stand. The image of an earth so overcrowded that people have to battle each other for standing room is a vision of a world where men *must* be enemies. It is the product of minds that accept the ancient, barbaric belief in human conflict and project it into an inevitability of the future. For those who believe that the gains of some men must always be at the expense of others, it is the ultimate way of arguing that all human progress will eventually be at everyone's expense, that civilization will culminate in a world unlivable for everybody.

This preposterous notion was popularized some years ago by the best-selling environmental book of all time, *The Population Bomb* by Paul Ehrlich. In what the author himself labelled an "absurd" exercise, he projected the current rate of growth for an astonishing length of time, 900 years, to arrive at the conclusion there would be 100 people per square yard of the earth's surface, including the oceans. A look at the present population reveals why Ehrlich had to go to such an extreme to try to make his case. With a space allotment one hundred times more generous—one person per square yard—the entire population of the world today would fit in an area one-and-a-half times the size of Rhode Island. With a space allotment 10,000 times larger than that in Ehrlich's projection, every human being now alive could still be accommodated in an area two-thirds the size of Texas. Such comparisons reveal little reason for regarding other men as a threat. Once again the idea that men are natural enemies, this time through overpopulation, can be spread only through exaggeration, in this case by a nine-century magnification of faulty assumptions.

Ehrlich's 1968 book predicted that hundreds of millions of people would die of starvation in the 1970s. The oceans would be dead by 1979. Flush toilets would be banned by 1974. Water pollution would increase hepatitis and dysentery by 500 percent. Air pollution would require urban residents to wear gas masks by 1980. There would be perpetual oil shortages, and rising sea levels would swamp cities in the 1980s. Every prediction by Ehrlich proved untrue, but in 1990 he recycled his alarmist views into a new book, *The Population Explosion,* which again forecast scenarios of doom in which men would inevitably be enemies by the very nature of their existence.

While men such as Ehrlich have stressed man's fertility as a threat, others have been complaining that progress itself is already producing overcrowding by increasingly concentrating the population in cities. Once again human interests are assumed to conflict as men are said to be creating urban congestion, to each other's detriment. But the proportion of the population in the United States living in large cities, those over 250,000, is the same as a half-century ago, and our cities are actually becoming *less* crowded, not more so. In the first half of this century, the population density of central Boston, for example, fell by two-thirds; Philadelphia, by roughly one-half. Central London now has less than one-fifth of the density it had in 1801. Even the slums are becoming less crowded. The Lower East Side of New York, "the great classic slum of the U.S.," today has less than one-third of the density it had in 1920. Central Harlem now is only one-half as populous as a generation ago.

The argument of overcrowding, as B. Bruce-Briggs has pointed out, is often stated in such terms as: "70 percent of our population lives on 2 percent of our land,"[1] which sounds terrible. But, he continues, simple arithmetic reveals that 2 percent of our land is 40 million acres, which means 3 to 4 people (an average family) per acre.[2] That's hardly a condition to alarm even the claustrophobic.

Even more important than the figures themselves, however, is the fact that the uncoerced distribution of population is the one which people find most beneficial, however uneven it may be. Why should a more uniform distribution be preferred to one which is of greater utility to people? Cities are fundamentally voluntary associations. No one, at least in our society, is forced to live in an urban environment; he will suffer no violence from the law or his fellows simply because he chooses to live in the country. The majority of people live in an urban environment because it is to their advantage to live in close proximity to others, because they benefit from the ways in which their interests are in agreement with those of other people. Urban development is a consequence of human interests coinciding rather than conflicting. The many conveniences of city life are simply expressions of this.

If "crowding" the bulk of the population on a small percentage of land is bad for people, why are they willing to pay so much to live that way? Why does urban land sell for so much more than rural land when it produces no crops or minerals and is usually regarded as less scenic? The higher values of urban lands represent the worth of their relationships to other people and their activities—an added value that would not occur if those relationships were on balance detrimental rather than beneficial. That they are *extremely* beneficial is shown by the fact that the slightly more than one percent of our land which meets the U.S. Census Bureau's definition of "urbanized area" has a value one-and-one-half times greater than all other lands combined.

One of the incidental benefits of the uneven distribution of population is that it makes possible an amenity which the opponents of urbanization claim it destroys: open space. By using urban lands intensively, we are able to afford the luxury of millions of vacant acres for recreation and environmental purposes. Back in 1970, when the overpopulation hysteria, just getting underway, led to the scare that we would run out of space, Professor Dennis H. Wrong observed that there is "more open space in the United States today than there was a generation ago."[3] In the 1960s one-third of all counties in the nation actually lost population, a trend which continued in the 1970s and 1980s. In 1920, state and national parks and wildlife areas totaled 8 million acres. By 1974 they were 73 million acres. Now they total more than 87 million acres. The National Wildlife Refuge System, begun by Theodore Roosevelt in 1903 with a three-acre island in Florida's Indian River, now encompasses more than 90 million acres. In 1995 the House Resources Committee reported that federal land set aside for conservation purposes grew to 271 million acres from 51 million in thirty years.

It isn't the advanced societies which require greater land areas for living but the more primitive ones, who use it less efficiently. In *America's Land & Its Uses,* Marion Clawson, former director of the Bureau of Land Management, states:

> Given their technology, the Indians had probably reached the numbers that represented the carrying capacity of the land. All of the area of the present United States that was habitable at all was occupied by some tribe or tribes; *there were no empty lands.*[4]

In addition to the argument that our cities are too dense, it is also argued—often by the same people—that they are not dense enough: that there is too much urban sprawl. Men are thus depicted as enemies in either case, whether they develop the land densely or sparsely. But in the latter case, as in the former, there is little real basis for concern. There is certainly no eminent danger that the trend to less dense development, though it requires greater area, will exhaust our land surface. Even if we add to the Census Bureau's urban land acreage all land used for transportation through rural areas, including highways, roads, railroad rights-of-way, and airports, the total accounts for only 3 percent of our land. In order to justify government land use controls, however, whether for density or sprawl or any other purpose, the men of force always attempt to portray the market actions of men as a threat. For example, though we are in no danger of being swallowed up by urban sprawl, Senator Henry Jackson, an advocate of federal land use controls, made it sound as if we were by warning that "each new decade urban growth will absorb 5 million acres." But this warning was converted from sinister to silly by Mr. Bruce-Briggs' simple arithmetic:

> This [Jackson's statement] sounds terribly serious until we remind ourselves that the nation has 2 billion acres and that 5 million acres is a quarter of one percent of the total land area. At the rate described by Jackson, it would require 400 years to "absorb" ten percent of the nation.[5]

Thus, even *if* urban sprawl were undesirable, men would have little to fear. But it is not undesirable. It is what most Americans want, as survey after survey demonstrates. A low-density suburban environment is what most Americans consider the ideal place to live. People in other countries exhibit the same preference. The suburbanization trend is worldwide. Urban sprawl is not inimical to a better life; it *is* "the better life" for most people.

THE FOOD SUPPLY

A major concern of those who fear overpopulation is that it will result in food shortages. The exponents of this belief dogmatically repeat over and over that the population is growing faster than the food supply. Hence they view members of the human race as enemies with whom they must clash for the available food. More people, more shortages, more conflicts. The trouble with this sequence is that it is founded on a false premise, a premise that is absurd on its face, and thoroughly refuted by abundant historical evidence.

The dogma that the population is growing faster than the food supply is tantamount to arguing that consumption fundamentally exceeds production. An impossibility. Nothing can be consumed without first being produced. If food production is inadequate to sustain the growing population, upon what are all the additional people subsisting? The population would have ceased growing long ago if food production had not grown at least as rapidly.

Man has been around for considerably more than a million years, perhaps closer to two million years, yet he remained relatively few in number until only about 10,000 years ago. What brought about a change then? The invention of agriculture, which enabled an increase in the food supply and permitted the population to grow.

Every subsequent increase in world population has likewise been supported by increased food production. Even during the 1960s, when world population grew more rapidly than ever in history—and when the clamor about overpopulation was loudest—food production was increasing twice as fast. These facts, documented by United Nations Food and Agriculture Organization statistics, were readily available to Ehrlich and others promoting the overpopulation hysteria.

But in the same way that the critics of the Industrial Revolution ignored facts which didn't fit their theoretical assumptions, so did Ehrlich and other critics of population ignore the facts about food production. The truth simply didn't fit with their preconceived idea of the necessity of human conflict. Just as the invader mentality couldn't understand how the factory system could enrich some people without depriving others, neither could it understand how more people could be fed without depriving others of food. In both cases the invader mentality couldn't grasp the significance of production.

Every prophet of overpopulation, from Malthus in the 18th century to the Ehrlichs of our own time, has projected past consumption without being able to visualize future gains in production—and then demanded that his shortsightedness serve as the basis of policy for the world. Such men have never fed the world's people nor advanced them in any other respect. Human progress, whether in food or anything else, has come not from the men who declared limits to human knowledge but from those whose minds exceeded the known limits. The fact that lesser minds are unable to conceive of this process is no reason for assuming it cannot continue. They have always assumed so and always been wrong.

Malthus was unable to anticipate new fertilizers and insecticides, new agricultural machinery, and new methods of food storage and distribution. Yet all these things came about, and the world, though more populous, was better fed than in his own time. With each advance, the shortsighted pessimists claimed the date of mass starvation was merely postponed a little. Nearly two centuries after Malthus they were still saying so. Scarcely had the modern anti-population-growth movement gained popularity when Dr. Norman Borlaug suddenly revealed advances in plant genetics which enormously improved agricultural yields, in most cases by several hundred percent. Whereupon the prophets of disaster said this "Green Revolution" would only postpone widespread world famines for perhaps two decades at most.

In 1991 Dennis Avery, a fellow of the Hudson Institute and author of *Global Food Progress 1991,* wrote that the latest demographic study "shows Third World birth rates slowing more rapidly than anyone had predicted. And Third World food production continues to rise twice as fast as its population."[6]

When the white man arrived in North America, there were only a few million inhabitants on the whole continent. That was all the land could support with the technology of the Indians. Since they were often at the brink of starvation, they would have found it inconceivable that a few centuries later the same land would nourish more than 300 million inhabitants, nourish them better, and still yield surplus food to be exported to the rest of the world. But such phenomenal gains are neither the beginning nor the end of the story of food production. The vast improvement in the yield of food in America is only part of the 10,000-fold improvement that began with the discovery of agriculture. No doubt the people of the Neolithic Age, who required some tens of square miles per person, would have been as astonished by the productivity of the people of Jericho as the Indians of Columbus' time would be by America's food supply today.

Are we to believe that the trend toward greater food supplies, which has been going on for 100 centuries, must now come to an end? More likely we are simply like the people who lived throughout this period, amazed by gains once others demonstrated them, unable to visualize what is yet to come.

Those who assert that food supplies cannot continue to increase are in the contradictory position of claiming knowledge of the unknown. They would have to know all that which is as yet uninvented and undiscovered in order to know that it will be inadequate. They would have to be omniscient. Far from knowing the future, they don't understand the past and are even less aware of the colossal potential of even our present technology. If just the land now cultivated were done so as efficiently as in the Netherlands today, the world could support 60 billion people—ten times the expected world population of the year 2000.

Only 2.9 (!) percent of the world's surface is presently under cultivation, according to a United Nations Environment Programme fact sheet. The basins of the Amazon and Congo Rivers alone contain a *billion* acres that could be used for agriculture. The cultivation of unused lands, however, is only the beginning of the possibilities for increasing food production.

Improvements in irrigation, new fertilizers, more efficient machinery and farming techniques, and the development of high-yielding varieties of crops have been steadily increasing production. In the United States, for example, the corn yield per acre increased 600 percent in thirty years and 1000 percent in this century. Corn contest winners in 1996 were getting more than 300 bushels per acre. And we have by no means reached the end of the line for such increases.

> "If anything should have played out, corn should have," says Ralph Hardy, president of Cornell University's Boyce Thompson Institute, a leading center of plant biotechnology research. The highest corn yields achieved each year in Iowa are nearly five times the world average—and they are increasing at a rate of 125 pounds per acre each year, more than double the average world gain.[7]

Furthermore, the technology of higher yields is not destructive of the environment but beneficial to it. In 1995 the Hudson Institute's Dennis Avery wrote:

> High yields are currently saving 10 million square miles of wildlife habitat from being plowed down for low-yielding crops. That's equal to the land area of North America. Herbicides are helping us fight soil erosion to a standstill with conservation tillage.[8]

In the 1980s—the time by which the prophets of doom of the 1960s and 1970s had predicted worldwide famines would already have occurred—there was such a glut of farm surpluses on world markets that it had driven prices so low that American farmers were going bankrupt in unprecedented numbers. The "Green Revolution," ushered in by Dr. Norman Borlaug's high-yielding varieties of wheat, rice and corn, was turning chronically food-short countries into food exporters. Thanks to the new technology, by 1987 even India, where the government for so many years had thwarted food production, had so much wheat that it was subsidizing exports. In 1983 Indonesia was the world's largest importer or rice; four years later this fifth-most-populous nation in the world was a small exporter of rice. Saudi Arabia, having raised agriculture out of the sand, had more surpluses than it could even store and was donating wheat to Egypt. The European Community, a major importer a decade earlier, was now a major exporter. "The world's ability to produce grain has outrun its ability to sell grain," said Morton Sosland, publisher of *Milling and Baking News* and a 40-year observer of the industry.[9] So much for the nonsense about the world's population growing faster than its food supply.

Further gains are on the way. Research has shown that the world's most important food crops can be further improved by genetic engineering. Scientists are now able to manipulate the DNA within the molecule to get desired genetic traits and then grow whole plants from the single cell. This opens up incredible possibilities for genetically superior crops.

Totally different methods may also be devised for improving agricultural yields. In Germany, for example, a number of power companies are disposing of waste heat—"thermal pollution"—from both nuclear and coal-fired plants by pumping cooling water from them through pipes beneath the surface of farmland. Raising soil temperatures in this manner significantly increases production. Several "agrotherm" experimental stations have been operating for three years. Here are some of the results:

> Corn grows about 3 feet taller; potatoes can be harvested 4 weeks earlier, and their yield is 69 percent higher; the sugarbeet crop is 70 percent up; soybeans...yield 2.2 tons per acre, compared with an average of 0.8 tons in U.S. natural soybean-growing areas. Cotton, peanuts and eggplants, crops entirely foreign to Germany, sprout in the Agrotherm experimental stations. Even pineapple is being tried.[10]

It is worth noting, too, that the gain in power plant efficiency alone justifies the method. The agricultural gain is pure bonus. Once again industrial progress by some people brings an incidental benefit, in this case more food, to others.

U.S. News & World Report, September 12, 1994, stated:

> A recent study by Paul Waggoner of the Connecticut Agricultural Experiment Station in New Haven backs up the claim that food production is for the foreseeable future limited only by human ingenuity, not natural resources. The gross productive potential of the Earth—set by available land, climate and sunlight for photosynthesis—is sufficient to produce food for a staggering 1,000 billion people. Even without irrigation, available water is sufficient to grow food for 400 billion....

While the yield from agriculture is growing and the end is nowhere in sight, the yield from aquaculture is even more dramatic and perhaps of even greater potential. The most productive oceans yield substantially less than one pound of fish per acre per year. But with commercial trout farming, yields of 90,000 to 130,000 pounds per acre per year are being obtained. An annual yield of one pound of fish per *gallon* is possible. "Silo culture," the stacking of fish tanks atop each other, makes "vertical" farming practical and efficient.

It takes six pounds of cattle feed to produce one pound of livestock, but one pound of farm-raised catfish can be grown on 1.7 pounds of feed. The production of farm-raised catfish has skyrocketed. It grew from only one-half million pounds in 1969 to 19 million pounds in 1976 and to 280 million pounds in 1987—and that's just in the United States. "Catfish production has doubled every third or fourth year," says Dr. George S. Libbey, a fisheries biology professor at Purdue University. "Nothing else in agriculture even comes close to that."[11]

Despite the phenomenal growth of catfish farming, there is plenty of potential for future expansion. "There are literally hundreds of thousands of acres of land suited to catfish farming in the Delta area of Mississippi which can be put into production as the industry expands in the future," said Mr. S. I. Hinote before an International Seafood Conference in Montreux, Switzerland.[12] There are over 1000 species of catfish in the world, and there is no technical reason catfish production elsewhere in the world couldn't be as prolific as in the U.S. As of January 1, 1996 the U.S. was producing 500 million pounds of catfish annually by 1,320 operators from only 167,000 acres of water, and production elsewhere in the world was minuscule. Now a way has been found to alter the genes of female catfish to produce neutral offspring, which grow larger and feed more efficiently.

Shrimp farming is still in its infancy in the United States, but American firms are already producing crops in Central and South America for marketing in the U.S. The worldwide catch of shrimp has stabilized for the past ten years, but aquaculture production has risen rapidly. From 78,300 tons in 1982, it rose to 217,000 tons in 1985 and to 733,000 tons in 1994.

Crawfish, a "substitute lobster" for many people, are being grown commercially in ever-increasing quantities that threaten to create near-term oversupply problems for the producers. Crawfish "farming" began in Louisiana in the 1970s with stock trapped wild in the state's Atchafalya Basin. By 1996 approximately 90,000 pond acres, most of it in Louisiana and Texas, were producing more than 100 million pounds of this delicacy annually. Crawfish thrive on pond vegetation, pasture grass, or rice and do not require prepared feeds, as catfish and trout do. Furthermore, after the first year, crawfish usually reproduce naturally, obviating the need for expensive hatchery operations.

World production of pen-raised salmon rose almost tenfold from 1980 to 1986. Thanks to Alaska's production, the U.S. salmon harvest ballooned from a mere 7.6 million pounds in 1980 to 894 million pounds in 1993—yet Alaska's share of the world salmon market has dropped. The January 30, 1995 issue of *Forbes* states:

> The development of farmed salmon has almost doubled the global supply of the fish while chopping Alaska's share of the world salmon market from 46 percent to 32 percent in the past decade....
>
> Why not farm salmon in Alaska? Good question. Answer: Prodded by the powerful commercial fishing interests, in 1987 the Alaska state legislature first placed a moratorium on and then banned outright the farming of any creatures with fins. Score one for Chile.

Chile has emerged from nowhere to become the world's second-largest producer of farm-raised salmon, after Norway. It has sharply increased its exports to Japan, where 40 percent of the world's salmon is consumed. And it has increased its exports to the U.S. from 4.6 million pounds in 1989 to 50 million pounds in 1994. Both Alaska and the state of Washington could vastly increase salmon production if fish farming were allowed. In the wild only about 10 percent of salmon fry survive whereas 90 percent survive on fish farms. Dan Swecker and his wife Debby spent 5 years and $500,000 battling the political system and the Sierra Club in trying to get a saltwater salmon farming permit in Washington. No luck. "Americans, I think, do not favor free trade,"[13] says Francisco Ruiz Tirado, a director of the Association of Chilean Salmon & Trout Farmers.

Farm-raised oysters can be cultivated in 16 months instead of the normal 72. Yields may be as high as 20,000 pounds per acre. Private aquaculturists already produce more than half of the U.S. oyster harvest of 50 million pounds, yet this is only a small fraction of what might be produced.

Clams are not as easy to raise as some other seafoods, but with the right environment it's possible to raise 500 clams per square meter. Cherrystone Aqua-Farms, one of the largest aquafarm clam producers on the East Coast, bought 2 million seed clams in 1984 and harvested 300,000 clams in 1986. The next year it harvested 700,000. In 1988 the company produced 35 *million* seed clams—the most anyone had ever produced—many of which it sold to other producers. Dr. Michael Peirson of Cherrystone Aqua-Farms said the company aimed to grow 20 million clams to market size annually. But in 1996 Dr. Peirson stated that production was approaching 70 million market-sized clams annually and that with expansion efforts already underway the company would be producing 100 million market clams within two years. To put this fantastic production into proper perspective, compare it to the natural production from the entire state of Virginia of 44 million clams. Yet Cherrystone has only about 150 employees and produces all this food from a very small area. The company plants 2 million clams per acre.

Tilapia, an African food fish, is being grown in such diverse places as Florida, Louisiana, Idaho and Arizona. Other species of fish are being raised experimentally. Paul D. Schacter, president of Tankulture Foods, raises St. Peter's fish in a 20,000 gallon tank in an old Chicago brewery. This white-fleshed species, native of the Nile River, thrives on potato peels and celery tops, which Schacter obtains free from produce suppliers and supermarkets. Professor Harold Calbert of the University of Wisconsin has been raising 1400 pounds of perch and walleyed pike annually in an old dairy barn. He raises perch in 9 to 11 months that are comparable to 3 to 4 year old lake fish and can sell them for one-third less.

The main reason aquaculture hasn't grown more rapidly is government regulation. In some states one must obtain as many as 30 permits before starting operations. A report by Frost & Sullivan states: "Individuals in the fish farming industry have stated that State and Federal regulations are the most serious problems that are encountered in establishing or operating a fish farming operation."[14]

Some day kelp, a common seaweed, may be used for livestock feed, fertilizer and fuel. It is nature's fastest-growing plant, growing as much as two feet a day and reaching lengths of 150 to 200 feet. The daily prunings from a 100,000 acre "kelp plantation" could provide fodder for cattle and sheep to feed 500,000 to 800,000 people and yield 43 million cubic feet of synthetic methane gas and great quantities of crop fertilizer besides.[15]

At the 166th national meeting of the American Chemical Society, scientists from Anheuser Busch announced they had developed a technique for making protein from baker's yeast. The protein is about the same quality as that found in soybeans. What is most surprising about this new food source is its tremendous growth rate. Under proper conditions 300 pounds of yeast will grow to 100,000 pounds in just 72 hours.[16] With such fecundity even Malthus and Ehrlich would have difficulty adhering to the idea that the human race is growing faster than the food supply.

Greater production is not the only way of increasing the amount of food available. Better packaging and distribution can effectively increase the supply by reducing spoilage. One quarter of all the cereal grains produced in the world go to waste every year. It is commonly assumed that the most advanced societies are the most wasteful; but advancing technology, which increases agricultural yields, also decreases waste. In the United States the food spoilage rate averages 15 percent. In Third World countries it is often 50 percent. In Honduras many bananas that used to be wasted are now canned as puree and exported. Irradiation, mentioned in Chapter Seven as a method of ensuring safer food, is also a method of preserving food and dramatically reducing the waste that occurs from spoilage.

Chapter Eleven
PRIVATE VERSUS PUBLIC: HARMONY OR CONFLICT

Takers favor collectivism because it's so consistent with invader methods and beliefs. It's a scheme for "distributing" the wealth of others through organized force; nothing about it is geared to the production or protection of wealth. The system forcibly displaces the very economic processes by which the minds of men create material values. Collectivism removes economic decisions from the private sector, where they are determined by the minds of the citizens, and places them in the public sector, where they are determined by the government's power to threaten physical violence.

Relying on force for satisfying their wants, the neo-invaders believe it can bring social as well as material gains. They expect to bring about social tranquility through government-enforced uniformity. In line with their belief that those with greater wealth must have acquired it at others' expense, the collectivists believe idyllic harmony will prevail among men when economic inequalities are eliminated. Instrumental to this goal is the uniform sharing of economic power through political control and the concept of public ownership.

But collectivism can never bring the peaceful paradise its advocates promise. By its very nature it must *create* conflict. A society can be harmonious only to the extent its members agree to their interactions. Since it's difficult to get everyone to agree on anything, much less everything, the collective approach can't possibly satisfy everyone. Increased collectivism must bring increased dissatisfaction. It compels uniform compliance instead of allowing for human diversity. In a society based on individualism, rather than collectivism, no one is forced to interact with others. Human relations can be harmonious only where an individual, instead of being forced to combine with others, can separate his affairs from theirs and interact when he agrees with others and abstain when he doesn't. This individuation is possible only under the political system of *laissez faire* capitalism. And the means of implementing this individuation in economic transactions is that which collectivism always seeks to destroy: the individual's property rights.

As an illustration of the conflict bred by the collective approach, consider again an example used in an earlier chapter, that of a new public school. If a majority in a school-bond election vote for a new school, the minority will have cause for resentment since they will have to help pay for something they didn't want. If the majority vote against the issue, those who desire the new school can hardly be blamed for regarding the victorious voters with hostility for preventing it. On the other hand, if the building is not a public school but a private one, or a private bank or store, those who don't want it won't experience the resentment of having to pay for it. Nor will those who desire such a building have cause for hostility toward those who don't if the minority is still free to construct it, something the defeated advocates of the public school cannot do.

As another example, consider the vast lands owned by the federal government. Conflicts in their use arise simply because they are public. There is no way to reconcile the demands made for mineral leases, grazing rights, timber rights, scenic or other recreational uses of these lands. It's impossible for the government to allocate lands equitably to such different purposes and to avoid resentment among the various interest groups involved. Any use will be opposed by every group favoring another. Aggregating the many interests in society under public ownership can only breed hostility; each group is set against others by the system itself. The only way these diverse interests can be sorted out is through private ownership. A free market would allocate the land best suited to each purpose and in an amount proportional to the economic demand for it in society. Property rights permit people to separate their land uses according to their separate interests.

The concept of public ownership in itself creates the invader's situation of one man's gain being another's loss. No matter how public property is allocated, its use by some people will preclude its use by others with equal title to it and reduce the total available for them. Since everyone in society regards himself as the public, he resents losing some of "his" property to anyone. And if no allocation is made—the assumption being that what is public is available to everyone—then the hidden conflict becomes highly visible. The best illustration of this, depicted endlessly in western movies, is the range wars that went on between the cattlemen, sheepmen and farmers over the use of federal "open range" land. Modern conflicts arise not only among different types of uses, such as mineral exploitation or timber cutting versus recreational use, but even among different uses of the same general type. For example, within the category of recreational use, conflicts have arisen between snowmobilers and cross-country skiers, between fishermen and water skiers, and between motorcyclists and members of the Sierra Club over the use of public areas.

Through much of our history, it was the policy to transfer land as quickly as possible from the government to private hands. The Homestead Act of 1862 is perhaps the best example of this though not the only one. The policy of conveying lands to the citizens promoted peace as well as prosperity: peace, by eliminating the kinds of conflict epitomized by the range wars; prosperity, by entrusting the land to the productive management of the people rather than the profligate management of government. But in recent decades there has been a pronounced trend back to public ownership, back to social conflict—settled now by political battles rather than frontier gunfire—as collectivist policy has increasingly supplanted the private-property approach of our forebears. Politicians vie with proposals for a new national park, another wilderness area, an addition to a national forest, or some other public project, itself a seat of controversy. Not only are private lands being taken away in this manner, but so-called public lands are in many cases being withdrawn from use by the people. For example, according to R. L. Smith, President of Michigan Technological University:

> In 1968 only 17 percent of public lands were excluded from mineral exploration and development under the Mining Law. By 1974 this had risen to 67 percent or an area equal to all of the land east of the Mississippi River except Maine.[1]

It is the essence of the invader mentality to regard other people, particularly productive people, as enemies and to try to take their property by force for one's own utilization. Today private lands are seized, just as the grain at Jericho was, by organized force for satisfying the desires of those controlling that force. Only now those desires are called "public." And in the same way that the ancient barbarians had to work up a certain zeal for their invasions, the neo-invaders have made a righteous cause of seizing private property for their own—"public"—purposes. The seizure, however, is only the beginning of the conflicts. Making land public simply opens its use to dispute by conflicting interests throughout society, all members of the public, all with equal title to it, all attempting to determine its use by their political clout, with a corresponding loss to others.

The same kind of conflicts posed by public ownership of land, as well as the contrast with the peaceful alternative of private property, can be seen in the application of these forms of ownership to animals. Wild game is considered public until individuals take possession of it. So when anyone shoots a deer, an elk or a pheasant, the public has lost one of these animals. One man's gain is everyone else's loss. But if a farmer butchers a pig, a cow or a chicken, other people don't consider it a loss. The animal being private property in the first place, members of the public cannot lose what was never theirs. The farmer gains, otherwise he wouldn't slaughter the animal, but his gain is not a loss to society.

Further conflict arises from the attempt to reconcile public ownership of game with the private ownership of land. By enforcing his right to prohibit trespassing, the land owner can prohibit the public from access to "their" game. And through game laws, the public can prohibit the land owner from taking game on his own property, even when it is destroying his crops. In which case, of course, the public's wildlife gain is the farmer's loss. Public gain at private expense.

The conflicts that appear when the collective approach is applied to land and animals will also appear when it is applied to anything else. Take timber, for example. If trees are regarded as a public resource, then every tree that is cut down represents a loss to society. The lumber somebody gains is considered to be everyone else's loss. Private gain at public expense. If the trees are privately owned, of course, the public can't be said to have suffered a loss any more than in the case of the farmer butchering his own animals.

Collectivism doesn't permit people to sort out their differences and act on them without clashing; it structures human interests so that they *must* oppose each other—which reinforces the invaders' belief in the necessity of human conflict. The concept of public ownership makes anybody's gain somebody's loss—which is consistent with the invaders' experience. And the view that anyone's gain from the land, the animals or the trees leaves correspondingly less for others fits with the invaders' view of values as being static, because both fail to allow for productivity.

It's important to remember that while land can't be increased in amount, as animals and trees can, neither can it be consumed. We are no more likely to run out of land than we are to run out of iron or aluminum or sources of energy. The amount of land is fixed, but its value depends on its usefulness—which can be increased. To quote Marion Clawson again:

> Our concern, as individuals and as citizens, is not really with the acreage of land, but with the products and services of land. These depend not only on the area and the characteristics of the land, but also upon the inputs of labor, capital, manage-

ment, and technology in various productive processes. The volume, variety and scope of these inputs has risen greatly over the years, and promises to rise more in the decades ahead. As a result, the products and services of land are not in danger of running out.[2]

There is nothing in the collectivist method which would favor the production of animals or trees or improving the productivity of the land. On the contrary, there is every evidence of the exact opposite, of the consumption of these values when they are public. For example, concerning the federal open range land in the last century, Professor Samuel P. Hays writes:

> Cattle and sheepmen roamed the public domain.... Cattlemen fenced range for their exclusive use, but competitors cut the wire. Resorting to force and violence, sheepherders and cowboys "solved" their disputes over grazing lands by slaughtering rival livestock and murdering rival stockmen.... Absence of the most elementary institution of property law created confusion, bitterness, and destruction.
>
> Amid this turmoil the public range deteriorated rapidly. Originally plentiful and lush, the forage supply was subjected to intense pressure by increasing use.... The public domain became stocked with more animals than it could support. Since each stockman feared that others would beat him to the available forage, he grazed early in the year and did not permit the young grass to mature and reseed. Under such conditions the quality and quantity of available forage rapidly decreased; vigorous perennials gave way to annuals and annuals to weeds.[3]

This process depleted the range by perhaps more than two-thirds from its virgin condition, according to Hays. Murray Rothbard links the overgrazing of public range land to the onset of the "dust bowl."[4] And just a few years ago the Council on Environmental Quality reported that much federal grassland was in "desperate condition" due to overgrazing. In 1993 more than half of all federal range land was in either poor or fair condition, according to the U.S. General Accounting Office.

Government has also squandered timber and animal resources entrusted to its stewardship. The federal government actually fostered the shearing of much of America's forests through government leases. It also traded away rich timber lands in exchange for an uneconomic railroad network. In its attempt to subsidize the westward expansion of the railroads, the government awarded tracts of land ten miles, and sometimes fifteen miles, on either side of rail lines as inducements to construct them.[5] As a result, the location of rail lines was influenced by the availability of free timber land instead of being determined strictly by the demand for transportation. Railroads were sometimes built where there was no economic demand for them simply in order to acquire the timber en route.

THE ANIMALS

The federal government presided over the virtual extermination of the buffalo. When the white man arrived, there were, according to the best estimates, 50 to 70 million buffalo in North America. Some authorities estimate over 100 million. There were none of the cattle we have today. Yet now there are far more cattle here than there ever were buffalo. The cattle are privately owned; the buffalo, largely public.

The disappearance of the buffalo, like that of much of America's forests, was primarily the result of government policies. The government's "open range" policy, of course, was deleterious to the buffalo but was only one of the factors involved. Another was the government's policy of killing the buffalo as a means of subduing the Indians. Still another was the government's persistent refusal to aid the buffalo even when its numbers had become alarmingly small. Time after time Congress refused to act. At one point it strongly argued that the buffalo was a "pest" that ought to be exterminated. And when Congress finally did pass a bill for the conservation of the buffalo, President Grant vetoed it. It's not as though the disappearance of the buffalo was an accident that nothing could have prevented. The government had many opportunities and failed them all.

In 1872 there still were seven million buffalo. Fifteen years later specimen hunters for New York's American Museum of Natural History couldn't find a single buffalo during an entire three-month expedition. By 1900 the once-vast wild herds had dwindled to a mere *twenty* animals, these being in Yellowstone National Park. But even with so few left to watch over, and these confined to federal land, the United States government with all its mighty power—and its usual incompetence— failed to prevent 16 of these last 20 from being slaughtered by poachers.

It certainly wasn't government that saved the buffalo from extinction. It was private concern and private property. Many people find this surprising because the conflicts inherent in public ownership have led them to think that human interests must conflict and that the private interests of others must run counter to and be destructive of that which they consider of value. But in the same way that the conflicts created by public ownership lead to some men benefiting from the destruction of values, such as the buffalo, private ownership leads to some men benefiting from the preservation and production of them. Other men then benefit, too, because human interests are not inherently in opposition. The history of the buffalo is instructive in this regard.

One individual, it may have been a Pend d'Oreille Indian named Walking Coyote, roped two male and two female buffalo calves to start a small private herd. From this grew the great Allard-Pancho and Conrad herds in Montana after the previous disappearance of every last buffalo in the public domain there. In the Panhandle, Colonel Charles Goodnight lured a few wild calves to his ranch, where he protected them. Mitchell Pablo, a half-Mexican half-Blackfoot Indian orphan who became a cattle baron, acquired a small herd of buffalo in 1883. He threatened drastic reprisals against anyone who hunted his private herd, and under his stewardship the herd increased rapidly. In 1906 Pablo was ready to sell, but even at that late date Congress refused to buy. So he sold to the Canadian government. The 691 buffalo he shipped in the next few years to Canada's vast 17,300 square mile Wood Buffalo National Park grew to a herd of 14,000 in a half century.

It was these few men, acting in their own interests and by means of private property, who preserved the buffalo and later furnished the animals for restocking national parks and other public lands. Even the restocking, for which the government is quick to claim credit, depended heavily upon private initiative. The 18,000-acre National Bison Range, which Congress belatedly established in 1908, came about only because of the American Bison Society and the publicity surrounding the shipment of Pablo's herd to Canada. The American Bison Society, founded in 1905 by Theodore Roosevelt, raised $50,000 in voluntary contributions for the National Bison Range and stocked it with 34 buffalo.

The story of the pronghorn antelope's survival is essentially the same as that of the buffalo. Under public stewardship the once-plentiful antelope all but vanished. It was saved from extinction by the protective actions of private citizens and later restocked over a much wider area by the government.

The survival of the tule elk, a dwarf species half the size of the familiar elk of the Pacific Northwest, was even more precarious but followed the same general pattern. These magnificent little animals once roamed California in great numbers, but today they are so scarce that most Americans have never heard of them. Rancher Henry Miller found the last remnants of the species *Cervus nannodes* hiding in the tules (bullrushes) on his huge estate. Declaring his property a sanctuary for the "Tule Elk," he saved them from extinction and coined what was to become their common name.

When Miller's herd grew, it furnished the animals with which the U.S. Biological Survey (forerunner to the U.S. Fish & Wildlife Service) attempted to restock other areas of the state. The government failed in these attempts except for a few animals shipped to a temporary paddock in Yosemite National Park. But it was not the policy of the National Park Service to maintain captive animals, and scientists warned that extended survival required a free-roaming herd and greater numbers.

Walter Dow, a businessman and rancher, thought the tule elk should do well in the Owens Valley, owned by the City of Los Angeles for water rights, and adjacent public lands restricted for water-shed protection. It took several years for the numerous government agencies to approve the transfer. Then, to avoid the failure of earlier government transfers, Dow himself made the crates for the 27 elk and personally supervised the transfer to the Owens Valley, completed October 10, 1933.

The tule elk thrived on their new terrain, but the shortage of beef in World War II brought demands for grazing permits there and for elk meat—a classic illustration of the conflicts over the use of public lands. A series of "managed" hunts became the policy of the Fish and Game Commission, whose objective on occasion was to eliminate as much as half of the 300-member herd. A World War II veteran described one of these slaughters as "an assault on the hapless elk by truck convoy, walkie-talkie radio communications, and airplane harassment that is nothing short of warfare."[6]

In 1967 the Los Angeles City Council voted to establish a tule elk refuge on the city-owned property, but jurisdiction over the land rested with the independent Department of Water and Power, which refused to comply. In 1969, when the Fish and Game Commission authorized another "managed" hunt, the city council requested that the Department of Water and Power prohibit hunting on its lands; but the department again refused to comply. In 1972 the last free-roaming herd of this species, under government management, numbered only 291 animals although the City of Los Angeles alone owned 183,000 acres of elk range in the Owens Valley.

While the government has done a miserable job of preserving and protecting some species, such as the buffalo and the tule elk, it has actually financed the destruction of others as a matter of policy. Through bounties and other predator-control programs, the government has driven some species to the edge of extinction.

Despite the government's horrible performance in natural resources, its powers regarding them have continued to grow, just as other government powers have and for the same reason. So many people have been led to believe that force is the answer. They have accepted the principle of gain through force without examining whether or not it is effective or appropriate.

What makes people so ready to accept the use of force here, as elsewhere, is the assumption of an enemy, whom force must conquer. Man—particularly civilized man—is said to be the villain and a threat to the one million species that now inhabit the earth. It is commonly believed that the disappearance of species is the inevitable result of human progress. But more than ninety-nine percent of all the species that have ever existed are already extinct—and almost all of them disappeared before the human race even came into existence! Once again Mother Nature is the biggest offender, having herself wiped out nearly all of the species she has created.

Progress itself can hardly be said to be reducing the number of living things on the planet. Clearly it has had adverse effects on certain species, but for others it has produced beneficial consequences that are invariably overlooked. There are, for example, more deer in America today than when Columbus set foot on our shores. Logging has increased their food supply. They browse on new shoots in logged-over areas, but the edible parts of mature trees are beyond their reach. Deer have also adapted very well to living on the fringes of agricultural areas and taking advantage of man's food production. Even in the populous state of New York deer have been increasing. The annual harvest there of about 200,000 deer is many times larger than the state's total deer population back in the 1920s.

There are now thousands of coyotes in the Northeast. They have trickled east through a circuitous route through Canada and now flourish on the region's swollen deer supply. Eastern coyotes often weigh about 50 pounds, about twice the size of Western coyotes. Cougar sightings have increased throughout the East. And New York recorded its first moose-car accident in 1990.

Various other animals, such as raccoons, opossums, geese and many other kinds of birds, have similarly increased. Wild turkeys have increased over 250 percent in 18 eastern states over the past 15 years, according to a USDA survey. Even the hated crows, which have been killed relentlessly and have had no government protection at all until recently, are more numerous now than in Columbus' time. And Americans are not only feeding but caring for 108 million dogs and cats plus assorted other pets. Remember that there are countries, such as in the Orient, which are not "plagued" with progress, where food is scarce and dogs are eaten.

Besides incidentally increasing the food supply for other animals, man's progress has made it unnecessary for him to depend as he once did on wild animals not only for food but for furs. With this pressure lessened, some fur bearers are now making surprising recoveries. In my home state of Minnesota, for example, there are now more beaver and raccoons than there were decades ago. In 1974 state hunters and trappers took 73,000 raccoons, compared to only 5,000 forty years earlier. In 1981 a total of 208,000 raccoons were taken; in 1988 the total was 304,000. Beaver, once feared near extinction, were closed to trapping in Minnesota in 1909 and remained closed for thirty years. Now, however, they are plentiful enough to allow regular trapping seasons. In 1974, 12,000 beaver were taken; in 1981 the number was 46,000; in 1988 it was 132,000. By 1992 beaver were becoming so numerous in some areas of the state that they were causing erosion of stream banks, endangering trout habitat, and causing other environmental damage; state officials in charge of protecting them were *asking* for help in trapping them to reduce the overpopulation.

Of course, some species have not been able to adapt to the changes man has brought to the environment. But there have always been environmental changes and species which failed to adjust to them. That's why no less than 99 million species are already extinct.

The outstanding example of extinction attributed to man is that of the passenger pigeon. Yet even without the slaughter that occurred, it is doubtful that the bird could have survived. While the lowly crow was intelligent and adaptable, the pigeon was not even though it was probably the most abundant species on earth.

The pigeons were rather stupid and, like other communal creatures, their responses were deeply grooved. When some of the pigeons in a flock were forced to veer suddenly away from a diving hawk, other following birds would blindly execute the same maneuver in the same place—like water flowing around an invisible stone—long after the hawk had gone.[7]

They were, as you can see, slow to adjust. This characteristic was evident in situations far graver than flying around a spot where a hawk used to be. Following those before them, the pigeons invariably continued to roost in the same trees even when they were grossly inadequate and downright dangerous.

Their attachment to some of these roosts was astonishing. They clung to them despite the fact that they sometimes had to fly so far afield for food that they did not get back until midnight, despite insufficient perching space within the roost itself (which forced the birds sometimes to pile up two and three deep on the branches while searching for a foothold), and despite appalling onslaughts from humans.[8]

Witnessing a crowded roost, Audubon wrote:

Here and there the perches gave way under the weight with a crash, and falling to the ground, destroyed hundreds of the birds beneath, forcing down the dense groups with which every stick was loaded.[9]

Among the habits which the pigeon couldn't change was that of living in extremely large flocks. Apparently it just couldn't survive on any other basis.[10] Inexorable changes in the environment would have made it impossible for flocks so large and so unadaptable to follow their traditional feeding habits. So large were the flocks that they often darkened the sky for hours. In 1810 the ornithologist Alexander Wilson, watching for several hours a flock more than a mile wide, calculated it was 240 miles long and contained 2,230,272,000 pigeons. Later studies have calculated that the yearly food consumption of such a flock would fill a warehouse 10 stories high, 100 feet wide and 25 miles long. That's a lot of beechnuts and acorns. Although man has multiplied the abundance of many types of food, the supply of these, on which the pigeons depended, definitely diminished.

It is difficult, too, to imagine the pigeons surviving amid the structures of our modern society. These low-flying birds never learned to evade even the modest rural structures of the 18th and 19th centuries, massacring themselves in great numbers against the walls of barns and houses. How would they have survived among our proliferation of buildings, bridges, poles, wires, billboards and antennas? The pigeons were so stupid that, although they could fly beautifully alongside one another, they couldn't cope with other pigeons flying directly toward them. Head-on collisions of flocks produced "severe damage."

So the disappearance of the passenger pigeon was probably inevitable. It should not, however, be thought of as an unmitigated environmental disaster, because the pigeons themselves were destructive of the environment. Of even a new roosting area, Audubon wrote,

> The dung lay several inches deep, covering the whole extent of the roosting place, like a bed of snow. Many trees, two feet in diameter, I observed, were broken off at no great distance from the ground; and the branches of many of the largest and tallest had given way, as if the forest had been swept by a tornado.[11]

In older roosting places, some of which had been used intermittently for centuries, the environmental damage was much worse. Maitland Edey writes that some areas

> were totally ravaged for miles, there remaining only the skeletons of the largest trees, and of these only the thickest branches. Everything else was dead, killed long ago by the dung which sometimes lay two or three feet deep on the ground.[12]

One wonders, if the passenger pigeon had somehow survived, whether the Environmental Protection Agency would tolerate it.

One wonders, too, if those who lament that we are polluting our environment ever thought about what 50 million buffalo did to the landscape. Settlers were picking up buffalo "chips" for fuel years after the buffalo disappeared. (Men were cleaning up the litter and pollution left by "nature"!) Think about all the nitrates and phosphates that washed into lakes and streams from buffalo dung. And think of the great clouds of dust stirred up by herds of stampeding buffalo.

The sad story of the passenger pigeon is well known, but few people know the story of a magnificent bird saved from extinction by man's tampering with the environment. No, it wasn't a deliberate scientific effort on behalf of the bird. It was an unexpected consequence. In altering the environment for their own interests, men incidentally created ideal conditions for the giant Canada goose, thought to have been extinct for decades. When a large flock of them was discovered several years ago, it wasn't in some remote, secluded wilderness. It was in the heart of a city! Surrounded by homes, industry and traffic, the flock had lived for years on Silver Lake in the middle of the city of Rochester, Minnesota. No one remembers when they first came there, and for years no one paid any special attention to them. Everyone thought they were just "regular" geese. They stayed in the bustling urban environment year-round because warm water discharged from the city's public utility plant kept the lake from freezing over. At first there were only a few of these geese, but every year there were more. There were thousands by the time a visiting biologist realized that, although resembling the more familiar Canada geese, these were just too big—half again as large. Curious, he investigated further. In scientific books he found a description of an "extinct" waterfowl which matched those he had seen.

The only threat to the Rochester geese these days is not from man and his progress but from government. The Minnesota Pollution Control Agency (PCA) recommended that the warm water discharge from the utility plant be limited to three degrees above the temperature of Silver Lake instead of 15 to 85 degrees above it, under which the geese had flourished. Stressing that every alternative to protect the geese would be explored, including the possibility of a variance from the regulations, PCA Director Grant Merritt nevertheless questioned whether the geese outweighed the effects of thermal pollution.[13]

There is nothing inherent in the nature of animals such as, say, the buffalo and the pheasant, that would prohibit them from being as abundant as cattle and chickens. Indeed, in the case of the buffalo there are many reasons why they could be even more abundant. Though almost twice the size of a domestic cow, a buffalo subsists on one-third less grazing land and eats grass that cattle won't touch. It withstands blizzards, droughts and food shortages far better than cattle. Faced with a shortage, the wily buffalo will even ration food for himself. Buffalo meat is at least as tasty as beef, which it resembles. It's prized in gourmet restaurants. It's tenderer, finer grained and has a lower cholesterol content than beef.

The reason cattle and chickens are so plentiful is that people can profit from *producing* them. Public ownership creates the conditions of an invasion where it's impossible to profit from production, where men can gain *only* by destruction. No one could make a profit from raising buffalo while the government was providing them free for the taking. Men could gain only by taking them, by destroying them.

Instead of applying the concept of private property to game animals, where profit would mean production, those who have insisted on regarding game as public have been driven by their own premise to think in terms of invader economics. They can think of gain only from destruction. They assume that allowing profit from game would only deplete it, not make it more abundant. So long as it is public, they are right. But instead of making it nonpublic, they have attempted to make it nonprofit. Invariably they have succeeded. Laws abound prohibiting commerce in wild game. Enacted in the hope of conserving these animals, they have instead made them scarcer, because it is now in no one's economic interests to produce or even conserve them. A farmer knows that he can profit from raising an extra row or two of corn by plowing the cover along the edge of his field. He can earn nothing from the pheasants that might live there.

Most farmers are ardent conservationists, love of nature being one of the strongest attractions to farming. Most farmers would be happy to feed and shelter game if it made economic sense. Many do now to some extent even when it doesn't. Let them profit from the pheasants as they do from the corn, from deer and buffalo as they do from hogs and cattle, and we shall not have to lament the scarcity of any of these animals. Nor shall we have to have licensing, closed seasons, game wardens or public refuges at taxpayers' expense to ensure their survival.

Denmark is a small country and has 5 million people. "But yes, we have hunting. Lots of it. Game is plentiful," says Egon Sorensen, head of that country's Department of Game Management, Advisory and Wildlife Planning Service. He tells why:

> We have high populations of game because the owner of the land owns the game. The land owner sells the hunting rights to hunters, then the hunter owns the game he kills. The hunter also can sell the game he shoots on commercial markets.
> Last year, hunters took something like 2,000 red deer, 30,000 to 35,000 roe deer, 700,000 to 800,000 pheasants, 200,000 gray partridge, 300,000 hare, 700,000 ducks and 60,000 red fox.[14]

Denmark has no government-imposed bag limits, although Sorensen's agency sets the hunting seasons.

In the United States hundreds of stockmen now raise buffalo for meat. Private game farms and shooting preserves across the country raise assorted animals from all over the world for hunters. Texas' 80,000-acre Y.O. Ranch, for example, offers hunting every day of the year. For most species no license is required. Hunters without guns are lent them at no cost and pay only for the ammunition they use. Yet there is no shortage of game. The ranch has Siberian ibex, African oryx, Corsican rams, sika deer from Japan, aoudads from North Africa, nilgai, blackbuck antelope and a few other species. Hunters pay only for what they kill.

These exotic animals can be bred and raised profitably because the government has no public supply of them that it dumps on the market free, thereby destroying the market, as it did with the buffalo and continues to do with deer, ducks, pheasants and other game which it "manages." Moreover, by offering exotic animals, enterprises such as the Y.O. Ranch can operate free of the licensing and other restrictions which apply to local species. Yet even without such so-called protection, the private stocks are in no danger of being exterminated. In fact, there are more scimitar-horned oryx on the private game ranches in Texas than in their native territories in Africa, where they are under government protection. And the Y.O. Ranch alone boasts more blackbuck antelope than are left in their native territories of India and Pakistan.[15]

Private herds are conserved because it's in the owners' self-interest to do so. It's ridiculous to argue that depletion will result from men profiting by the killing of these animals. Farmers profit from the slaughter of hogs and cattle, and yet we aren't running out of those animals. As with farmers, it would be foolish for the owners of private game herds to kill too much of their stock. In both cases men are interested in maximizing profits. Harvesting too many animals would reduce next year's profit. Liquidating the herd would eliminate all future profits. It would also be economically foolish not to harvest any of the animals and to allow a herd to grow beyond the carrying capacity of its range, an event that would kill many of the animals with no return at all. The greatest total profit is obtained through a large *sustained* yield, which is obtained by maintaining a herd as close as practicable to the capacity of its range. The truest conservationist couldn't ask for more.

Observe that the economic incentive for conserving the animals, whether wild game or farm animals, is possible only through private property. The owners forego the profits of disposing of all of their animals at once in order to reap greater rewards over a period of time. But if the animals are public, the economic incentive is the exact opposite: it is to dispose of them for any immediate gain before others do. Public ownership has acted to deplete wildlife in exactly the same way that it caused the depletion of federal "open range" land in the last century. It removes people's economic interest in the future of the resource.

Public ownership is economically wasteful because it is anti-mind. It acts against man's ability to plan his actions over time, reducing him to the range-of-the-moment actions of an animal. Private property, like money, permits men to exercise that distinctive human capability for postponing immediate rewards in favor of greater future ones. It is ironic that concern for preserving something for the future is invoked as a reason for making it public, because doing so always creates economic demand for immediate consumption. Public ownership is therefore doubly destructive of resources. It promotes consumption while destroying the market for preservation and production.

It is to counter the economic demand for immediate consumption, brought about by public ownership, that the government then attempts forcibly to restrict that consumption. The demand, though artificially stimulated, is very real, but the *economic* means of dealing with it are eliminated. Hence the government rations demand by licenses, bag limits, closed seasons and even queuing. The apparent "necessity" of such measures—in the absence of the price mechanism to ration a scarce commodity, or the profit motive to conserve it—is then taken by the advocates of force as confirmation that only coercion can solve the problem.

The record shows the exact opposite, that government cannot solve the problem of conservation. It is evidence of people's confidence in force *on principle* that so many still look to government as the key to wildlife abundance when all the facts are to the contrary. Government has failed in wildlife management not only in our own country but elsewhere. On the other hand, a market economy, in the few instances where it has been allowed to operate in this field, has succeeded admirably in proliferating game animals, even when handicapped to some extent by government policy. Organizations such as the Y.O. Ranch, for example, have had the artificial handicap of having to start their herds by buying second generation animals from European zoos or other private sources, because government regulations prohibit public agencies from selling even surplus animals to private buyers.

Kemp and Ruby Savage, a retired couple in South Carolina, make a handsome income raising quail. Actually, they earn more from the sale of eggs from the 20,000 quail they house than from the sale of birds themselves. The returns aren't only financial. Kemp says, "They're nice birds...nice birds. They've brought me satisfaction, and that's something to say."[16] Many more people would raise all sorts of game birds if they weren't discouraged by the government regulations involved.

As with other wildlife habitat, wetlands have disappeared because the farmer couldn't profit from them. Game laws prevented it. Waterfowl were public, free. But here the government didn't stop at eliminating the market for preserving wildlife habitat; it actually financed its destruction. For decades the government used tax money to subsidize the draining of wetlands, sacrificing conservation to buy farm votes. Then the politicians, and many misled environmentalists, portrayed agricultural progress as the enemy of the waterfowl and government as the only means of conquering this villain. So politicians began spending tax money for the opposite purpose, to preserve wetlands and even to create them. This tactic bought them the environmental vote.

Nothing but government, it was claimed, could save the marshes and the ducks. With its tax powers, its powers of eminent domain, its sprawling bureaucracy and all the political propaganda about its environmental accomplishments, the federal government now has 4.7 million acres of wetlands. But private organizations, including hunting and conservation clubs, without any of the government's powers, have quietly set aside 5 to 7 million acres of wetlands in this country. Even these figures understate the case considerably because a great many ducks breed on private property not set aside specifically for that purpose. According to Jim Kimball, former Minnesota Conservation Commissioner, "Ninety-eight percent of the ducks on this continent are raised not on refuges, public wetlands or waterfowl production projects but on privately-owned land."[17]

One private organization, Ducks Unlimited, has acquired 2 million acres and has improved habitat on an additional several million privately-owned acres. As of 1992 this group had spent $693 million to improve 4.3 million acres of habitat in Canada, 1.1 million acres in Mexico and 560,000 acres in the United States. Furthermore, its efforts are even more effective because it preserves wetlands in the Canadian breeding grounds where 80 percent of our ducks are hatched. U.S. law prohibits federal duck stamp money from being used outside the country. Ducks Unlimited also has accomplished 1200 water control projects to protect against both drought and flood, and these have benefited 60 different mammals and 19 types of fish as well as 250 species of birds. All this from a nonprofit organization. Think what could be accomplished if the full economic incentives of the market were unleashed.

THE TREES

In the case of timber lands, just as with grazing lands and wildlife, public ownership creates demand for immediate consumption of the resource while destroying the economic incentives for production and conservation. When the government owns the land and leases it for logging, the lessee can profit *only* from cutting the trees, not from planting or conserving them. Moreover, the incentive is to lease and cut *now,* to get the timber before others do—in the same way that stockmen tried to get the forage of the federal "open range" land before others did. As Murray Rothbard put it, it is to the best interests of the lessee "to use the resource as intensively as possible *in the present.*"[18] Thus public ownership, far from fulfilling the collectivist dream of preserving "our heritage" of these natural resources for the future, has been accomplishing the exact opposite.

> In the American West and in Canada, most of the forests are owned, not by private owners but by the federal (or provincial) government. The government then *leases* their use to private timber companies.... In this situation, the private timber company does not own the capital value, and thus does not have to worry about depletion of the resource itself. The timber company has no economic incentive to conserve the resource, replant trees, etc. Its only incentive is to cut as many trees as quickly as possible, since there is no economic value to the timber company in maintaining the capital value of the forest. In Europe, where private ownership of forests is far more common, there is little complaint of destruction of timber resources. For wherever private property is allowed in the forest itself, it is to the benefit of the owner to preserve and restore tree growth while he is cutting timber, so as to avoid depletion of the forest's capital value.
>
> Thus, in the United States, a major culprit has been the Forest Service of the U.S. Department of Agriculture, which owns forests and leases annual rights to cut timber, with resulting devastation of trees.[19]

In 1989 Lawrence Solomon, executive director of Environment Probe, a Toronto-based environmental organization, wrote:

> The government of Ontario has a problem with the way many of its small, private woodlot owners tend their forests: They won't cut down their trees....
>
> Deforestation and the degradation of Ontario's forest land make the papers every day in Ontario, but it isn't the private sector, which owns less than 10 percent of Ontario's timber that is to blame. The deforestation is occurring in the government's land.... When [private owners] do sell their trees, they tend to avoid clear-cutting and they hold out for prices that are typically two or three times those set by the government for timber.
>
> Sweden has more standing forest today than at any time in its past.... Unlike Canada, most of the forest land is privately owned, but the government of Sweden, too, has a problem with its small woodlot owners: Sweden's forest industry has become a major importer of wood because the smallholders don't want to cut down their trees fast enough. Each year, Sweden grows 100 million cubic meters of wood while harvesting only 70 million cubic meters, leaving a large and growing surplus on private ground.
>
> Neighboring Finland also has a huge forest industry and, like Sweden, has more forest than ever before.... [But small woodlot owners] were refusing to cut their wood out of "their gut reaction...to leave the trees alone."
>
> In Third World countries, too, the state encourages the plunder of the forest while the traditional owners of the forest— whether individual property owners or, more often, small village or tribal communities—vainly attempt to stave off remote governments. In Brazil's Amazon basin, the government has subsidized the tearing down and burning of a forested area bigger than all of France over this past decade. Subsidies of various kinds have deforested other regions of Latin America, several Asian countries, and much of Africa, often after decentralized forest holdings fell under central government control.
>
> Because governments around the world have such an abysmal record, environmentalists like the World Resources Institute, a UN-funded Washington think tank, have come to favor returning state lands to private owners and local communities, which, on the whole, have maintained their lands far better. Private owners don't cut at a loss, they don't cut for employment, and they manage their forests not as an undifferentiated commodity but as multi-purpose properties with timber being but one asset.[20]

There are 750 million acres of forests in the United States. Fully one-third—an area greater than all of Norway, Sweden, Denmark, Austria, Switzerland and Ireland combined—is set aside for wilderness areas, state and national parks, wildlife refuges, scenic rivers, etc. A further 135 million acres, principally national forests, are publicly owned and managed for timber; it is from this category that government leasing occurs. Only 65 million acres are owned by the forest products industry. The balance of the country's forests belong to other private owners, mostly small farmers.

More of the nation's forest products come from the industry's 65 million acres than from the government-managed 135 million acres. But don't jump to the conclusion that industry is merely depleting its resource faster. Just as with privately-owned game and farm animals, maximum profit from privately-owned forests is obtained by operating the asset for sustained yield. Concerned with continuing profits, the industry is actually growing 13 percent more timber than it is cutting—and this figure has been rising steadily since the 1920s. We're not running out of timber any more than we're running out of food or metal or energy. Timber is becoming more and more abundant and has been doing so for a long time. Up to the year 1925 a total of only one and a half million acres had been reseeded. That much is now planted every year. In recent years tree planting has been broadened further by extending it to abandoned cropland, which—thanks to our increasing agricultural productivity—is no longer needed for growing food.

The number of acres planted in trees in the U.S. has risen about 2000 percent since 1930, according to the U.S. Department of Agriculture. The U.S. Forest Service estimates that 65 percent of the Northeast is covered with forest, compared to 35 percent a hundred years ago. Four million trees are planted in the United States *every day*—85 percent of them by private owners. Forest cover has also been increasing in Western Europe; it rose 30 percent between 1971 and 1990.[21]

Because industry has an economic incentive to increase rather than deplete the capital value of the forests it owns, it not only plants timber but cuts underbrush, controls drainage, protects against fire and pests, and takes other measures to promote tree growth. As a result, industry is growing 52 cubic feet of wood per acre per year, according to the U.S. Department of Agriculture, compared to only 32 cubic feet for government-managed land. Thus private property and the profit motive, instead of depleting the resource for shortsighted gain as is so often alleged, actually encourage reinvestment which enhances the resource.

With public lands there is no economic incentive for reinvestment. According to Robert B. Pamplin, Chairman and President of Georgia-Pacific, "Congress has failed year after year to allocate enough money from government timber sale receipts even for reforestation and other proper management."[22] The American Forest Institute reports that the federal government has 5 million acres in need of reforestation and another 13 million—almost ten percent of its commercial-type forests—in need of improvement because of forest fires, disease or other reasons. It appears that instead of reinvesting its timber receipts in the forests themselves, the government has spent the money for political purposes. *Some* people have benefited from political spending at the expense of *all* the people, the public, to whom the resource is said to belong. Despite their lofty rhetoric, government leaders have attached a higher priority to preserving and enhancing their own power, through politically popular spending, than to preserving and enhancing the capital value of the forests. In fact, they've been draining revenue from the latter to pay for the former, all the while clamoring that only government could preserve the forests for future generations and that private enterprise would sacrifice the resource for an expedient profit.

Instead of sacrificing the resource, the industry, in its pursuit of profit, has ingeniously devised ways to produce more of it. It has developed supertrees. Fir now grows in 40 to 50 years to a size that used to require 80 to 100 years. Similar genetic improvements have been achieved with Southern pine. Experimental work is being conducted in fertilizers in the hope of further accelerating growth.

In addition to producing more timber, the industry is using it more efficiently. The National Geographic Society observes:

> Operators have learned to use up to 80 percent of a log, compared with perhaps 50 percent some 20 years ago. A number of uses, ranging from mulch to auxilliary fuel, have been found, even for tree bark.[23]

The industry has developed such products as plywood, particleboard and hardboard as means of utilizing wood resources more fully. Particleboard, widely used for flooring underlayment, is made mainly from shavings, formerly waste. Our affluent society is not wasting more; it's wasting less. Such economies are in the industry's self-interest, but they have the secondary effect of conserving timber resources. Conservation is not the victim of profits; it is a consequence of them.

Most Americans have no conception of the strides the industry has been making in increasing the nation's timber supply. But there is another misconception that is even more common: that consumption is growing rapidly. It is generally assumed that population growth, advancing technology and rising living standards are consuming our forests at an accelerating rate. Hence, as with other resources, it is argued that we must change our life style now or face exhaustion of the resource later. But the facts are a real surprise. Only in the economic boom of the 1970s did *total* lumber consumption even manage to climb back to the peak that existed before World War I. Though our population has grown enormously, per capita consumption is much lower now than before World War I due to more efficient use of lumber, as well as advances in the use of other building materials.

> For a typical 320 square foot log cabin, our forebears used 70 trees. And burned what was left over.
> Today, that same number of trees would provide a 3500 square foot home—plus enough tissue and paper products for an average family—for over 30 years![24]

The timber industry, and other industries as well, have been increasing operational efficiency and reducing the waste of raw materials because they can thereby increase profits. It is the very fact that government operations are non-profit that makes them inefficient and wasteful. According to Pamplin, the government wastes 6 to 8 *billion* board feet of lumber every year in the form of dead or dying trees which are not harvested.[25] (This figure is only for the government's commercial-type forests and does not include the 250 million acres set aside for parks, wilderness areas, etc.) That kind of waste would never occur on private property; the selfish desire for profits would prevent it.

A corollary of the invader assumption that anyone's gain must be someone else's loss is the belief that if no one gains, then nobody else will lose. On this basis, the nonprofit comes to be viewed as the economic ideal. If there are no profits, then they can't be at anyone's expense; no one else loses, right? Wrong. *Everybody* loses! The 6 to 8 billion board feet of lumber wasted represent an economic loss to every member of the public, to whom the resource belongs. And in the same way that profits from this timber, if it were sold, would represent material gains for others, that is, the purchasers, the economic loss instead represents a material loss: the loss of enough lumber for a quarter of a million homes annually. In turn, this material loss means that the available supply of lumber is less than it would be, and so prices are higher. Every purchaser of lumber, therefore, is also paying an additional expense. Non-profit management by the government is the most expensive thing in the world. We simply can't afford it.

In 1986 the General Accounting Office reported that much of the timber cut in national forests is sold at a loss.

> In two regions of the Rocky Mountains, over 96 percent of the sales didn't cover costs.... Some sales apparently didn't even come close. Harvests in the Monongahela National Forest in West Virginia returned only 25 cents on every dollar spent, and harvests in the Beaverhead National Forest in Montana returned only 32 cents.... Wyoming's Bighorn National Park recovered a mere 21 cents on the dollar.[26]

The Forest Service does make a profit on the national forests on the Pacific Coast. The one-third of the national forests located here produce three-fourths of the agency's revenues. However, these are the "irreplaceable coastal rainforests, which are being logged at record rates.... The Wilderness Society fears that America's remaining rainforests, most of which are controlled by the Forest Service, could disappear within 15 years."[27]

On November 1, 1990 the Interior Department released an audit showing that mismanagement of some of the world's most productive timber lands cost the government at least $90 million since 1986. The report said that failure to perform thinning, fertilization and other maintenance resulted in fewer trees that could be cut and could result in losses of $1.7 billion over the 60 to 80 year life cycle of the forests.

On October 2, 1995 congressional auditors reported that the federal government spent $1 billion more to log national forest in the previous three years than it received in receipts. Thus the trend of losses continues year after year after year.

As another illustration of the waste from nonprofit timber management, consider the deliberate burning of tons of valuable cedar in two national forests. The fires were lit by the Smokey-the-Bear agency itself. In February 1976 the *Spokane Weekly Chronicle* reported that the United States Forest Service had paid a private contractor

$12,250 to stack 300,000 board feet of cedar into about 30 huge "decks" for massive bonfires in the Clearwater National Forest. Some of the logs were 6 to 8 feet in diameter. A district ranger explained that the material had to be removed and couldn't be sold, but it doesn't seem the agency tried very hard. Why should it? Since it's a nonprofit agency, it had nothing to gain. But can you imagine a private company burning something that could be sold?

Del W. Roby, a small cedar mill operator just twenty miles away, said he would have bought the cedar if he had heard about it before the burn. Dennis L. Arave, the operator of a larger mill at Orofino, 100 miles away, said he asked the forest service about buying the decks but wasn't given a chance. A Spokane operator said he and his family had to go on welfare that winter because he couldn't buy enough cedar to keep his mill open.

In the Kanisku National Forest 100,000 board feet were burned at about the same time as the fires in the Clearwater forest. Loggers in the area said there have been other fires, too. Some listed specific times and locations, but they refused to give their names because they feared "retaliation" by the forest service. One logger said, "I could tell you a lot of stories like this, but if I spoke out, I may never get another contract."[28] Although fear is ineffective for producing values, it seems to be effective for hushing up their waste.

The facts overwhelmingly demonstrate that private ownership is far more effective in perpetuating forests incidentally than public ownership is by direct intent. As a further bit of evidence, consider the example of Georgia-Pacific Corporation. Begun in 1927 with only $6000 cash and $6000 in borrowed money, the company now owns well over 3 million acres in the United States, on which it is growing more trees than it cuts. In only a half century this vast forested acreage was acquired and is being constantly upgraded and protected, all without the expenditure of any tax money.

Here's another instructive example. About a half century ago Boise-Cascade Corporation offered the State of Minnesota a burned-over tract of land in exchange for other, forested acreage. The company argued that its offering had considerable recreational potential. The state flatly disagreed. So the company set about to restore the land for its own use, commercial timber. In doing so—a process begun long before environmental concern became a national fad—the company incidentally created a scenic asset and a favorable habitat for wildlife.

By the early 1970s the land was yielding a moderate amount of pulpwood. It also had one of the highest deer populations in the state and had become so attractive that, although previously rejected for a state park, it was now selected for a *national* park. Those championing this Voyageurs National Park claimed that government had to rescue this "natural" asset from the clutches of the wicked timber industry. They said the land should be made public before it was *spoiled* and so it could be enjoyed by all the people. But the alleged "enemy," Boise-Cascade, was already providing what amounted to a free public park on its land, with campgrounds, a canoe route and portage system, hunting camps, 25 miles of snowmobile routes and other recreational facilities, all at no cost to the taxpayer.

Once the property became a national park, the conflicts began. Hunting became a hotly contested issue. Some groups wanted to ban snowmobiling. Jurisdictional disputes arose between state and federal authorities. The state contended it had jurisdiction of the water surface, but the federal government disagreed. The state attempted to strengthen its water argument by making all land within the park a state wildlife refuge. Meanwhile, on another front, local residents formed a Concerned Citizens Committee to fight the National Park Service policy of no hunting. A spokesman for the group said the people in the area were duped by promises the state would not seek a national park unless hunting would be allowed. He said, "If you live here and you like to hunt, there is no place to go. For 100 miles to the south and to the west there is nothing but peat bogs."[29]

In 1994 the Minnesota United Snowmobilers Association, the state's largest snowmobile group, with 15,000 members, sued federal officials to reopen parts of Voyageurs National Park closed to snowmobiling. The federal law establishing the park in 1971 specifically provides for snowmobiling, a common activity there before the existence of the park; but a 1992 "biological opinion" by the Wildlife Service resulted in a partial ban to avoid adverse effects on wolves and eagles. Earlier, a federal appeals court in 1992 rejected an appeal by seven environmental groups on the incompatibility of snowmobiling in the park and ruled that snowmobiling could continue. The 1994 lawsuit contended that the "biological opinion" failed to provide any evidence of harm from snowmobiling.

For a quarter of a century there has been a continuing dispute—and a string of lawsuits—over how Voyageurs National Park should be managed in relation to the interests of the various factions involved. In August 1995 members of Congress even journeyed to the remote town of International Falls, Minnesota, where a joint U.S. House-Senate committee hearing was held in a local high school to try to resolve the conflicts. These included the issue of snowmobiling and various proposals to open several lakes to motorized boats and to allow trucks to haul canoes and boats over three portages, measures to which the "preservationists" were adamantly opposed. The committee also heard an appeal from a group lobbying to declassify the area as a national park, an event not likely to occur but one which demonstrates the deep dissatisfaction among the local populace. The congressional hearing did nothing to settle the conflicts. So the wrangling continues, as it has for more than twenty years. Try to tell the people of that area how public ownership brings peaceful sharing and is to everyone's benefit. But better keep your voice low.

Consider this, too: if public ownership can't find a way to accommodate the interests of various factions concerning this tiny geographic area, how can it possibly be expected to do so on a national scale? If national legislators who personally visit this locality and listen to the concerns of people can't come up with an answer, how can they possibly do so for localities they never visit and people who never even have a chance to voice their opinions?

Incidentally, the economic benefits that Voyageurs was supposed to bring to the area—which were the basis for obtaining local support for the proposed park—never materialized. The *Star Tribune,* Minnesota's largest newspaper, on August 13, 1995 noted: "[I]t clearly has not been the economic boon to northern Minnesota that was promised.... [T]he visitors never came; use levels generally have been about 20 percent of predictions." The park employs only 41 people full-time.

The timber issue that has received the most publicity is that of the redwoods in California. Once again the facts are quite different from the common assumptions. Instead of their homeland being drastically reduced by civilization, the redwoods are growing today on 85 percent of their original area. Moreover, according to John Miles, a prominent consulting forester, "These forests have been converted from a generally overmature, decadent condition to one of fantastically vigorous growth."[30] Contrary to popular myths about their longevity, most redwoods die of old age in 500 to 800 years; only a few live more than 1000 years.

There never were more than 100,000 acres of the real giants. Before the Redwood National Park, twenty-eight state redwood parks already contained 100,000 acres, including 50,000 acres of virgin big trees and more than 1,500,000 trees altogether. The Redwood National Park set aside 30,000 additional acres,[31] yet there is still pressure to have the government acquire more.

The redwood, which reseeds rapidly, is America's fastest growing conifer, maturing in less than a man's lifetime; a 200-foot giant can be grown in 100 years. By the year 2000 industry will have logged off its virgin trees, but then it will be harvesting mature second-growth timber on a sustained-yield basis. As Harold A. Miller, President of Miller Redwood Company, testified before a U.S. Senate hearing, "We are developing our properties on a permanent basis and we operate our forests on a plan of perpetual yield."[32]

There is nothing surprising about that policy. It's common throughout the industry. It's the logical consequence of the attempt to maximize profits from the resource. To insure its own future profits, Miller Redwood aims to establish 10 trees for every one it cuts.

The profit motive could work even more effectively for the preservation of redwoods, particularly the largest trees, if it weren't for the economic distortions created by public ownership. The recreational market could offer "perpetual yield" for managing forest lands on a "permanent basis," but government has destroyed this market for preserving the trees in the same way it destroyed the market for preserving the buffalo. Just as no one could profit from the buffalo (except by destroying them) while there was a huge public supply free, no one can now profit from the recreational aspects of the trees while the government is dumping its huge supply on the market "free." The only way the industry can now profit from the trees is by cutting them down. Yet even without the economic rewards which a free market would provide, the redwood industry has opened more than 300,000 acres of its private timberlands to public recreation. Think what would happen if the full market incentives were allowed to function in this field.

Because recreational and industrial uses are not incompatible but complementary, even a very nominal charge for private park use would have an important economic effect. It would be highly desirable add-on income because it would add almost nothing to costs. It would be a market that companies would seek and for which they would *compete* as they do now for automobiles, soap or deodorants. Or lumber. Why not have all the benefits of competition, including the abundance of supply and constant upgrading of product, in the field of scenic parks? In this competition the largest trees would have a premium, which they do not have in the lumber market, where wood is priced the same for trees of all sizes. While this factor is not one on which proper timber management is crucially dependent, it nevertheless demonstrates that a freer market would provide more incentive, not less, for conservation.

Of course, a private park system would be opposed by those who say that everyone should be allowed to enjoy the redwoods free. But that's exactly the attitude many people used to have toward the buffalo and the Western range land and which led to their depletion.

In any case, the redwoods aren't free. All the acreage that has been, or will be, set aside (except gifts, of which industry is the largest donor) is paid for through taxes and inflation. Far from being free, public parks and recreation areas are paid for by everyone. But not everyone uses them. Most Americans will never see a redwood, or Voyageurs National Park, yet all are paying for them. Once again some people are enjoying a benefit at others' expense. Just like at Jericho.

The fact that many public parks are widely used demonstrates an economic demand that would support them without government assistance. In the present circumstances, however, the users are not paying the costs of that support. Which is why they want the parks public and why they always want more of them. As long as other people can be forced to pay for their desires, why not?

The biggest threat to the redwoods isn't from industry but, unwittingly, from those who want them left untouched, a policy which could be fatal to the trees. According to Dr. Edward C. Stone, professor of forestry at Berkeley, the trees can no longer be left alone and expected to survive, because conditions have changed:

> Down the ages, fire and silting have been recurring phenomena, and as a result, stands of almost pure redwood developed. But during the last 30 years or so, fire has been excluded, and so competitive Douglas fir and tan oak seedlings are now common throughout the forest. If we totally control flooding, the fir and oak will become established and gradual displacement of the redwood will begin.[33]

Fire poses no threat to the redwoods, whose thick bark is extremely fire resistant. Flooding left silt deposits, which contained mineral nutrients essential to the redwoods. Without these processes human intervention is necessary. In the words of Dr. Stone:

> Our big task now is to actively *manage* the big trees—
> perhaps with burning, herbicides, even the chain saw—if we are
> to preserve our spectacular exhibit for future generations.[34]

THE WATERS

The principles of public and private ownership which are so evident with land, animals and trees are also evident in regard to water and fish. Lakes, rivers and streams in the United States have always been considered public. They have been the aquatic equivalent of western "open range" land and have been degraded and depleted for the same reasons. It is to no one's economic interests to preserve or enhance these resources, because they are public; rather, it is to everyone's interests to exploit them before others do. In the same way that western stockmen tried to graze their animals before others used up the available forage, fishermen have tried to catch the available fish before others got them. In the same way that no one could profit from planting grass on public grazing lands, or even allowing it to reseed naturally, no one can profit from restocking public waters or allowing them to attain an abundance of fish naturally.

Nor is there any economic incentive for maintaining the water quality of public water bodies. Once again people can profit only from the use of the public asset, not from its capital value. It's not surprising, therefore, that water assets have been used in ways which have reduced their capital value through pollution. Just as people could profit only from depleting public forests and game animals but not from conserving or producing them, they could likewise profit from degrading public waters but not from preserving or enhancing them.

Even when the very purpose of public ownership is preservation of a natural resource, making it public leads to its degradation instead. Take the federal government's "Wild Rivers" program, for example. Obviously it was intended to preserve the natural character of certain waterways from the activities of modern man. But once again, just as with other natural resources, the fact of public ownership led to increased consumption in the present. It also eliminated any incentive for preservation. Here is a description of these consequences on one river, the St. Croix, by a local newspaper, the *Burnett County Sentinel* of Grantsburg, Wisconsin:

> It wasn't too many years ago when the St. Croix River
> area was a peaceful, slow-moving and relaxing place where one
> would have to look hard to find recreationalists and debris.

Now, this is all pleasant memories.

With the coming of the St. Croix National and Scenic Wild Riverway, and its promotion by the Department of Interior's national park service, the St. Croix has changed into a busy freeway of canoes, a haven for campers and a public dumping ground....

On the river you can see beer cans glistening in the sunlight as they lay on the bottom. You can also notice the remains of what were previously healthy trees that met their demise for a camper's fire. And, last but not least, the peace and serenity of the wilderness is lost in an echo of loud voices of persons enjoying themselves at the expense of others.[35]

From this example it's not hard to see how people come to regard others as enemies when it comes to the use of public resources. Public ownership once again creates the invader's situation of some people benefiting at the expense of others. Everyone demands to use the resource because he is part of the "public," and no one has an economic interest in preserving it because it belongs to others, who are equally demanding in its use. There is both the incentive and the means for everyone's enjoyment to be at everyone else's expense. No one can benefit from other people's use of the resource; he can only lose by it. But if the resource were private property, the owner could benefit from other people's use by charging them; and this income would provide the incentive and the means for ensuring the quality of the resource.

By providing lakes and rivers "free," the government has destroyed the market for maintaining and upgrading them. And by preventing private ownership of these resources, the government has created a monopoly for itself, just as it has done with postal service. No matter how ineptly the government has managed the nation's water resources, or the postal service, the citizens have had nowhere else to turn. No one has been permitted to offer better lakes and rivers than the public ones, no matter how degraded they became. Government has foreclosed the possibility of competition.

Would a body of water such as Lake Erie ever have become polluted if it had been private property? Of course not, because a private corporation would have had an economic interest in maintaining its capital value. The lake would obviously be worth far more clean than polluted. If its water quality deteriorated, corporate income would drop from such sources as swimming, boating, fishing and homes and industries requiring clean water. Instead of leading to pollution, the profit motive would lead to the upgrading of water quality, just as it does with every other product and service in the marketplace.

A private corporation would guard the worth of the lake in the same way it guards any other asset. If anyone were polluting the lake, the private owner would seek damages in the same way that you or I would seek compensation if someone smashed into our automobile or caused any other property damage.

While the profit motive would protect water resources, the non-profit nature of government works in the opposite direction, toward the degradation of the resource. Government has no economic incentive for upgrading or even maintaining the quality of its product. Is it surprising, then, that water quality deteriorated for decades under government management? It took until 1970 for the federal government even to enforce its powers under the Rivers and Harbors Act of 1899 to require permits for dumping industrial waste into navigable waters. Can you imagine a profit-making organization allowing valuable assets to deteriorate for 71 years before using the power available to it to safeguard them? But government, being nonprofit, had nothing to gain from protecting those assets promptly. For the same reason, the government did little about Lake Erie until 1972 even though its pollution was an object of growing concern since the 1940s.

The supposed virtue of waters being public is that it permits everyone to use them without cost. But when such uses as swimming and fishing are free, there is no way their value can be an economic factor in sustaining them. There is no way an economic preference for these uses can be established, no market for their preservation, and no way in which consumer use can be translated into economic support for them. As a result, these uses become front line economic casualties. It is by not allowing the clean water uses to pay for themselves that polluting uses became economically dominant.

Those who think it terrible that anyone should have to pay for use of a swimming beach, and that some people would thereby be denied, should consider how many people were denied swimming as a result of its being free. Swimming has been free in Lake Erie, but by 1969 one-half of the beaches on the United States side were closed because of pollution. Near Cleveland fecal bacteria frequently reached concentrations 100 times the safe limit for swimming.[36]

And who has been the biggest polluter of Lake Erie, or of the rest of the nation's waters? Government itself. Local governments have been the principal culprits, through municipal sewage. In 1981 New York was still dumping 151 million gallons of *raw* sewage into the Hudson River daily. The City of Detroit has historically been the largest polluter of Lake Erie. As recently as 1978 it was dumping 28,000 pounds of phosphorus and almost a million tons of solids into the lake every day via the Detroit River. More than 100 other city governments have also polluted Lake Erie. By 1975 only 59 percent of municipal sewage on the American side of the lake was receiving adequate treatment.[37]

The magnitude of municipal pollution of Lake Erie is evident from cost estimates for proper waste treatment. In 1976 the Environmental Protection Agency (EPA) estimated it would require $17 billion to upgrade municipal sewage plants to adequate standards. By comparison, the cost to industry for the corrective measures it would require was estimated at $2 billion.[38]

Industry isn't even in second place as a polluter of Lake Erie. Storm water runoff from farms and city streets brings more pollution into Lake Erie than all its industries.[39]

Another major polluter—cited as such by President Nixon in his April 15, 1970 congressional message on the Great Lakes—has been the U.S. Army Corps of Engineers. For decades this agency has polluted Lake Erie and other navigable waters with contaminated dredgings from federal projects. This is the same agency charged with policing industrial discharges through federal permits under the Rivers and Harbors Act of 1899.

According to EPA estimates, ninety percent of all major industries met the agency's water quality standards by July 1, 1977 but only one-half of the nation's municipal governments did so. It would take another five to ten years for some of the latter to comply. Detroit wasn't providing adequate treatment for all of its sewage until 1980, four years behind schedule. New York wasn't in compliance until the mid 1980s, and it was dumping the sludge from its sewage treatment plants into the ocean until June 30, 1992. San Francisco didn't even start to upgrade its sewage treatment facilities until 1976. Ray Burgess, public works director of Baton Rouge, Louisiana admits that for five years his city had "done all that was possible to resist"[40] building new sewage-treatment plants. Even former EPA administrator Russell Train acknowledged that the industrial polluters "are far and away ahead of municipalities"[41] in meeting federal water quality goals.

In a report to Congress on February 14, 1989, EPA stated that two-thirds of the nation's public wastewater treatment plants now have "documented water quality or public health problems." The cost of improvements would require all of the EPA's current $4.9 billion annual budget for the next 17 years.

Treatment plants are only part of the problem. Most older U.S. cities, especially Eastern ones, have combined storm and sanitary sewers which overflow during rains. In Cleveland such overflows carry more than a million pounds of phosphorus into Lake Erie annually. Of Chicago's overflow problem, city engineer Frank E. Dalton said, "It's the equivalent of four million people, every fourth day, walking down to the Chicago River and depositing their raw wastes."[42] The problem was so severe that Chicago undertook a "Deep tunnel" project that cost more than the Alaska pipeline. It wasn't completed until 1985. Separating combined sewers in other major cities isn't expected to be completed until at least the year 2025.

In May 1996 the cities of Minneapolis, St. Paul and South St. Paul completed a ten-year project costing $332 million to separate storm and sanitary sewers, ending the diversion of raw sewage into the Mississippi River due to overflows created from storm water. As recently as 1984 these cities had dumped an annual average of 4.6 billion gallons of raw, untreated human sewage into the river. Yet these municipalities have been not among the worst performers in recent years but among the best! In 1996 reporter Dean Rebuffoni wrote:

> The pollution created by old combined sewers is a nation-wide problem: About 1,200 cities, including most of the largest, have such waste systems. And, apparently, no other major urban area has done as much as the Twin Cities and South St. Paul to correct the problem.[43]

Why, then, has the public been given the impression that industry is primarily responsible for pollution of the nation's waterways? Once again those advocating force had to stir up hostility in order to rally people to their method. They had to depict an enemy that would incite the public to resort to force. And people certainly wouldn't accept force as the solution if they realized that it had caused the problem, that the institutions of force—governments—were by far the worst polluters, and that the real enemy of a clean environment was not industrial progress but collective ownership, not private enterprise but the concept of public property. Lake Baikal in the former Soviet Union is no less polluted because the government-run industries around it belonged to "the people."

Wilfred Beckerman spoke of water pollution in the Soviet Union:

> There are innumerable other well publicized instances [besides Lake Baikal] of serious pollution and environmental damage in the U.S.S.R. Timber resources have been badly managed, leading to extensive erosion and other unfavorable environmental effects.... Two great inland seas, the Caspian and the Aral, seem to be facing serious problems of water depletion as well as pollution.... According to an article in the weekly journal *Nedelya* Siberia might be deprived of pure water in 10 or 15 years time.[44]

Dr. Petr Beckmann on conditions in two other former communist countries, Czechoslovakia and Poland:

> In parts of Czechoslovakia, mothers are officially advised not to give their babies tap water without boiling it first.[45]
>
> In Poland, the government has divided water into four categories, ranging from No. 1, drinking water, to No.4, unfit even for industrial use—presumably useless for anything at all. From 1977 to 1980, the fraction of this "water No. 4" has risen from 32 percent to 48 percent.
>
> Thus blooms the environment when it is no longer recklessly despoiled by capitalist greed, nor raped by the race for profits, but protected by those who are exclusively guided by good for the people.[46]

Those who think the environment can be protected by simply passing more laws should take note of the fact that there was no shortage of such laws in the Soviet Union. Dr. Thomas DiLorenzo of the University of Tennessee at Chattanooga writes:

> In the Soviet Union there was a vast body of environmental law and regulation that purportedly protected the public interest, but these constraints had no perceivable benefit. The Soviet Union, like all socialist countries, suffered from a massive "tragedy of the commons".... Where property is communally or governmentally owned...resources will inevitably be overused with little regard for future consequences.... [T]he inclination is for each individual to abuse or deplete the resource before someone else does.[47]

Nor is the environment any better in the poor countries which have no industry to blame. Wilfred Beckerman again:

> In very poor countries pollution is commonly of the kind that was found in nineteenth-century Britain or other Western nations, particularly pollution of water on account of poor sanitation arrangements and absence of appropriate sewers and the like. This is often accompanied by excessive urban densities, together with high unemployment, causing environmental degradation of many kinds. There is no doubt that economic growth is the only way that the poorest two-thirds of the world's population can eliminate the pollution and environmental degradation that always go hand-in-hand with poverty.[48]

In the United States the obvious desire to gain support for government action wasn't the only reason the advocates of force attempted to focus the blame for pollution on industry rather than on government, where it belonged. According to their preconceptions, industry *had* to be guilty. That was the only conclusion which fit their underlying assumptions that human interests are in opposition and that some people's gains must be at others' expense—assumptions valid for the use of force but not for production and trade. Since industry made profits, these gains were assumed to be at others' expense; government was presumed nonpolluting because nonprofit. Industry, moreover, acted for its own interests—which were assumed to be in opposition to the "public interest," to which selfless politicians were so conspicuously dedicated.

Once again, it is public property which creates situations where men's interests must be in opposition and where selfish pursuit must be at others' expense. Rivers are a case in point. A community gets its water from upstream and deposits its sewage downstream. So there is no way it can benefit from cleaning up its own effluent; the benefits all go to those downstream. Since eliminating its pollution is not in its own interests, each river community has tended to use the river *at the expense* of everyone else further down. The fact that the rivers are public has permitted them to do so.

Until only a few years ago pollution was invariably *accepted* by government at all levels, usually for political reasons. The local governments that were the worst offenders were usually those with the greatest political power, the cities with the most votes, such as New York, Detroit and Philadelphia. In the first 182 years of our history only three cases of water pollution were heard by the U.S. Supreme Court, and all were cases of states suing other states or local governments.[49]

Those who are inclined to blame the sorry state of our waterways on the fragmentation of political power among many local governments and state and federal agencies have only to look at the example of the Soviet Union to realize that centralized political control doesn't solve the problem either. And government's performance at the national level in our own country has certainly been less than inspirational with respect to water resources. For almost its entire history our federal government itself has been a prime polluter and condoned pollution by others, particularly other levels of government. Jonathan H. Adler, Associate Director of Environmental Studies at the Competitive Enterprise Institute, writes:

> Under the Clean Water Act, politically preferred polluters are treated more favorably than others. Municipal polluters face cleanup goals that are often less stringent than those of industrial polluters, and their cleanup schedules are far more lenient. Yet, to the rivers and fish, pollution is pollution.
>
> This problem of unequal treatment is compounded by the prevalence of citizen suit provisions in the Clean Water Act and other environmental laws. Although it may sound good to allow any citizen or citizen group to force the government to enforce pollution laws (and to allow the citizen or group to recoup legal costs), what it means is that special interest groups can effectively determine the enforcement priorities of government agencies. Many of the environmental organizations that engage in citizen suits have an anti-business bias. As a result, private industry is subject to more legal actions than either agricultural activities or governmental facilities, even though both of the latter are greater sources of water pollution. Indeed, between 1984 and 1988, environmentalist citizen suits against private industry were more than six times as common as suits against governmental facilities.[50]

The problem is not which level of government, or which political faction, controls water resources. Rather it is that they are public at all and managed by any government for political advantage instead of being private property, managed for profit. The profit motive would lead to managing the resource to best serve society, in order to gain income, while conserving and if possible enhancing it for its capital value.

Just as the profit motive in a free market would work in favor of a better environment, it is because government can undertake unprofitable projects that it can do so much environmental damage. Consider, for example, the Garrison Diversion Project, a project to irrigate North

Dakota farmland with water from the Missouri River. Its estimated cost of $500 million would amount to $300,000 for each family provided with irrigation. That would be uneconomic enough in itself, but the project will result in *fewer* acres for agriculture: more existing farmland will be taken out of production through flooding and canals than will be brought into production through irrigation. Once again a government enterprise proves to be a net loss for society.

Once again the benefits provided by government to some people are at other people's expense: at the expense of the taxpayers; at the expense of farmers who have lost their farms or seen their sugar beets rot in the ground (because, although the surface of their land is not flooded, government dams have altered the hydraulic gradient of rivers, thereby raising the ground water table); and at the expense of other farmers, whose wells went dry when government ditches cut off their natural underground supply.

In 1974 a Ford Foundation study by 24 economists, engineers, ecologists and lawyers concluded that the benefits of the Garrison project were "substantially less" than the costs. It stated that the project "has no economic justification and can be carried out only at a net loss of economic welfare to the nation."[51]

So far so bad. It gets worse. The economic losses from the project are matched by environmental losses. The U.S. Fish and Wildlife Service, after initially supporting the project, took a closer look. At least one government biologist lost his job because of his views, but eventually his agency branded the Garrison project "a net loser." The agency estimated that 80 percent of the state's National Wildlife Refuge acreage would be "negatively impacted." Many different kinds of environmental damage are being produced. One little known to the general public is described by James Nathan Miller as follows:

> Arid and semi-arid regions have heavy concentrations of salt in their soil. When you irrigate this soil, you can't just sprinkle the water on the land and forget about it. If you do, you will produce a build-up of salty water in the ground that will eventually poison your crops. So irrigation farmers must bury drainage pipes in their fields to flush the salt to the nearest stream. (Garrison will have 2000 miles of such drainage pipes.) *The resulting salt pollution can be serious enough to render a river's water undrinkable.*[52] (Italics added)

This pollution is the result of a government project—the same government that poses as the champion of clean water.

Miller notes that the Garrison project is not exceptionally worthless. "Quite the contrary," he says. "Its significance is that it's an average, run-of-the-mill worthless project, typical of many others now being built in the name of irrigation, flood control and barge transportation."[53]

Because of objections stirred up by the Garrison Project, the government ordered a $1.2 million study of alternatives. This study, which took two years to complete, was released February 23, 1979. It showed that *none* of the six scaled-down alternatives had a favorable cost-benefit ratio. And even though a more modest version was adopted, the cost was now 40 percent higher than the earlier $500 million price tag.

In 1985 the U.S. Secretary of the Interior reduced the irrigation acreage of the Garrison Project to 131,000 acres from 250,000 acres. This trimmed-down version would require an additional $906 million beyond the $213 million already spent.

In 1988 a study released by the Bureau of Reclamation showed the government to be spending $534 million annually to provide cheap irrigation water to Western farms, many of which produce surplus crops that reap federal farm-subsidy payments. The report said farmers in North Dakota supplied by the Garrison Project will be charged $39.78 for water that cost $758.90 an acre to deliver.[54]

On July 29, 1996 the General Accounting Office released a report on 133 irrigation projects in 17 western states. The report said these cost the federal government more than seven dollars for every dollar received from the farmers who use the water.

Government's mismanagement of public waters has not been limited to those inland. The federal government presided over the precipitous decline in New England coastal fishing in the same way it presided over the disappearance of the buffalo. In both cases the government didn't even make a serious attempt to conserve the resource until it had almost disappeared; instead the government gave it away to all takers. With coastal fishing, too, the fact the resource was public stimulated consumption while destroying the economic incentive for production and preservation. Men could profit only from taking fish, or buffalo, not from raising them or conserving them for the future.

Waters beyond the territorial limits are being depleted for the same reason as within them: because they are public. The only difference is that international waters are being depleted by many countries while coastal waters within territorial limits are depleted by only one. But in neither case is there any economic incentive for producing or conserving the oceans' stock. So even if government controls were extended over the oceans, either through world government or by extending national juris- dictions, the only economic incentive would still be for consumption, just as it is in waters already under national control. The oceans have been depleted not because of the absence of government controls but because of the absence of private property.

It's no coincidence that the enormous productivity of aquaculture mentioned in the last chapter is taking place on private property, not in the vast, public oceans. While relatively tiny tracts under private ownership are yielding truly astonishing amounts of trout, catfish, shrimp, clams and other foods, the fertile and immense oceans— covering 137 million square miles—are being depleted. Because they are public. Haddock have virtually vanished from their traditional waters. Cod and hake are not far behind. Sardines are down in the Bay of Biscay and other areas where they were once plentiful. The herring population dropped 90 percent in just ten years.[55]

Cod were so thick off the coast of America when explorer John Cabot arrived in 1497 that his crew caught them in baskets. On March 22, 1994 *The Wall Street Journal* noted:

> The 1993 U.S. cod catch was only about 49 million pounds, according to a federal estimate. That's down 19 percent from 1992, and the lowest since 1973. The catch is expected to decline further, fisheries scientists say. Canada is even worse off: Cod fishing on the Grand Banks of Newfoundland is now banned. Cod has been called "commercially extinct," and more than 30,000 people have lost jobs.

Governments around the world have not only failed to prevent overfishing; they have subsidized it. The United Nations Food and Agri- culture Organization (FAO) estimates that the global fishing fleet costs about $92 billion a year to operate but brings in revenues of only $70 billion. The difference is largely made up by subsidies from govern- ments to fishermen and their boat builders.

A report by the FAO in 1993 said that 13 of the the 17 principal fishing zones in the world are either depleted or in steep decline. An article in *The New York Times* in March 1994 states that "most fishing areas are free-for-all, as anglers try to catch as many fish as possible before a rival does." Thus the "tragedy of the commons" is repeated in the oceans just as it was with Western public range lands.

The Atlantic bluefin tuna may be regarded as extinct for all practical purposes. In the winter of 1991-1992 a single fish was auctioned in Tokyo for $68,503, or $94.65 a pound. In 1994 that species was being sold for $350 per pound in Tokyo restaurants. "The last buffalo hunt is taking place in the oceans," says Carl Safina, a senior scientist at Scully Marine Center on Long Island, N.Y. Commercial and sport fishermen each blame the other—just like the cattle ranchers and sheep farmers of the Old West. "They may both be right," says Michael Sutton of the World Wildlife Fund. "It won't matter. There won't be any tuna for anyone."[56]

It was the invention of agriculture which led to the concept of private property. Before agriculture there was neither the need nor the opportunity to develop private ownership of land. Among the few primitive societies that still subsist by hunting and gathering, the communal approach to property is the rule even today. And their standard of living reflects it. The historical advance of human living standards, the rise of civilization depended on agriculture, and agriculture required the development of property rights. If men were to make the land productive, they had to be assured that the harvest of their labors wouldn't be reaped by others. The concept of public ownership isn't an advanced concept of civilization but a precivilized anachronism. It's a primitive carry-over from some 10,000 years ago, before Jericho, before men first began to live by making the earth productive.

The oceans today are regarded in the same way as the land was before agriculture. Their productive potential is as undeveloped as that of the lands still occupied by primitive tribes who live by hunting and gathering. Men today can obtain wealth from the oceans only on a hunting-and-gathering basis. They roam the oceans as they roamed the land for a million years before Jericho, taking whatever food they can find but doing nothing to produce it. On the seas men are still "takers" rather than "makers" because they failed to develop property rights there as they did with the land. Aquaculture, like agriculture, will not be practical in the oceans until men can be assured that the harvest of their labors will not be reaped by others.

It is discouraging to see so little progress in the establishment of private property rights in the oceans. But it is frightening to witness the popular political trend for making privately-owned land public again, as it was in precivilized times.

PATTERNS OF DEVELOPMENT

It is sometimes argued that private property can't meet the complexities of modern civilization, but the truth is the exact opposite. *Only* through private property can men sort out complex interests and create the intricate patterns of activity that civilization requires.

Civilization is a consequence of human ideas, and private property is the means by which men can peacefully implement their ideas at no one else's expense. To the extent that the prerogatives of private ownership are diminished or distorted, the role of men's minds is reduced. Every attempt to use government power to modify people's behavior in the use of property rests on the faulty premise that force is superior to thinking, that human activities can be "improved" by coercion. The results speak for themselves.

Earlier in this chapter it was noted that government attempts to subsidize the westward expansion of the railroads resulted in a less efficient rail network than a free market would have provided. Without the artificial incentive of free timber lands, or other government benefits, private railroads would have been extended only in accord with the demand for transportation. The government could only provide a less intelligent solution: it could stimulate wasteful overbuilding, or else prevent construction of needed facilities; and it could substitute only inferior locations for the superior ones dictated by economic demand.

Similarly, every other attempt to "direct" the use of private property through government stimulation or controls results in too much of something, too little of it, or puts it in the wrong place. Yet none of these problems occurs without government intervention. In a free economy men tend to employ their property in ways complementary to others because the greatest profits can be obtained from doing so—just as private railroad companies could obtain the greatest market profits from the best locations for rail lines. As Adam Smith explained two hundred years ago, every individual seeks to employ his capital for his own advantage, but this pursuit "naturally, or rather necessarily leads him to prefer that employment which is most advantageous to society."[57] And because men's interests aren't naturally in opposition, many harmonious consequences are produced incidentally which couldn't be foreseen or provided for by central authority. The following story illustrates the point perhaps better than anything else could.

After Vasily Isaev, deputy mayor of Moscow, visited Houston, Texas, he commented that it had an "impressive" city plan in contrast to other American cities where development appeared to be "carried out with the plans of private firms rather than the cities."[58] But Houston has no plan at all; it is one of the few cities without one in the entire country. It is also the nation's largest city without a zoning ordinance. To a stranger, the best example of uncontrolled private development, the largest unplanned, unzoned city in the United States, appeared more orderly than the planned and regulated American cities.

Houston is a perfect example of Adam Smith's contention that "by pursuing his own interests [a man] frequently promotes that of society more effectually than when he really intends to promote it."[59] In seeking only his own selfish gain, he is led as if by an "invisible hand" to advance society in ways which he does not intend or understand.

Chapter Twelve
SEND THE BILL TO THE·VICTIMS

An army produces nothing. It only consumes. It exists entirely on the productivity of others, either because they support the army or because they fall victims to it. In America these two sources are one and the same for the army of bureaucrats and politicians. The American people are supporting the army which is plundering them. They are financing the invasion against themselves.

Defense is a cost which productive people are, or should be, willing to pay, as they would insurance, in order to protect themselves against the danger of far greater loss. The invader's aim is the opposite. It is to seize a gain rather than to prevent a loss. The cost of an offensive army is borne in the hope of capturing far greater worth. Such a gain, of course, can only be other people's loss, which it is the purpose of their defense to prevent.

The army of bureaucrats and politicians is large and growing for two reasons. The first is the popular misconception that fellow citizens, free men functioning under liberty, are enemies against whom this large standing army must be kept to protect the individual. The second, often disguised under the first, is the popular desire to use this army for offensive purposes rather than defensive ones: to attempt to *gain* something through regulations, restrictions or government programs, which *always* mean losses for other people.

The army of bureaucrats and politicians doesn't produce values any more than a military army does. The administration of government regulations and restrictions rests on the threat of physical force, as the definition of the word "enforcement" tells us. Bureaucrats can no more create economic worth by threatening force than an army can by actualizing it.

The explosion in government size came late in our history. A century and a quarter after Americans obtained their independence the cost of all government—federal, state and local—amounted to only $20 a year per person. The breakdown was as follows: six dollars at the federal level, two at the state, and twelve at the local level. In 1995 governments at all levels in the United States spent more than was on deposit in all the banks in the nation.

It took 186 years for the federal budget to reach $100 billion. It then took only nine years to reach $200 billion, another four to reach

$300 billion, and only two more to exceed $400 billion. We then passed six of these hundred-billion-dollar landmarks in the next ten years; the federal budget reached the trillion dollar level for the first time in 1987. In 1994 it was over $1.5 trillion.

The federal government is spending at the rate of $2.8 million per minute. The interest alone on the money it borrows costs $378,000 per minute. The annual cost of just the interest paid by the federal government is now greater than the entire federal budget of only 20 years ago. By 1992, 62 cents of every dollar in personal income tax was going for interest on the national debt; and at the current rate of growth, interest on the debt will equal all personal income taxes by the year 2004.

The head of the General Accounting Office has stated that the waste in the federal government totals $180 billion annually. This is equal to 37.6 percent of all personal income taxes paid to the federal government in 1992. Add this to the 62 percent of personal income tax that goes for payment of interest on the debt, and 99.6 percent of all personal federal income tax may be viewed as going for waste and interest on past waste.

Although government borrowing creates an enormous financial burden for the future, Americans have also been shouldering an increased burden in the present through rising taxes. Between 1970 and 1981 federal income taxes for individuals rose more than 300 percent, personal tax payments to the states and localities rose 380 percent, and property taxes doubled. Federal taxes were increased four times in the years 1982 to 1989, and they were raised again in 1990, 1991, and 1993. State and local governments increased taxes by $10.3 billion in 1991, and the states hiked taxes by another $15 billion in 1992.

State payrolls continue to grow. In the period 1988-93 forty-two of our fifty states showed public sector employment growing faster than private sector jobs.

By 1993 there were more government employees in the United States than there were people working in manufacturing. According to the Bureau of Labor Statistics, there were 18.7 million government employees and only 18.1 million workers in manufacturing. And government employees are paid more. A report by the American Legislative Exchange Council, an organization of state legislators, says that from 1980 to 1990 public-employee pay increased six times faster than private pay.

Government spending is, of course, at its worst at the federal level. Despite its past profligacy, our federal government is committed to even greater spending in the future. The National Taxpayers Union calculates that federal obligations total more than twice the gross national product of every country on earth. The numerous federal tax increases have been far outstripped by increases in federal spending.

The financial condition of the United States is even worse than it appears, because federal bookkeeping doesn't conform to accepted accounting standards. In 1974 one of the nation's most prestigious accounting firms, Arthur Andersen and Company, found that the government's true deficit was *thirty times* the figure reported by the government. In 1984 the reported national debt was $2.2 trillion; by the end of 1995 that had more than doubled, to over $4.8 trillion, with each person's share exceeding $18,300.

But the official national debt figure doesn't include the huge unfunded liabilities of the Social Security System, Medicare, and military and civil service pensions. Together these total an additional $14.4 trillion. Nor does the official national debt figure include anything for certain contingent liabilities, such as federal deposit insurance, and guarantees of private pensions and stockholders' brokerage accounts. The savings and loan crisis is an example of a contingent liability that came due.

THE CHAIN OF LOSSES

Earlier chapters showed how economic gains lead to others. Profits and technological advances become the base for further progress. They also create a variety of unintended secondary benefits for other people. The economic losses inflicted by government intervention have the opposite effect. They lead to even greater losses through greater government activity—more laws, more controls, more bureaucrats to "correct" the problems—while creating a variety of unintended secondary losses throughout society.

As the army of nonproductive people increases, the productive population which must support them is reduced. Costs are larger, but there are fewer people to pay them. And because the government takes an increased share of earnings, the producers find it more and more difficult to raise their productivity. There is simply less money available for reinvestment in wealth-producing enterprises.

But that is only the beginning of the chain of losses precipitated by more government. The increased regulations restrict the scope of action for generating new wealth.

In addition there is a further loss in the productive work force, because workers are shifted *within* industry from productive tasks to nonproductive ones, to reading regulations, filling out forms, and making required reports. These tasks consume capital as well as reduce the number of productive workers. So those remaining must produce even more to cover these costs, and even less capital is available for employment in productive operations.

The chain of losses continues. There are financial costs, direct and indirect, but there are also human costs and even environmental ones. Here are some specific examples of the different costs.

THE COSTS OF COMPLIANCE

Between 1986 and 1992 Congress enacted 10 major pieces of legislation to regulate business, including, in 1990 alone, the Clean Air Act, the Americans with Disabilities Act, and the Nutrition Labeling and Education Act. These will greatly increase the costs to Americans in future years as various provisions are scheduled to take effect and the full cost of the required spending will be realized. But even before this latest regulatory splurge, the costs were already staggering.

The ten billion sheets of paper Washington bureaucrats handle every year would fill Yankee Stadium 51 times over. According to the Grace Commission, the federal bureaucracy, which shuffles all this paperwork, occupies 2.61 billion square feet of office space. That is equivalent to all the office space in our ten largest cities multiplied by four.

In 1995, federal statutes and rules ran to 100 million words. It would take eight years just to read them.

According to the Tax Foundation, the annual paperwork required by the tax laws alone consumed 5.4 billion hours of private individuals and corporations in 1994. That's the equivalent of 2,596,152 people working 40 hours a week for a year without vacations. Just to fill out approximately 480 different tax forms. This vast human effort produces no wealth or progress. In fact, it preempts people from using that time and energy for productive enterprises.

For most American corporations, the cost of filling out their federal income tax forms is greater than the taxes that they pay. According to Arthur Hall, an economist with the Tax Foundation, ninety percent of U.S. corporations (those with assets of less than $1 million), incur compliance costs of 390 percent of the taxes they pay. In other words, for every $100 the government receives in taxes, it costs those small companies $390 dollars to fill out the forms. For the Fortune 500 companies the cost of income tax compliance runs over a billion dollars annually, or an average of $2.11 million per company. The total annual cost of tax compliance for all businesses and individuals is $192 billion. That's just for the costs of the paperwork, not for the actual taxes. Businesses must function as record keepers and tax collectors for the IRS, sending more than a billion reports annually to the agency—with copies to the taxpayers by first class mail.

Then there are environmental forms and other regulatory compliance costs. In an article published in 1995, Dr. Murray Weidenbaum and Representative David McIntosh, Chairman of the House Subcommittee on Regulatory Affairs, cited a figure of 6.5 billion hours for filling out these government forms and keeping required records for the year 1991.[1]

Standard Oil of Indiana has about 100 employees working full-time just to handle the administrative load created by government regulations. The information it has had to supply to just one federal agency, the energy department, occupies more than 636 miles of computer tape. Every year the company files about 24,000 pages of federal reports and 225,000 pages of supplementary data. The company also finds it necessary to make 27,000 phone calls a year to Washington, twenty times the number it made before there were federal energy regulations.

Exxon filed one mammoth report in 1974 that ran 475,000 pages. It was for the Federal Energy Administration. But there are 44 other federal agencies with which Exxon must file 379 reports at frequencies from once a week to once a year. Then there are 465 other reports that the company must submit regularly to state agencies. The cost to the American petroleum industry of just complying with government reporting requirements would finance the drilling of six hundred oil wells annually.

The Federal Power Commission (FPC) for years required natural gas producers to fill out a 428-page form in quadruplicate. The agency claimed it needed the information to regulate the price of natural gas. One company estimated it took 17,000 accountant hours to gather the required information and complete the form.

But the FPC form, formidable as it is, is dwarfed by an application that Eli Lilly and Company submitted to the Food and Drug Administration. It ran 120,000 pages and weighed over a ton. The company is forced to spend more time on government paperwork than it is able to spend on research for cancer and heart disease combined. The paperwork also adds fifty cents to the price of every prescription filled with the company's medicine.

The same company also makes weed killers, for which it must obtain approval of the Environmental Protection Agency (EPA). At a hearing before the Commission on Federal Paperwork, Richard Wood, chairman of the board of Eli Lilly and Company, displayed a 153-page computer-printed index of submittals to the EPA. Each *entry* on each of the 153 pages represented a separate document of from three to 3000 pages in length.

Until the last days of 1995, trucking companies were still submitting 16,000 pages of rate tariffs to the Interstate Commerce Commission *every working day*. These were being stacked floor to ceiling in 14 corridors of the ICC building, the Tariff Examination Room and the Cancelled Tariff Library. All this regulatory paperwork served no possible function since the deregulation of the trucking industry fourteen years earlier. Nevertheless, trucking companies kept submitting the papers because no one told them to stop and they were afraid of being found guilty of some violation if they didn't continue. And even though it admitted it had no use for these papers, the ICC continued to collect them because Congress hadn't repealed the Interstate Commerce Act. It finally did so at the end of December 1995.

A study by the Brookings Institution estimated the cost of just the 1970 Clean Air Act and the 1972 Water Pollution Control Act at perhaps $500 billion over the first ten years. That may have been conservative. In 1994 EPA said that the clean water act alone was costing Americans $60 billion per year. A 1995 survey by the U. S. Conference of Mayors said that full compliance with the clean water act would cost as much as $99 billion per year.

The 1970 Clean Air Act resulted in the American steel industry spending one quarter of its capital investment over the next decade just for pollution control equipment. The environmental laws of the 1970s added $18 to $20 per ton to the price of American steel, $250 per ton to the price of copper, and 15 to 20 cents per gallon to the price of gasoline. The higher costs are still reflected in the prices we pay today as the costs of maintaining compliance with the regulations continue—and additional regulations have added to these costs. In 1992 Robert Stempel, head of General Motors, stated that the 1990 Clean Air Act would consume 25 to 28 percent of GM's capital investment budget. The acid-rain provisions of that act add at least another $5 per ton to the price of steel and $80 per ton to the price of aluminum. Electricity has also become more expensive for the consumer. Ohioans pay $898 million more annually; Georgians, $396 million more; and Virginians, an extra $417 million.

In 1990 the EPA itself estimated that its pollution-control regulations were costing Americans $115 billion annually. The agency estimated the cost of compliance during the first twenty years of its existence, 1970 to 1990, at $1.4 *trillion*. It estimated compliance during the next decade will cost an additional $1.6 trillion—not counting the cost of the 1990 Clean Air Act. The 1970 Clean Air Act was 50 pages; the 1990 act was 1,110 pages.

The 1990 Clean Air Act required oil companies to sell a cleaner-burning gasoline by 1995 than they knew how to make. Aside from the enormous research costs of trying to find such a gasoline, as of 1995 the refiners had spent $5 billion just for "upgrading existing facilities and building new ones to make and store the gasoline. They reconfigured pipeline shipping and cleaned out holding tanks to meet the stringent requirements calling for the reformulated fuel to be untainted by conventional gasoline."[2]

Still another cost was the estimated 6000 high-sulfur coal-mining jobs that were lost by 1995 as coal-fired utilities made their first round of emission cuts required by the 1990 legislation. Say goodbye to another 9000 high-sulfur mining jobs by the year 2000.

The total loss of jobs will be much higher than those in just the coal mining industry. S. Fred Singer, professor of environmental science at the University of Virginia, former EPA official, advisor to the Energy Department, and chief scientist of the U.S. Transportation Department, said the 1990 Clean Air Act would

> raise the cost of gasoline, cars, electricity and food. And some 200,000 people will be thrown out of work—coal miners, auto workers, and employees in small businesses that cannot cope with the regulations. But never mind! We'll get federal money to retrain these people. The country will surely need more lawyers and lots of environmental consultants who can figure out what the Clean Air regulations mean.[3]

In fact, the EPA itself says that the Clean Air Act requirements will create 20,000 to 40,000 jobs by the end of the decade, just the kind of jobs Dr. Singer describes. So 20,000 to 40,000 jobs will be *misallocated* from productive work to bureaucratic paperwork and other

uneconomic tasks that drain society. This is already happening. For
example, Counterpoint Publishing Inc., of Cambridge, Mass., describes
itself as "a company whose only reason for being is to help people
handle the sheer volume of regulations issued by the federal government."[4] Many people are kept (artificially or uneconomically) busy in
this new "industry" because "as many as 2,000 to 4,000 regulations will
change in any two-month period,"[5] says Brian Gurnham, president of
ERM-Computer Services Inc. His company sells optical-disk updates
every two months on federal and state environmental regulations.

The 1990 Clean Air Act means about 150,000 small businesses
have to obtain clean air permits, says Dr. Murray Weidenbaum.

> Just to obtain one set of the permits will force a small
> company to spend between $10,000 and $15,000 to collect the
> data and do the paper work. The monitoring devices needed to
> track emission rates will cost an additional $10,000 to $50,000.[6]

That's just for the Clean Air Act. Then there's the 1990 Pollution
Prevention Act, which will require each manufacturing facility with 11 or
more employees to report on how it uses any of 300 different chemicals.

In 1992 a reporter for *The Wall Street Journal* was shown a picture
of an employee of the Bernhardt Furniture Co., Lenoir, N.C., standing
beside a stack of regulations just for the disposal of cleaning rags. The
employee is 6 feet 2 inches tall, and the stack is slightly taller than he is.
Mr. Alex Bernhardt, president of the company, says it "could easily
spend twice as much on (environmental) compliance in the next five
years as on research and development and new machinery and equipment"[7] combined.

Mereco Technologies Group Inc. must compile information on
800 chemical products to satisfy state and federal rules. The company
has only 14 employees. It had to hire three full-time chemists just to
prepare the company for compliance.

It's no trick to create jobs. What really matters is creating jobs that
produce wealth rather than drain it. The Soviet Union and other socialist/
communist countries used to boast that they had no unemployment, but
their economies nevertheless spiraled downward until they collapsed.
Their government-created jobs didn't create wealth; they consumed it.
Only the private sector can create jobs that aren't net losers to society.

The Americans with Disabilities Act was an attempt to provide
benefits to an unfortunate minority at others' expense, and the expense

is turning out to be horrendously larger than previously thought. Congress put the cost of compliance at $2 billion per year, but the cost will be at least $100 billion over the next five years, according to Robert Genetski, a Chicago consultant.[8] He says it will cost $45 billion just to bring the nation's office buildings into compliance. The American Hospital Association says it will cost $20 billion to bring hospitals into compliance. Tens of billions more will have to be spent for equipping trains, buses, restaurants, rental cars, public facilities, and for legal and administrative expenses.

The overall cost of regulation is not only astronomical but continues to climb despite the few examples of deregulation. Thomas Hopkins, an economics professor at Rochester Institute of Technology estimated that the regulatory costs for all the nation's businesses in 1988 were $450 billion. His estimate for 1992 was $564 billion. This agrees closely with a 1992 estimate by David Littman, senior economist at Manufacturers National Bank in Detroit, of a gross annual cost of $562 billion for federal regulation.[9] That's twice the cost of the defense budget and far larger than the losses in the savings and loan debacle, the largest financial disaster in the history of the world. And the saving and loan debacle was a one-time event while the regulatory costs are incurred every year. Still, the cost of regulation continues to escalate. According to the General Accounting Office, it topped $647 billion in 1994.

Most people have difficulty grasping the magnitude of government costs because the numbers are so large. For people whose income is measured in thousands of dollars per year, figures in millions are vaguely perceived as immense. Figures in billions are incomprehensible. Here are two comparisons which may improve one's perspective of these large numbers. If a million one-dollar bills were stacked up, they would be about as high as a 57-story building; but if the stack were to contain a billion dollars, it would reach 107 *miles* into the sky. If a person were to spend $1000 per day, he could spend a million dollars in less than three years; but to spend a billion dollars at the same rate would require 2739 years.

If we use the GAO's figure of $647 billion given earlier as the annual cost of federal regulation and divide by the number of households in the U.S., we arrive at $6,712 per household. That's just for the *direct* costs of regulation. If one includes the *indirect* costs, the figure is much higher. Well-known economist William J. Laffer III says the total cost of government regulation for Americans is a minimum of $10,922 annually per household and may be as high as $20,376.

INCREASING CONSUMER COSTS

The regulatory costs of the paperwork, administration, and such items as pollution control equipment are, of course, passed on to the consumer. But these aren't the only ways in which prices are raised. Sometimes, the very *intent* of regulation is to raise prices of consumer products! In this the government runs completely opposite to the history of human progress.

Take food, for example. The inventions of agriculture, the plow, the reaper, the tractor have all made food more plentiful and cheaper. Mass production in processing, improvements in storage and transportation, and efficiencies in marketing have all increased the availability of food and also lowered costs.

Government has been working in the opposite direction. It has been trying to make food scarcer and more expensive. For example, federal farm price support programs have been used to assure artificially high prices, and the government has required and even financed the destruction of agricultural products in order to make them scarcer. The government has also paid farmers for not growing crops in order to make them less plentiful and higher priced.

Federal intervention in agriculture began with Franklin Roosevelt's "New Deal." During the Great Depression the government paid farmers to destroy crops and animals rather than sell them to the public at low prices. The administration promoted the burning of potatoes, the wasteful killing of hogs, and the plowing under of food crops and cotton. It also bought farm products and stored them, at additional cost, to keep the public from getting them at low prices. Meanwhile consumers were paying higher prices for the same commodities to be imported. By 1933 the federal programs in wheat and cotton alone had cost $300 million. Twenty years later the government owned more than $5 billion worth of agricultural commodities, on which the storage costs alone were averaging one-half million dollars a day.

Over the years government farm programs have changed, but they still run counter to the economic trend of 10,000 years of progress. They still attempt to make foods artificially expensive and scarcer. Today, for example, federal law allows price-fixing and strict limits on competition in the production and sale of many agricultural items, mainly dairy products, nuts, fruits and vegetables. Agricultural co-ops enjoy a privileged status under the law and use what are known as "marketing orders" from the government to control the growing of these commodities, their flow to market, and often their prices. The result is that consumers are forced to pay much higher prices for these agricultural commodities. The loss isn't only financial.

Food is lost, too. Fourteen thousand tons of cherries were left to rot in orchards in 1972 because of a marketing order intended to keep prices up. In that same year Ocean Spray, a co-op which controls 85 percent of the nation's cranberry market, reported that 600,896 barrels of cranberries that were held off market went to waste. A federal marketing order was also responsible for the intentional destruction of about one-quarter of California's cling peach crop and the pulling up of 8,600 acres of peach trees in 1970. These kinds of losses have been occurring year after year for decades. In 1989 James Bovard, an analyst for the Cato Institute, wrote:

> Each year, marketing orders from the Agriculture Department force farmers to abandon or squander roughly 500 million lemons, 1 billion oranges, 100 million pounds of raisins, 70 million pounds of almonds and 7 million pounds of filberts. The main purpose of this federally mandated waste is to cause an artificial shortage of certain fruits and nuts and drive up prices.[10]

In 1992 Bovard wrote:

> It is a federal crime for California farmers to sell nectarines less than 2 and 3/8 inches in diameter and peaches less than 2 and 7/16 inches in diameter.[11]

When a farmer was found selling smaller fruit to inner-city buyers in Los Angeles, he was presented with a federal injunction and the threat of a $100 fine per box of fruit. Bovard continues:

> Federal regulators apparently feared that allowing poor blacks to pay lower prices for small fruit would make it more difficult for the Agriculture Department to force the rich to pay higher prices for large fruit.[12]

A 1988 Agriculture Department study estimated that consumers and taxpayers would save $1.4 billion annually if restrictions on reconstituted milk were removed. Milk is 87 percent water. Removing the water would lower transportation costs and allow low-cost production to be shipped to high-cost areas and reconstituted. But the government wants to protect high-cost areas from low-priced competition—at the expense of the consumer.

By similar protectionist "logic," the government restricts imports of dairy products to 2 percent of domestic production. So consumers are forced to buy American milk, cheese and butter at prices substantially above world prices. According to Bovard, "Thanks to import barriers and marketing order restrictions, dairy prices have been between 30 and 200 percent higher than they might otherwise have been."[13] In 1989 Rod Leonard of the Community Nutrition Institute in Washington said that federal policies add $6 to $7 billion per year to the cost of dairy products for American consumers. Annual subsidies for each American diary cow exceed the per capita income for half the population of the world.

U.S. domestic sugar prices are almost double the price on the world market. In recent years the price discrepancy has at times been even greater. The federal government, however, limits sugar imports, preventing consumers from getting this low-priced sugar in order to "protect" the high U.S. price. According to the U.S. Commerce Department, this protectionism costs Americans $3 billion a year for this one commodity.

The price of U.S. peanuts is also double the world price. For decades the federal government has prevented its citizens from buying cheaper foreign peanuts by import restrictions that, until 1995, limited the amount coming into this country to about two peanuts per year for each citizen. That restriction was eased in the name of "free trade" by the Clinton Administration's General Agreement on Tariffs and Trade (GATT)—but was replaced by a 155 percent tariff on peanut butter imports! That's hardly a victory for free trade.

An Agriculture Department study of ten federal farm programs showed that they resulted in $12.1 billion in higher prices to consumers in 1987. Yet the government would take no steps to end these uneconomic programs.

In 1992 a study by the Organization for Economic Cooperation and Development estimated that federal farm programs cost Americans an extra $80 billion per year in agricultural subsidies and higher food prices. Of course, the argument is always made that these government programs benefit the farmers. These programs are just another means by which government attempts to benefit some people at other people's expense, just like our earlier examples in the chapters on taxation and regulation. And just as in those earlier examples, the costs always exceed the benefits. In a study published by Cambridge University Press in 1992 two Australian economists, Rod Tyers and Kym Anderson, show that every dollar that federal farm programs put in the pockets of U.S. farmers costs the U.S. taxpayers and consumers $1.26. The more such programs attempt to benefit a particular industry or segment of the economy, the worse off we are as a nation.

Agriculture isn't the only industry in which government protectionism adds to consumer costs. Federal restrictions add $2,500 to the average cost of a Japanese auto and $7 billion to steel costs every year, according to the Center for the Study of American Business. The Council of Economic Advisors estimates that trade restrictions add 50 percent to the cost of imported clothing for American consumers. In 1993 the International Trade Commission estimated that tariffs and quotas on apparel and textiles cost Americans $15.85 billion annually.

In December 1994 Congress approved a new international trade agreement popularly known as GATT. While the Clinton Administration trumpeted this as a triumph for free trade, *U.S. News & World Report* called the intricate 22,000-page agreement "a tortuous road to freer trade pockmarked with protectionist potholes"—some of which "could outlast portions of the new road itself." The magazine said:

> The new trade pact takes aim at the barriers, committing rich countries to dismantle quotas and convert them to tariffs by 2005, and then to negotiate these tariffs downward. Yet underlying this long-term commitment is a rich tapestry of protection. In fact, the countries that signed the trade accord put off dismantling most of their quotas until 2004; that means that almost half of all clothing imported into the United States will still be brought in under costly quotas for 10 more years. But 2004 now looms as an especially painful day of reckoning for rich countries—and some analysts worry that domestic apparel manufacturers will lobby to push back the deadline even further as it approaches. Moreover, under the deal, wealthy nations can actually impose new quotas if imports surge unexpectedly over the next 10 years. And even the agreement's tariff cuts fall short of freeing up trade. When all the scheduled cuts are completed, U.S. consumers still will pay an average of 18 percent on clothing imports and more than 15 percent on imported textiles like wool.[14]

James Bovard on the same subject:

Clinton administration policy makers have finagled numbers and exploited loopholes so that the U.S. government will continue protecting the domestic textile industry far longer than most experts expected at the time the GATT agreement was signed. This will mean that American consumers will pay tens of billions of dollars in higher clothing prices in the coming years than they would have paid.[15]

Higher taxes in the United States have also been making food and everything else more expensive. They are an additional cost which must be passed along in higher prices for the products. According to the Tax Foundation Inc., there are 151 different taxes built into the price of a loaf of bread. In Indiana, the state in which the count was taken, the grocer paid four federal taxes and the baker eight. The grocer and the baker also paid 15 state taxes. The mill which supplied the flour paid seven federal and eight state taxes. The railroad carrying the flour paid five federal taxes and state taxes in every state through which the product was transported. Similarly, the companies supplying sugar, salt, milk, shortening, milk solids and yeast and the railroads carrying these items paid dozens of other taxes.

The same study revealed that there are 100 taxes on an egg and no less than 600 on a house. The increase in these hidden taxes, which the customer pays indirectly, has contributed to the rising cost of everything the consumers buy.

An article in *The Freeman* in October 1994 explained the costs and regulations governing a lemonade stand in Boston:

Opening a stand requires permission from five different government entities. Licenses and permits for a lemonade stand cost $335. Fifty-five dollars covers the cost of a city Hawkers' and Peddlers' license from the Division of Standards. A mobile food permit from the Health Division runs $100, while registering a business with the City Clerk costs $30. For $15 a square foot the Department of Public Works will issue a permit to sell on public sidewalks. Furthermore, Boston requires lemonade stand operators to carry $500,000 liability insurance policies. What half-million dollar damage a lemonade stand can inflict, I cannot fathom....

The old-fashioned lemonade stand must comply with dozens of ordinances. For example, 105 CMR 590-004(A)5 requires sugar to be in its original container identifying it by common name and 590.009 grants the Board of Health jurisdiction of the length of employees' fingernails. If the lemonade is made in a residential kitchen, only immediate family members residing in the household may prepare it for retail sale (590.028F), and washing machines and dryers located in the kitchen may not be in operation while the lemons are squeezed (590.028G (15). At least once a day, food pushcarts must report to a fixed food establishment (such as a restaurant) for supplies, cleaning, and servicing (590.029(1)).

THE COST OF DELAYS

The delays imposed by government create another category of losses. For example, the "Big John" hopper cars mentioned in Chapter Five weren't approved by the ICC for two years. So for two years shippers had to pay the higher prices connected with the older cars. When Laker Airways proposed to cut transatlantic air fares by more than 50 percent, the CAB delayed six years before approving the request. So there were six years of unnecessarily high costs for air travelers.

For every bit of production and trade which is made more expensive and more difficult, there are many more which are never begun. It's impossible to calculate the losses from business not even attempted because of the specter of government interference, but just the losses from attempts which had to be abandoned are enormous. For example, in 1975 Dow Chemical abandoned plans for a $500 million petrochemical complex near San Francisco. After two years of effort and $10 million in costs, the company had been able to obtain only four of the required 65 permits. Yet a senior air district official described the Dow project as "a very clean industrial plant" and noted, "I'm not sure *anything* can be built there under our rules."[16]

Five years were consumed by the environmental review of the proposed Kaiparowits generating plant in Utah. By then, 1976, the cost of the plant had ballooned to $3.5 billion from $500 million even though the plant was to be only half the original size. Still needing 220 permits from 42 federal, state and local agencies, the utility companies abandoned the project.

When the West End Radio Company in Tracy, California, routinely petitioned the Federal Communications Commission (FCC) for a station license, no one could have imagined how long it would have to wait. Thirty years later it was still waiting. In all that time the FCC said it wasn't able to reach a decision despite an enormous file on the application. Another company, Olympic Broadcasting in

Carmichael, California, also had to wait three decades for the FCC to process it's license application.

In April 1975 the Federal Power Commission dismissed an application to build a hydroelectric plant in the Pacific Northwest. The matter had been before the commission for 19 years.

Thirteen years after the Union Pacific Railroad requested permission from the ICC to acquire the Rock Island Line, the commission declared in favor of giving the railroads essentially what they asked for in the first place. But by then the Union Pacific didn't really want the merger any more. The Rock Island Line, which had been marginally profitable when the proceedings started, had been forced to operate for so many years without the efficiencies of the proposed merger that it had gone bankrupt. And years of operating at a deficit, when there was insufficient money for maintenance, left the line so debilitated that three-quarters of a billion dollars would be required to put it back in shape.

On March 2, 1994 U.S. Labor Secretary Robert Reich ruled on one of the largest discrimination cases submitted under contract compliance laws. The case had been pending for 17 years through the administration of six labor secretaries. It alleged gender discrimination by Honeywell Inc. against about 100 women beginning 22 years earlier. Of course, the government's decision doesn't necessarily end the case since Honeywell announced it may appeal. Secretary Reich said only about half of the 100 longest-pending cases in his department have been disposed of and three are older than the Honeywell case.

The government's longest-running lawsuit against a corporation was a suit by the National Labor Relations Board against Milliken & Co. It consumed 24 years.

When the Federal Trade Commission failed conspicuously to prove its charge of a "shared monopoly" of the breakfast cereal market by Kellogg's, General Mills and General Foods, it finally dropped the case— after spending eleven years and millions of dollars of taxpayer money.

In 1996 75-year-old Eugene Simons finally received two leases from the Bureau of Land Management to mine on 5,000 acres of federal land in Sweetwater County, Wyoming. He had applied for the leases 29 years earlier. He had met all the requirements back then, and, in fact, the agency had approved his leases on paper. But agency bureaucrats refused to give him the actual leases for the next 29 years. Instead they stalled, appealed, reviewed, scheduled hearings, canceled hearings, fabricated regulations, negotiated, demanded economic studies, demanded more studies, demanded more time, and finally decided Mr. Simons needed a permit from another federal agency (the Forest Service). "I cannot see how we can legally and ethically change the rules in the middle of the game," wrote one district supervisor. "Inaction by the BLM is entirely responsible for this fiasco. I will not participate in a bastard project."[17] Mr. Tom Sansonetti, a former top lawyer at the Interior Department (which includes the BLM) said, "Cases like Gene Simons' are just not that unusual. There are dozens of people spread all throughout New Mexico, Utah, Idaho and Montana in similar situations."[18]

The delays of lengthy government hearings and reviews increase financial losses in the form of legal fees and related costs. For the Southern Railway in the case of the "Big John" hopper cars, these costs amounted to $2 million. In the Rock Island merger case the cost of a transcript alone, at sixty cents per page, amounted to $29,000. About one-half million dollars is believed to have been spent in this way by the railroads involved, just for records of the case. Rock Island paid an additional $1.3 million in legal fees. With the legal fees of Union Pacific and various other railroads which became involved, plus an assortment of related expenses, the total cost of the attempted merger has been estimated at $137 million.

Delays and mounting costs are intrinsic to the system of government regulation. The regulators have nothing to gain from prompt action and everything to lose by it. Any benefits from their decisions will go to the industries, not to themselves. But an incorrect decision will bring criticism upon themselves. The regulator may be reprimanded and his chance for advancement diminished. The agency may even have its budget cut or be swallowed up by another agency through reorganization. The only incentive, therefore, is to avoid error; there are no rewards for constructive action or promptness.

The best way to avoid error is to avoid decisions. The next best course is to have as much data on hand as possible in order to minimize the possibility of error if a decision must be made. So the regulatory bureaucracies tend to put off decisions and to accumulate data. In the same way that these agencies have nothing to gain from their decisions, they likewise have nothing to lose from the delays. Nor are they the ones who pay the expense of gathering the data they request. These losses are borne by the regulatory victims.

THE COST OF MISTAKES

The bureaucrats don't pay the cost of their mistakes any more than they pay the costs of their delays or indecisions. These are simply another category of losses inflicted on the American people. An individual or a company may be right and the government wrong, but the cost of proving one's innocence may well be greater than the penalty for being guilty. The sheer injustice of the system is absurd.

When the government charged three salt companies, Morton, International and Diamond Crystal, with price-fixing, the maximum fines, if they were found guilty, would have been $150,000. But they were not found guilty. Two and one-half years later a jury found them innocent. However, the cost of defending themselves, of legal fees and assembling the data for their case, came to $775,000.

Celanese Corporation has admitted spending $100,000 in legal fees to prove its innocence in just two affirmative action cases. Sources close to the cases have estimated that the total cost to the company was closer to $300,000.

Nor are big companies the only ones placed in this predicament. When an OSHA inspector arrived at Blackie's Boatyard in Newport Beach, California, the company had only six employees. One of them was working in a boat tied to the pier. The inspector asked, "What would happen if he fell in the water?" The owner of the boatyard, Blackie Gadarian, replied, "He would stand up. The water's only three feet deep all along the pier."[19] Nevertheless, Gadarian was notified that he had violated the OSHA ladder regulation, Section 1501.84 (c) (4), and was subject to a fine of up to $1000.

He asked to see the rule and a month later received a 248-page document. He could find nothing in it relevant to his alleged violation. A request for clarification brought a 48-page supplement. It said only that there had to be a ladder in the vicinity of a boat repair dock.

Since Gadarian already had four ladders near his pier, he refused to pay the fine, which OSHA had set at only fifteen dollars. Certainly it would have been far easier and cheaper to pay the small fine, but he wanted to prove his innocence. So he argued his case against a battery of government lawyers before a federal hearing examiner and various other officials. It was a four-hour ordeal, but he won.

While this last case was a small one, it is illustrative of how government regulations lead to a whole series of losses. First, a great deal of money was wasted by the government in employing people to write absolutely senseless regulations and sending inspectors around to enforce them. Then a productive worker had to take time away from his work to familiarize himself with a 248-page regulation and a 48-page supplement. Then he was faced with a direct financial loss in the form of a fine or the greater loss of still more time to prove his innocence. Compliance with the inspector's demand would have also meant additional financial loss, the expenditure for a ladder installation which no one would have used. Finally, contesting the fine pointed out the existence of a host of other nonproductive people on the public payroll, namely, the government lawyers, hearing examiner and other officials, whom Gadarian and the rest of the productive workers are supporting.

THE HUMAN COST

Still another loss from government intervention is one that can't be measured in dollars and cents. It is a cost that is paid in human suffering, in physical pain and even death. It results from government delaying the use of new medicines, inhibiting or precluding their development, or compelling the use of products more dangerous than others available. In other cases government has advocated products or sponsored medicines which turned out to be more hazardous than the dangers they were supposed to prevent.

The case of nitrazepam has already been noted in Chapter Five. The anti-asthma drug beclomethasome dipropionate is a similar example. For years it couldn't be used in this country even though literally millions of doses had been used in foreign countries without any adverse effects. Meanwhile, the drugs being used in this country for the same purpose produced all sorts of bad side effects, including facial disfigurations.

The FDA's commissioner bragged in 1981 that his agency's approval of beta blocker drugs would save 17,000 lives per year. But by the same token, the same number of people must have needlessly died every year during the seven years it took FDA to grant that approval. Thus the FDA was responsible for well over 100,000 deaths from just the delays of this one administrative action.

Similarly, 3,500 kidney cancer patients died because of the FDA's delays in approving Interleukin 2. Fatal heart attacks killed 150,000 people waiting for the FDA to approve TPA, which dissolves blood clots. Furthermore, when research conducted by the National Institutes of Health found that a change in dosing strategy of TPA improved the survival rate of heart-attack patients, the FDA prevented this information from being disseminated.

> The new dosage regimen [for TPA] was deemed an off-label use and the drug's developer was barred by the FDA from telling doctors and patients about the new approach. In the process, Dr. Kessler's policies endangered thousands of heart patients. Indeed, several studies have shown that the absence of timely information on appropriate—and usually off-label—uses of drugs is implicated in 15 % to 30 % of the drug-related deaths or life-threatening drug reactions in hospitals.[20]

As with the other regulatory agencies, the FDA has nothing to gain from approving progress in the field which it regulates. If a new drug turns out to be a boon to mankind, it will bring no benefits to the FDA. The company that developed it will make the profits, and the scientist responsible may become famous. The regulators will remain in obscurity. But should a drug prove hazardous, the government will be criticized for approving it and the regulators will be under fire. They therefore have great incentive to delay drug approval and none to accelerate it. The victims of their delays are all the unseen, unnumbered sufferers whose pain could be relieved, whose health could be improved or whose lives could be extended by the pharmaceutical products they are prevented from obtaining.

For every drug that government delays coming on the market there are many more which are not discovered or developed because of the regulations. Sir Arthur Fleming, the discoverer of penicillin, has said he wouldn't have gone ahead with the wonder drug of the century if current drug-testing requirements had been in effect then. The reason is that it is now necessary to test first on animals, and penicillin gives far more adverse reactions in dogs than in humans. Fleming says that if he had had to perform the animal tests, he would have seen a tremendous adverse reaction and been scared off; and penicillin, which has saved so many lives, alleviated so much suffering, and restored so many people to health, would have remained unknown.

Phosphates

When the environmental movement started, the initial concern about clean water resulted in great furor over phosphate in detergents. If the greedy soap companies were only concerned about profits, then, by golly, government was going to look out for people's true concerns and protect the environment. States, cities and counties across the nation rushed to pass laws banning phosphate detergents. The federal government asked industry to accelerate the development of substitute products. But in April 1971 the Surgeon General of the United States issued a stunning statement:

> In respect to efforts to displace phosphates from detergents, it should be realized that tests conducted thus far indicate that some of the currently used substitutes for phosphates are clearly toxic or caustic and pose serious accident hazards, especially for children. Other substitutes not yet fully tested may also be toxic and/or caustic.... Let me amplify my concern.... Such materials measured in quantities as little as a fraction of a teaspoon may cause severe damage to the skin, eyes, mouth, throat, larynx, esophagus or stomach on contact.

He characterized the various phosphate substitutes as posing a "serious risk of irreversible loss of sight, loss of voice, ulcerations and blockage of the esophagus, severe skin burns and even death." The banning of phosphate detergents had led to those safe products being replaced by ones which were extremely dangerous.

Combustible Sleepwear for Children

Here is another example of how government intervention with the best of intentions can end up producing grave danger instead. In July 1972 the Consumer Product Safety Commission issued Federal Standard DOCFF3-71 establishing rigid flame-retardancy requirements for children's sleepwear. While the impression was given that industry didn't care if children burned as long as it could make profits, the government postured as the champion of child safety.

So clothing manufacturers had to make costly adjustments in production. Cotton, which was used in 56 percent of children's sleepwear in 1971, was used in only 13 percent by 1975. The synthetic fibers which took its place were treated with the chemical "Tris" in order to meet the government's flame-retardancy standards. As a result, about 20 million children became exposed to a chemical which can be absorbed through the skin—a chemical which definitely can cause genetic damage and very possibly cancer.

Then government had the opportunity of again posing as the champion of child safety by demanding the recall of the products. The impression was created—officials certainly did nothing to correct the public's view—that such dangerous products were the result of a profit-oriented economic system while nonprofit government was the hero of human health.

As it turned out, the danger of death or injury from combustible sleepwear was greatly exaggerated in the first place. Researchers at the University of California at Berkeley have since shown that government figures on these casualties were *ten times* too high.[21] And by far the major cause of all fire deaths (at least six times larger than the next most common cause) is smoking—an activity not frequent among those under age six, those the regulations were supposed to protect.

In place of a greatly exaggerated threat from fire accidents, a vastly greater danger had been introduced into children's sleepwear because of Federal Standard DOCFF3-71. This loss in safety also created enormous economic losses. First there was the expense of shifting production to meet the required standards. Then 20 million garments had to be recalled from the stores, a loss which led to eleven manufacturers being faced with bankruptcy. The "Flammable Sleepwear Scare," like all other such government scares, left the public worse off—both economically and health-wise—than if the government had done *nothing*.

The Swine Flu Fiasco

Another example in the category of human costs is the swine flu scare. The federal government issued dire warnings that a deadly epidemic was about to descend on the American people. Then came a federal crash program to inoculate millions of Americans. It came to an abrupt halt, however, after an outbreak of adverse reactions to the vaccine. The most severe of these was a rare neurological disorder called Guillain-Barre syndrome.

Mark Waldvogel was a healthy, athletic, high school senior when he received a swine flu vaccination. He developed the Guillain-Barre syndrome from it, and he is now a paraplegic, confined to a wheelchair for life.

Waldvogel and no less than 1100 other victims filed lawsuits against the government. A total of 3800 people filed claims—the first step toward a lawsuit. The government was slow to compensate the victims of its vaccination program for their injuries, adding to their misfortune. Three years after the disastrous vaccinations the government had settled only 196 of the claims and lawsuits. And the swine flu epidemic never materialized.

Energy Efficient Homes

Radon is an inert, radioactive gas arising from the decay of uranium that is present in small amounts practically everywhere in the earth's crust. The gas gets trapped in homes with insufficient ventilation as it emerges from the ground, building foundations, and the water supply piped through the ground. The danger is not from the gas itself but from the products of its own radioactive decay, which lodge in the lungs, where they can cause cancer. The only known prevention is adequate ventilation. Now, remember the energy efficient homes widely promoted by the Carter Administration as a means of fuel conservation? They sacrificed ventilation for fuel efficiency. Had the administration achieved its goal of energy-efficient homes, the result would have been 10,000 fatal lung cancers per year, according to the authoritative Dr. Bernard Cohen of the University of Pittsburgh.[22] Government, by going against the market, was once again trading a greater value for a lesser one: 10,000 lives per year for a few barrels of oil.

Death by Fuel-Efficiency Standards and Ethanol

In another anti-market action, the federal government forced Americans to trade lives for fuel-efficient cars. A study by Robert Crandall of the Brookings Institution and John Graham of the Harvard University School of Public Health concluded that the "fuel economy regulation inevitably leads to smaller, lighter cars that are inherently less safe."[23] The study said that the fuel economy standards applied to 1989 cars would result in 2,200 to 3,900 more traffic deaths over the next decade, and an additional 11,000 to 19,500 serious injuries. Once again, the "heavy hand of government" inflicts damage in unexpected ways.

On February 19, 1992 a federal appeals court in Washington, D.C. overturned the government's Corporate Average Fuel Economy (CAFE) program because of its lethal effect in reducing the availability of larger, safer cars. The court accused the National Highway Traffic Safety Administration of "papering over the issue," "fudging the analysis," "disingenuously obscuring," and "cowering behind bureaucratic mumbo-jumbo."

In 1994 Professor Graham wrote:

> [C]hampions of proposals to save energy by enhancing vehicle fuel efficiency are only beginning to acknowledge how many additional deaths and serious injuries among motorists are caused each year by the sale of smaller and lighter cars. My best

estimate is that current proposals to raise new car fuel economy standards to 40 miles per gallon from 27 miles per gallon will eliminate the safety gains from airbag technology.[24]

The government's support of ethanol also exacts a toll in human life. By subsidizing ethanol with a tax credit to gasoline marketers, the federal government has diverted money to the ethanol industry and away from the Highway Trust Fund. Between 1983 and 1996, according to Treasury Department calculations, the ethanol tax credit cost the fund $5.9 billion in lost revenue. The Highway Trust Fund finances roads and bridges, and safer roads and bridges obviously save lives. No lives are saved by ethanol, but $5.9 billion could have bought significant life-saving improvements in the nation's highway system.

The Asbestos Scare

As of 1995, asbestos removal in schools across the nation, which had been mandated by EPA, had cost at least $35 billion. But by 1992 even the head of EPA admitted that this gigantic and costly program wasn't necessary or in the public interest. The money has been wasted. There was no threat from asbestos in place in the schools. There never had been. EPA should have known better, you say? EPA *did* know better!

> [T]he health data used by EPA and the HEW agencies were contrived. An opinion was substituted. All available data were not used…deleted information showed what science panels in England and Canada had already concluded: **Asbestos in buildings is not a health hazard.**[25]

That charge is made by John E. Kinney, Diplomate, American Academy of Environmental Engineers. Michael J. Bennett, author of *The Asbestos Racket,* states that there have been dozens, if not hundreds, of studies—some ten and even twenty years earlier—that had shown there was no danger from the asbestos, as EPA had claimed. He charges:

> The EPA also ignored its own scientific review of the study used to justify a ban on asbestos in schools. The EPA's own scientific panel denounced the study as "unconvincing," "greatly overestimated," "scientifically unappealing," and "absurd."…
> The United States government through EPA has, in the words of Justice Oliver Wendell Holmes, been "crying 'fire' in a crowded theater." The government's actions have been so

irresponsible that, were it a private corporation, it could, and should be, arrested for incitement to riot.[26]

EPA initially forecast 67,000 cancer deaths per year from asbestos. That figure was subject to widespread ridicule throughout the scientific community. Two prominent British epidemiologists charged EPA estimates were for "political, rather than scientific, purposes." One of them said the danger from asbestos was equal to smoking a half a cigarette in a lifetime.[27]

When EPA issued its mandate for the removal of asbestos from schools, it dropped its estimate from 67,000 to 3,300 to 12,000 cancer deaths per year. Later it dropped the number to 88. By 1991 the figure EPA was using for all cancer deaths from current use of asbestos in the United States was 20 per year—"and that figure is believed by the scientific community to be greatly exaggerated,"[28] says Michael Bennett. A federal judge, in striking down a 1989 EPA prohibition on a wide range of asbestos products, noted that toothpicks, which cause about one death per year (from accidental swallowing) are more than twice as risky as asbestos products.

The risk of lung cancer from asbestos is also distorted by data which include smokers. "Almost all lung cancers seen in asbestos workers have been among smokers," says R. S. Mitchell of the University of Colorado School of Medicine. "Asbestos is regarded as a promoter, not initiator, of lung cancer."[29]

There is a very dangerous type of asbestos, a hard asbestos called crocidolite; but it is so uncommon that it is commercially produced in only one place on earth, in Africa, and there in only small amounts. Another hard asbestos, amosite, is also dangerous but less so. However, the only type of asbestos mined in the United States, Canada and the Soviet Union is the common soft asbestos, chrysotile, which is relatively benign. This is the only type of asbestos used for insulating buildings in the United States and Canada.

Chrysotile, or "serpentine," asbestos has long twisted fibers that usually cannot penetrate into the lung's air sacs and are easily expelled from the lungs. The hard, or "amphibole," asbestos has fibers small enough to penetrate the air sacs and are seldom eliminated from lung tissue.

The shipyard workers in World War II who later developed lung cancer were working with crocidolite asbestos imported from Africa for naval vessels because of its extreme resistance to corrosion from salt water. Scientists all over the world were aware of the important health difference between hard and soft asbestos. EPA, however, chose to ignore the difference in order to make the danger sound more frightening and thus ruthlessly exploit people's fears for the safety of their children.

While the public was predictably frightened, professionals were not. Dr. James R. Dunn, a past President of the American Institute of Professional Geologists, describes a tour he took with a group of other scientists in 1985 of the "worst superfund site in Arizona," a closed chrysotile asbestos plant. They toured "without benefit of face masks or protective covering of any type."

> All of the hundred or so people on our buses went through the plant, many collected samples of chrysotile ore, and all were perfectly aware that they were breathing asbestos fibers and that they were getting fibers on their clothes probably to take home with them. And many would also take the ore samples back and further expose their families. Were these some kind of stupid or ill-informed beings from another planet? Hadn't they heard about the dangers? No, quite to the contrary, they were very well-informed scientists who knew that the danger to them was so trivial that it was about like the probability of getting hit by a meteorite. Most of them knew, for example, that the families of workers at Canadian asbestos mines living in mining camps, sometimes with their homes surrounded with asbestos-bearing waste rock, were in no more danger of getting lung cancer than the average Canadian. They also knew that asbestosis takes years of exposure to atmospheres clouded with asbestos fibers before any problem could develop. In a very real way these scientists were, quite unintentionally, "voting with their feet," showing as clearly as possible their disdain (1) for the fears of so many citizens, (2) for the "reporting" and veracity of most newspapers, and (3) for the accuracy of our government's conclusion regarding the dangers from chrysotile asbestos.[30]

In the largest study ever made on chrysotile exposure, 11,000 Quebec asbestos miners and others with "high" exposure for as long as twenty years were found to have less risk of lung cancer than the general public. These results are documented in a 1991 report by the Health Effects Institute in Cambridge, Mass.

Despite massive and compelling evidence to the contrary, on August 8, 1994, OSHA—not EPA, but OSHA—said it "is reaffirming its position that chrysotile is as dangerous as other forms of asbestos."

The agency announced it was issuing new, more stringent standards for asbestos in the workplace, even for chrysotile.

In the San Francisco area there are many large outcrops of asbestos-bearing rock containing about 50 percent chrysotile asbestos. Yet "although local people have been drinking chrysotile-rich water and breathing chrysotile-rich air for lifetimes, there is no cancer epidemic in that area of California."[31]

Indeed, we have all been breathing, drinking and eating asbestos, though usually in lesser amounts than people in San Francisco. A National Academy of Sciences committee estimated the "natural" amounts of asbestos in air and water.

> The committee said that "natural" air (air sampled in areas remote from industrial civilization) might contain about .01 fiber per cubic centimeter, and that "natural" water might contain about 10^4 to 10^6 fibers per liter.... [I]f this even approaches accuracy, all Americans have been inhaling, drinking, eating, and washing themselves with asbestos fibers all their lives.[32]

The United States has more than 400,000 miles of asbestos cement pipe, which supplies drinking water to scores of millions of Americans without any evidence of health damage.

It turns out that removing asbestos insulation from buildings results in greater exposure to the asbestos than from leaving it sealed in the walls. Tests have shown that when asbestos is undisturbed in buildings, breathing the air in those buildings is the same as breathing outdoor air. The Health Effects Institute report says that even if the entire U.S. population worked for twenty years in buildings containing the most dangerous kind of asbestos (not chrysotile), mesothelioma (a cancer linked to asbestos) would increase, at most, by ten cases per year, to about 410 cases annually from 400 cases.

But when asbestos is removed from buildings, the fibers become airborne, lodge in the building's ventilation system, and then remain at elevated levels in the air inside the building for years. So the government's policy of removing asbestos from schools resulted in children inhaling *more* asbestos, not less. Moreover, workers involved in the asbestos removal were exposed to much higher levels of asbestos, particularly since an estimated 50 to 75 percent were not following recommended procedures.

In one high school where even an OSHA official admitted that the asbestos removal was "as well run and controlled as is feasible," airborne asbestos levels rose tenfold after removal. A year later the levels were even higher. "We spend an awful lot of taxpayer money [on asbestos removal] without decreasing risk,"[33] said Gerard Ryan of OSHA's Denver office.

In 1992 EPA reported that asbestos levels had risen two years after asbestos removal projects in nine of seventeen New Jersey high schools. Nevertheless, in 1993 industry consultant Olin Jennings estimated that $80 billion will be spend on asbestos removal over the next 20 years, thanks to government policy.

Even worse, the asbestos insulation is replaced with more dangerous alternatives. Dr. Dunn says, "Man-made mineral fibers (fiberglass, rock wool, etc.) are much more carcinogenic than the common chrysotile asbestos."[34] His conclusion is based on "two major scientific reports" (by Saracci et al. and Enterline and Marsh) covering 41,876 workers in Europe and the United States. Once again the government increased rather than decreased the health risks to the public, because the dangers of the alternatives were not considered.

The government asbestos rules also pose other safety risks. Despite our government's plans to phase out the use of asbestos in other products, including automobile brake linings, a letter from the U.S. Embassy in Stockholm to the Swedish Foreign Ministry on August 16, 1985, concerning a proposed Swedish ban on asbestos, said such a ban was unjustified:

> Nor does scientific evidence indicate that asbestos-containing brake linings constitute a hazard to health.... The performance of the braking systems of vehicles which were originally designed with asbestos linings could be seriously impaired if asbestos-free linings are used as replacements. This may result in the *creation of serious safety problems*. The U.S. Government does not believe that the brake linings of U.S. vehicles imported into Sweden constitute a threat to the environment and health."[35](Italics added)

How then could they be a threat to the environment and health in the United States?

We do know of another instance in which the replacement of asbestos led to "the creation of serious safety problems." Remember the Challenger disaster, the space shuttle which resulted in a fiery death for its astronauts in 1986 because of the failure of an O-ring? After 77 successful flights of Titan III rockets, the government told the manufacturer of this proven component to remove asbestos from the premises because of EPA regulations.[36] So a modified putty was substituted for asbestos in the O-rings, with spectacularly disastrous results. As might be expected, neither the government nor the media focused on the real reason the O-ring failed.

Other Human Costs of Environmental Regulations

As was pointed out in Chapter Eight, EPA regulations are responsible not only for deaths in this country but for untold millions of foreign deaths. Tens of millions of people around the world have died from malaria alone because of EPA's ban on DDT. According to figures of the Pan American Health Organization, 10,000 Peruvians died and a million became ill due to cholera in the years 1991 to 1995; that was the human cost when chlorination of drinking water was severely cut back because of EPA's alarmist concern over a possible slight risk of cancer from water purified in this way. Nobody knows how many people may have died in Uganda because the government there didn't provide clean water to its people because of EPA. The country had only asbestos-cement waterpipe and couldn't afford the metal or plastic pipe demanded by the U.S. Agency for International Development (AID) because of EPA's ban on asbestos products. So no water pipe was installed.

Even the ban on CFC's will have an enormous cost in human health and lives, especially in the poorer countries of the world, which will be deprived of the health benefits of low-cost refrigeration and air conditioning. Dr. Ellsaesser notes that the substitutes for CFCs

> will be less efficient, require larger volumes of working fluid and heavier compressors, be more subject to burning and explosion, and be more hazardous to those coming into direct contact with them.
>
> For all these reasons freon [CFC] replacements will make refrigeration and air conditioning more expensive and hazardous. Unless we can all look forward to unlimited affluence, this means that refrigeration and air conditioning will be less widely used. Has any one calculated the health consequences of this? United States health statistics show a dramatic decline in deaths caused by diseases such a stomach cancer when refrigeration was introduced and cardiorespiratory deaths when air conditioning was introduced.[37]

Dr. Dixy Lee Ray states:

> CFCs are non-volatile and non-toxic and present no direct hazards to living organisms. Until CFCs were developed, many people died from toxic fumes of ammonia, methyl chloride, and sulfur dioxide, which were often used as refrigerants.
>
> In 1929, more than 100 people died in a Cleveland hospital from a leak in the refrigeration system.... Not only are CFCs safe, but all of the proposed substitutes have turned out to be very expensive, and some are toxic, flammable, and corrosive.... Replacing *just* the refrigerated transport for food moving to market would cost more than $150 *billion*.... Because of the severe effect on transportation and storage of food due to the loss or greatly increased cost of refrigeration, estimates indicate that between 20 to 40 million people will die yearly from hunger, starvation, and food-borne diseases.[38]

The lack of refrigeration in poor countries due to the ban on CFCs will also kill people because the integrity of many medicines, vaccines and the blood supply for surgery and transfusions requires refrigeration. Even this, however, will not be the end of the chain of losses.

The ban on CFCs will exact a price in human deaths in still another manner. Halon, a type of CFC, plays a critical role in fire-fighting. Dr. Ray says, "Countless lives have been saved by using halons to put out fires in aircraft, in ships and submarines, and in many industrial facilities. What will replace halon?"[39]

The Human Cost of the Economic Cost

When regulations slow the rate of economic growth, there is a cost in human lives. A lower standard of living than would otherwise occur results in people dying prematurely from such things as a poorer diet, operating less safe automobiles or other machines, or taking additional risks in other ways because they can't afford healthier, safer alternatives.

According to a study by the National Center for Policy Analysis, one additional death results from the reduction in living standards caused by an increase in regulatory costs of $5 million to $12 million. On this basis, even *if* EPA regulations saved lives, those saved would be far outnumbered by those dying as a result of the regulations. EPA's figure that its regulations are costing $115 billion annually translates into 9,545 to 23,000 fatalities per year. That agency's estimate of $1.4 trillion for regulatory compliance during the first twenty years of its existence means 108,600 to 280,000 deaths due to the regulations during this period.

And where are the health benefits? An EPA-funded study by econometricians Hazilla and Kopp couldn't find *any!* Presumed benefits from clean air and water—for example, fewer work days lost through illness—could not be found. Once again government policies have been sacrificing a greater value for a lesser one: many lives for so few (if any) that they are statistically undetectable.

The cost of a single theoretical life saved by EPA regulations is so astronomical as to be absurd. Yale Law School Professor E. Donald Elliott, a former EPA general counsel, says, "I saw rules costing $30 billion"[40] (per theoretical life saved.) For the 1990 EPA regulation on wood preservatives the rate was even higher: $5.7 trillion. "This implies a willingness to spend the entire GNP to avoid a single hypothetical premature death," say Brimelow and Spencer in an article in *Forbes.*[41] Obviously, there are many ways such vast amounts of money could be spent that would save an enormously larger number of lives. EPA regulations, however, force people to spend more for less.

Brookings Institution economist Robert Crandall says any health benefit from EPA regulations "must be very small, much less than 1 percent of GNP."[42] But the Hazilla and Kopp study concluded that the real gross national product in 1990 was at least 5.8 percent lower than if there were no federal clean air and water regulation.

The Hazilla and Kopp study was probably too conservative. An unpublished study for the Office of Technology Assessment, cited by Mr. Crandall, showed that productivity in the manufacturing sector alone was 11 percent lower by the mid-1980s than it would have been without OSHA and environmental regulations. That 11 percent would translate into $140 billion a year in lost productivity in today's economy—and even more additional deaths annually than the 9,545 to 23,000 from the direct costs of the environmental regulations.

That's just for the environmental regulations. If we use the General Accounting Office's estimate, cited earlier, of $647 billion as the total annual cost of all federal regulations in the United States, the human cost is 53,900 to 129,400 deaths per year due to the economic effects on living standards from the direct costs of complying with federal regulations. Even those figures don't count the impact of lost productivity and innovation, which is significant. For example, Dr. Murray Weidenbaum says the Civil Rights Act, with its affirmative action program, has resulted in indirect costs far larger than the direct costs of complying with the regulations:

> This law lengthens the amount of time that many jobs stay vacant. Any employer subject to affirmative action requirements who simply goes out and hires people does so at his or her peril. In order to reduce—but not eliminate—the likelihood of being sued, prospective employers must go through a lengthy and expensive process that includes advertising in specified types of media. The advertised position must stay open long enough to provide those interested with an adequate opportunity to respond.
>
> Precise measures of the total costs imposed by civil rights laws and regulations are illusive. Nevertheless, Peter Brimelow and Leslie Spencer came up with an aggregate estimate of $236 billion a year or approximately 4 percent of the gross domestic product.... [T]he direct compliance expenses of private business necessary to respond to civil rights rules are estimated at...$5-8 billion a year. Educational institutions spend $11 billion annually.... These direct costs are clearly very substantial. However, the truly huge costs imposed by these regulations—the remaining $220 billion plus—are *indirect, such as the opportunities forgone because of the diversion of management time, energy, and resources.*(Italics added)[43]

These indirect costs of $220 billion translate to an additional 18,333 to 44,000 deaths annually.

Researcher R. L. Keeney calculates that each increase of $1 billion in interest payments on the national debt causes about 200 fatalities.[44] He also estimates that a $100 regulatory cost for a household with a $20,000 income causes about 5 deaths per million per year. (Those with higher incomes have fewer fatalities.) However, the regulatory costs are not $100 per household but at least $6,712 per household. Thus government regulations are not only fantastically deadly but are most lethal to the lower classes, those who are said to be most in need of regulatory protection.

THE ENVIRONMENTAL COSTS

Our last category of losses from government intervention is environmental. It includes the way in which regulations have compelled the waste of natural resources and led to environmental degradation— and have created additional financial losses at the same time.

For example, the National Commission on Productivity has estimated that the ICC regulation requiring truckers to return empty after making a delivery wasted 200 million gallons of fuel annually in addition to wasting $250 million. While the government passed laws to force the auto companies to reduce auto emissions even though the technology for doing so was unknown, the exhaust from needless burning of 200 million gallons of fuel was added to the atmosphere every year even though the solution for its elimination was obvious. No new technology was required. Because of the Clean Air Act of 1970, the four American automobile companies assigned over 8000 engineers and technicians to work full-time on trying to meet government requirements for emission-control devices. But look at the exhaust emissions that would have been eliminated by the simple procedure of abolishing one regulation! The politicians who professed such concern about air pollution in the 1970 legislation, and who attached such "urgency" to the problem, waited ten years—until deregulation of the trucking industry—to eliminate this one wasteful, polluting regulation.

On one of its plants Armco Steel was required to install special pollution-control equipment which would remove 21.2 pounds of iron oxide dust every hour. The equipment was run by a 1020 horsepower electric motor. But to generate the amount of electricity needed to run that motor, the utility company spewed out 23 pounds an hour of sulfur and nitrogen oxides and other gaseous pollution.

Another casualty of clean air legislation was recycling through refuse-to-energy plants:

> The obvious alternatives to landfills are recycling and burning. Recycling produces a number of materials, most importantly fertilizer; and burning produces steam for both district heating and electric power. Contemporary refuse processing plants, which automatically sort and then process the refuse, can reduce the volume of waste to some 10 to 15 percent …. This was the way many municipalities went until 1977, when the Clean Air Act put refuse-to-energy plants out of business. The result, in many cases, was dirtier air, not cleaner. Philadelphia, for example, rejected the proposal of a garbage-to-energy plant because of the difficulties of complying with the clean air legislation. Instead, the air is now being polluted by the notoriously unclean diesel engines of the trucks hauling thousands of tons of garbage all the way to Virginia every day.

As a matter of fact, burning garbage is cleaner than burning coal, at least when judged by the combined amount of nitrous oxides, sulfur oxides and hydrogen chloride produced per kilowatt-hour of electricity.[45]

In 1972 Dr. Joseph T. Ling, director of environmental engineering and pollution control for the 3M Company, calculated the cost and the environmental impact of modifying an existing 3M plant so that its effluent would meet U.S. Public Health Service standards for drinking water. The plant was already providing secondary waste treatment. Dr. Ling described his conclusions in testimony before the House Committee on Public Works. Here are some excerpts:

> In order to do this, we would have to spend $25 million for capital investment and $3.5 million at least for maintenance and operation per year.
>
> But that is not the point. The point is that, while we are using this money, we have to buy necessary equipment, concrete and steel, to build this facility. In addition to that, we have to purchase 9,000 tons of chemicals to make this operation run. This includes sulfuric acid and caustic carbon, etc.
>
> In addition to these 9,000 tons of chemicals, we have to purchase approximately 1,500 kilowatts of electricity.
>
> Also we have to use 19,000 tons of coal to produce the steam for this particular operation. We figured we probably would remove about 4,000 tons of pollutants from the water of this plant.
>
> In order to do this operation, we would produce 9,000 tons of chemical sludge and about 1,200 tons of fly ash from the boiler, 1,000 tons of sulphur dioxide, and 200 tons of nitrogen oxide in terms of air pollution.
>
> This is only about 3M Company. How about the 9,000 tons of chemicals purchased from someone else in the country? In order, then, for him to produce 9,000 tons of chemicals for us to use for this particular process, according to the *Encyclopedia of Chemical Technology*...he would need 15,000 tons of natural resources...and he would also need additional power to do that job.
>
> Meanwhile, he would produce 6,500 tons of sludge. That is, solid wastes.
>
> How about the 1,500 kilowatts of electricity? According to the data published by the U.S. Public Health Service, he would have to use 6,000 tons of coal to produce these 1,500 kilowatts. Meanwhile, he would have to emit 350 tons per year of sulphur dioxide, 60 tons of fly ash, and 60 tons of nitrogen oxide, plus 100 million BTU's per year waste heat....

How about the steel supply that we bought for the steel tank and the concrete tank? I would have to go to the calculation for the steel manufacturing and the cement operations, which I did not do.

From just the use of these major cycles I draw the conclusion: In order to remove approximately 4,000 tons of pollutants from this particular plant, we would have to use more than 40,000 tons of natural resources.

We would produce approximately 19,000 tons of waste material in terms of solid wastes or air pollution. That is four times as much as we removed from our plant....

If you looked into 3M's effluent pipe, yes, you would get a clear effluent. But you go up a little bit higher to look at the overall environment for the country and you would find that we created a lot more pollution than we have removed from the plant.[46]

Of course, Dr. Ling's testimony was ignored by the committee before which he was testifying and by the rest of Congress as well. He wasn't saying what they wanted to hear.

Congress, and other advocates of regulation, wanted to hear that regulation was necessary and would be beneficial. But twenty years later the Brookings Institution's Crandall found that for several pollutants the adjusted reduction rate has actually been less than was occurring in the 1960s, before EPA existed. Furthermore, Crandall says it's not clear that the controls were responsible for whatever reduction occurred after they were imposed. "Assertions about the tremendous strides the EPA has made," he says, "are mostly religious sentiment."[47] Several scholarly studies now support the assertion that the quality of our environment was improving faster in the 1960s, before the federal government got into the act, than in the 1970s.[48]

In the same way that reduced economic growth from environmental and other regulations has shortened people's lives, it has also adversely affected the environment. In 1994 Bruce Bartlett, a fellow at the Alexis de Tocqueville Institution, wrote,

[T]he evidence suggests that the best way to eliminate [environmental degradation] is to increase the rate of economic growth. Growth leads to more efficient production and invariably leads to reduced pollution.... The ironic conclusion, therefore, is that existing environmental regulation, by reducing economic growth, may actually be reducing environmental quality, or at least slowing the rate of improvement.[49]

In 1995 Brian Wesbury, chief economist for the U.S. Congress, wrote: "If the economy had grown at 4% per year over the past 30 years (as it did between 1947 and 1967), real GDP per capita would be $10,300 higher today."[50] We would have a much higher standard of living today *and* a cleaner environment. And hundreds of thousands of needless deaths from government regulations would have been avoided.

The cleaner we try to make our environment, the less we get for our money. For example, to go from 98 percent removal of particulate matter from smokestacks to 99.8 percent requires four times the energy as to go from zero to 98 percent.

In 1972 an EPA report on noxious emissions from automobiles stated that the cost of eliminating them would be 8.1 times greater than the damage they cause.

In 1976 Dr. Lewis J. Perl, vice president of National Economic Research Associates, noted that the National Commission on Water Quality estimated the benefits from the Federal Water Pollution Control Act at about $55 per household per year by 1983. He thought that estimate might well be high but "in any event the cost of achieving the gains would amount to some $40 billion per year or about $500 per household."[51] The costs, then, would be about ten times the benefits.

Dr. Perl calculated that for a particular plant then under construction the cost of meeting existing air quality standards was 11.4 times greater than the benefits. For the nation as a whole he estimated the cost-benefit ratio at 13 to 1. For new standards then under consideration in Congress, he calculated the cost-benefit ratio at 33.5 to 1. Thus during this period when government was supposedly doing more and more for the environment it was sacrificing the taxpayers' dollars for less and less in return.

In addition to the financial costs there may be some surprising environmental costs from getting the air and water too clean. According to Philip West, director of the Institute for Environmental Sciences at Louisiana State University,

> Even as we decry excessive pollution, it would be sensible to recognize that certain long-term, and sometimes indirect, benefits are derived from many types of pollution and, therefore, that we can go too far in our quest for "pure" air and water.[52]

Murky water and dusty air play vital, beneficial roles in the food chain, says West, a man with more than 40 years experience in environmental research. He notes, for example, that large fish are unable to find food in the pristine waters of the Bahamas, which lack residues of agricultural, industrial, and municipal wastes. The situation is very different in the Gulf of Mexico.

> The Mississippi River flushes the North American heartland and discharges its murky brew into the currents of the Gulf of Mexico.
> If the Mississippi as it passes New Orleans and Baton Rouge were distilled water, Oysters Rockefeller and Oysters Bienville would never have been invented, for there would be few, if any, oysters in the Gulf....
> Moreover, the shrimp, crab, pompano, trout, red snapper, red fish, grouper, flounder and other marine delicacies that abound in the Gulf also owe their existence to the contaminants carried by the fresh but impure waters of Ol' Man River and his unclean relatives.[53]

West notes, too, that without dust in the air there would be no rain or clouds; atmospheric moisture collects on tiny dust particles to start the condensation process. Air also contains oxides of nitrogen, ammonia, and other such "contaminants" that become plant nutrients and soil fertilizers when carried to the ground by rain.

PART III
REAPING AND RAVAGING

Chapter Thirteen
THE HARVEST OF REASON

THE SEED: INDIVIDUALITY

The power of a herd or a pack of animals is the power of its numbers. It is the collective physical strength of its members. It can be exercised only when the members behave alike, as when a herd stampedes or a wolf pack attacks. Any deviation from the standard behavior of the group diminishes the power of the group.

The tribe is an outgrowth of the herd. It grew out of the need for collective physical strength either for aggression or self-defense. And the power of the tribe, like that of the herd, depends on uniform behavior. Not surprisingly, therefore, tribes developed various ways to standardize behavior, to limit the individualization of their members. Individualism was the basic threat to tribal power.

The mind being the means by which men might vary their behavior from that of others, it was against the mind that tribal pressures for conformity were allied. Superstition and authority militated against new ideas. The power of the mind was held in check by the power to threaten pain, either through imaginary demons or through primitive brutality. When innovation and independence would bring pain, it was to ritual and conformity that men were conditioned to look for guidance and satisfaction.

The tribe provided a measure of physical and emotional security, but by its very nature tribal power was set against the only process by which human progress could occur. For men to advance, they had to begin thinking for themselves. They had to leave the beliefs and routines established by others and assume the risks and responsibilities of following their own minds. The invention of agriculture, or any other step in the rise of civilization, could not have occurred in any other manner. Human progress, the flowering of the intellect which distinguishes us from the animals, has been a process of graduating from the collective action of the herd or tribe to the individual action of the independent mind.

SPROUTING

When Copernicus challenged the established view of the universe, he did so without any new instruments or information. The only thing that was new was his thinking. The telescope had not yet been invented; it didn't appear until a hundred years after he began working on his idea. His miserable wooden instruments, with lines marked off in ink, were less precise than those of the Greek astronomers Hipparchus and Ptolemy, who lived in Alexandria fourteen centuries earlier. Copernicus saw nothing in the heavens that they had not seen. In fact, he used their data to build his theory. But he refused to accept their conclusion, which had been universally accepted for so long, that the earth was stationary with the sun revolving about it. He followed his own mind, not the beliefs of other men, however overwhelming their numbers down through the centuries.

The same powers of the human mind that restructured man's concept of the universe also restructured his concept of himself. Observation and analysis of nature, by which Copernicus had discovered the truth of the heavens, were the means by which Andreas Vesalius discovered the truth of the human body. In the same year that Copernicus published his brilliant theory, Vesalius published his daring book on anatomy, *On the Fabric of the Human Body.* It, too, challenged accepted ideas set down fourteen centuries earlier, by a man named Galen. As in the case of Copernicus, Vesalius had no new technology or data not available to others. The bodies on which he based his drawings and descriptions were no different from those of other men, but he saw in them what others had not seen or even bothered to investigate. He was thinking for himself.

The importance of the specific truths discovered by Copernicus and Vesalius is obvious. They established new directions in astronomy and medicine. Less obvious but even more important was the wider effect they had on men's philosophical outlook. They changed men's whole approach to knowledge in general. An intellectual revolution occurred. The very word "revolution" developed a meaning which is not astronomical but which was derived from the effect of Copernicus' work, *On the Revolutions of the Heavenly Spheres.* What was so revolutionary was the idea that truth was to be determined by rational proof based on sensory evidence, not by human authority or the revelation of scriptures. Copernicus and Vesalius taught men to look to nature and to their own minds for answers, not to dogmas set down by others.

Galileo furthered both the Copernican theory and the revolution in knowledge which it precipitated. He stressed the observation of nature and developed the experimental process we call the scientific method. With it he built the foundations for the science of mechanics: he conducted his famous experiments with falling bodies and made hundreds of less well-known studies of the pendulum, the flight of projectiles, elasticity and resistance of solid bodies, and many related subjects. He also built a telescope, with which he discovered four moons of Jupiter and was able to make the first maps of the surface of the earth's moon. But more importantly, his telescope enabled him to see that the ancient theory of Ptolemy did not work, that Copernicus was indeed right.

Few people were convinced. Galileo wrote to Kepler that he was "the first and almost the only person"[1] who was. Galileo invited professors opposing the Copernican theory to examine his telescope and look through it. They refused. One scientist declined "because it would only confuse him."[2] Galileo was saying: the truth is self-evident if you will only look and *use your own minds*. They didn't. Instead they used the power of authority: physical force. Their reply, in effect, was: *drop your mind.* Pain—the essence of authoritarian power—was employed toward that end. Galileo was shown the Inquisition's instruments of torture, twice, and told they would be used unless he recanted. No primitive tribe could have thought of more brutal ways of inflicting pain. With civilization the methods had changed but not the purpose. The object of Galileo's trial, in the words of Professor Bronowski, was "to show men of imagination that they were not immune from the process of primitive, animal fear."[3] The threat was sufficient; Galileo recanted. And intellectual leadership passed from Italy to the north, just as Galileo had said it would. It never returned.

To the north was Kepler. At first a mystic and a speculative dreamer, he turned to sober observation and developed a zeal for factual accuracy which became the basis of his discoveries. Following the Copernican theory and aided by improved telescopes, he calculated the orbit of Mars. But after six years and nine thousand folio-sheets of calculations in his small handwriting, his results clashed with certain observed positions of Mars by up to eight minutes of arc.

For 2000 years the circle had been assumed to be the ideal geometric form. Perhaps it was the ancient invention of the wheel that led men to such reverence. In any case, it was dogma that celestial motions were at uniform rates through perfectly circular orbits. Like Copernicus before him, Kepler now had to decide whether to cling to an ideal at odds with reality or to give preeminence to reality and the power of his own mind to grasp it. He had to choose between an idea supported by everyone else and one supported only by its own rationality. Kepler stuck to the facts, discarded the circular ideal and, upon further study, concluded that planetary orbits were elliptical. He was able to formulate laws for them, thus turning the Copernican theory from a general description of the sun and planets to a precise, mathematical one.

What enabled Kepler to do so was his realization of a cause-and-effect relationship between the sun and the planets. Nobody had even suspected the existence of a physical force between them, but Kepler was convinced that physical causes operate between celestial bodies just as between earthly ones. His concern with causality is evident in the title of his most famous work, *A New Astronomy Based on Causation Or Physics of the Sky.* Kepler reasoned that the planets were governed by some force emanating from the sun, that the more distant planets moved more slowly because the sun's force diminished with distance, just like light, and that there must be some simple, mathematical relationship between a planet's speed and its distance from the sun.

Although Kepler made a start toward causal explanation, his accomplishments, like those of Copernicus and Galileo, were essentially descriptive. The great causal explanation came from a man who combined the separate discoveries of those three men into a magnificent, unified system. He was one of the very greatest minds the human race ever produced, Sir Isaac Newton.

Newton perceived that the force which Galileo had studied in his experiments with falling bodies was the same force that Kepler found to emanate from the sun and control the movements of the planets. Newton had discovered universal gravitation. The laws of mechanics on earth, which Galileo had investigated, were shown to be applicable throughout the universe. With his own powerful achievement in mathematics, Newton was able to demonstrate that all matter and motion were governed by a single set of *universal principles.* His predecessors described *how* bodies moved in the heavens and on earth; he explained *why* they moved as they did.

One advance had led to another. Each great man's achievement was not inimical to the progress of others but created conditions enabling them to advance further. Each new discovery had beneficial consequences beyond its original significance. Seemingly unrelated ideas, such as those of Galileo and Kepler, were combined to provide the base upon which further progress was pyramided.

Thousands of years earlier the most ancient civilized achievements had led to a multiplicity of others. Agriculture, the domestication of animals, the wheel turned out to be useful not only in the specific way intended but in many more that were incidental and totally unexpected. Now men's achievements in astronomy and physics were leading to further progress not only in those specific sciences but in completely different fields. Newton ushered in the Age of Enlightenment, an age that saw men find more and more ways to apply their minds, with astonishing results on the practical as well as the theoretical level.

A string of practical inventions followed in quick succession: hard paste porcelain (1708), iron smelting with coke (1709), the steam pump (1712), the threshing machine (1732), the flying shuttle for weaving (1733), Sheffield silver plate (1742), mayonnaise (1756), the steam engine (1769), the spinning jenny (1768), the water closet (1778), the cotton gin (1793),

Theoretical science, too, was making great strides. In chemistry, for example, Henry Cavendish discovered hydrogen; Joseph Black, carbon dioxide; and Lavoisier, oxygen. With Lavoisier's explanation of oxidation the ancient mystery of fire was solved. The mystery of another of nature's most spectacular phenomena, lightning, was solved by Ben Franklin with his famous kite experiment in 1752, in which he showed that lightning was electricity.

With their new mastery of the physical world, it was not surprising that men began to apply the same successful mental process to ethical, social and political subjects. Newton had taught men that there were universal principles of physical order which could be discovered by studying the *nature of things.* Men now began studying the *nature of man,* in quest of universal principles of social and political order.

The most important of these early studies were those of John Locke, an ardent devotee of Newtonian thought. Locke, who had been a medical student, saw how medical progress developed from observation and analysis of the human body. Profoundly influenced by his own experience in natural science, he attempted to develop an orderly system of political thought based on natural rights, just as Newton had developed an orderly system of physics based on natural laws.

It was no accident that the Founding Fathers of America were so concerned with the concept of *natural* rights and that Thomas Jefferson employed phrases from Locke's work in the Declaration of Independence. It was a time when the towering achievement of Newton had a pervasive influence. Tom Paine was voicing the approach common to his time when he wrote, in the introduction to *The Rights of Man,* "that Man must go back to Nature for information." That was what Newton had urged men to do. It was what Franklin had done in regard to lightning and what Locke had done in regard to human rights. And it was typical that a man like Franklin, for example, the quintessential Founding Father, would apply the same reasoning to political issues that he had to natural science, just as Locke had done. The same reasoning which led men to both a theoretical understanding of the world and to practical inventions for enhancing their lives also led them to the greatest political invention ever made. It was at once profoundly theoretical and immensely practical. It was founded on *universal principles of human nature.* It was the Constitution of the United States.

Civilization is built on ideas, and our civilization was built on the foundations of thinking which began with the Renaissance. The American Revolution was the culmination of the intellectual revolution which began with Copernicus.

Copernicus reoriented man's view of the universe; he shifted the center of celestial order from the earth to the sun. The Founding Fathers reoriented man's view of government; they shifted the center of political order from the State to the individual.

THE FERTILE CLIMATE

It is one of those neat coincidences of history that the revolutionary works of Copernicus and Vesalius were published in the same year, that a new understanding of the universe was accompanied by a new understanding of man himself. But it's not quite as surprising as it might at first appear. Both grew out of a common intellectual climate.

It is another neat coincidence, but again not altogether surprising, that the Declaration of Independence and Adam Smith's *The Wealth of Nations* appeared in the same year, 1776. These, too, were products of the same intellectual climate. The success of human reason in the natural sciences, which led men to apply the same rational thinking to political theory, likewise led them to apply it to economics.

If the Declaration of Independence may be compared in its revolutionary significance to the work of Copernicus, Adam Smith's work is the counterpart of Vesalius'. Vesalius showed how men function physically; Smith showed how they function economically. Vesalius explained the working relationships within the human body; Smith explained them between human beings.

In the natural sciences rational inquiry had led to the discovery of universal principles, or natural laws, such as the law of gravity. In politics it led to the recognition of natural rights and the American attempt to structure human laws on that basis. In economics it led to the development of natural principles of production and exchange, such as the law of supply and demand and Say's law of markets.

Like the laws of physical science, these economic laws operate automatically, naturally, without human supervision. The mercantilist theory, which prevailed up to that time, had held to the necessity of close government supervision of the whole economy. The mercantilists, who believed wealth was fixed, assumed any nation's gain was always another's loss. Government economic supervision was deemed necessary to make sure that international trade was as one-sided as possible. Governments were supposed to protect their industries, prohibit skilled workers from emigrating, and strive for a favorable balance of trade by taxing and restricting imports, encouraging exports, hoarding the medium of exchange, and acquiring and developing colonies for the benefit of the mother country.

Smith held that these policies were not the basis of a nation's wealth, that wealth was created by an entirely different—and *natural*—process. "Little else," he said, "is required to carry a state to the highest degree of affluence from the lowest barbarism but peace, easy taxes, and a tolerable administration of justice; all the rest being brought about by the *natural course of things*." Then, in a statement which revealed the common ground between the economic and political ideas of the American revolution, he continued, "All governments which thwart the natural course are unnatural, and, to support themselves, are obliged to be oppressive and tyrannical."[4]

Here, then, was how the results of human reasoning applied in such different directions as politics and economics had come together as part of a magnificent, unified philosophy of individualism. It was very much like the apparently unrelated works of Galileo on earthly mechanics and Kepler on planetary orbits turning out to be part of a universal, integrated system.

ORGANIC DEVELOPMENT: NATURAL RIGHTS

If, as the Declaration of Independence states, "all men are created equal," it is in the sense that each man has an equal right to life, that class or blood line is not the basis of rights, that *life itself* is. The right to life is the basic right from which all others are derived.

The basis of rights is thus a *natural* phenomenon. Rights are not an arbitrary convention but a logical derivation from a physical reality: a man's existence.

A "right" is defined as "a just and fair claim." As an adjective, the word "right" means "in conformity with fact, reason, or some standard or principle." The two meanings are related. A claim can be "just and fair" only if it is "in conformity with fact, reason, or some standard or principle."

Clearly a man has a "just and fair claim" to his own life. From the fact of his own life, all other rights are derived by reason through recognition of the physical principle of cause and effect. Liberty is the political recognition of the fact that a man's actions are the effects of the life within him, which is the cause. It is the right to life, the source of action, which is the basis for the right to act in any way that does not infringe on the corresponding rights of others. The boundary of such infringement can be comprehended as a physical reality: the initiation of physical force against the lives and property of others. Liberty being a natural right, it has a natural, physical limit.

The right to property has a similar basis and limit. Property is the effect of which labor is the cause. If a man has the liberty to labor for himself, can he logically be denied the effects of his labor? If he is so denied, then he does not really have a right to his life since his life is the source of his labor. Property is the recognition of the causal relationship between a man's actions and their material consequences. It is the legal means by which men can provide themselves with the physical means for sustaining and satisfying their lives without the use of force against each other. It is the hallmark of a civilized society, where men deal by reason rather than force.

Property rights are inextricably tied to the rights to life and liberty. All three are simply different aspects of the nature of man—and those governments which have been most vigorous in attacking property rights have inevitably been the greatest violators of life and liberty. The posed opposition of "human rights versus property rights" is an absurdity because property rights *are* a human right. Property, as such, has no rights. The term "property rights" simply means the right of humans to possess property.

The phrase "life, liberty and property" was a familiar one to the Founding Fathers because Locke's work had become an integral part of

American political philosophy. So much so that Jefferson was accused by some, most notably his fellow Virginian Richard Henry Lee, of simply copying Locke's work in writing the Declaration of Independence. Jefferson replied that he didn't consult other literature while he was writing but "did not consider it as any part of my charge to invent new ideas altogether."[5] Rather, he said he intended simply to make "an expression of the American mind."[6]

Jefferson, however, substituted the words "pursuit of happiness" for the word "property" in Locke's triad of rights. The change was in no way intended to downgrade property rights. Jefferson and his contemporaries envisioned property rights as the principal means for the pursuit and attainment of happiness. Jefferson simply wanted to state the issue in wider terms. The new phrase was inclusive not only of property rights but of the purpose they were to serve, and that of human actions in general.

Jefferson referred to the rights to "life, liberty and the pursuit of happiness" as *"unalienable"* because they were derived from the nature of man and inseparable from it. It was because of their natural origin, too, that he said they were "self-evident." They could be known by direct observation and reasoning, just as man could know other truths of nature, and were not dependent upon political authority or mystical revelation.

The nature of human life makes still another aspect of human rights self-evident. It is that rights are inherently individual. A man can have a right to only his own life. If the right to life is an individual one, so must be all those which are based upon and derived from it. It can immediately be seen that this is indeed the case. The "pursuit of happiness" can only mean individual happiness. There is no such thing as the "public happiness" or the "national happiness."

Similarly, such rights as those to freedom of speech and freedom of religion are meaningless except as men speak or believe as individuals. The question of these rights could never arise if everyone were of the same mind, if they all had the same ideas and beliefs. These rights arise only because man is capable of *differing* from his fellows, of thinking for himself and forming his own convictions. The whole concept of rights implies safeguarding the individual differences which spring from the human mind. Liberty can only mean *individual* liberty, by which men think and speak and act each according to *his own mind.*

Property rights are the means by which individuals can implement their other rights in material terms. The concept of private property is the natural, universal principle for structuring social action, in a material context, on the supreme value of individual life. It is the only way that men can deal with their surroundings with respect for each other's lives. It is the only nonviolent basis for an economic system. John Adams warned,

> The moment the idea is admitted into society, that property is not as sacred as the laws of God, and that there is not a force of law and public justice to protect it, anarchy and tyranny commence.[7]

All the valid rights a man has, or can ever have, are the consequence of his own existence. There can be no rights of the majority or of society that each and every member of society does not possess as an individual. There can be no "public rights" just as there is no "public happiness." There can be no group rights, no rights of consumers, producers, blacks, whites, workers, employers or any other special group—no rights except individual rights. If there were, men would not be equal in terms of rights. And class, not life, would be the basis of rights.

Since rights are an attribute of individual life, not of human numbers, men acting together in the name of government have no more rights than any individual. Government, as the Declaration of Independence states, derives its just powers from the people. People cannot delegate to the government that which is beyond their rights as individuals. Since self-defense—a corollary of the right to life—is the only justification for the use of force by individuals, it is the only justification for government.

The Declaration of Independence states that it was "to *secure*"— Locke's phrase—the rights of life, liberty and the pursuit of happiness that governments were instituted. These rights in themselves limit government to the defensive function of safeguarding them, because any coercive initiative would violate them. The initiation of force *is* the violation of rights, and government is force. Just as it is the nature of man which determines the rights of the individual, it is the nature of force which determines the proper role of government.

Government is logically limited to a defensive role, too, by the principle of *equal* rights. Government cannot serve *all* its citizens equally if it violates the rights of *any* of them. To prevent government from violating anybody's rights, Americans devised the concept of *limited* government. The idea was to give government only enough power and authority for its proper function, no more.

In a defensive role government does not give anybody anything; it merely protects what is already theirs by "just and fair claim." Justice is the only item government can give without taking it away from somebody else. Anything else government might give it has to take from somebody, because force *by its very nature* can't produce anything. Any "positive" programs, any intervention in economic or social affairs, can only benefit some citizens at the expense of the natural rights of others. American government was not intended to play an "activist" role in human affairs because it could not do so without violating its fundamental purpose, which was to secure the natural rights of its citizens.

It was by making the individual the center of their political universe that the Founding Fathers were able to devise a government that served rather than violated human nature. Government, which had always been the master of men, was now made the servant. Its force was not to be used to bend men to the service of the State or other men—not even a majority—but to insure that each man remained his own master, free of subjugation of any sort. The primacy of individual rights meant that every human life was an end in itself. It was *not* the purpose of the individual to serve the State or other men, whatever their numbers. A man's purpose was to serve himself: to pursue his happiness to the limits of his liberty.

When individual rights are not the purpose of government, they will be sacrificed to whatever is, whether it be the wishes of the ruling few or of the masses. Government's purpose will not be to defend individual rights but to deny them, to subordinate the individual to the State for some alleged "greater good." The more anything is valued above the individual, the more freedom disappears and the more extreme are the measures government will use to violate rights in the name of "higher" goals. Witness in our own time the atrocities under Soviet rule in the name of collective good, detailed so vividly by Alexander Solzhenitzen, or those in France under the mercantilist doctrine of American colonial times. Alexis de Tocqueville noted that 16,000 people were slain by the French government for violating certain textile regulations. John Chamberlain writes that

> in Valence [France], on a single occasion, seventy-seven people were sentenced to be hanged for breaking economic regulations, fifty-eight to be broken on the wheel, and six hundred thirty-one were sent to the galleys.[8]

Such were the penalties for serving one's own economic interests instead of acting as the government deemed best for the country.

Whether government is man's servant or his master, whether it protects his rights or is the greatest violator of them, all depends upon whether or not the individual is the philosophical center of society. If he is, if individual rights are the reason for government, then it follows that it is right for the individual to go his own way, to differ, to think for himself and act for his own interests. It is regarded as positively good that he should do so.

If, on the contrary, society (read: tribe or herd) is the reason for government, then it follows that the individual must be subordinated to the collective. He must not be allowed to go his own way. He must not be allowed to think and act for himself. His behavior, rather than being directed by his mind for his own good, must be directed by central authority for the common good—the so-called "public interest." Government edicts replace individual thought as guides to action. The citizen must drop his mind and obey. It is regarded as positively good to make men conform rather than allow them to differ, for uniform behavior is viewed as the strength of collective action.

The great advances of America took place because its philosophy of individualism liberated the human mind. Individual rights can be exercised only by individual thinking. And *individual* thinking is the only kind there is, thinking being an internal process of the individual brain. Here, again, the system of natural rights can be seen to fit the system of nature, for nature has given every man a brain, not just those in authority. Directing society by central authority is certainly not in accord with the facts of nature.

In another respect, too, individualism fosters the use of men's minds. A government whose purpose is only to defend individual rights works to eliminate force (i.e., crime), thus leaving men free to determine their affairs by reason. Such a government serves only as a counterforce to negate the use of force by members of society.

Whenever government attempts more than a defensive function, it serves to negate the minds of its citizens. It counters not force but thinking. Individual rights and individual thinking go together; they are either exercised or violated jointly. And just as physical force is the means of violating rights, it is the means government employs against men's minds. It is the means by which government instills primitive, animal fear to paralyze the mind or to force men to surrender their ideas, as Galileo did. Whether men are broken on the rack, tortured in Siberia, or simply threatened with jail sentences and fines, government can mold society only by substituting the power of pain for the power of ideas.

In recent years it has become popular to characterize certain government programs as a "carrot-and-stick" approach. But government can't produce "carrots." It can get them only by applying its "stick" to somebody else. In the end, government's *only* power is the power of the "stick," the power of pain.

The American concept of *limited* government limited the power of pain as an instrument of policy because it limited the role of force. When individual reason replaced collective coercion in directing human lives, the pursuit of happiness replaced the power of pain as a social determinant.

FULL BLOOM

The Declaration of Independence is not a law or a part of our government. It is an ideological statement of the basic premises of American government. The Constitution of the United States is the translation of those ideas into an actual system of government.

When we understand the philosophy of individualism, as expressed in the Declaration of Independence, we can understand why the Constitution is fundamentally a negative document. In the seven original articles of the Constitution the words "no" and "not" appear 49 times, usually as restraints on government power. The first ten amendments, known as the Bill of Rights, are even more consistently negative: "Congress shall make *no* law" abridging freedom of religion or speech; the right to keep and bear arms "shall *not* be infringed"; "the right to be secure...against unreasonable searches and seizures shall *not* be violated"; "excessive bail shall *not* be required, *nor* excessive fines imposed, *nor* cruel and unusual punishments inflicted"; "the enumeration of certain rights shall *not* be construed to deny or disparage others retained by the people"; etc.

The Constitution evidences a negative tone because it was to be the people's protection *against* government. The Framers of our government explicitly stated that they regarded government itself as the greatest danger to individual rights. They hoped to limit this danger through a system of checks and balances and by specifically limiting the powers of government, all through a written constitution.

The Constitution was to be the individual's shield against the organized force of other men acting in the name of government. By limiting the role of force, the Constitution left reason unlimited. The great progress of America was not caused by government action; it resulted from limiting it, because human reason was then free to manifest itself in people's affairs without restraint or interference.

Individualism precipitated limited government. If it weren't for individual rights, there would have been no reason for limiting government. And it is because the individual is no longer considered as important as he was 200 years ago that government has expanded far beyond its original limitations.

In the same way that individualism led the Founding Fathers to the concept of limited government, it also led them to reject democracy as a form of government. And, again, it is because the individual is no longer so important in our society that democracy has become so favored.

Earlier this century Albert Jay Nock wrote that it was worth going through the literature of early America

> to see how the words "democracy" and "democrat" appear exclusively as terms of contumely and reprehension.... One sometimes wonders how our revolutionary forefathers would take it if they could hear some flatulent political thimblerigger [i.e., swindler] charge them with having founded "the great and glorious democracy of the West."[9]

Democracy was regarded contemptuously because it is incompatible with individualism. Democracy is a collectivist concept. It is "a form of government in which the supreme power is lodged in the hands of the people *collectively*."[10] It is a system of collective coercion, whereby every individual is forced to conform to the rule of the majority. The Founders sought a system of individual choice, where every man would be free to go his own way. They wanted a system where no man would have a master, not one where the majority would be the master, as in a democracy.

When they stated that their political experiment rested "on the capacity of mankind for self-government," the Founders did not mean collective political action. They meant each man's capacity for governing his own affairs. They were *not* referring to governing each other's affairs through a participatory political process. It is only because our own age is so collectivist oriented that most people immediately associate "self-government" with mass political action instead of with the individual governing his own life.

That the latter meaning is what the Founders understood by "self-government" is quite obvious from their own words and the kind of government they created. It is the only meaning that is consistent with their idea of limited government, of not entrusting government with a role in the everyday affairs of men in the first place. This view is supported by statements of the Founders themselves. For example, Jefferson, who though not democratic was more democratically inclined than some of the others, wrote, "We think experience has proved it safer, for the mass of individuals composing society, to reserve to themselves *personally* the exercise of all rightful powers."[11] In his first inaugural address he spoke of the need to leave men "free to regulate their own pursuits of industry and improvement." On another occasion he wrote, "I have no fear but that the result of our experiment will be that men may be trusted to govern themselves *without a master*."[12] (Italics added)

Was it a democracy, then, that was created by the men who founded our government? Certainly not. They intended to guard *against* democracy, which they regarded as evil. Edmund Randolph, Governor of Virginia, who was one of the leaders at the Constitutional Convention, who became the nation's first attorney general and later succeeded Jefferson as secretary of state, was emphatic on this point. He said the "general object" of the convention was "to provide a cure for the evils" traceable to "the turbulence and follies of democracy."[13]

Roger Sherman, Elbridge Gerry, Alexander Hamilton and various other delegates to the convention expressed similar views of democracy. Gerry, for example, labeled it "the worst of all political evils." John Adams, who was in Europe at the time of the convention, also despised democracy, as did most of the other prominent political figures of the day. Samuel Adams said, "Remember, democracy never lasts long. It soon wastes, exhausts, and murders itself. There never was a democracy that did not commit suicide." One of the greatest of the Founding Fathers, the man who is often referred to as the Father of the Constitution, has furnished us with one of the strongest statements against democracy. Writing in *The Federalist,* which is universally recognized as the most authoritative exposition of the Constitution, James Madison declared:

> [A] pure democracy...can admit no cure for the mischiefs
> of faction.... There is nothing to check the inducements to

sacrifice the weaker party.... Hence it is that such democracies have ever been spectacles of turbulence and contention; have ever been found incompatible with personal security or the rights of property; and have in general been as short in their lives as they have been violent in their deaths.[14]

By "faction" Madison meant what we would call special interest groups or pressure groups. He was referring to people united by a common interest or passion who employ collective strength to gain something at the expense of others in society: who attempt to gain through *numbers* what they are not entitled to as *individuals,* at the expense of the natural rights of other people. What made democracy so deplorable was that it rewarded and encouraged such behavior. For by its very nature—which is collectivist—democracy is based on *numbers* rather than *rights*. Their concern being individual rights, the Founders sought to protect those rights from the power of numbers, from democracy. They didn't want a government which some segments or "factions" of society could use as a means for ganging up on other people, plundering them through the political process.

The Founders wanted the people to be represented in government. The problem was how to give the *individual* a voice in government without submitting government to the *collective* power of raw numbers. It was highly desirable, as Madison expressed it, to structure government so that it would have a "tendency to break and control" the power of factions. These limitations on the collective power of the people were ingeniously integrated with the limitations on the powers of government.

One of the principal ways of limiting government was to separate its functions and balance them against each other. At the federal level three distinct branches were established, the executive, the legislative and the judicial. It was hoped that each would serve as a check against the others, that by guarding its own powers each branch would prevent the expansion of the others.

The same principles of separation and balance were intended between different *levels* of government as between the different *branches*. Powers were divided between federal and state levels. Only certain ones were assigned to the federal government, balanced by others reserved to the states. The states were intended to act as a check on the usurpation of federal power in the same way that the executive, legislative and judicial branches were to serve as checks upon each other.

Of the three federal branches, only one-half of one was organized on the democratic principle. The judiciary was *appointed*—for life. Hardly democratic. The president was to be elected not by the people but by an electoral college. Even the upper half of the legislative branch, the Senate, was not to be chosen by the people, being elected instead by the state legislatures. Only the members of the House of Representatives were to be elected directly by the people. That's all the democracy the Founding Fathers intended.

In classical theory, an unfamiliar subject today, there were three types of government: monarchy, oligarchy (or aristocracy), and democracy. These were, respectively, rule by one, rule by a few, and rule by the many. The Founders considered which of these types would be best suited to each of the branches of government. There was, for example, some discussion of whether the presidency should be held by a single individual or by a committee of three or even five members. In the end the monarchical principle seemed best suited to the executive branch. The Supreme Court and the Senate were oligarchical in principle, and only the House of Representatives was democratic. The resulting government certainly could not be called democratic. It was a *mixed* government drawn on the principles of the three classical types. With the separation and balance of the three *branches* of government, no one *type* would predominate. The result is best described not as any one of them but as a limited, constitutional republic.

The composite nature of government had implications for the selection of officeholders. Dr. Clarence B. Carson writes:

> A mixed government was desirable because there were differing functions of government which could best be entrusted to one, to a few, or to many. But, if the functions were best performed in this way, the division should not be watered down by having all the branches chosen by the same electorate.[15]

One of the most remarkable aspects of the Constitution was the way its various features harmonized intricately with one another. There was, as shown by Dr. Carson's explanation, good reason simply from the standpoint of a mixed government why the Founders considered it "very important that each branch be distinct from the other in the manner of selection."[16] But this same idea also fit neatly with their other objectives: maintaining the separation of the executive, legislative, and judicial functions; using the states to check and balance federal power;

and structuring government to "break and control" the power of factions among the people.

The electorate for the House was the people. For the Senate it was the states. But there was no convenient third electorate for the presidency. One had to be created: the electoral college.

Three separate electorates certainly served to "break and control" the power of factions or to mitigate the numerical power principle of democracy. They also promoted the independence of the separate branches of government. It was on this ground that the national legislature was ultimately rejected for choosing the president and the electoral college agreed upon instead. The Founders had no desire to create an additional political entity if existing ones could do the job. But, as Gouverneur Morris put it, if Congress performed the electoral function, the president would be a mere creature of the legislature. He could hardly act independently if he was indebted to legislators for his office.

The Convention considered a variety of methods for selecting the president. The matter was of great concern. James Wilson, one of the most astute delegates, called the issue "the most difficult of all on which we have had to decide."[17] The methods considered included election by the national legislature, by the state legislatures, and by the governors, as well as by special electors apportioned in various ways. Popular election was mentioned but was out of the question. As Roger Lea MacBride states in *The American Electoral College,* "…the conviction that Americans in the collective ought not to exercise that power *directly* eliminated it from the running as a possibility even before the Convention opened."[18]

Again the Founders demonstrated their distrust of democracy. But *indirect* election satisfied them where the democratic principle of direct election did not. It became the method for choosing both the president and the Senate. It gave the people a voice in government, even if indirectly, and yet it could serve to "break and control" the numerical power of factions. In addition it had many other virtues.

Indirect election promoted independent decisions, encouraging those elected to exercise their own best judgment. They could be more concerned with doing what was right rather than what was popular. Political decisions would tend to be made by superior thought rather than superior numbers.

Indirect election discouraged politicians from pandering to the public, from promising illicit gains in exchange for votes. Interposing a level of electors between the officeholders and the public diminished the political incentive for using governmental power *offensively,* to reward some factions—special interest groups—at other people's expense.

Indirect election was also a way of refining the ideas of the people. The Founders were well aware that not everyone had the same knowledge or ability to make political decisions. If people elected from among themselves those who were ablest, they in turn would be more likely to make a wise elective choice than the populace as a whole. Indirect elections thus tended to upgrade political selection by what Madison referred to as a series of filtrations. "The effect," he wrote, "is to refine and enlarge the public views by passing them through the medium of a chosen body of citizens, whose wisdom may best discern the true interest of their country."[19]

The Founders wanted to place political decisions in the hands of those best qualified to make them—not in the hands of the public at large. (The decisions they wanted left in the hands of the public were not political ones but those each man might exercise in his own affairs.) Jefferson once wrote to John Adams:

> I agree with you that there is a natural aristocracy among men. The grounds of this are virtue and talents.... There is also an artificial aristocracy, founded on wealth and birth, without either virtue or talents.... The natural aristocracy I consider as the most precious gift of nature, for the instruction, the trusts, and government of society.... May we not even say, that that form of government is the best, which provides the most effectually for a pure selection of these natural aristoi into the offices of government?[20]

That statement is by the same man who some years earlier had written that "all men are created equal." But there is no contradiction. For when he wrote that men were equal, he meant equal in terms of rights, which means: equally entitled to government protection of one's life, liberty and property. It did not mean that men were equal in competence to decide how to run the government or who should run it or that everyone should have an equal voice in determining such matters. The Founders were concerned with the *equality* of rights, but they were concerned with the *quality*—not the equality—of political judgment.

Here, then, was another objection to democracy. It treated men as equal in political judgment, yet nature had obviously made them unequal in this respect. Democracy simply didn't fit the nature of man.

The Founders, intent upon creating a government appropriate to the nature of man, knew that a political form so blatantly contrary to reality couldn't serve their purpose.

The original organization of the legislative branch furnishes perhaps the most exquisite example of how the Founders integrated all of their concerns to achieve a delicately balanced and intricately coordinated political structure. It gave the people representation, yet it limited the democratic effects which the Founders feared. It gave the states a means of checking the expansion of federal power. And it protected the small states from the large ones and vice versa. In short, it protected individual rights from the people, from the federal government, and from the governments of other states.

If representation in the legislature were made proportional to population, the large states would obviously be dominant and might pass laws to their advantage at the expense of the people in the smaller states. Of course, the large states objected to equal representation, where all states would have the same number of representatives irrespective of population. The solution was to have two legislative bodies, one of each type, a House and a Senate. Each state would have two senators, but its number of representatives in the House would depend upon its population. Any bills had to be passed by both legislative bodies in order to become law. So neither the large nor the small states could enact laws at the other's expense. Laws could be passed only if they were generally considered beneficial to both groups.

Members of the House were to be elected directly by the people. But this democratic feature was immediately balanced by the principle of indirect election in the Senate. The popular was to be balanced by the wise; the voice of the masses was to be balanced by the wisdom of a few who were more knowledgeable than the general public and selected from them by the filtering process of indirect election.

There were several reasons for using the state legislatures to elect the U.S. Senate. Their members would be more knowledgeable in governmental matters than the general public. Still, the public would be represented indirectly, because the state governments themselves would be chosen by the people—the filtering effect. The state governments were also a logical choice because they were completely independent from any of the three federal branches—the separation of powers. Furthermore, (and this is an important but much neglected point) through the selection of senators the states could act as a check on federal power—the principle of checks and balances. The Senate was the states' only means of representation in the federal government. It was the one vital link between the two levels of government.

In the same way that the House and Senate constituted a balance between the large and the small states, they also constituted a balance between the wishes of the majority and the rights of the individual. The House, being popularly elected would represent the popular views. Its members would necessarily be concerned with pleasing the majority; for if not, the majority would elect people who would. The House, therefore, could not be expected to safeguard the rights of individuals in the minority.

As noted earlier, there were certain functions of government which the Founders considered best performed by one, by a few, or by many. Safeguarding individual rights was not one of the functions best performed by the many, or the majority. It was a function best left to a few. The Senate was the logical few. All of the characteristics of indirect election worked to the advantage of this purpose. The Senate would be chosen from the better informed minority and might be expected to have a better understanding of individual rights than the general public. Not being directly elected by the people, senators could not be voted out by the majority if they upheld the rights of the individual. Nor could they perpetuate themselves in office by signing away the rights of minorities in exchange for the votes of the majority. It should also be added that one of the reasons for giving senators six-year terms of office, compared to only two years for House members, was so that the matter of their elections would have less bearing on their decisions.

The House and the Senate, then, formed a delicate balance between power and principle, between the collective power of *numbers* and the principle of individual *rights*. Since any proposed legislation had to pass both houses of Congress in order to become law, the many could not oppress the few. At the same time, the many were protected in the same manner from the concentration of power in the hands of a few.

The Founders feared for individual rights, particularly property rights, under a one-man-one-vote system and expected the Senate to provide the necessary protection. These points are unmistakably clear in the notes of the Convention.

Expressing his fear for property rights, Madison, in replying to Charles Cotesworth Pinckney at the Convention, stated:

> [T]hose who sigh for a more equal distribution of its [life's] blessings...may in time outnumber those who are placed

above the feelings of indigence. According to the equal laws of suffrage, the power will slide into the hands of the former. No agrarian attempts have yet been made in this country, but the symptoms of a leveling spirit, as we have understood, have sufficiently appeared in certain quarters[21] to give notice of future danger. How is this danger to be guarded against on republican principles?[22]

In the light of Madison's comments, says Irving Brant in *Storm Over the Constitution,* it "becomes possible to understand the early American hostility to democracy which so astonishes the Americans of this day when (if ever) they discover that the Fathers feared and detested the equalitarian spirit in government."[23]

Men are obviously not equal in abilities or ambition. In *The Federalist* Madison observed that differences in property arise from "the diversity in the faculties of men" and that "the protection of these faculties is the first object of government." In other words, the "first object" of government is to protect men's individuality, not to compel their uniformity or equality. "From the protection of different and unequal faculties," says Madison, "the possession of different degrees and kinds of property results."[24] This natural, logical process—which the Founders sought to protect—is, of course, completely contrary to the uniformity of men and property that is idealized by the proponents of democracy. As Madison stated:

> Theoretic politicians, who have patronized this species of government [i.e., democracy] have erroneously supposed that by reducing mankind to a perfect equality in their political rights, they would at the same time be perfectly equalized and assimilated in their possessions, their opinions, and their passions.[25]

Nature has not made men equal, nor is there any logical reason why they should be so in any respect except a negative one: equal protection against force. When men are equally protected in their rights, they will naturally be unequal in other respects. As Alexander Hamilton put it, "Inequality will exist as long as liberty exists. It unavoidably results from that very liberty itself."[26] In 1791 James Wilson wrote:

> When we say, that all men are equal; we mean not to apply this equality to their virtues, their talents, their dispos-itions, *or their acquirements.* In all these respects, there is, and it

is fit for the great purpose of society that there should be, great inequality among men.(Italics added)[27]

Under liberty the distribution of property is determined by the *natural, logical, cause-and-effect relationships* of production and free trade. It is a consequence not of force but of reason and labor, which flourish when force is banned from human society. Wealth is determined not by collective numbers but by individual talent and enterprise. Just as there is always a minority in whom these qualities exceed those of the general public, there will always be unequal material consequences where those differences are allowed to express themselves. The Founders believed government should protect the resulting differences in wealth *on principle and as a matter of right*—not try to level them out. Jefferson said,

> To take from one, because it is thought that his own industry and that of his fathers has acquired too much, in order to spare to others, who, or whose fathers have not exercised equal industry and skill, is to violate arbitrarily the first principle of association, "the *guarantee* to every one of a free exercise of his industry, and the fruits acquired by it."[28]

Now, contrast the view of the Founders with that of President Lyndon Johnson, who in 1965 said, "We seek...not just equality as a right and a theory but equality as a fact and as a result." It would not be unfair to say that the policies of our federal government in recent decades more accurately reflect the view expressed by LBJ than the diametrically opposite view of the Founders. We have reversed the role of government. Hamilton was right when he said, "Inequality will exist as long as liberty exists"; our government has been systematically taking away our liberty in pursuit of "equality as a fact and as a result." That this view has come to dominate American politics is certainly not a progressive development—just the opposite!—but it shouldn't be a surprising one. Twenty centuries ago Cicero observed that democracies usually choose a leader "who curries favor with the people by promising them other men's property."[29]

In the days of Jericho the material wealth was certainly distributed unequally. The people who produced it were the opulent minority, who by their ingenuity and labor had risen above the indigence of others. They were surrounded by vastly greater numbers of men who desired a more equal distribution of the world's riches and employed the collective strength of their numbers to get it. When Madison told the Convention that the Senate ought to be "so constituted as to protect the minority of the opulent against the majority,"[30] he puts himself squarely in defense of the American "people of Jericho," so to speak. And the rest of the delegates were virtually unanimous in agreeing with him. As Brant notes, Madison's speech expressed "the general thought of the Convention."[31] In the end only the Pennsylvania delegation voted for popular election of the Senate, although the Convention approved direct election of the House by almost the reverse margin. Only New Jersey voted against the latter, while Maryland was divided.

The political system established by the Founders was not to be a means by which the invaders among men could plunder the producers simply by substituting ballots for bullets, by using superior numbers as armed invaders would for "distributing" the harvest of other people's labors. Government was to be a system for the defense of men's rights, not a system for using government's power to threaten force in order to gain the same ends that invaders gain through outright violence.

There were various other undemocratic features built into the Constitution, by which the Founders hoped to avert the "tyranny of the majority." For example, it was certainly undemocratic to allow a single individual, the president, to veto legislative measures passed by majorities of both houses of Congress. And since a two-thirds majority is required to override a presidential veto, the negative vote of a single senator from a small state can equal the votes of both senators from a large state. A negative vote from a Rhode Island senator can cancel the affirmative votes of both senators from New York, a state whose principal city alone has many times the population of the whole state of Rhode Island. That's a far cry from a one-man-one-vote basis. It was also undemocratic to allow a vote of five of the mere nine men on the Supreme Court to overrule the elected representatives of the people by declaring their laws unconstitutional.

As the authoritative Dr. Morley aptly phrased it, "Obviously the outstanding characteristic of our whole system of checks and balances is its intent to make the United States safe *from*—not for—democracy."[32]

Chapter Fourteen
FROM DEFENDER TO INVADER

How did a government which was intended to leave men free to run their own affairs become one which now prevents them from doing so? Besides regulating virtually every economic activity of its citizens, the federal government is the biggest property manager, renter, mover and hauler, medical clinician, lender, insurer, mortgage broker, employer, debtor, taxer and spender in all history.

In this country government was supposed to be man's servant rather than his master. How, then, did we come to the point where the citizen must now toil more for the government than for his food, clothing and shelter combined? According to the Tax Foundation, Inc., in 1995 the average taxpayer labored 2 hours and 47 minutes a day to pay his taxes and 2 hours 32 minutes for food, clothing and shelter.

How did a government founded to protect the natural rights of men become the chief violator of those rights, in the name of equality? Instead of equal justice, the government now does injustice to men's natural rights in order to achieve economic and social equality. The government which, as Jefferson said, was not to "take from the mouth of labor the bread it has earned"[1] has become the principal agent for doing exactly that, for redistributing wealth from those who have earned it to those who haven't.

And it's not only the wealthy whom government has victimized. It's everyone. Through inflation government has robbed every laborer of the true value of his earnings, no matter how small. Why has government become the force for robbing men's earnings instead of protecting them?

How did a government structured to protect the people from democracy become increasingly democratic? The Founding Fathers regarded democracy as downright evil, yet it has now become the ideal. Why?

These diverse questions all have the same answer: the ideological displacement of the individual with the collective. It was the importance of the individual which led to a social system where each man could direct his own affairs, serve his own interests, and was entitled to keep his earnings. It was assigning the collective a greater importance than the individual that led to regulating him, to forcing him to serve government decreed goals rather than his own, to taking away his earnings to pay for them, and to democracy as a way of establishing collective control over him.

The philosophical shift from individualism to collectivism meant a shift of both means and ends. The end was no longer the individual but the so-called common good; the pursuit of happiness was replaced by the pursuit of the "public interest." As for means, reason was the means by which free men pursued their happiness because government, by protecting men's natural rights, barred them from using force. But with the shift in ends, force was the only means by which government could prevent men from acting for themselves and compel them to serve the common good. Thus, shifting the end from the individual to the collective necessarily meant shifting the means from reason to force. In this way the necessity of suiting actions to goals also fit the characteristic capability of the actor in each case: reasoning is inherently an individual process, being an internal operation of the brain; and force is the definitive method of government.

THE CULT OF UNIFORMITY

It was the shift from individualism and reason to collectivism and force which brought about the cult of uniformity, for several reasons. Uniformity is the best way of maintaining and maximizing collective power, just as in the case of the tribe or herd. Uniformity is the key to drawing the strength of the group and directing it to a common goal rather than to diverse individual interests. The power to bend the individual to national goals, whether social reforms or economic programs such as the five-year plans of socialist countries, is what collectivists consider so admirable about totalitarian governments and regard as the weakness of a free society. As a practical matter, too, national programs are facilitated by uniformity among the populace because central administration is geared to uniformity, not diversity, and it is much easier to control a herd than a multitude of disparate individuals.

Uniformity is also the key to fashioning the common goals toward which collective effort will be applied. For the more diverse the members of society are, the more varied are their concerns and the fewer are their common objectives. If collectivism is to maintain its relevance, and its power as well, society must be kept as uniform as possible. A system that requires common goals and actions has no place for the uncommon.

Uniformity is also the condition which does most to eliminate the necessity for individuals to think for themselves. It removes the need for the independent decisions, which diversity demands. It permits people to get by largely by following others, just as in a herd or tribe, and thereby avoid the responsibility of independent thought and action. Uniformity, then, is a condition as unfavorable to thought as it is favorable to force, as inimical to individualism as it is advantageous to collectivism.

Uniformity is irrelevant to individualism. In a system of individual liberty men are free to be uncommon. Wealth is distributed not according to evenness but according to reason: according to the logical cause-and-effect sequences of production and exchange chosen by the minds of the participants. The distribution of material values follows the same rational principle of causality that men had to grasp and utilize in order to produce every material value from the first stone tools and the first agricultural harvest to the most complex creations of our modern age.

Under collectivism the distribution of wealth follows not reason but force, not rational principle but relative power—the power to seize the effects which only reason could produce. Material values are obtained not through recognizing and respecting the principle of causality, upon which every civilized advance has depended, but through organizing political muscle of sufficient strength to break it, to violate the cause-and-effect relationships of production, trade and property.

UNIFORMITY AND DEMOCRACY

While a social system based on individualism distributes wealth according to reason, one based on collectivism distributes it according to collective force institutionalized in a political system. What makes democracy so appealing in this regard is that it offers an idealized measure of the collective force of the herd. What more logical standard can there be for the collective force of a herd than its numerical strength? A one-man-one-vote system is the political expression of *animal* power. Just as with the power of a herd, the measure of democratic power is the power of *uniform* action, the power of the greatest number acting in the same way.

A system where wealth is distributed from some people to others through democratic voting is founded on the "superiority" of physical, animal force over reason. The physical strength of numbers becomes the measure for the political muscle to break, to destroy, to *trample,* the rational cause-and-effect relationships of production, trade and property rights.

Democracy, of course, can distribute wealth to some people *only* by taking it away from others. It can no more create it than any other type of government can. Madison observed that democracy contained "nothing to check the inducements to sacrifice the weaker party." But this characteristic, which Madison and his contemporaries feared, is what makes democratic redistribution so acceptable to its advocates. They know that what is to be redistributed must be taken away from somebody, and democracy legitimizes the transfer on the basis of *strength against weakness*—an outcome appropriate to force. It legitimizes the *victimization* of the individual or the minority in order to benefit the majority simply because of their superior animal numbers.

Democracy not only represents the primitive power of animal numbers. It uses it to mold society to the homogeneity of the herd, which is indeed the democratic ideal. It rewards the common at the expense of the uncommon. It serves the herd by tearing down those who rise above the herd. It strengthens the herd by attacking the only threat to herd power: the thinking men who demonstrate that they do not need the herd, who live by productive ability rather than collective force. And by "equalizing" men, democracy maintains its collective political power in the same way that a herd maintains its collective physical power. Democracy creates an electorate of uniformities who will act together to perpetuate collective force as a way of life.

Liberty allows men to escape from the equality of the herd. Where men are free, where their natural rights are respected and protected, the natural inequalities in human ability will inevitably result in economic inequality. The only way government, democratic or otherwise, can attempt to make men equal economically is to make them *un*equal politically—to violate the natural rights of some in order to benefit others. Accordingly, the whole concept of natural rights—itself a product of reason—disappears under collectivism as political equality is replaced by the equality of the herd.

Rights are no longer natural but artificial, hence no longer "unalienable." Instead of being rationally derived from nature, they are determined arbitrarily by politics. Rights are no longer absolute but relative, no longer derived from the absolute fact of a man's own existence but from the relative facts of others' demands and political power—the power to take one's property or limit one's liberty for their advantage. In place of the natural rights to life, liberty and property, politicians invent and substitute a host of artificial ones—"rights" to all sorts of social or economic benefits at the expense of other people's earnings and freedoms, "rights" to just about anything that will appeal to the masses of voters and help to get themselves elected.

When the people of Jericho turned to agriculture, they escaped the "equality" which had characterized human existence for a million years. They left the uniformity of those who surrounded and out-numbered them. They were a minority who rose above the vast majority, and they did it without taking anything from anyone. They did it by productive ability, which had nothing to do with collective force. The invaders, on the other hand, with their animalistic reliance on physical force, created nothing. They gained only at others' expense.

A democracy needs a productive minority in the same way that the invaders needed the people of Jericho. The democratic process *creates* nothing. It represents collective physical force, which, like the invasions of Jericho, can bring material gains to some only by violating other people's natural rights, specifically their property rights. The only difference is that at Jericho the victims resisted. In a democracy they are expected to surrender their property without a struggle because they are *outnumbered*. This system is widely regarded today as very enlightened and "progressive." Which just goes to show that those who think so have as little understanding of progress as they do of property rights. But that, too, was true of the invaders 10,000 years ago.

MAKING ENEMIES

When government takes wealth from some to give to others, it produces exactly the kind of enmity *within* society as between the people of Jericho and the invaders, and for the same reason. As long as government is confined to a defensive function, as long as no one can gain material values from government, there are no victims to resent the loss. The more government attempts to benefit some segments of society, the more it must victimize others and create enmity on both sides. The victims resent those who attempt to capture their earnings; and the latter resent the former for opposing them, for resisting the redistribution of what the envious have-nots have been led to believe they are entitled.

Invasion remains unattractive when there seems to be nothing to be gained from it. Let it be proven advantageous and it will be common-place. Similarly, when there is nothing to be gained from government, there is little interest in politics. Let one faction demonstrate it can gain from government, and others will attempt to do so. And in the same way that the people of Jericho were forced to fight in self-defense, people who have no interest in politics are forced to become politically active because their wealth and rights are at stake. Thus, expanding the role of government beyond the defensive function stimulates political participation—but in the sense of moving society into battle and with the necessary concomitant of arousing hostility among the populace. As Frederic Bastiat wrote in *The Law:*

> If the law confined itself to safeguarding all persons, liberties, and property rights; if it were only the organization of the individual's right to legitimate self-defense...is it likely that we citizens would argue very much about whether the suffrage should be more or less universal? Is it likely that such a dispute would endanger the greatest good, the public peace?...
>
> But once let the disastrous principle be introduced that, under the pretext of organization, regulation, protection, or encouragement, the law can *take from some to give to others...* whether farmers or manufacturers or merchants or shipowners or artists or actors; then certainly, in that event, there is no class that does not demand, with good reason, to have a hand in making the laws; that does not vehemently claim its right to vote and to be considered eligible; that would not overthrow society rather than fail to obtain that right.[2]

Is it surprising, then, that the growing role of our government has been accompanied by growing violence and by the growth of revolutionary political groups in our society? Or that crime has increased, when government itself violates men's property rights and, by moving more and more issues from the private, *voluntary* sector to the political arena, has demonstrated that they are to be settled by *force?* Is it any wonder that democracies become, as Madison said, "spectacles of turbulence and contention"?

Bastiat continues:

> Even beggars and tramps will prove to you that they have an incontestable right to vote. They will say to you: "We never buy wine, tobacco, or salt without paying a tax, and part of the tax is given by law, in bounties and subsidies, to men richer than we are.... Since everyone exploits the law to his own profit, we too want to do so. We desire to have it grant us the *right to public relief,* which is the poor man's share of the plunder. To this end we must become voters and legislators, so that we may organize

the dole for our class in grand style, as you have organized protective tariffs in grand style for your class...."

What can one reply to such an argument? Yes, so long as it is admitted in principle that the law may be diverted from its true mission, that it may violate property rights instead of guaranteeing them, each class will want to make the law, whether to defend itself against being plundered or to organize plunder for its own profit.... In a word, people will be continually pounding on the door of the legislature. The struggle will not be less bitter within it....

Is there any need to prove that this odious perversion of the law is a perpetual cause of hatred, discord, and even social disorder? Look at the United States. There is no country in the world where the law confines itself more rigorously to its proper role, which is to guarantee everyone's liberty and property. Accordingly, there is no country in which the social order seems to rest on a more stable foundation.[3]

Bastiat wrote those words in the year 1850. He would no doubt be shocked by the explosive growth of American government in the twentieth century, but he would not be surprised that an explosion of social disorder has followed. He would regard it as inevitable, a consequence of the illusion "that it is possible to enrich all classes at the expense of one another."[4]

GOVERNMENT SWITCHES SIDES

Replacing limited government with Big Government has turned the function of government from protecting to plundering. The organized force of the American political system is now assisting the "takers" rather than defending the "makers." It is on the side of the invaders rather than the people of Jericho. Instead of protecting each man's right to his own productive efforts, our government has increasingly become the weapon by which factions within society can plunder each other. Expanding government has simply expanded the ways in which they can do so.

Now, legal plunder can be committed in an infinite number of ways; hence there are an infinite number of plans for organizing it: tariffs, protection, bonuses, subsidies, incentives, the progressive income tax, free education, the right to employment, the right to profit, the right to wages, the right to relief, the right to the tools of production, interest-free credit, etc., etc. And

it is the aggregate of all these plans, in respect to what they have
in common, legal plunder, that goes under the name of socialism.[5]

Observe that almost all of those examples of legal plunder which
Bastiat in France a century and a half ago grouped under socialism have
since come about in this country under democracy. (Notice, too, how
many of these, and many more like them, are proclaimed as "rights.")
Democracy has led to socialism because it, like socialism, is premised
on collectivism, not individualism. Both democracy and socialism deny
the primacy of the individual. Both substitute the relativism of numbers
for the absolutism of individual rights. Accordingly, both empower the
many to sacrifice the few in the name of the collective good, usually
referred to these days as the "public interest."

In a democracy the sacrifice of the few to the many is arranged
and sanctioned by voting. It is determined by numerical strength at the
polls. How could the collectivist premise be more obvious? How could
it possibly be given a more articulate political expression than in the
democratic concept of majority rule? Under this concept the majority
assumes the power to force supposedly free men not in the majority to
support programs against their judgment and counter to their interests.
In short, the majority possesses the legal authority to sacrifice the
minority—to violate their natural rights—in the name of the collective
good of society.

Subsidies, welfare programs, tariffs, the progressive income tax
and all the other socialist programs have been thrust upon us on the
grounds they have been adopted by politicians elected by the majority.
All these programs sacrifice some people to others. They do not create
wealth. They are really invasions, "the moral equivalent of war," to
borrow a phrase from President Carter, for they benefit some people
by the seizure of wealth from others. Under democracy any such
invasion is acceptable as long as it is popular, and getting elected
consists of promising plunder to the greater number while victimizing
the smaller number. Organized force is employed according to
popularity, not principle.

GANGING UP

All of the invasionary programs of democratic government do not
necessarily benefit the majority as a group. In fact, the more such
programs government attempts, the more difficult it becomes to find

others which will yield such broad results. There simply isn't sufficient uniformity among the populace for the majority to benefit in very many different ways. People's activities and interests are too diverse. This situation leads to two courses of attack for the political warriors. One is to turn the obstacle into an opportunity by introducing programs to make the populace more uniform.

The second is to attempt to benefit the majority piecemeal. Instead of programs for the majority as a whole, the politicians propose to benefit many factions separately, factions which, though each a minority, taken collectively constitute a majority. Instead of the battle lines being drawn simply between two sides, the majority and the minority, politics has become a many-sided conflict. Numerous warring factions contest with each other or combine for advantage against others.

Democratic politics has become the art of *putting together majorities,* of assembling the preponderance of votes by promising various factions legal plunder in return for being elected to conduct the invasions against other elements of society. And a system in which individual rights can be sacrificed to the majority quickly becomes one where those rights will be sacrificed to any minority faction which may be politically important to assembling a majority. Thus the idea of sacrificing the individual to the majority leads inevitably to sacrificing him to minorities as well.

As more and more programs are undertaken to placate various factions and win elections, the system ultimately sacrifices everybody to everybody else. More government programs mean more victims since every government benefit is somebody's loss. And when government permits and even promotes legalized plunder for some, everyone else will demand his share, too. The question guiding every voter becomes, "What's in it for me?" The politicians are only too happy to provide obliging answers. The result is a socialistic system of universal plunder which comes about under the name of democracy.

Once the collectivist premise is adopted, once it is accepted that the rights of the individual may be violated for the alleged good of others, there is no stopping the process short of sacrificing everyone. There is no individual against whom superior numbers cannot be assembled for some particular cause. There is no one, at least no one who has anything, against whom some assortment of other men cannot be gathered who can benefit at his expense. A political system functioning on this grisly basis is the logical extension of the original premise. The only way to prevent it from developing, or to reverse it once the process has begun, is to begin at the beginning: to start by recognizing and defending the inviolable supremacy of individual rights *on principle.*

What made the United States a country characterized throughout most of its history by production rather than plunder was that it rejected the collectivist premise from the very beginning. This was the one country founded on individualism, the one country whose government was instituted to secure the natural rights of the individual against the force of other men regardless of how superior their numbers might be. This same country has become a victim of creeping socialism, of growing political plunder, because it has increasingly substituted the collectivist premise for the supremacy of individual rights. Structural features of our original government which protected the individual have been dismantled, and the government has been made more democratic instead. Democracy is a form of government designed for the demands of the masses, not for protecting the rights of the individual.

At the end of the Constitutional Convention a woman, curious about what sort of government had been devised, stopped Ben Franklin and asked, "What have you given us?" He replied, "A republic, Madam— *if you can keep it."* We haven't. Increasingly we've turned it into a democracy.

AN INGENIOUS POLITICAL MECHANISM, HOW IT WORKED, AND HOW IT WAS DESTROYED

The electoral college possessed unique features for protecting the individual from the majority—unlike popular elections which many have advocated for determining the president. Because of the Founders' orientation to individualism and reason, the method they devised for selecting the president was geared not only to an intelligent—rather than a popular—choice but to safeguarding the rights of the individual against the superior numbers of other men. The Founders did not equate popularity with either wisdom or justice. In fact, they well knew that popular, or democratic, government possessed great potential for injustice to individual rights.

The electoral college is perhaps the least understood feature of our Constitution. Unfortunately, its original form was destroyed so early that it never had a chance to demonstrate its remarkable characteristics.

So great was the esteem in which George Washington was held by his contemporaries that he would have been their choice for president by any method of selection they might have adopted. Hence the electoral college proved nothing in picking our first president. It chose John Adams as vice president, which appears to have been a wise choice. Adams succeeded Washington as president and has generally been classed by historians as a "near great" president.[6]

The electoral college had had only that brief history when a crisis occurred in the election of our third president. It was an unusual circumstance which might not have occurred again. Or if it had occurred later on, after the electoral college had established the worth of its unique features, the adjustment that followed probably wouldn't have utterly destroyed them.

The electoral college had all the advantages of indirect election, just as the Senate did. Indeed, some of these seemed more pronounced by the fact that the electors were selected for one task alone. They would have nothing to gain politically, because after casting their ballots they would return to their private affairs. It seemed, therefore, that they would be even less susceptible to corruption or political pressure and more likely than ever to exercise the wisdom and independent judgment for which they were selected.

Each state's representation in the electoral college was equal to its representation in Congress, that is, to the total of its House members plus its senators. In this way the exact numerical composition of the legislative branch—which was acceptable to both large and small states—was mirrored in the electoral college. But that numerical composition was acceptable for the legislative branch only because there were two legislative bodies, with power divided and balanced between them. How was such a division and balance of power to be achieved in the single body of the electoral college? While power in Congress was divided between two houses, in the electoral college it was divided between two votes.

The method of voting was the electoral college's most ingenious and least appreciated feature. It was also the one which precipitated the crisis. Each elector was to vote for two men for president, at least one of whom had to be from outside the elector's own state. The candidate receiving the greatest number of votes would be the president. The runner-up would be the vice president.

An obvious advantage of the method was that it provided that the vice president would be the man regarded as second most qualified to be president, rather than just someone chosen to balance the ticket geographically or for some other political advantage. There were, however, subtler but even more important advantages to the system.

The requirement that each elector's votes be split between two candidates tended to "break and control" the power of factions. It cut the democratic power of numbers. It limited the political effects of the larger states' numerical strength and prevented them from dominating presidential elections.

While it might be expected that electors would show some partiality to candidates from their own states, this factor would be offset by the requirement that each elector cast at least one vote for someone outside his state. At least half of the votes were thus more likely to reflect merit rather than state politics. The voting was deliberately structured to minimize the influence of local political ties or indebtedness and to maximize the independent reasoning of the electors. Since electors could be expected to some extent to vote for leading figures from their own states—not only for political reasons but because they might know their qualifications better—such votes would in large measure cancel each other. Important and often decisive, then, would be those votes candidates would receive from *outside* their states, votes reflecting the impartial judgment of electors who had no political obligations and nothing to gain. The dominant power in electing the president would thus rest not with the states which had most to gain, by electing one of their own men, but with the votes from states which had *least* to gain, just as with the electors themselves. (The exact opposite would be true if the president were popularly elected.) Consequently, with the original system there would be little tendency to choose a president on the basis of gaining benefits for some at others' expense.

The electoral system of voting for two candidates had other fascinating implications. It might well be that the elector would feel obligated to vote for the most popular candidate among the people he represented. He might even be pledged to do so. But he would have a second vote to cast. Having cast one vote for the popular choice, he might be more inclined to exercise his own judgment on the second. Both would count the same. In this event the electoral college would represent a balance between the numerical power of the people and the independent judgment of the electors, and the choice of the president would reflect some combination of the two.

No less intriguing would be the consequences if the elector reflected popular sentiment in his second vote as well. Suppose instead of exercising independent judgment he cast the second vote for the second most popular candidate in his constituency.[7] In the individual elector's votes a second place would be just as good as first place. Both votes would be equal. *The majority would have no advantage*—with obvious implications for the security of minority rights. There would be little political incentive for making lavish campaign promises to gain the votes of the majority at the expense of the minority if the minority were equally important politically.

With such a system it would also be possible for a man to be elected president who did not carry a single state in popular vote. He could accumulate a winning total of electoral votes by finishing second in a great many states if several different candidates won in those states, each winning only a few. In this situation the man with all the second place finishes would indeed have the broadest political support across the country. Under today's system he wouldn't get a single electoral vote.

If a candidate could receive electoral votes for finishing second in a given state or district, the whole power structure of the two-party system wouldn't have developed in the way that it has.[8] Where the winner takes all the votes as under the present system, there can be only two significant parties, both contesting the *majority* position. Only the majority on a state-wide basis has any representation in the electoral college. One party is the majority; the other hopes to become the majority and has the best chance of doing so. All its hopes and its influence rest on becoming the majority, because it has no representation as a minority. If, however, each elector cast two votes for the presidency, one representing whoever came in second, both the majority and the principal minority would be represented. There would be a political value to being that minority, not just to being the majority. Second place would be worth fighting for, whereas only first place is today. As a result, third parties could effectively contest the second position for the same reason that only two can do so for the top spot in the present winner-take-all system.

Under the present two-party system the greater the dominance of one party in a state, the less important the other becomes, because the more remote is its chance of becoming the majority, which is the only way of winning electoral votes. Under a two-vote electoral system, where the runner-up would receive the second vote, the greater dominance of one party would make it more attractive for third parties to compete. In a state where, let's say, eighty percent of the people vote for one party, a third party would need to gain only little more than half of the remaining twenty percent to obtain electoral representation.

Under the present two-party system, the greater the dominance of one party, the less sensitive it is to the rights of individuals in the minority, because the more difficult it becomes for the minority to protect themselves. Under a two-vote electoral system, with the second vote representing the runner-up, the minority represented by that vote would have the electoral power to balance the majority regardless of the size of that majority. For example, if the runner-up had only twenty percent of the popular vote in a state or district, compared to eighty percent for the majority candidate, the former would have the same electoral power to balance the latter as if the vote totals were 49 to 51 percent or even 50-50. Thus the two-vote electoral system was another ingenious method of protecting the rights of individuals in the minority from the power and desires of the majority.

We will never know whether or how the electoral college would have utilized these possibilities had its original form been retained, but the potential was there. It was intrinsic to the mechanism. The original electoral college was structured for a diffusion of power and for balancing the interests represented by majority and minority candidates. Presidential elections were not mere popularity contests. Candidates of the minority had far more significance than they can ever have under the present system, and the minority was not effectively limited to only a second party. It was far easier for third parties to be competitive and influential.

Why, then, didn't the system survive? In 1800 Thomas Jefferson and Aaron Burr had the same number of electoral votes. The tie occurred because the electors didn't perform as they should have by voting for the two finest men for the presidency, MacBride writes:

> It is probable that few people outside his own circle wanted him [Burr] to be president—and if the Electors had voted according to their own convictions he would never have been a real contender for the job.[9]

Burr got his electoral votes because the electors assumed Jefferson would be president and cast their second vote for the *vice* presidency instead of for another man for the presidency. They didn't want Burr for president, but he was politically powerful in New York, the nation's largest state, and would also balance the ticket by being from the North. (Jefferson was from Virginia.)

The Constitution provided that in case of a tie, or if no one had a majority of electoral votes, the House of Representatives would choose the president. In this way the Founders again arranged for the selection of the president by the filtering process of indirect election. House members, who were elected by the people, would in turn elect the president. The large states' numerical strength in the House was equalized by the fact that presidential balloting there was by states.

When the Jefferson-Burr contest went to the House, the scoundrel Burr made a bold attempt to gain the presidency. He collaborated with the opposition members in the House and persuaded them to vote for him for president. After 35 ballots the contest was still deadlocked. Finally, to end the crisis, Alexander Hamilton prevailed upon several of his party members to cast blank votes and allow Jefferson to be elected.

As a result, the Constitution was amended, by the Twelfth Amendment, to prevent such an incident from occurring again. The electoral college was altered to provide for separate ballots for the president and vice president, with each elector casting one vote for each. Gone were all the advantages of the two-vote system.

It was no longer necessary that half of a state's electoral votes for president be for someone from outside the state. So overnight the large states doubled their power to advance their own candidates for the presidency. Instead of power being diffused, as formerly, it was now concentrated.

Along with increasing the power of the large states, the new electoral method increased the power of popular majorities. The minority, which might have been represented by the second electoral vote under the original system, either through the free choice of an elector or by a second-place finish, no longer had any representation. Where the system once gave the minority some measure of protection against the power of the majority, it now amplified the power of the majority instead.

Without the requirement of splitting votes between two candidates, block voting for a single candidate became the practice. It assumed a power that it never could have attained under the old system. By casting its votes as a block, a state could increase its electoral power relative to those states which still divided their votes among two or more candidates. To maintain its share of influence, every state soon found it necessary to cast all its electoral votes as a block. The system which originally mitigated the power of superior numbers was turned into one which exemplified them.

While the new system limited electors to a single choice on their ballots, the block-voting practice dictated that it would be the popular choice. Although the electors might have voted individually on the basis of their own minds, there was no way they could do so collectively. Voting collectively, as a block, inevitably meant voting on a physical rather than an intellectual basis, voting on the basis of herd power rather than reasoning. The electoral system, which was originally designed to reflect superior judgment, became a mechanical system where that judgment could not be exercised.

After the Jefferson-Burr crisis, some change was clearly needed. In my opinion the change should have been to have separate ballots for president and vice president but to allow each elector two votes for each. This arrangement would have prevented another Jefferson-Burr situation and yet preserved the essential advantages of the original two-vote system. As with the present system, it also would have provided for the election of president and vice-president from the same party, an event which would have been unlikely under the original system.

It took a long time for the damage done by the Twelfth Amendment to surface. There were at least three reasons for the delay. One was simply that the American people for so long remained predominantly individualistic. They adhered to the ideas of liberty and limited government and in general didn't expect government to provide an answer for every human need, problem or desire. Second, it wasn't until the twentieth century that communications media were developed to the extent that presidential candidates could reach large numbers of people directly and frequently to bid for their votes with promises of benefits at other people's expense. Third, so long as the Senate was structured to protect the rights of the individual, a president was severely limited in his ability to get programs of political plunder through the legislature.

CONVERTING THE MACHINERY OF GOVERNMENT TO A WEAPON OF PLUNDER

If one were to try to define a watershed between individualism and collectivism as the dominant principle of American government, no more fitting date could be chosen than the year 1913. It was probably the worst year in history for damage to the structure of our political system. It was the year that saw the passage of the income tax, the Federal Reserve Act, and the Constitutional amendment for the popular election of senators. No alterations of our system of government have done greater damage to the concept of individual rights, have led to the plundering of more wealth, have done more injustice or caused more suffering to more Americans than these.

Popular election of senators transformed the Senate from a bastion for defending individual rights to a means by which the majority could overrun them. If senators or senate candidates wouldn't support legislation to benefit the majority at the expense of others, the voters, or rather the majority of them, would almost always put others in office who would.

All of the benefits which the politicians were to promise ever more lavishly to the voters as the years went by had to be taken from somebody. Here's where the income tax and the Federal Reserve System came in handy.

It was easy to sell the public on the income tax, because the majority could envision themselves benefiting at the expense of the wealthy few. Of course, that supply of victims quickly became insufficient. As government promised more and attempted more, it had to tax more. When it became a system of universal plunder, with programs to benefit everybody at everybody else's expense, it was victimizing everyone through taxes, not just the wealthy few. Instead of the majority being better off, as promised, *practically everybody* was worse off! Almost everyone was receiving less in government benefits than he was paying in taxes.

The losses were becoming too great to be paid solely through taxes. Although the income tax ballooned far beyond what its original sponsors could have imagined, revenues were increasingly insufficient. Losses escalated as government programs expanded, because those programs were inevitably net losers. It was political suicide to raise taxes to the level necessary to pay for these programs. It would be all too obvious to the voters that they were losing far more than they were gaining through the system. So it became politically necessary to resort to inflation, which the Federal Reserve System facilitated so conveniently. As Big Government undertook to provide more and more for everyone, it resorted increasingly to the ultimate means of plundering everyone.

The constitutional government established in the United States two centuries ago was an intricately balanced mechanism. All the pieces were interconnected. They actuated and regulated each other to make the system work as it was intended. Altering one part altered the functioning of the others and, consequently, the operation of the entire mechanism. Popular election of senators destroyed essential internal regulators, and the political machine in Washington began to accelerate wildly.

There was no longer any brake in the legislative branch against the tendency to promise political plunder in exchange for votes. At the same time, a brake on the expansion of federal power was also removed, so programs proliferated for delivering that plunder. The power of the *states* to select senators had been a built-in control against the expansion of federal power.

Today there is no field in which the authority of the states hasn't been usurped by the federal government in its ever-widening role. State sovereignty is a joke. The states are mere departments of Big Government which operate at the sufferance of Washington. They can perform only those functions Washington permits and in the way that it allows.

The Tenth Amendment, which reserved to the states or to the people any powers not specifically delegated to the federal government by the Constitution, has become meaningless, because the states have no practical way of resisting the federal usurpation of these reserved powers. The Constitution gives the federal government no authority whatever in education, agriculture, medical care and dozens of other fields in which federal intervention is now commonplace. The states would have been able to limit this cancerous expansion of federal power if they had retained the ability to protect their sovereignty by their representation in the Senate.

It should be noted that there wouldn't be much danger of the states plundering the people and violating their rights to the extent the federal government has. The fact that there are many states would prevent any one of them from being too oppressive; people could too easily move to another state. Furthermore, the ambitions of state governments would always be limited by the fact they don't have the power of inflation, as the federal government does. The Constitution forbids any state from making anything but gold or silver legal tender.

The Supreme Court was the final defense against the unconstitutional expansion of federal power. It resisted for a while, but not for long. Eventually it even came to champion federal intervention rather than individual rights.

This turnabout of the Supreme Court was yet another consequence of the earlier structural changes in the federal government. Supreme Court justices are nominated by the president and must be approved by the Senate. When the alteration of the electoral college gave increased power to majorities, and when the Senate became popularly elected, it was only natural that men who became presidents and senators were more concerned with majority favoritism than with individual rights. It was only natural, too, that presidents would tend to nominate, and the Senate to approve, men for the Court who had the same philosophical orientation as themselves. There were a few exceptions, and some Supreme Court justices changed their philosophy after their appointments. But eventually the Supreme Court came to be dominated by men who were as oriented to the masses as earlier justices were to individual rights.

Whereas the earlier justices were primarily concerned with protecting the individual *from* force, the new breed of justices wanted to benefit the masses *by* force. In trying to justify the use of government power for what they regarded as the collective good, these "judicial activists" substituted good intentions for reason and Constitutional principles. They warped logic to fit their righteous desires. Instead of adhering to the language and intent of the Constitution, they fabricated excuses to accommodate federal programs they favored.

For instance, in the case which upheld federal intervention in agriculture, *Wickard v. Filburn* (1942), a farmer contested the government's authority to enforce acreage planting allotments. He had planted 23 acres of wheat when the government had allotted him only eleven. He was fined for the excess—even though the grain was never marketed. It was consumed by livestock on his own property. The Court held that if he had not fed the excess wheat to his stock, he might have bought feed, and that feed, even if produced locally, *might* have affected the price of other wheat in interstate commerce. Therefore, the federal government's intervention in agriculture was "justified" by its authority to regulate interstate commerce.

By similar illogic, the Court has declared that elevator operators carrying people between floors of a building are engaged in interstate commerce.

Much of the federal regulations with which we must contend rest on the twisting of language and logic to tie them to the interstate commerce clause of the Constitution. Yet that clause was never intended to give the federal government any positive role—not even in genuine interstate commerce. It was included solely to prevent the states from obstructing commerce across their borders. In Madison's words, authority over interstate commerce was not given to the federal government "to be used for...positive purposes," but only as "a negative and preventive provision against injustice among the states themselves."[10]

In an excellent book which should be read by every American, *We Hold These Truths,* Lawrence Patton McDonald writes:

> Inherent in the entire Constitution, though not expressly stated, is the ancient principle that *the intent of the law-giver is the law.* A written Constitution would be an absurdity and a nullity if that principle were not inherent in it. If a judge can interpret the Constitution or laws to mean something obviously not intended by the original makers—if he can decide that the Constitution does not mean today what it meant yesterday, and if his ruling becomes binding upon the nation—then the nation's Constitution and laws are meaningless. If judges can "reinterpret" the law whenever they wish, to make it more suitable for some contemporary conditions (with them determining what that "suitability" is), then the nation is ruled by judicial despots, not by law.[11]

Chapter Fifteen
THE QUIET CONQUEST

We come now to the question of how a people who once loved freedom above all else were gradually led to accept, even prefer, the yoke of government control. How was America transformed from a nation of self-reliant individuals to one whose people look continually to Washington, D.C. for solutions?

It was the observance of individual rights that made the United States a land of political liberty and, consequently, economic progress. But although America demonstrated that the system of individual rights was incredibly superior for solving all sorts of problems, in one critical area it chose the *opposite* system. The extent to which this deviation undermined individualism, capitalism and freedom is almost impossible to overestimate.

In one critical area Americans generally came to accept the collectivist premise that alleged social good is more important than individual rights—and is to be achieved by violating rather than honoring them. The primacy of the individual was denied because—as is always the case—the cause was considered so noble, so pure, so lofty. The cause this time was education. Americans accepted the idea of forcibly taking some people's money to educate other people's children—the moral equivalent of robbing a bank if the money is to be used for a "good purpose."

The true moral character of public education was disguised by referring to it in collectivist terms as taxing everybody's wealth to educate everybody's children, all in the name of the collective good of society, of course. But not everybody had children, nor did those who had them all want them educated in exactly the same way. The essential fact is that the system violated every individual's right to his own earnings, to employ them as he saw fit, whether for education or anything else. Some people's education was placed ahead of other people's rights and paid for at their expense.

At the same time, the parents lost the right to select the kind of education they wanted for their children. And without the economic effects of market selection and free competition, the quality of public education deteriorated badly. The "new math" and the "look-say" method of teaching reading, which have proven so disastrous, could never have become widespread in a free market educational system, where parents would have a choice and could send their children to schools employing methods that worked. It was the government's *monopolistic* control over education which permitted it to force an increasingly inferior product on the public while the goods and services produced in the free market were constantly being upgraded.

During the long slide in public education the National Assessment of Educational Progress reported that fewer than one in 100 seventeen-year-olds now had the mathematical skills to balance a checkbook. *The Wall Street Journal* reported, "Many schools discover kids using 'new math' can't divide 100 by 10."[1] In 1991 the Carnegie Commission on Science, Technology and Government reported that 47 percent of the nation's 17-year-olds could not convert nine parts out of 100 to a percentage. In 1992 Benno Schmidt, president of Yale University, wrote:

> Nearly half of all high school students have not mastered seventh-grade arithmetic. American 13-year olds place near the bottom in science and math achievement in international comparisons.[2]

TRAINING LITTLE INVADERS

The shocking failure of public school methods, which are unsuccessful in teaching even the most basic educational skills, is paralleled by an even greater failure in ideology. The mere example of the system itself is devastating. For if children are led to believe that it is proper to obtain an education through organized force, will they not believe it proper to obtain other things in the same manner? Should we be surprised when the students themselves attempt to gain other ends by force and the campuses become scenes of violence? And should we be surprised that even those who do not favor student violence generally favor achieving the same ends through the organized force of government? If it is right for government to rob a bank, or rather the rest of society, for one "good purpose," why not fund a lot of others the same way?

Furthermore, the students see that their teachers support themselves in exactly this fashion, by money taken through coercion, through the government's power to threaten physical violence. No wonder the schools teach "invader economics." The teachers live by it. It is with perfect consistency that they advocate Big Government, that they teach an unlimited number of "good purposes" can be achieved by government seizing wealth to pay for them—in the same way it pays for the students' education and the teachers' salaries. An educational system dependent upon government will inevitably glorify government's powers to tax and spend.

It is not merely because of their own vested interest in the system that educators preach "invader economics." They really know no other. Most have no understanding of a free market, which is not surprising since so many have never held jobs outside the teaching field. And only about half of the nation's 60,000 social studies teachers, who are those most likely to teach economics, have had any formal training in the subject; moreover, that training is in the "new economics" rather than classical free market economics. These economic illiterates are unable to visualize how free enterprise would function in education. Should the question arise, the teachers will undoubtedly tell the students that free enterprise would be unworkable in education. Yet private companies provide most of the educational materials used in the public schools, the books, desks, pens, paper, audio-visual equipment, computers, etc. They also provide employee training in highly technical subjects for tens of thousands of workers throughout industry.

IBM is training 22,000 of its employees daily—the equivalent of a major university—at a cost of $1.5 billion annually. The American Society for Training and Development estimates that business is spending $210 billion annually on training and education. Compare this to a total budget of about $250 billion for all education kindergarten through 12th grade in the U.S.

Most of the education provided by business is job training, but a surprising, and growing, amount is for basic education. More and more companies are providing classes in such fundamentals as reading and writing—which people should have learned in the public schools but didn't. A few, such as General Motors, even pay workers for attending literacy classes during working hours. Columnist George Melloan observes, "Employers, through taxes, help pay for the public school system that does not meet their needs and then must pay again to remedy its failures."[3]

If privately-owned businesses are able to teach basic skills, which the public schools have failed to do, why are we sticking so doggedly to the concept of government-run schools? We may ask ourselves: why would the British people stick so doggedly for so many decades to the concept of government-run coal mines when they were such failures compared to the private mines? Or, why would the Soviets stick to the concept of government-run agriculture for 70 years when it was so clearly inferior to private farming? We're the same way with education. We keep pouring more and more money and effort into a government-run system even though its failures are more and more apparent, but we will not trade it for a privately-run one. We will not do so even though evidence abounds that private schools throughout their long history have outperformed the public ones. We will not do so even when private businesses—whose main business is not even education—are able to provide the basic skills which public schools have so conspicuously failed to provide.

Defenders of the public school system will immediately reply, "What about the people who couldn't afford private schools? If schools were privately-owned and run for profit, there would be poor people whose children would be uneducated." Well, observe that the same arguments could be made about coal or food: what about the poor people who couldn't afford coal (or food)? If coal mines (or farms) were privately-owned and run for profit, there would be poor people who would freeze (or go hungry). Yet we know that is not the case. Just the opposite is true. When individuals are free to serve *their own interests* by profiting from coal and food, other people will find these commodities more available and economic *as a consequence*. There is a cause-and-effect relationship between the primacy of the individual and the beneficial effects to others in society, and that relationship cannot be reversed without disastrous effect. If the individual is not allowed to act for his own interests, if he is not allowed to make a profit, if his right to the pursuit of happiness is to be subordinated to other people's need for coal, food, or education, then there will be a shortage of these effects in society. Because the cause has been eliminated.

The way to improve education is to remove it from the public sector. It cannot be reformed any more than Soviet agriculture or British Coal could be reformed and still be government run. Melloan notes that businesses "find that it is easier to do their own training than to try to reform public education."[4] Government-run enterprises can't be reformed because the *only* way government can operate them is by acting against the primacy of the individual: by attempting—through force—to obtain the effect by acting against the cause.

Most efforts to reform economic education in our public schools consist of trying to get the schools to adopt textbooks favorable to capitalism rather than socialism. It is a futile effort. A tax-supported educational system is the antithesis of capitalism. It is hoping for far too much to expect the schools to teach capitalism when they themselves function in the diametrically opposite way. Expecting the teachers in a socialistic school system to teach capitalism would be like expecting the invaders of Jericho to teach agriculture. It is a subject they simply do not understand and one which is completely counter to their own way of life. As a result, our schools are not training our children to be thinking, productive individuals; they are training them to be little invaders.

For example, one school textbook, *Poverty and Welfare* by Bennett and Newman, teaches how to apply for welfare but not how to apply for a job. Pages 62 and 63 contain a welfare application form, but there is no job application form. This and many other shocking examples are cited in *Textbooks on Trial* by James C. Hefley. Many of the following are taken from this book, which is the account of a Texas couple's investigations prompted by what they saw in their own children's school books.

A Global History of Man by Stavrianos *et al.* declares on page 444: "…Marxism turns people toward a future of unlimited promise, an escalator to the stars." At a hearing before Texas' State Textbook Committee Dr. Robert H. Selby, head of the History Department at Le Tourneau College, stated that the book "reveals a very clear support of Marxism."[5] Dr. Anthony Kubeck, Chairman of the Department of History and Political Science at the University of Dallas and a distinguished authority on the Far East, said that the description of Chinese history "is one-sided, leaning toward a sympathetic view of Mao Tse-tung's brand of Communism…. It simply is not accurate to describe Communist China as the author does."[6] Yet the State Committee voted to accept the book.

Economics for Our Times by Augustus H. Smith has one page on free enterprise, six pages on socialism and communism—defensive of liberal socialism—and two *chapters* on Big Government. So upset by this book was Morgan J. Davis, Chairman of the Board of Humble Oil and vice chairman of the Texas Committee On Education Beyond the High School, that he wrote a letter of protest to the governor of Texas. Calling the book "an out-and-out advocate of the welfare state and a system of socialism," he continued, in part:

> There are many, many passages in this book which either openly advocate a governmentally controlled economy or infer that such an economy is the ideal for which we should strive.

It is difficult for me to see how a student who accepts the
text as written could be other than an embryo socialist in his
thinking.[7]

The same book brought this editorial comment from a Texas
newspaper:

Economics for Our Times is unsuitable as a textbook
because of its lack of objectivity and real accuracy in discussing
the economy of this country historically—both through omission
and constant out-of-proportion presentation of government as a
solution to individual and commercial economic problems. The
authors have expounded what might be called "central statism."[8]

The State Committee approved the book.

The American Economy by Sampson *et al.* makes a weak case for
free enterprise and a strong case for communism. Then it states on page
409 that communists are convinced of the superiority of their system
while suggesting (page 396) that Americans may turn to revolution to
correct the problems of free enterprise.

Economics: Principles and Practices by Brown and Wolf mini-
mizes the benefits of free enterprise and lauds government economic
management. Pictures display the United States at its worst and the
Soviet Union at its best. The heavy emphasis on American problems is
accompanied by the implicit message that capitalism cannot solve them.

The Capitalist System by Edwards, Reich and Weisskopf
is described in a sales brochure by the publisher, Prentice-Hall, Inc.,
as follows:

This second edition of THE CAPITALIST SYSTEM will
give your students a strong background in the *Marxist
perspective* on the American Capitalist System....
Part I illustrates briefly but vividly some of the *forms of
oppression* that are so prevalent and so intractable in the United
States today. Part II lays the basic theoretical groundwork for a
Marxist analysis of capitalist society. Part III explains and
evaluates the workings of the contemporary stage of capitalism
in the United States—*monopoly capitalism.* Parts IV and V
analyze *specific forms of oppression* (inequality, sexism, racism,
economic crises, imperialism) in the U.S. today. In examining
the current situation, these chapters seek to throw light on
potential contradictions that are likely to shape future changes in

the capitalist system. Part VI explores the authors' vision of a *socialist alternative to capitalism* and considers some of the possible strategies for achieving such a society.[9]

Economics is not the only subject being slanted to fit the collectivist viewpoint. History has been rewritten to support it. For example, there can be no doubt whatsoever that the authors of our Constitution, by providing the liberty for each man to serve his own interests, intended to leave each man to the concern of *his own* welfare. Yet *Our American Government* by Dimond and Pflieger, page 37, says the exact opposite:

> The Constitution was to be the basis for building a nation in which the welfare of each person was to be the concern of all.

From the same book, page 9, here is another example of collectivist thinking imputed to the Founders:

> The good of all was thought by the framers of the Constitution to be superior to the rights of the individual.

That statement is simply not true. Consider, as just one bit of evidence, the fact that the Constitution contains a Bill of Rights and does not say that exceptions may be made for the good of all. Those rights are supreme and absolute. The Founders obviously did not consider the "good of all" to be superior to them. Consider, too, that the Declaration of Independence states man's rights to life, liberty and the pursuit of happiness are "unalienable." It does not say "...unalienable unless superseded by the good of all."

Many books, such as *Our Nation's Story,* discuss the Constitution without ever mentioning one of its most important aspects—that it was intended to *limit* the powers of the federal government.

But the last word in distortion may be *Many Peoples, One Nation,* edited by P. I. Rose. Page 88 contains the following:

> No nation on earth is guilty of practices more shocking and bloody than is the United States at this very hour.
> Go where you may and search where you will. Roam through all the kingdoms of the Old World. Travel through South America. Search out every wrong. When you have found the last, compare your facts with the everyday practices of this

nation. Then you will agree with me that, for revolting barbarity
and shameless hypocrisy, America has no rival.

We do not need to roam the kingdoms of the Old World. We need
look no further than the Soviet Union, which modern American
textbooks have been so fond of praising. According to Alexander
Solzhenitzen, the most reliable estimates indicate about seventeen
persons per year were executed in Czarist Russia. The Spanish
Inquisition, at the height of its persecutions, executed about ten persons
per month. But in the years immediately following the Bolshevik
Revolution the Soviet government was executing more than a thousand
persons per month. Three decades later that government was executing
40,000 people per month!

In addition to the executions, huge waves, numbering in the
millions, were imprisoned, tortured and sent to slave labor camps—
tantamount to a death sentence for many. There was the wave of 1929-30
"which drove a mere 15 million peasants out into the taiga and the
tundra.... This wave poured forth, sank down into the permafrost, and
even our most active minds can hardly recall a thing about it.... And
after it was the wave of 1944 and 1946 when they dumped whole nations
down the sewer pipes."

In *The Gulag Archipelago,* from which that quote is taken,
Solzhenitzen describes the torture: human beings were lowered into acid
baths; skulls were squeezed with iron rings; prisoners "would be trussed
up naked to be bitten by ants and bedbugs"; "a ramrod heated over a
primus stove would be thrust up their anal canal"; "a man's genitals
would be crushed beneath the toe of a jackboot." In "the luckiest
possible circumstances, prisoners would be tortured by being beaten to a
bloody pulp."

Yet, to repeat, an American fifth grade textbook published in 1974
contains these words: "No nation on earth is guilty of practices more
shocking and bloody than is the United States at this very hour....
Search where you will...compare your facts with *the everyday practices*
of this nation. Then you will agree with me that, for revolting barbarity
and shameless hypocrisy, America has no rival."

Those textbooks with passing references to the evils of communism in the Soviet Union often did so as though they were a thing
of the past long before there was any evidence of reform there. Here
are a few examples from pages 592 and 593 of *Land of the Free*

by John W. Caughey: "...Russia HAD one ruling party.... All other parties WERE suppressed...speech and writing WERE controlled. Critics WERE jailed or killed.... In practice Communist Russia WAS as brutal a police state as Mussolini's Italy or Hitler's German." (capitalization added)

That book was published in 1971, long before anyone ever heard of Gorbachev or *perestroika.* The brutality and oppression continued for many more years. In 1989 there was still only one political party although restraints on speech and criticism of the government were relaxed, thanks to Gorbachev. Obviously the authors of such textbooks were enamored with Soviet socialism and endeavored to portray it in a favorable light totally unwarranted by the actual facts of the time.

In 1995 Professors Jackstadt and Sanera reviewed nearly 100 textbooks and found misinformation not only on history and government but on environmental issues. Writing in *The Freeman,* October, 1995, they state:

> [S]chool textbooks, with rare exceptions, teach children that acid rain is a major crisis which is killing forests, fish, crops.... Nearly every text fails to mention the findings of the largest study of acid rain ever conducted [The National Acid Precipitation Assessment Project,]...that "There is no evidence of widespread forest damage from current ambient levels of acidic deposition [acid rain] in the United States."
>
> In the textbooks, the tenuous global warming hypothesis is almost always covered as a fact....
>
> Nowhere is the environmental education bias in the textbooks more comprehensive than in the area of the alleged world population crisis. With rare exceptions, the texts use a graph that shows the acceleration of population growth over the last 500 years.... These texts are misleading because they fail to tell children that since the 1960s the rate of population growth has declined.... Most texts go on to demonstrate the catastrophic effects of population growth by discussing dwindling food supplies and mass starvation, yet most of this information is either grossly exaggerated or simply untrue....
>
> The texts also send the message that <u>government activity is the only way that environmental problems will be solved</u> [Underlining added.] The Glenco [a Macmillan subsidiary] text *Biology: An Everyday Experience* discusses the energy crisis in these terms. "The supply of fossil fuels is being used up at an alarming rate," the text warns. "Government must help save our fossil fuel supply by passing laws limiting their use."

While the textbooks are somewhat limited in what they can do to teach political action skills, special political action handbooks for teachers and students have been developed....

The political activism in the classroom is the direct result of...state-level environmental education laws....[For example,] Washington state's Framework for Environmental Education asks teachers to "foster the idea that involvement in the political and legal process is paramount to resolving environmental issues."

Should we be surprised, then, that voters have turned increasingly to government to resolve these issues? And should we be surprised that the news media—largely a product of public education—practices "advocacy journalism" that slants news reporting in favor of governmental solutions?

In September 1996 M. Sanera and J. S. Shaw wrote:

Our own review of over 140 textbooks and nearly 170 environmental books written for children shows that on major issues, the "education" is strictly one-sided....

The EPA's Environmental Education Division has done nothing to address such problems of exaggeration and bias—or even to recognize they exist. Just the opposite, in fact.... A couple of years ago, moreover, the EPA issued an "Environmental Science Education Materials Review Guide," which stated that materials are to "reflect EPA policy on the topics explored." The EPA is shamelessly advocating political action, and it won't tolerate any deviation from its positions.[10]

EDUCATIONAL THEORY AND POLITICAL THEORY

Public education has become anti-capitalistic because it has nothing in common with capitalism. It is slanted toward socialism or communism because it shares their collectivism. It is this affinity which makes it possible for so many educators to dismiss not only the shortcomings but even the atrocities of Marxist governments. It also explains such things as why *Land of the Free* contains only two brief paragraphs on the famous black leader Booker T. Washington, who advocated self-improvement through education and hard work, and two lengthy, laudatory articles on another black, W. E. B. DuBois—a Marxist.

The fundamental contradiction between America's collectivist school system and its basic capitalism should have been resolved by making the schools capitalistic enterprises. Instead it was resolved in the other direction. The educators undertook to reform America. As early as

1899 John Dewey, one of the leaders of the Progressive Education movement, said that "educational theory...becomes political theory, and the educator is inevitably cast in the struggle for social reform."[11]

The Progressive Education movement aimed at nothing less than the complete social reconstruction of America. Another leader in the movement, Professor George S. Counts of Columbia University, declared in his 1932 monograph *Dare the School Build a New Social Order?* that capitalism "must be replaced" by "some form of socialized economy."

Both Dewey and Counts were key members of the American Federation of Teachers (AFT), a Marxist organization from its inception in 1916, which spearheaded the drive for "an educational program for a socialist America." Another organization became even more powerful in that drive. Though not originally Marxist, the National Education Association (NEA) followed the lead of the AFT and by the 1930s was both Marxist and militant.

ANTI-INDIVIDUALISM

Anti-capitalism means anti-individualism. Dewey's anti-individualism ran deep. He even tried to explain that most fundamental human process, the inherently individual act of thinking, as a collective phenomenon:

> "It thinks" is a truer psychological statement than "I think."...The stuff of belief and proposition is not originated by us. It comes to us from others, by education, tradition, and the suggestion of the environment. Our intelligence is bound up, so far as its materials are concerned, with the community life of which we are a part. We know what it communicates to us, and know according to the habits it forms in us. Science is an affair of civilization not of individual intellect.[12]

Despite the existence of a patent office, which records the individuals who think up inventions, Dewey denied the role of the individual mind in technological progress:

> The stationary engine, the locomotive, the dynamo, the motor car, turbine, telegraph, radio and moving pictures are not the products of either isolated individuals nor of the particular economic regime called capitalism.[13]

In the same way that denial of the individual mind was central to the Progressive Education movement, so also was denial of the self. As Professor Counts explained,

> Throughout the school program the development of the social order rather than the egoistic impulses should be stressed; and the motive of personal aggrandizement should be subordinated to social ends.[14]

MOLDING THE CHILD TO THE HERD

According to the doctrine of permissiveness preached by Dewey, teachers were not supposed to set standards or impose an order on the learning experience. The "primary source of social control"[15] in the schools, said Dewey, was to be the group, not the teacher. Thus, instead of being guided by the wisdom of the teacher, the child was to be brought under the control of the herd. He was to be guided by relativism rather than principle, by the shifting mood of the collectivity of his contemporaries rather than by any standards of reason or knowledge, which it used to be the teacher's function to impart. It was perfect training for democracy.

Dewey wrote:

> This movement is charged with promotion of "relativism" in a sense in which the latter is identified with *lack of standards.*[16] (Italics added)

Dewey prattled endlessly about democracy and even wrote a book entitled *Democracy And Education.* For him democracy was "an unquestioned good,"[17] and yet he admitted, "I don't know just what democracy means in detail...at the present time. I make this humiliating confession the more readily because I suspect that nobody else knows what it means in full concrete detail."[18] Speak for yourself, Mr. Dewey. Some of us know all too well.

Chapter Thirteen, *The Harvest of Reason,* showed the vital role of universal principles in scientific and social progress. It was man's understanding first of natural laws and then of natural rights which made it possible for him to master his environment and free himself. The results were expressed in material affluence and political liberty.

Dewey, on the other hand, throughout his long career continually rejected any idea of universal principles. He did not believe in either natural laws or natural rights. His view was not only completely counter to the basis of scientific and material progress but had the effect of working against freedom. It placed man back under the control of others, from whom he had been freed by the development of political liberty under the concept of natural rights. Dr. Carson explains:

> Dewey did not believe in natural law and natural rights. His belief in freedom had no such foundation, if it had any foundation at all. There was no arbiter for Dewey beyond what is and what the people want, no natural laws limiting what the people may do and have, nothing beyond the majority to which to appeal. Hence, he placed no limits upon the power vested in the people and did not believe that there were any. *Total* power would be vested in the people.[19]

A form of totalitarianism, that's what Dewey envisioned. And the child was being prepared for it from the day he first entered a public school, where he was brought under the social control of the group, where he was taught not so much to develop his mind as to drop it and submit to the herd.

Instead of teaching the student to think, the schools taught him to adjust. "Life adjustment" became more important than academic skills. Having jettisoned the standards of knowledge and intellectual development, the schools instead emphasized "social values." They replaced any objective standards or reason or truth with social relativity, so that the student would be guided not by principles but by whatever was acceptable to the herd which surrounded him. Again, it was perfect training for democracy. It is revealing, too, that the NEA credo asserts that education must serve democracy. As Dewey said, "Educational theory...becomes political theory."

Making the child submissive to the group was a process that cultivated uniformity, as in a herd or tribe. For when the child was trained to be dependent upon the approval of the group, he would emulate the group rather than think for himself. He would conform rather than develop independence and individuality. He was conditioned to find satisfaction in belonging to the herd rather than rising above it, in being common rather than excellent, equal rather than unequal.

Schools no longer were institutions to develop excellence. They *lacked standards* for it. Many stopped grading the students. In others grading became a formality with little relation to performance; "grade inflation" resulted in higher levels of grading even though performance was declining. Graduation requirements were lowered. So were the levels of proficiency required for advancement to the next grade. Sometimes these were eliminated; if you were present with the herd, you passed, whether you had learned anything or not. Educational policy was concerned more with pushing the largest possible herd through the school system than with developing the minds of the students. Intellectual quality was dropped in order to make the herd as large as possible.

If belonging to a herd was good, belonging to a bigger herd was better. The ideal was a world herd, where global uniformity would be assured through global authority. World government became an explicit aim of the Progressive Education movement, as its leaders frequently stated. It is not surprising, therefore, to find a textbook say:

> Allegiance to a nation is the biggest stumbling block to creation of international government. National boundaries and the concept of sovereignty must be abolished.... Opinion favorable to international government will be developed in the social studies in the elementary school.[20]

And in *The Story of American Freedom,* the Allied forces in World War II have been renamed the "United Nations" forces although the UN didn't even exist at the time. It wasn't founded until after the war.

Just to show how uniform everyone is, textbook authors took to knocking down heroes, portraying them as really no better than anyone else, if as good. Deliberate distortion was employed to show how "equal" great men are to the rest of the human herd. One short example is illustrative. Mel and Norma Gabler, whose story is told in *Textbooks on Trial,* found a text stating that George Washington had a violent temper. Then they found an earlier book by the same publisher. It had the same statement—but more. It said: "George Washington had a violent temper, *but* he kept it under masterly control." Leaving off the last half of that sentence completely changed the meaning. The obvious intent was to make the message derogatory.

The uniformity which was being cultivated in the schools both permitted and necessitated centralized control of the educational system. Commonness facilitated centralization, and the worship of uniformity demanded it; for only under centralized administration would everyone get exactly the same education. And if everyone's education were not the same, then, it was argued, there would be social inequality, an intolerable injustice.

At the same time, centralized educational control was necessary to remove the comparison and the threat of competition from schools offering different methods and subject matter. The public schools couldn't stand comparison or competition, even among themselves, any more than the Postal Service can afford to have others delivering mail. It wouldn't do, for example, to have some schools still teaching "old math" instead of "new math," turning out mathematically superior students, and exposing the folly of the new method. The increasing centralization of educational authority extended the scope for enforcing uniformity among the schools as well as the children.

It is significant, too, that the NEA has opposed having private businesses contract to teach reading in public schools on the basis of pupil achievement. It would be embarrassing, if not downright disastrous, to the public schools to allow private enterprise to demonstrate that it could teach reading more effectively than they could. What if the idea spread? What if private companies started teaching history and economics and told students all about individual rights and limited government and free market economics?

The same arguments for uniformity in education could be applied just as well to the press. Obviously, if people do not all read the same newspaper, they are not all equally informed. Horrors! Social injustice! But it is the diversity of free expression which offers the best chance for truth to be discovered and propagated, and the same is true in education. As Bastiat put it:

> Obviously, if people could agree on the best possible kind of education, in regard to both content and method, a uniform system of public instruction would be preferable, since error would, in that case, be necessarily excluded by law. But as long as such a criterion has not been found, as long as the legislator and the Minister of Public Education do not carry...infallibility, the true method has the best chance of being discovered and of displacing the others if room is left for diversity, trial and error, experimentation, and individual efforts guided by a self-regarding *interest in the outcome*—in a word, where there is freedom. The chances are worst in a uniform system of education established by decree, for in such a system error is permanent, universal, and irremediable....
>
> I could make the same observation about the press, and, in fact, I hardly understand why those who demand a uniform

system of state education do not demand a uniform state press. For the press is also a kind of education. ... Either the state is infallible, and we can do no better than to let it take entire control over men's minds; or it is not, and in that case it is no more reasonable to turn education over to it than the press.[21]

The virtues of freedom of the press are widely recognized by Americans. Yet those who condemn any idea of government standards for the press as a form of censorship often endorse educational censorship in the form of government standards for the schools. Freedom of choice ought to be as applicable to education as to the press, and it would surely be as beneficial.

With the massive entry of the federal government into education in the early 1960s, the social reconstruction long sought by public educators could proceed much more rapidly than when control was fragmented and localized. Uniformity would be universal. From now on there would be no escape. There would be no alternative or competitive educational choices which might interfere with bringing the child under the control of the herd. There would be no escape from indoctrination into collectivism and from subordinating the child's education to collectivist goals. There would be no economic choices in public education by which parents could express a preference for the intellectual development of their children over using the children as tools for social policy. When a group of educators went to Washington and proved conclusively that there were no problems of school construction or teachers' salaries that could not be met at the local and state levels, Francis Keppel, then Commissioner of Education, replied, "You don't understand; with your plan we couldn't achieve our social objectives."[22]

THE WEEDS GROW

Sowing the seeds of democratic socialism for decades in the elementary and high schools led to the blossoming of radicalism on college campuses. *U.S. News & World Report* of January 25, 1982 reported that at a time when Ronald Reagan's conservative views prevailed in Washington and throughout the nation, the number of Marxist professors on campus was increasing. One of them, Bertell Ollman, of New York University, said, "More and more students and faculty are being introduced to Marx's interpretation of how capitalism works." His book *Alienation: Marxist Conception of Man in Capitalist Society* was being used as a textbook in more than 100 universities. A leading distributor reported that orders for left-wing educational books increased 40 percent over the previous year. Sales by the largest left-wing publishing house were now exceeding 400,000 volumes annually.

Here are a few excerpts from these college texts of the 1980s. *The New Socialist Revolution* by Michael Lerner:

> Immediately the socialists take control of the U.S. economy, a high level of material prosperity will be possible in the United States and much of the rest of the world.

The Left Academy by Mark Kesselman:

> The United States is the only advanced capitalist society without a large, working-class-based socialist party.... This helps to explain why...the United States is virtually unique among [industrialized nations] in lacking adequate facilities, such as housing and medical care, essential for decent subsistence. In the absence of a strong socialist movement, capital and the state have been less responsive to the interest of workers and the poor.

Schooling in Capitalist America by Samuel Bowles and Herbert Gintis:

> We venture to suggest that all of the glaring inadequacies of political democracy in the United States are attributable to the private ownership of the means of production and the lack of a real economic democracy.

After that kind of teaching on our campuses, should we be surprised that nearly a quarter of U.S. college seniors attribute a famous saying of Karl Marx to the work of our Founding Fathers? In 1989 a Gallup Poll disclosed that 23 percent of college seniors believed that Marx's phrase "From each according to his ability, to each according to his need" is part of the U.S. Constitution.

In 1996 Paul Samuelson's *Economics* was still the most widely-used economic textbook on American campuses, being used by 1.5 million college students. In fifteen editions since 1948 this book has indoctrinated students with the message that big government is the key to economic stability and growth. In the 12th edition (1985) Samuelson wrote that since 1928 the Soviet economy "has outpaced the long-term growth of the major market economies."

By the time Samuelson's 13th edition appeared, in 1988, Gorbachev's policy of "glasnost" had opened the window on the failure of the Soviet economy for all to see. News articles such as we have quoted in our first chapter describing the failure of the Soviet system were regularly appearing in Western newspapers. The Soviet Union was approaching its ultimate collapse. Nevertheless, in the 1988 edition of his book Samuelson wrote, "The Soviet economy is proof that, contrary to what many skeptics had earlier believed, the socialist command economy can function and even thrive." While devoting numerous pages to the "success" of the Soviet Union and Communist China, the book gives one paragraph to Germany's spectacular economic recovery after World War II and says almost nothing about the successes of Japan, Hong Kong and Taiwan.

In an article in the *Los Angeles Times* in November 1991 Ann Rosenhaft, secretary of the Socialist Party USA estimated that there were 10,000 Marxist professors in U.S. colleges and universities. The collapse of communism in the Soviet Union and Eastern Europe has had little effect on their thinking. Most claim the communist governments in those countries "distorted" socialism and their demise will open opportunities for a new look at socialism. Marxist economics professor Samuel Bowles of the University of Massachusetts at Amherst says the old communist governments were "like a millstone around our necks." Now, he says, "I've never known my leftist colleagues to be so euphoric."[23] Charles Sykes, a journalist who covers education, writes:

> They are totally unembarrassed by what has been happening in Eastern Europe [i.e., the collapse of communist governments]. It has left them utterly unfazed. I would be extremely surprised if this was even a minor glitch to most academic Marxists. These are still very good times for Marxist scholars.[24]

On September 6, 1994, *The Wall Street Journal* led off an article on education with the sentence: "Marxism may be dead in most of the world, but it's alive and well here in the United States—at least on college campuses."

A January 3, 1996 article by Lynne V. Cheney, former chairman of the National Endowment for the Humanities, quotes Prof. Richard Ohmann of Wesleyan University as boasting, "We work in whatever ways we can toward the end of capitalist patriarchy." Wesleyan's 1996 course catalog says of an American Studies course regularly taught by Prof. Ohmann: "The course challenges the hierarchy, oppression, and exploitation in modern American culture with a variety of critical analyses and alternative proposals.... Topics cover an introduction to current trends in leftist thought, including anarchism, ecology, feminism, Marxism, and ethnic perspectives.... Projects have included guerrilla theater, community organizing, and campus activism."[25]

The same article by Cheney quotes Prof. Vivian Ng of the University of Oklahoma as saying, "I do political work, both inside the classroom and outside it.... My students came around and I converted them." Cheney says: "In freshman composition classes from coast to coast, many students are being taught not about the well-composed paragraph but about how deeply mired in racism, sexism and capitalism our nation is and about the necessity of transforming it into the vision of the left."

Chapter Sixteen
OVERVIEW

Every educated man in Ancient Greece knew that the earth was round and spinning on its axis. A thousand years later everyone "knew" it was flat. History has other examples, too, of knowledge which was lost and had to be rediscovered, sometimes many centuries later.

Today there seems to be little danger that scientific or technical knowledge will be lost, but an understanding of the importance of the individual has already all but disappeared. The crucial role the philosophy of individualism has played in man's progress has been almost totally obscured—even in history's most outstanding example of it. In the United States, with the most spectacular record of human advancement ever, that record has been rewritten in collectivist terms. The individualism of the Founding Fathers, which was the intellectual foundation of their political system and all the wealth and progress that followed, has been systematically expunged.

Today it is heresy to assert what was once widely known in this country. It is as heretical to assert that the individual is the proper center of our social system as it was for Galileo to assert that the sun is the center of our solar system.

In Galileo's time the institutions of learning were controlled by central authority, which assured uniformity of educational doctrine and made error "permanent, universal and irremediable," to use Bastiat's phrase. The Ptolemaic theory of an earth-centered universe was not only unquestioned but unquestionable. Today democracy is not only unquestioned but unquestionable because the center of social order is misplaced; and that error has likewise been made "permanent, universal and irremediable" by the uniformity of an educational system under centralized authority.

For centuries men held astronomical ideals that clashed with the facts of reality. Today they hold political ideals that do so.

For centuries men held to the ideal that planets must advance at uniform rates through circular orbits. Today it is an unquestioned ideal that society must advance at uniform rates for all its members and that everyone must be as equal as the radii of planetary orbits were once thought to be.

When Kepler discovered that the theoretical ideal clashed with reality, he had to choose between the two. He chose reality. Collectivists faced with the same decision usually make the opposite choice. So in love with their socialistic ideal are they that rather than give it up they will either ignore reality or attempt to bend it to fit their theory. Had they been astronomers rather than social reformers, they no doubt would favor moving the planets into uniform, circular progressions rather than replacing their theory with one appropriate to nature. They would be calling for "astronomical reform" instead of "social reform."

It's not easy for people to discard seemingly idealistic theories which are in fact contrary to nature. Even mankind's greatest thinkers have sometimes locked their minds on them, creating enormous mental blocks to the truth. For example, although Copernicus developed the revolutionary idea that the earth revolved about the sun, he clung stubbornly to the ideal of the circle for orbits. At one point it occurred to him that they might be elliptical, but he crossed out that passage in his manuscript. It did not appear in the printed copy. Orbits simply *had* to be circular.

Galileo saw comets through his telescope, yet he rejected their existence. Seeing their paths were elliptical, he concluded they must be optical illusions.

Before Darwin's work on evolution there was abundant evidence, both in nature and in the work of other men, to suggest that species were not immutable. But just as with the belief in circular orbits, men were too blinded by their adherence to false theory to accept the obvious. When the famous biologist T. H. Huxley learned of Darwin's discovery, his first remark was how "extremely stupid" he himself had been not to have thought of it. The idea suddenly seemed so simple and obvious.

Someday the generally accepted social theories of our age will seem as false as the generally accepted astronomical and biological theories of the past seem to us. The idea that people must be uniform through society will be recognized as no more correct than that planetary motions must be uniform through space or that species must remain uniform through time. It will all seem so simple and obvious. People will probably remark how "extremely stupid" it was not to have made the realization earlier, because the evidence is so abundant that men are not uniform and that nature never intended them to be.

In fact, it is the *lowest* forms of life which are most uniform. Those which are highest on the evolutionary ladder exhibit the greatest diversity, the widest individual differences. Only a theory of government that allows for human differences, for "the diversity in the faculties of men," as Madison put it, can be truly in accord with the nature of man.

Equal rights, correctly speaking, mean only that men are entitled to equal protection against force, which means: the liberty to be *unequal* in every other respect. Any attempt by government to make men equal in any other respect necessarily violates their rights, their liberty. Schemes for economic or social equality are always at the expense of liberty. Men can have either liberty or equality. Not both. And unless the herd is to be preferred to the human, there is no reason not to choose liberty.

Uniformity throughout society is not the only false political ideal for which discrediting evidence is obvious, overwhelming and yet overlooked. There is one even more fundamental. Men someday will probably be amazed not only that it endured so long but that it ever became generally accepted in an advanced civilization in the first place.

It is the idea that wisdom resides in the majority, that what is right is what is believed by the greatest number of people. Democracy is based on this fallacy. It presumes that wisdom is defined by popular opinion. It encourages people to equate the two, because it functions as though there were no difference. But if truth were determined by popular opinion, the world would still be flat. In no other field except government is an idea today presumed to be correct simply because of the number of its adherents. Almost 300 years after Newton demonstrated the universal nature of truth the belief persists that standards of truth which apply everywhere else do not apply to politics.

Since at least the Renaissance the various branches of knowledge have been coming together. The Renaissance showed that reality was consistent not only throughout the different sciences but even the arts. The laws of perspective, by which painters of that period discovered they could create the impression of a third dimension, were scientific, mathematical laws. And because the painters studied anatomy and dissected corpses in order to be able to draw the human figure better, the science of medicine advanced hand-in-hand with the art of painting.

Despite increasing specialization in the sciences in modern times, the standards for recognizing truth in them are universal, and knowledge is cross-confirming and complementary rather than contradictory. For example, the sciences of chemistry and biology utilize the same logic (so does every other science) and have converged in biochemistry. And advances in electronics have revealed the electrical nature of chemical reactions in biological processes, for example, the electro-chemical impulses transmitted through nerve cells. Three scientific disciplines have thus come together. Modern sciences have been converging in the same way that political and economic thought converged with each other and with science in the 18th century. But now that the universal nature of truth is more evident than ever, politics operates on an entirely different standard and proceeds contrarily. While the sciences extend our knowledge of man's nature, our government increasingly acts in contradiction to man's natural rights. The disparity has grown as democracy has increased.

Millions of people who would not accept popularity as the criterion of truth in any profession nevertheless accept it unquestioningly in any political issue. It would be absurd to submit questions of medical diagnosis or surgery to popular vote. Yet people who would scoff at submitting their bodies to medical decisions made in such a manner routinely acknowledge the "wisdom" of submitting their lives to political decisions made in exactly the same way.

It would seem desirable to have as few issues as possible determined by democratic vote and as many as possible resolved in the manner of private medical decisions, but the trend to Big Government does the opposite. It takes away people's opportunity to make their own decisions and moves those decisions to the political level, where they are determined in an entirely different way by an entirely different standard.

There is no correlation at all between democratic rule and the laws of logic, between the majority and the truth. Popularity and rationality are completely different concepts. One is a physical criterion; the other, an intellectual one. The democratic principle of numerical power corresponds not to reason or to any intellectual standard but to physical force, and a very primitive concept of force at that. It provides the consistency of correlating the physical force of government with some measure of the force of the herd but proves nothing about the rationality of political decisions or actions.

Leaving people to make their own decisions, to *personally* exercise all rightful powers, as Jefferson put it, leaves those decisions to the standard of rationality. Furthermore, rational decisions in a free society are rewarded in the marketplace while errors are self-liquidating.

A limited government, which limits democracy as much as it does anything else, limits the extent to which popularity can displace rationality as the basis for human decisions. It limits the extent to which animal numbers can replace a man's own mind in determining his destiny.

Some people favor majority rule on the grounds it's better than having a minority rule the majority—*as though those were the only two choices.* The assumption, of course, is that government is an instrument of plunder and that it's better to have the majority plunder the minority rather than the other way around. But there is a third possibility. Obvious as it is, it is overlooked by those who have locked their minds on the idea of a collective solution. The third possibility is to have nobody rule anybody else, to leave each man to rule himself. True "self-government," as the Founders intended that term. The individualistic solution.

It would mean human affairs would be decided by men individually by reason rather than collectively by democracy. It would mean that decisions now made on a political basis would instead be made on the same intellectual basis by which men arrive at the truth in medicine or astronomy or by which they make decisions in their businesses or personal affairs when they have the freedom to do so.

Individualism would mean stripping government down to its essential function of defense and restoring to every individual the liberty that government has been steadily taking away in the name of democracy. It would mean government would no longer be an instrument of plunder, as it has become under democracy. The sole function of government would be the protection of the individual's natural rights. Any other purpose would be rejected *on principle* as inconsistent with and destructive of human rights.

The tendency for democracy to become a system of plunder was foreseen long ago by the English historian Thomas Babington Macaulay. Writing in 1857 to his American friend Henry Randall, he lamented, "I have long been convinced that institutions purely democratic must, sooner or later, destroy liberty or civilization or both." Once we begin the cycle of "tax and tax, spend and spend, elect and elect," he prophesied that

> either civilization or liberty must perish. Either some Caesar or Napoleon will seize the reins of government with a strong hand; or your republic will be as fearfully plundered and laid waste by barbarians in the twentieth century as the Roman Empire was in the fifth—with this difference, that the Huns and Vandals who ravaged the Roman Empire came from without, and that your Huns and Vandals will have been engendered within your own country by your own institutions.

NOTES

NOTES TO CHAPTER ONE

1. *Star Tribune,* Nov. 9, 1987.
2. *The Wall Street Journal,* Aug. 18, 1987.
3. *The Wall Street Journal,* July 20, 1995.
4. *The Wall Street Journal,* Nov. 12, 1986.
5. *ibid.*
6. *ibid.*
7. Dr. John A. Sparks in *The Freeman,* Nov. 1978.
8. *The Wall Street Journal,* July 10, 1985.
9. *ibid.*
10. *ibid.*
11. Translated and reprinted by *The Minneapolis Star and Tribune,* July 31, 1983.
12. *U.S. News & World Report,* June 2, 1975.
13. *The Wall Street Journal,* Aug. 20, 1975.
14. Reprinted in *The Minneapolis Star,* Aug. 22, 1975.
15. Henry Grady Weaver, *The Mainspring of Human Progress* (Irvington-on-Hudson, N.Y.: The Foundation for Economic Education, Inc., 1954), p. 66.
16. *The Bank Credit Analyst,* Sept. 1978.
17. *The Wall Street Journal,* Aug. 21, 1979.
18. *Christian Economics,* June 28, 1960.
19. *ibid.*
20. Jim Dobbs, *It's Your Move* (Austin, Texas: Jim Dobbs & Associates, 1962), p. 135.
21. *Reason,* Jan. 1986.
22. *The Wall Street Journal,* Feb. 24, 1988.
23. *The Wall Street Journal,* March 9, 1989.
24. *The Wall Street Journal,* Oct. 2, 1995.
25. *ibid.*
26. William Manchester, *American Caesar* (Boston: Little, Brown and Company, 1978), pp. 469-471.
27. Douglas MacArthur, *Reminiscences* (New York: McGraw-Hill, 1964), p. 283.
28. Courtney Whitney, *MacArthur, His Rendezvous with History* (New York: Alfred A. Knopf, 1956), p. 503-504.
29. Roger A. Freeman, *The Growth of American Government: A Morphology of the Welfare State* (Stanford, Calif.: Hoover Institution Press, 1975), p. 109.
30. William E. Simon, *A Time For Truth* (New York: McGraw-Hill, 1978), p. 40.
31. William C. Wooldridge, *Uncle Sam, The Monopoly Man* (New Rochelle, N.Y.: Arlington House, 1970), p. 24.
32. *The Wall Street Journal,* Dec. 20, 1972.
33. *Moneysworth,* Sept. 1, 1975.
34. *Reason,* July 1978.
35. *The Wall Street Journal,* June 6, 1990.
36. *Phi Delta Kappan,* April 1975.
37. *The Wall Street Journal,* July 11, 1988.
38. *The Wall Street Journal,* July 5, 1988.
39. *The Wall Street Journal,* April 18, 1989.
40. *Barron's,* Jan. 21, 1974.

41.   *The Minneapolis Tribune,* July 18, 1979 and *The Freeman,* July 1979.

42   *The Wall Street Journal,* July 25, 1995.

43.   *The Wall Street Journal,* Aug. 24, 1983.

44.   Rose Wilder Lane, *The Discovery of Freedom* (New York: Arno Press & *The New York Times,* 1972), pp. 126-27.

45.   *The Freeman,* July 1987.

46.   Elgin Groseclose, *Money and Man* (New York: Frederick Ungar Publishing Co., 1967), p. 104-5.

NOTES TO CHAPTER TWO

1.   George R. Stewart, *Man: An Autobiography* (New York: Random House, 1946). Quotation from the abridgement in *The Reader's Digest,* July 1947).

2.   *ibid.*

3.   Dr. Bronowski writes of the Bakhtiari, one of the few remaining nomadic tribes: "They have only the simple technology that can be carried on daily journeys from place to place. The simplicity is not romantic; it is a matter of survival. Everything must be light enough to be carried, to be set up every evening and to be packed away again every morning...

      "It is not possible in the nomad life to make things that will not be needed for several weeks. They could not be carried. And in fact the Bakhtiari do not know how to make them.... The Bakhtiari life is too narrow to have time or skill for specialization. There is no room for innovation, because there is not time, on the move, between evening and morning, coming and going all their lives, to develop a new device or a new thought—not even a new tune." Jacob Bronowski, *The Ascent of Man* (Boston: Little, Brown and Company, 1974), p. 62.

4.   *ibid.,* p. 73.

5.   *ibid.,* p. 74.

6.   G. Himmelfarb, *Darwin and the Darwinian Revolution,* (New York: Anchor Books, 1959), p. 239.

7.   Siemens and Halske.

8.   John Chamberlain, *The Enterprising Americans* (New York: Harper & Row, 1961), p. 147.

9.   Rose Wilder Lane, *The Discovery of Freedom* (New York: Arno Press and The New York Times, 1972), p. 231.

10.   Samuel C. Burchell, *Age of Progress* (New York: Time Inc., 1966), p. 52.

11.   The Suez Canal was closed by Arab-Israeli fighting in 1967 and remained closed for eight years.

12.   Edith Hamilton, *The Greek Way to Western Civilization* (New York: The New American Library, 1948), p. 22.

13.   Felix Morley, *The Power in the People* (Los Angeles: Nash Publishing, 1972), p. 83.

NOTES TO CHAPTER THREE

1.   Jacob Bronowski, *op. cit.,* p. 69.

2.   *ibid.,* p. 88.

3.   John Stuart Mill, *Principles of Political Economy* (Ashley edition), p. 881.

4.   William A. Rusher, "A Cold, Calculated Road to Peace," *Human Events,* May 31, 1975, describes a research program which confirms this point. Professor

R. J. Rummel, Director of the PATH Institute of Research on International Problems, at the University of Hawaii, carried out a 12-year computer study based on millions of facts such as exports, migration, treaties, wars, mail, United Nations votes, etc. These facts were analyzed in relation to such social characteristics as national wealth, degree of industrialization, population, ideology, political institutions, race, religion, education and others. Says Rusher: "According to the computer, what is related to conflict is power, and power alone. But the level of conflict is not, as so many people suppose, lowest where two nations have equal power. On the contrary, to quote Professor Rummel directly, the maintenance of peace 'requires a dominance of power: peace is a condition of power inequality.'"

NOTES TO CHAPTER FOUR

1. *The Minneapolis Tribune,* Dec. 21, 1975.
2. *The California Mining Journal,* Oct. 1976.
3. *The Journal of Commerce,* Nov. 19, 1976.
4. *Business Week,* Jan. 30, 1989.
5. *Reason,* Feb. 1989.
6. Donald Lambro, *The Federal Rathole* (New Rochelle, N.Y.: Arlington House, 1975). Several other government expenditures listed in this chapter are also from Mr. Lambro's book. Others are from publications of the National Taxpayers Union, including its *Taxpayer's Liability Index* and its monthly periodical *Dollars and Sense.*

NOTES TO CHAPTER FIVE

1. *The Wall Street Journal,* March 7, 1989.
2. *Star Tribune,* June 26, 1992.
3. *The Wall Street Journal,* Dec. 29, 1975.
4. *U.S. News & World Report,* Oct. 6, 1975.
5. Melvin J. Grayson and Thomas R. Shepard, Jr., *The Disaster Lobby* (Chicago: Follett Publishing Company, 1973), p.156.
6. Sam Peltzman, "The Effects of Automobile Safety Regulation," *Journal of Political Economy,* Aug. 1975.
7. John Adams, *Risk* (London: UCL Press Limited, University College London, 1995).
8. *The Wall Street Journal,* March 17, 1994.
9. *ibid.*
10. *ibid.*
11. *The Freeman,* April 1990.
12. William Wardell and Louis Lasagna, *Regulation and Drug Development* (Washington, D.C.: American Enterprise Institute, 1975).
13. Henry G. Grabowski, John M. Vernon and Lacy Glen Thomas, "The Effects of Regulatory Policy on the Incentives to Innovate: An International Comparative Analysis," Dec. 1975. (Paper presented at the Third Seminar on Pharmaceutical Public Policy Issues in Washington, D.C., on Dec. 15, 1975.)
14. *The Wall Street Journal,* April 6, 1976.
15. Sam Peltzman, *Regulation of Pharmaceutical Innovation* (Washington, D.C.: American Enterprise Institute, 1974), pp. 72, 82, 89.

16. *The Wall Street Journal,* March 27, 1985.
17. *The Wall Street Journal,* Dec. 15, 1995.
18. *Access to Energy,* May 1986.
19. *The Wall Street Journal,* April 4, 1996.
20. Melvin D. Barger in *The Freeman,* April 1975.

NOTES TO CHAPTER SIX

1. A noted Egyptian traveler of the sixth century, Cosmas Indicopleustes, wrote that "it is with their gold piece (the *bezant* of Constantinople) that all nations do trade; it is received everywhere from one end of the earth to the other." Quoted in Elgin Groseclose *Money and Man* (New York: Frederick Ungar Publishing Co., 1967), p. 50.
2. Murray N. Rothbard, *What Has Government Done to Our Money?* (Santa Ana, Calif.: Rampart College, 1974), p. 3.
3. Elgin Groseclose, *op. cit.,* p. 178.
4. Our hypothetical examples assume, of course, that the change in the supply of the given commodity, or money, is the *only* change that occurs. But a real economy is never static; there can be changes in supply due to factors such as technology or weather and in demand because buyers, for a variety of reasons, alter the subjective value they place on the various products available to them. All of which means that in a dynamic economy there will not be a neat mathematical relationship between changes in the money supply and price levels. An increase in the money supply will mean higher prices than otherwise, but because of the other variables the increases will not be in exact proportion.
5. *ibid.,* p. 66
6. Donald J. Hoppe, *How to Invest in Gold Stocks* (New Rochelle, N.Y.: Arlington House, 1972), p. 35.
7. *Myers' Finance Review,* No. 91, April 24, 1970.
8. *ibid.*
9. Hilaire Belloc, *The Mercy of Allah* (Westminister, Md.: Christian Classics, Inc., 1973), p. 293-4.
10. In recent years we have seen this deception attempted on an international scale through the introduction of Special Drawing Rights, the so-called "paper gold" of the International Monetary Fund. Clearly this is nothing but the policy of the sultan in Belloc's essay practiced on a global level.
11. Henry Hazlitt, *What You Should Know About Inflation* (New York: Funk & Wagnalls, 1968), p. 24.
12. The goldsmiths were not the first to create artificial bank credit in this manner. Earlier the Venetian government, badly in need of funds, organized a new government bank for the purpose of creating a credit to its own account without a corresponding deposit. The Venetian example, however, seems to have been unrelated to the subsequent banking practices of the English goldsmiths, from whom modern banking developed.
13. Government securities, and certain other securities, may also be purchased by the Federal Reserve Open Market Committee. In this case the purchase is made from a dealer rather than directly from the U.S. Treasury. The dealer is paid with a check drawn on a Federal Reserve Bank, which he deposits in a member bank. Such a deposit then becomes the reserve for multiple credit expansion in the same manner as before.

14. Henry Hazlitt, *op. cit.,* p. 124 f.
15. Harry D. Schultz, *Panics & Crashes* (New Rochelle, N.Y.: Arlington House, 1972), p. 113.
16. *Gold Newsletter,* Vol. IV, No. 12, Dec. 1975.
17. Gerald Swanson, *Hyperinflation: Lessons from South America* (Richmond, Virginia: Figgie International, Inc., 1986).
18. Elgin Groseclose, *Fifty Years of Managed Money* (New York: Books Inc., 1966), p. 155.
19. *ibid.,* p. 154. See also Murray Rothbard, *America's Great Depression* (Kansas City: Sheed and Ward, Inc., 1975), pp. 92-93. Rothbard notes that "Demand deposits required roughly 10 percent reserve backing, while time deposits needed only 3 percent reserve."
20. Elgin Groseclose, *op. cit.,* p. 156. Milton Friedman and Anna J. Schwartz in *A Monetary History of the United States 1867-1960* (Princeton, New Jersey: Princeton University Press, 1963), assert that the Fed was not inflating in the 1920's. A thorough and convincing refutation of this assertion is given by Rothbard in *America's Great Depression.*
21. *Congressional Record,* Dec. 13, 1913.
22. Donald J. Hoppe, *op cit.,* p. 79.
23. *The Freeman,* Oct. 1975.
24. Milton Friedman and Anna J. Schwartz, *op. cit.,* p. 10, conclude that before the Federal Reserve, "The blind, undesigned, and quasi-automatic working of the gold standard turned out to produce a greater measure of predictability and regularity—perhaps because its discipline was impersonal and inescapable—than did deliberate and conscious control exercised within institutional arrangements intended to promote monetary stability."
25. Elgin Groseclose, *op cit.,* p. 215.
26. Keynes probably first used this phrase in 1923 in his *Tract on Monetary Reform,* but he employed it on a number of occasions throughout his career to emphasize his concern with the short term.
27. Elgin Groseclose, *op cit.,* p. 195.

NOTES TO CHAPTER SEVEN

1. F. A. Hayek, *Capitalism and the Historians* (Chicago: The University of Chicago Press, 1954), p. 22.
2. *ibid.,* p. 9-10.
3. *ibid.,* p. 17.
4. *ibid.,* p. 16.
5. Ludwig won Mises, *Human Action* (New Haven, Conn.: Yale University Press, 1949), p. 615.
6. Hayek, *op. cit.,* p. 17.
7. *ibid.,* p. 19.
8. *ibid.*
9. Quoted in Hayek, *op. cit.,* p. 21.
10. Hayek, *op. cit.,* p. 176.
11. Ayn Rand, *Capitalism: The Unknown Ideal* (New York: The New American Library, Inc., 1967), p. 112.
12. Hayek, *op. cit.,* p. 180.
13. *ibid.,* p. 178.

14. *ibid.,* p. 180.
15. *ibid.,* p. 181.
16. Grayson and Shepard, *op. cit.,* p. 153.
17. *U. S. News & World Report,* June 14, 1976.
18. See Murray L. Weidenbaum, *Business, Government and the Public* (Engle-wood Cliffs, N.J.: Prentice Hall, 1977).
19. *The Minneapolis Star,* Sept. 10, 1976.
20. *The Minneapolis Tribune,* March 25, 1976.
21. *Nation's Business,* May 1968.
22. *ibid.*
23. *ibid.*
24. *ibid.*
25. *The Freeman,* Nov. 1994.
26. Elting E. Morrison and John M. Blum, eds., *The letters of Theodore Roosevelt,* 8 Vols. (Cambridge: Harvard University Press, 1951-54), vol. 5, p. 340.
27. U.S. Congress, House, Committee on Agriculture, *Hearings on the So-called "Beveridge Amendment" to the Agriculture Appropriation Bill,* 59th Congress, 1st Session, 1906, p. 194.
28. *The Freeman,* Nov. 1994.
29. From a promotional piece written by Jack London and personally approved by Sinclair. See Mark Sullivan, *Our Times: The United States, 1900-1925;* vol 2: *America Finding Herself* (New York: Charles Scribner's Sons, 1927), p. 473.
30. Elizabeth M. Whelan and Frederick J. Stare, *Panic in the Pantry* (New York: Atheneum, 1977), p. 166.
31. *ibid.,* p. 167.
32. *The New York Times,* March 13, 1979.
33. Whelan and Stare, *op. cit.,* p. 167.
34. *Report by the Comptroller General of the United States: Does Nitrite Cause Cancer? Concerns About Validity of FDA-Sponsored Study Delay Answer.* General Accounting Office, Jan. 31, 1980. HRD-80-96.
35. Steven R. Tannenbaum, "Ins and Outs of Nitrites," *Sciences,* January 1980, p. 7.
36. Edith Efron, *The Apocalyptics: Cancer and The Big Lie* (New York: Simon and Schuster, 1984), p. 408.
37. *Human Events,* Jan. 5, 1980.
38. *The Wall Street Journal,* Feb. 14, 1984.
39. *ibid.*
40. *Newsweek,* April 9, 1984.
41. *Access to Energy,* May 1989.
42. That EPA's decision to ban Alar was not based on science but on the agency's political sensitivity to public opinion is underscored by these facts: 1) EPA issued a joint declaration with the FDA and the U.S. Agriculture Dept. stating: "There is not an imminent hazard posed to children in the consumption of apples...despite claims to the contrary," 2) The research arm of the World Health Organization concluded that "neither Alar nor its breakdown product UDMH are carcinogens," 3) This same conclusion was reached by the British Advisory Committee on Pesticides in 1989, and 4) The National Cancer Institute compared the risk of eating an apple with that of a well-done hamburger or a peanut butter sandwich.
43. *World Research INK,* March 1977.

44. *Newsweek,* April 9, 1984.
45. Efron, *op. cit.,* p. 155.
46. William R. Havender and Leonard T. Flynn, *Does Nature Know Best?* (Summit, N.J.: American Council on Science and Health, 1987), pp. 18-19.
47. *IARC,* Vol. 10, 1976.
48. Efron, *op. cit.,* p. 175.
49. *Access to Energy,* Oct. 1986.
50. Efron, *op. cit.,* p. 91
51. *ibid.,* p. 13.
52. *ibid.,* p. 121, 413, 423.
53. *ibid.,* p. 406.
54. W. J. Hayes, *Toxicology of Pesticides* (The Williams and Wilkins Co., 1975), p. 98.
55. G. Claus and K. Bolander, "Environmental Carcinogenesis - The Threshold Principle: A Law of Nature," in *Pollution and Water Resources,* Columbia University Seminar Series, Vol. 15, Part I (1983), p. 160.
56. Leonard T. Flynn, Pesticides: *Helpful or Harmful?* (Summit, N.J.: American Council on Science and Health, 1988), P. 20.
57. Efron, *op. cit.,* p. 421.
58. M. Alice Ottoboni, *The Dose Makes the Poison* (Berkeley, Calif.: Vincente Books, 1984), p. 35.
59. Elizabeth C. Miller, "Some Current Perspectives on Chemical Carcinogens in Humans and Experimental Animals: Presidential Address," *Cancer Research,* 38 (1978):1491.
60. FDA's Jacqueline Verrett, quoted in Efron *op. cit.,* p. 91.
61. Quoted in Efron, *op. cit.,* p. 292.
62. Efron, *op. cit.,* p. 292.
63. Efron, *op. cit.,* p. 293.
64. *FDA Consumer,* Feb. 1985.
65. Flynn, *op. cit.,* p. 47.
66. *Science,* Oct. 31, 1989.
67. *The Wall Street Journal,* Feb. 14, 1984.
68. *ibid.*
69. *ibid.*
70. Whelan and Stare, *op. cit.,* p. 126.
71. *Congressional Record,* July 28, 1978.
72. *The American Spectator,* June 1993.
73. Havender and Flynn, *op. cit.,* p. 33.
74. Whelan and Stare, *op. cit.,* p. 126.
75. Grayson and Shepard, *op. cit.,* pp. 183-84.

NOTES TO CHAPTER EIGHT

1. *The New York Times,* April 20, 1971.
2. *The Minneapolis Tribune,* Sept. 28, 1971.
3. Grayson and Shepard, *op. cit.,* p. 49.
4. *Technology: Journal of the Franklin Institute,* 1994, Vol. 331A, pp. 135-45. In this same article Dr. Ellsaesser asks: "Do these graphs suggest that the quoted statements by our leaders [about air pollution becoming worse] were based on something other than sound information? How could they have gotten away

with such statements before a free and unbiased press? The answer is that the press was neither unbiased nor interested in uncovering the truth."

5.   NAS/NRC (National Academy of Sciences/National Research Council). Proceedings of the conference on health effects of air pollution, 1973 October 3-5, prepared for the Committee on Public Works, U.S. Senate, Serial No. 93-15, Washington, D.C: Government Printing Office, 1973.

6.   *The Wall Street Journal,* Aug. 29, 1990.

7.   *The Wall Street Journal,* May 1, 1992.

8.   *Access to Energy,* May 1988.

9.   *Rethinking the Ozone Problem in Urban and Regional Air Pollution* (Washington, D.C.: National Academy of Science, 1991)

10. *Science,* July 2, 1993.

11. Dr. Beckmann calculates that, based on U.S. Dept. of Energy figures, ethanol has a net energy loss of 3.1 MBTU per ton of corn and residue.

12. *The Wall Street Journal,* Sept. 28, 1989.

13. *ibid.*

14. John E. Kinney, *Danger in Environmental Policy* (Louisville, Ky.: National Council for Environmental Balance, 1990), pamphlet B-90-1.

15. *The Wall Street Journal,* Aug. 29, 1990.

16. *Human Events,* Jan. 11, 1975.

17. *Update,* Winter 1976. (Publication of the University of Minnesota.)

18. *Public Works,* October 1980.

19. *The Wall Street Journal,* June 30, 1987.

20. *Update,* Winter 1976.

21. *The Wall Street Journal,* July 31, 1995.

22. Dale E. Linvill, W. J. Hooker and Brian Olson, *21st Century Science and Technology,* Sept.-Oct. 1989.

23. *EPA Study: Battling Smog: A Plan for Action, No. 93,* Center for the Study of American Business at Washington University, St. Louis, Mo., Sept. 1989.

24. *The Minneapolis Tribune,* Oct. 29, 1978.

25. *Industry Week,* Aug. 17, 1970.

26. *Human Events,* Jan. 11, 1975.

27. John J. McKetta, Jr., *Acid Rain - 1987 Update* (Louisville, Kentucky: National Council for Environmental Balance, 1987), pamphlet 52.

28. *The Wall Street Journal,* June 28, 1984.

29. I. W. Tucker, *Fallout From the Environmental Volcano of the 1970's* (Louisville, Ky.: National Council for Environmental Balance, 1981), pamphlet 26.

30. *California Mining Journal,* June 1976. (Story also in *The Los Angeles Times and Arizona Republic.*)

31. John J. McKetta, Jr., *Acid Rain - What is the Real Story?* (Louisville, Ky.: National Council for Environmental Balance, 1985), pamphlet B-85-1.

32. *The Wall Street Journal,* June 28, 1984.

33. *Access to Energy,* Aug. 1980.

34. John J. McKetta, Jr., *op. cit.*

35. John J. McKetta, Jr., *Acid Rain - 1987 Update* (Louisville, Ky.: National Council for Environmental Balance, 1987), pamphlet 52.

36. (London) *Economist,* April 14, 1984.

37. Barry Commoner, *The Closing Circle* (New York: Alfred A. Knopf, 1971), p. 31.

38. John Maddox, *The Doomsday Syndrome* (New York: McGraw Hill, 1972), p. 143.
39. *Access to Energy,* April 1984.
40. *Access to Energy,* July 1988.
41. *ibid.*
42. *Access to Energy,* Sept. 1987.
43. *The Wall Street Journal,* March 23, 1989.
44. *The Wall Street Journal,* April 16, 1987.
45. R. S. Stolarski and M. R. Schoebert, 1986, "Further Interpretation of Satellite Measurements of Antarctic Total Ozone," *Geophysical Research Letters,* Vol. 13, p. 210.
46. Dixy Lee Ray and Lou Guzzo, *Environmental Overkill* (Washington, D.C.: Regnery Gateway, 1993), p. 35.
47. *ibid.*
48. *ibid.,* p.34.
49. *Access To Energy,* July 1992.
50. *Reason,* June 1992.
51. Aslam Khalil and R. A. Rasmussen, 1989, "The Potential of Soils as a Sink of Chlorofluorocarbons and Other Man-Made Chlorocarbons," *Geophysical Research Letters,* Vol. 16, pp. 679-82.
    Khalil, Rasmussen and M. Y. French, 1989, "Emissions of Trace Gases From Chinese Rice Fields and Biomass Generators," *Chemosphere,* 1989, Vol 20, pp. 207-66.
52. H. B. Singh, L. J. Salas and R. E. Stiles, 1983, "Methyl Halides In and Over the Eastern Pacific," *Journal of Geophysical Research,* Vol. 88, pp. 3684-90.
53. Dean A. Hegg, Lawrence F. Radke, Peter V. Hobbs, et al., 1990, "Emissions of Some Trace Gases From Biomass Fires," *Journal of Geophysical Research,* Vol. 95, pp. 5669-75.
54. *Access to Energy,* Dec. 1983.
55. *The New York Times,* Aug. 14, 1975 stated that "there were many signs pointing to the possibility that the earth may be heading for another ice age." *Science* magazine, Dec. 10, 1976 said: heading "toward extensive Northern Hemisphere glaciation." *The Christian Science Monitor,* Aug. 27, 1974 reported that armadillos were retreating south, that "the North Atlantic is cooling down about as fast as an ocean can cool," and that glaciers "have begun to advance." *International Wildlife,* July 1975, claimed that "a new ice age must now stand alongside nuclear war as a likely source of wholesale death and misery." The National Academy of Sciences wrote in 1977 that "evidence as diverse as the duration of arctic snow cover, animal migration, sea surface temperatures and microfossils on the ocean floor suggest a trend [leading to a new ice age] is upon us."
56. *Star Tribune,* Dec. 8, 1988.
57. *ibid.*
58. *Minneapolis Star & Tribune,* June 17, 1986.
59. *Star Tribune,* Dec. 30, 1988.
60. *Global Warming Update, Recent Scientific Findings* (Washington, D.C.: George C. Marshall Institute, 1992).
61. *The Wall Street Journal,* Dec. 4, 1989.
62. *IAEA Bulletin,* No. 2, 1989.
63. *Science,* Nov. 5, 1982.
64. *National Review,* October 5, 1992.

65. *ibid.*
66. *The Wall Street Journal,* Dec. 26, 1995.
67. *The Wall Street Journal,* June 12, 1996. See also replies in "Letters to the Editor," June 25, July 11 and Aug. 13, 1996.
68. *The Wall Street Journal,* Jan. 15, 1996.
69. *Star Tribune,* April 27, 1996.
70. D. L. Ray and Lou Guzzo, *op. cit.,* pp. 26-27.
71. *Champs Elysees,* Paris, Dec. 1991.
72   *Star Tribune,* Sept. 5, 1989.
73. John Maddox, *op. cit.,* p. 120.
74. Robt. H. White-Stevens, *Coercive Utopians Unleash Insect-Vectored Diseases on Man, Part 2* (Louisville, Ky.: National Council for Environmental Balance, 1978), pamphlet.
75. *ibid.*
76. *The Wall Street Journal,* May 25, 1994.
77. *Nature,* Nov. 28, 1991.
78. *The Wall Street Journal,* Sept. 12, 1989.
79. John L. Wong, *Cancer: What to Fear, What Not to Fear* (Louisville, Ky.: National Council for Environmental Balance, 1987), pamphlet B-87-3.
80. *Access to Energy,* Aug. 1976.
81. J. Gordon Edwards, *Saving Lives With Pesticides* (Louisville, Ky.: National Council for Environmental Balance, 1983), pamphlet 35.
82. *Human Events,* Feb. 22, 1975.
83. *U.S. News & World Report,* Aug. 16, 1976.
84. *The Minneapolis Tribune,* May 6, 1976.
85. *The Canadian Mining and Metallurgical Bulletin,* Sept. 1979.
86. *ibid.* Also, John Maddox, *op. cit.,* p.117 says: "The seas as a whole contain 25-100 million tons of mercury, most of which has found its way there during the geological history of the earth by the breaking down of rocks and by the activities of volcanoes. The production of mercury in the world as a whole is at present no more than 10,000 tons a year, which means that even if all of it were immediately dumped into the oceans, it would take between 2,500 and 10,000 million years to double the concentration of mercury in the sea."
87. *U.S. News & World Report,* Aug. 16, 1976.
88. *The Wall Street Journal,* April 13, 1990.
89. The concern proved unfounded when Japanese biologists found a natural oil-eating bacterium in mud on the sea bottom near Suruga Bay. Though it had obviously been there a long time, it had caused no adverse environmental effect. French researchers have also reported a similar discovery.
90. *The Wall Street Journal,* April 13, 1991.
91. *America's Future,* Nov. 1991.
92. Dan Smoot, *The Business End of Government* (Belmont, Mass.: Western Islands, 1973), p. 131-2.

NOTES TO CHAPTER NINE

1. John Maddox, *op. cit.,* p. 77.
2. Barry Commoner, *The Closing Circle* (New York: Alfred A. Knopf, 1971), p. 122.
3. Dirck Van Sickle, *The Ecological Citizen* (New York: Harper Row, 1972), p. 25.

4. John Maddox, *op. cit.*, p. 107.

5. Wilfred Beckerman, *Two Cheers for the Affluent Society* (New York: St. Martin's Press, 1974), p. 187.

6. *Commodity Year Book 1976,* (New York: Commodity Research Bureau, Inc., 1976), p. 345.

7. John Maddox, *op. cit.,* p. 106.

8. *Access to Energy,* June 1995.

9. *The Wall Street Journal,* Nov. 30, 1976.

10. Wilfred Beckerman, *op. cit.,* pp. 176-77.

11. *Commodity Year Book 1976,* p. 7.

12. Estimate by Commodities Research Unit, London, based on data on metallic concentrations in *Encyclopedia Britannica.*

13. Wilfred Beckerman, *op. cit.,* p. 175.

14. Anton G. Pegis, "Encroachment of Competing Land Uses on *Mineral Development," Mineral Industries Bulletin,* July 1976 (Colorado School of Mines Research Institute).

15. Jane Jacobs, *The Economy of Cities* (New York: Random House, 1969), Vintage Books Edition, p. 124.

16. *The Freeman,* Sept. 1975.

17. *Access to Energy,* June 1, 1977.

18. *The Freeman,* Sept. 1975.

19. *ibid.*

20. *The Wall Street Journal,* April 4, 1996.

21. *The Wall Street Journal,* Oct. 1995.

22. *The Mining Record,* Dec. 8, 1976.

23. *The Journal of Commerce,* Feb. 1, 1977.

24. *The Northern Miner,* July 21, 1977.

25. *Access to Energy,* Feb. 1976.

26. *The Wall Street Journal,* May 16, 1995.

27. *The Wall Street Journal,* July 25, 1995.

28. Petr Beckmann, *Eco-hysterics and the Technophobes* (Boulder, Colo.: The Golem Press, 1973), p. 114.

29. *Access to Energy,* Dec. 1976.

30. *The Northern Miner,* Dec. 30, 1976.

31. *Access to Energy,* Dec. 1976.

NOTES TO CHAPTER TEN

1. For example, Dr. John Maier, Associate Director of the Rockefeller Foundation, uses these figures in *As We Live and Breathe: The Challenge of Our Environment* (Washington, D.C.: National Geographic Society, 1971), p. 203.

2. *The Alternative,* June/July 1976.

3. *New York Times Magazine,* Aug. 2, 1970.

4. Marion Clawson, *America's Land & Its Uses* (Baltimore: The Johns Hopkins Press, 1972), p. 16.

5. *The Alternative,* June/July 1976.

6. *The Wall Street Journal,* Sept. 19, 1991.

7. *U.S. News & World Report,* Sept. 12, 1994.

8. *The Wall Street Journal,* Dec. 12, 1995.

9. *The Wall Street Journal,* April 6, 1987.

10. *Access to Energy,* Dec. 1976.

11. *The Indianapolis Business Journal,* Jan. 4-10, 1988.
12. *Quick Frozen Foods International,* Jan. 1987.
13. *Forbes,* Jan. 30, 1995.
14. Frost & Sullivan, *Fish Farming, Processed and Fresh Fish Markets* (New York, 1981).
15. *The Minneapolis Tribune,* Sept. 10, 1976.
16. *The Chicago Tribune,* Sept. 4, 1973.

NOTES TO CHAPTER ELEVEN

1. *The Northern Miner,* Jan. 13, 1977.
2. Marion Clawson, *op. cit.,* p. 2.
3. Samuel P. Hays, *Conservation and the Gospel of Efficiency* (Cambridge: Harvard University Press, 1954), pp. 50-51.
4. Murray N. Rothbard, *For a New Liberty* (New York: MacMillan Publishing Co., Inc., 1973), p. 264.
5. In the 19th century 10 percent of public land was given to the transcontinental railroads. The Union Pacific received one-tenth of the state of Nebraska— 4,845,997 acres!
6. *EQM,* Aug. 1972.
7. *Life,* Dec. 22, 1961.
8. *ibid.*
9. Quoted in *ibid.*
10. Maitland Edey states, "As long as there were pigeons at all, they tended to come together. In the end, when the flocks were broken up and the survivors were forced to exist separately or in scattered groups of a few dozen or a few hundred birds, they seemed incapable of doing so." *ibid.*
11. Quoted in *ibid.*
12. *ibid.*
13. *The Minneapolis Tribune,* Feb. 16, 1975.
14. *The Minneapolis Tribune,* May 27, 1979.
15. *The New York Times,* April 1, 1973.
16. *Free Enterprise,* June 1976.
17. *The Minneapolis Tribune,* April 28, 1968.
18. Murray N. Rothbard, *Power and Market* (Menlo Park, Calif.: Institute for Humane Studies, Inc., 1970), p. 50. See also pp. 139-40.
19. Murray N. Rothbard, *For a New Liberty,* p. 263.
20. *The Wall Street Journal,* Aug. 25, 1989.
21. *Science,* April 3, 1992.
22. From an address to the Garden Club of America, Augusta, Ga., April 2, 1974.
23. National Geographic Society, *op. cit.,* p. 108.
24. From a Georgia-Pacific advertisement in *The Wall Street Journal,* Oct. 11, 1977.
25. From an address to Sales & Marketing Executives International, Portland, Ore., May 21, 1975.
26. *The Wall Street Journal,* April 18, 1986.
27. *The Wall Street Journal,* Aug. 25, 1989.
28. *Spokane Weekly Chronicle,* Feb. 12, 26, 1976.
29. *The Minneapolis Tribune,* Sept. 9, 1976.
30. *The Reader's Digest,* Dec. 1966.

31. The Redwood National Park is 58,000 acres, but this includes 27,468 acres previously within state parks.
32. *The Reader's Digest,* Dec. 1966.
33. *ibid.*
34. *ibid.*
35. Quoted in *The Minneapolis Star,* Aug. 10, 1976.
36. *The Reader's Digest,* May 1969.
37. *The Wall Street Journal,* Aug. 31, 1976.
38. *ibid.*
39. *ibid.*
40. *The Wall Street Journal,* Oct. 13, 1976.
41. *ibid.*
42. *The Wall Street Journal,* Aug. 7, 1980.
43. *Star Tribune,* May 18, 1996.
44. Wilfred Beckerman, *op. cit.,* p. 32.
45. *Access to Energy,* Nov. 1987.
46. *Access to Energy,* April 1986.
47. *The Freeman,* March 1992.
48. Wilfred Beckerman, *op. cit.,* p. 97.
49. Missouri v. Illinois and the Sanitary District of Chicago, 1906; New York v. New Jersey, 1921; and New Jersey v. New York, 1931.
50. *The Freeman,* March 1995.
51. Quoted in *The Reader's Digest,* Nov. 1976.
52. *ibid.*
53. *ibid.*
54. *Star Tribune,* March 9, 1988.
55. *Chicago Tribune,* Dec. 10, 1973.
56. *Star Tribune,* Oct. 4, 1992.
57. Adam Smith, *The Wealth of Nations* (New Rochelle, N.Y.: Arlington House, n.d.), II, p. 27.
58. *AREA Bulletin,* Dec. 1975.
59. Adam Smith, *op. cit.,* p. 30.

NOTES TO CHAPTER TWELVE

1. *The Wall Street Journal,* Feb. 23, 1995.
2. *The Wall Street Journal,* Aug. 22, 1995.
3. *The Wall Street Journal,* May 23, 1990.
4. *The Wall Street Journal,* June 12, 1992.
5. *ibid.*
6. *The Wall Street Journal,* March 2, 1992.
7. *The Wall Street Journal,* June 15, 1992.
8. *The Wall Street Journal,* Feb. 19, 1992.
9. *The Wall Street Journal,* April 21, 1992.
10. *Star Tribune,* April 28, 1989.
11. *The Wall Street Journal,* Aug. 11, 1992.
12. *ibid.*
13. *The Wall Street Journal,* May 9, 1989.
14. *U.S. News & World Report,* Dec. 5, 1994.
15. *The Wall Street Journal,* July, 5, 1994.
16. Quoted in the *California Mining Journal,* Aug. 1976.

17. *The Wall Street Journal,* July 31, 1996.
18. *ibid.*
19. *The Reader's Digest,* May 1975.
20. *The Wall Street Journal,* April 4, 1996.
21. *Science,* Jan. 7, 1977.
22. B. L. Cohen, "Health Effects from Radon from Insulation of Buildings," *Health Physics* Dec. 1980, pp. 937-941.
23. *Journal of Law and Economics,* April 1989.
24. *The Wall Street Journal,* May 18, 1994,
25. John E. Kinney, *Bad Politics not Good Science Sets Public Environmental Policy* (Louisville, Ky.: National Council for Environmental Balance, 1991), pamphlet B-91-1.
26. Michael J. Bennett, *The Asbestos Racket* (Bellevue, Wash.: Free Enterprise Press, 1991), p. 14, 31.
27. Sir Richard Doll of Oxford University, quoted in *ibid.*
28. *ibid.,* p. 41.
29. *Access to Energy,* April 1988.
30. James R. Dunn, *Asbestos - Let's Get the Facts Straight* (Louisville, Ky.; National Council for Environmental Balance, 1985), pamphlet 47.
31. Dunn, *op. cit.*
32. Efron, *op. cit.,* p. 407.
33. *The Wall Street Journal,* March 22, 1993.
34. Dunn, *op. cit.*
35. *Access to Energy,* Dec. 1986.
36. *Nature,* Feb. 27, 1986.
37. *21st Century,* Summer 1990.
38. Dixy Lee Ray and Lou Guzzo, *op. cit.,* pp. 43-49.
39. *ibid.,* p. 45.
40. *Forbes,* July 6, 1992.
41. *ibid.*
42. *ibid.*
43. *The Freeman,* Nov. 1994.
44. R. L. Keeney, "Mortality Risks Induced by Economic Expenditures," *Risk Analysis,* Vol. 10 (1990), pp. 147-159. Keeney also calculates one fatality for each $5 million in increased expenditures caused by government regulations.
45. *Access to Energy,* Jan. 1987.
46. Quoted in *The Wall Street Journal,* Aug. 1, 1972.
47. *Forbes, op. cit.*
48. See: Paul W. MacAvoy, *Industry Regulation and the Performance of the American Economy* (New York: W. W. Norton & Co., 1992), pp. 96-103; Paul Portney, *Public Policies for Environmental Protection* (Washington, D.C.: Resources for the Future, 1990); Robert W. Crandall, *Controlling Industrial Air Pollution: The Economics and Politics of Clean Air* (Washington, D.C.: The Brookings Institution, 1983), p.19.
49. *The Wall Street Journal,* Sept. 14, 1994.
50. *The Wall Street Journal,* Dec. 28, 1995.
51. *The Wall Street Journal,* Aug. 10, 1976.
52. *The Minneapolis Star,* Feb. 22, 1979.
53. *ibid.*

NOTES TO CHAPTER THIRTEEN

1. Quoted in Hans Reichenbach, *From Copernicus to Einstein* (New York: Philosophical Library, 1942), p. 23.
2. *ibid.,* p. 24.
3. Jacob Bronowski, *op. cit.,* p. 216.
4. From a paper to a Glasgow economic society in 1755, quoted in John Chamberlain, *The Roots of Capitalism* (Princeton, N.J.: D. Van Nostrand Company, Inc., 1953), p. 23.
5. Quoted in Felix Morley, *op. cit.,* p. 73. See also John C. Miller, *Origins of the American Revolution* (Boston: Little, Brown and Company, 1943), Chapt. VIII.
6. Adrienne Koch and William Peden, eds., *The Life and Selected Writings of Thomas Jefferson* (New York: Random House, The Modern Library, 1944), p. 719.
7. Philip B. Kurland and Ralph Lerner, eds., *The Founders' Constitution* (Chicago: University of Chicago Press, 1987), vol. 1, p. 591.
8. John Chamberlain, *op. cit.,* p. 20.
9. Albert Jay Nock, *Our Enemy the State* (New York: Free Life Editions, Inc., 1973), pp. 59-60.
10. *The New Twentieth Century Dictionary* (unabridged).
11. Edward Dumbauld, ed., *The Political Writings of Thomas Jefferson* (New York: Liberal Arts Press, 1955), pp. 48-49.
12. *ibid.,* p. 77.
13. Quoted in Morely, *op. cit.,* p. 5. Also, "our chief danger," said Randolph at the Convention, "arises from the democratic parts of our [state] constitutions.... None of the contitutions have provided sufficient checks against the democracy." See Max Farrand, ed., *The Records of the Federal Convention of 1787* (3 vol., New Haven, Conn., 1911), 1:26-27. Historian Forrest McDonald (in *E Pluribus Unum*) notes that Randolph's comments were the sentiments of "all but a handful" of the delegates.
14. Madison *et al., The Federalist* (New Rochelle, N.Y.: Arlington House, n.d.), p. 81.
15. Clarence B. Carson, *The Rebirth of Liberty* (New Rochelle, N.Y.: Arlington House, 1973), p. 205.
16. *ibid.*
17. Max Farrand, *The Framing of the Constitution of the United States* (New Haven: Yale University Press, 1913), p. 164.
18. Roger Lea MacBride, *The American Electoral College* (Caldwell, Idaho: The Caxton Printers, Ltd., 1953), p. 25.
19. Madison, *op. cit.,* p, 82.
20. Adrienne Koch and William Peden, *op. cit.,* p. 632-3.
21. He was referring to Shay's Rebellion.
22. Quoted in Irving Brant, *Storm Over the Constitution* (New York: The Bobbs-Merrill Company, 1936), pp. 210-11.
23. *ibid.*
24. Madison, *op. cit.,* p. 78.
25. *ibid.,* P. 81.
26. On the floor of the Constitutional Convention, June 26, 1787.
27. Philip B. Kurland and Ralph Lerner, *op. cit.,* p. 555.
28. *ibid.,* p. 573.

29. Will Durant, *The Story of Civilization, Part III: Caesar and Christ* (New York: Simon and Schuster, 1944), p. 165.
30. Quoted in Brant, *op. cit.,* p. 227.
31. *ibid.*
32. Morley, *op. cit.,* p. 259.

NOTES TO CHAPTER FOURTEEN

1. Adrienne Koch and William Peden, *op. cit.,* p. 323.
2. Frederic Bastiat, *Selected Essays on Political Economy* (Princeton, N.J.: D. Van Nostrand Co., Inc., 1964), p. 58.
3. *ibid.,* pp. 58-59.
4. *ibid.,* p. 61.
5. *ibid.,* pp. 61-62.
6. See Morten Borden, ed., *America's Ten Greatest Presidents* (Chicago: Rand McNally, 1961), p. 4.
7. The states might well require this. In the same way that some states now legally bind their electors to vote for the candidate with the most popular votes, under a two-vote electoral system they might require the electors to vote for the two most popular candidates.
8. It is usually assumed that the Founders failed to foresee the development of the two-party system, but they may well have intended to prevent it. It certainly cannot be said that the idea of a two-party system never occurred to them. For example, in 1780 John Adams, referring to the Massachusetts Constitution, wrote, "There is nothing which I dread so much as a division of the republic into two great parties, each arranged under its leader, and concerting measures in opposition to each other. This, in my humble apprehension, is to be dreaded as the greatest political evil under our Constitution."
9. Roger Lea MacBride, *op. cit.,* p. 31.
10. Quoted in Lawrence Patton McDonald, *We Hold These Truths* (Seal Beach, Calif.: '76 Press, 1976), p. 46.
11. *ibid.,* p. 32.

NOTES TO CHAPTER FIFTEEN

1. *The Wall Street Journal,* May 31, 1973.
2. *The Wall Street Journal,* June 5, 1992.
3. *The Wall Street Journal,* June 21, 1988.
4. *ibid.*
5. James C. Hefley, *Textbooks on Trial* (Wheaton, Ill.: Victor Books, 1976), p. 83.
6. *ibid.,* p. 84.
7. *ibid.,* p. 40.
8. *Tyler Morning Telegraph,* quoted in ibid., p. 57.
9. Quoted in *The American Spectator,* January 1978.
10. *The Wall Street Journal,* Sept. 4, 1996.
11. Quoted in Lawrence A. Cremin, *The Transformation of the School* (New York: Alfred A. Knopf, 1961), p. 100.
12. John J. McDermott, ed., *The Philosophy of John Dewey* (New York: G.P. Putnam's Sons, 1973), p. 713.
13. *ibid.,* p. 654.

14. Quoted in John H. Snow and Paul W. Shafer, *The Turning of the Tides* (New York: Long House, 1956), p. 30.

15. Joe Park, *Selected Readings in the Philosophy of Education* (New York: Macmillan, 1963), p. 143. See also Clarence B. Carson, *The Flight from Reality* (Irvington-on-Hudson, N.Y.: The Foundation for Economic Education, 1969), p. 289.

16. John Dewey, *Problems of Men* (New York: Philosophical Library, 1946), p. 12.

17. Clarence B. Carson, "The Concept of Democracy and John Dewey," *Modern Age,* Spring 1960. A reflection of confused thinking, Dewey's use of language was incredibly imprecise. Dr. Carson has counted no less than thirty different meanings of the word "democracy" in Dewey's writings. No wonder Dewey was not sure what it meant. See Carson, *The Fateful Turn* (Irvington-on Hudson, N.Y.: The Foundation for Economic Education, 1963), pp. 237-42.

18. Dewey, *op. cit.,* p. 56.

19. Carson, *The Fateful Turn,* p. 247.

20. Quoted in Hefley, *op. cit.,* p. 201.

21. Bastiat, *op. cit.,* p. 131.

22. Quoted in *Vital Speeches,* Sept. 1, 1965.

23. *Insight,* Oct. 8, 1990.

24. *ibid.*

25. *The Wall Street Journal,* Jan. 3, 1996.

GENERAL BIBLIOGRAPHY

Anderson, B. A., *Economics and the Public Welfare.* Princeton, NJ: D. Van Nostrand Co., Inc., 1949.

Barbash, Fred, *The Founding,* New York: Simon and Schuster, 1987.

Bastiat, Frederic, *Selected Essays on Political Economy.* Princeton, NJ: D. Van Nostrand Co., Inc., 1964.

——*Economic Sophisms.* Princeton, NJ: D. Van Nostrand Co. Inc., 1964.

——*Economic Harmonies.* Princeton, NJ: D. Van Nostrand Co., Inc., 1964.

Beckerman, Wilfred, *Two Cheers for the Affluent Society.* New York: St. Martin's Press, 1974.

Beckmann, Petr, *Eco-hysterics and the Technophobes.* Boulder, CO: The Golem Press, 1973.

——*The Health Hazards of NOT Going Nuclear.* Bolder, CO: The Golem Press, 1976.

Blumenfeld, Samuel L., *Is Public Education Necessary?* Boise, Idaho: The Paradigm Co., 1985.

Bronowski, Jacob, *The Ascent of Man.* Boston: Little, Brown and Company, 1974.

Carson, Clarence B., *The Fateful Turn.* Irvington-on Hudson, NY: The Foundation for Economic Education, 1963.

——*The Flight From Reality,* Irvington-on-Hudson, NY: The Foundation for Economic Education, 1969.

—— *The Rebirth of Liberty.* New Rochelle, NY: Arlington House, 1973.

Chamberlain, John, *The Roots of Capitalism.* Princeton, NJ: D. Van Nostrand Co., Inc.,1953.

——*The Enterprising Americans.* New York: Harper and Row, 1963.

Del Mar, Alexander, *A History of the Precious Metals.* New York: Augustus M. Kelly, 1969.

——*The Science of Money.* New York: Burt Franklin, 1968.

Edwards, J. Gordon, *Saving Lives With Pesticides.* Louisville, KY: National Council for Environmental Balance, 1983.

Efron, Edith, *The Apocalyptics: Cancer and The Big Lie.* New York: Simon and Schuster, 1984.

Flynn, Leonard T., *Pesticides: Helpful or Harmful?* Summit, NJ: American Council on Science and Health, 1988.

Freeman, Roger A., *The Growth of American Government: A Morphology of the Welfare State.* Stanford, CA: Hoover Institution Press, 1975.

Friedman, Milton, *Capitalism and Freedom.* Chicago: University of Chicago Press, 1962.

Friedman, Milton and Anna Jacobson Schwartz, *A Monetary History of the United States 1867-1960.* Princeton, NJ: Princeton University Press, 1963.

Friedman, Milton and Rose, *Free To Choose.* New York: Harcourt Brace Jovanovich, 1990.

Fumento, Michael, *Science under Seige.* New York: William Morrow and Co., 1993.

Garrett, Garet, *The People's Pottage.* Caldwell, Idaho: The Caxton Printers, Ltd., 1965.

Grayson, Melvin J. and Shepard, Thomas R. Jr., *The Disaster Lobby.* Chicago: Follett Publishing Co., 1973.

Groseclose, Elgin, *Fifty Years of Managed Money.* New York: Books Inc., 1966.

—— *Money and Man.* New York: Frederick Ungar Publishing Co., 1967.

Hamilton, Edith, *The Greek Way to Western Civilization.* New York: The New American Library, 1948.

Havender, William R., and Flynn, Leonard T., *Does Nature Know Best?* Summit, NJ: American Council on Science and Health, 1987.

Hayek, F. A., *Capitalism and the Historians.* Chicago: The University of Chicago Press, 1954.

——*Individualism and Economic Order.* Chicago: The University of Chicago Press, 1948.

——*The Road to Serfdom,* Chicago: The University of Chicago Press, 1962.

Hazlitt, Henry, *The Critics of Keynesian Economics.* New Rochelle, NY. Arlington House, 1977.

——*Economics in One Lesson.* New York: Harper and Brothers, 1946.

——*The Failure of the "New Economics."* Princeton, NJ: D. Van Nostrand Co., 1959.

——*What You Should Know About Inflation.* New York: Funk & Wagnalls, 1968.

Hospers, John, *Libertarianism.* Los Angeles: Nash Publishing, 1971.

Jacobs, Jane, *The Economy of Cities.* New York: Random House, 1969.
——*Cities and the Wealth of Nations.* New York: Random House, 1984.
Johnson, Paul, *Enemies of Society.* New York: Atheneum, 1977.
——*Modern Times.* New York: HarperCollins, 1991.
Koch, Adrienne and Peden, William, eds., *The Life and Selected Writings of Thomas Jefferson.* New York: Random House, 1944.
Lane, Rose Wilder, *The Discovery of Freedom.* New York: Arno Press & The New York Times, 1972.
MacBride, Roger Lea, *The American Electoral College.* Caldwell, Idaho: The Caxton Printers, Ltd., 1953.
John Maddox, *The Doomsday Syndrome.* New York: McGraw-Hill, 1972.
Madison *et al., The Federalist.* New Rochelle, NY: Arlington House, n.d.
Maine, Sir Henry Sumner, *Popular Government.* Indianapolis: Liberty Classics, 1976.
McDonald, Forrest, *E Pluribus Unum: The Formation of the American Republic 1776-1790.* Boston: Houghton Mifflin Co., 1965.
McDonald, Lawrence Patton, *We Hold These Truths.* Seal Beach, CA: '76 Press, 1976.
McKetta, John J., *The World Doesn't End Here.* Louisville, KY: National Council for Environment Balance, 1974.
Mencken, H. L., *Notes on Democracy.* New York: Farrar, Strauss & Giroux, Inc., 1977.
Mises, Ludwig von, *The Anti-capitalistic Mentality.* Princeton, NJ: D. Van Nostrand Co., Inc., 1956.
——*Human Action.* New Haven, CT: Yale University Press, 1949.
——*Omnipotent Government: The Rise of the Total State and Total War.* New Rochelle, NY: Arlington House, 1969.
——*Socialism.* London: Jonathan Cape, 1972.
——*The Theory of Money and Credit.* New Haven, CT: Yale University Press, 1953.
Morley, Felix, *The Power in the People.* Los Angeles: Nash Publishing, 1972.
Nock, Albert Jay, *Our Enemy the State.* New York: Free Life Editions, Inc., l973.
Ottoboni, M. Alice, *The Dose Makes the Poison.* Berkeley, CA: Vincente Books, 1984.
Rand, Ayn, *Capitalism: The Unknown Ideal.* New York: The New American Library, Inc., 1967.
Ray, Dixy Lee and Guzzo, Lou, *Environmental Overkill.* Washington, DC: Regnery Gateway, 1993.
Reisman, George, *The Government Against the Economy.* Ottawa, IL: Jameson Books, 1979.
Rickenbacker, William F., *Death of the Dollar.* New York: Dell, 1968.
Rothbard, Murray, *America's Great Depression.* Kansas City: Sheed and Ward, Inc., 1975.
——*Conceived in Liberty,* New Rochelle, NY: Arlington House, 1975.
——*For a New Liberty.* New York: Macmillan Publishing Co., Inc., 1973.
——*Man, Economy, and State,* 2 Vols. Los Angeles: Nash Publishing, 1970.
——*Power and Market.* Menlo Park, CA: Institute for Humane Studies, Inc., 1970.
——*What Has Government Done to Our Money?* Santa Ana, CA: Rampart College, 1974.
Rougier, Louis, *The Genius of the West,* Los Angeles: Nash Publishing, 1971.
Salsman, Richard M. *Breaking the Banks: Central Banking Problems and Free Banking Solutions.* Great Barrington, MA: American Institute for Economic Research, 1990.
——*Gold and Liberty.* Great Barrington, MA: American Institute for Economic Research, 1995.
Shelton, Judy, *Money Meltdown.* New York: Macmillan, 1994.
Simon, Julian L., *The Ultimate Resource.* Princeton, NJ: Princeton University Press, 1981.
Simon, Julian L. and Herman Kahn, *The Resourceful Earth,* New York: Basil Blackwell, 1984.
Smith, Jerome F., *The Coming Currency Collapse.* New York: Books In Focus, Inc., 1980.
Snyder, Carl, *Capitalism the Creator.* New York: Macmillan, 1940.
Sutton, Antony C., *The War on Gold.* Seal Beach, CA: '76 Press, 1977.
Weidenbaum, Murray L., *Business, Government and the Public.* Englewood Cliffs, NJ: Prentice Hall, 1977.

Whelan, Elizabeth M., and Stare, Frederick J., *Panic in the Pantry.* New York: Atheneum, 1977.

Weaver, Henry Grady, *The Mainspring of Human Progress.* Irvington-on-Hudson, NY: The Foundation for Economic Education, Inc., 1954.

Wooldridge, William C., *Uncle Sam, The Monopoly Man.* New Rochelle, NY: Arlington House, 1970.

INDEX

THE TROJAN PROJECT
A Novel of Intrigue about Reshaping America

by
EDMUND CONTOSKI

One man's vision of America, from *The Trojan Project:*

"In a free society people would have a right to make their pursuit of happiness the standard for all their decisions in the exercise of their rights. The individual, not the government, would be the sole judge of that standard, and there would be no appeal beyond the voluntary consent of other people's minds....There would be none of the 'tyranny over the minds of men' that we have by the federal government overseeing all our economic decisions and threatening us with fines and jail sentences to enforce that tyranny....[The individual] has a right to make all economic choices without *any* government interference because it's *his* life....

"I don't like to think of [my children] being yoked together with their contemporaries like beasts of burden pulling a $5 trillion debt down the highway of life—the load of other people's 'good' purposes. I'd like to think of them growing up in a country where they would be free to fulfill their own dreams, where they could pursue their own happiness instead of being shackled to pull the collective load of everyone else's shortcomings, failures, mistakes, inabilities, 'needs' and 'inequalities.' It used to be said that this was a country where people could rise as high as their abilities would take them. We never hear that any more. That was the America where individual rights— man's natural rights—were paramount, where people were free to use their abilities for themselves. They were free to be unequal. Now we hear only about everything that's wrong and unequal in society and how government must take away more and more of everyone's money and freedom for collective solutions—in the 'public interest'—in order to *level* society rather than allow people to reach heights. This is the America where government has invented phony 'rights' to displace man's natural rights, where 'rights' are made deliberately unequal in order to try to *level life.*"

"Jefferson said: 'The legitimate powers of government extend to such acts only as are injurious to others.' It's not the purpose of government to protect men from actions injurious to themselves. When you try to protect people from their own bad decisions, you're protecting them from life itself. You're depriving them of the right to live by their own minds. You're condemning them to a less than human existence on the grounds they're incompetent to live a truly human one.... You treat the citizens of this country as though they're all hopelessly senile or as children who can never be regarded as grown up enough to make decisions and be responsible for them."

6 by 9 inches. Quality paperback. Price: $17.95
To order this book, see back of this page.

Books by Edmund Contoski available from American Liberty Publishers:

MAKERS AND TAKERS
How Wealth and Progress are Made and
How They are Taken Away or Prevented $24.95

THE TROJAN PROJECT $17.95
What can one man do when he finds himself up against the most dangerous men in America? His only weapons are intellectual: a keen analytical mind and rational morality. His opponents have vast resources of money and power—and no moral limitations on their use.

The tale begins with a series of puzzling events. Cars are being moved mysteriously at night without anyone knowing who moves them or why, and food is disappearing. One man discovers what causes these strange happenings, but he doesn't know the full story. When finally he does, he learns his own life is in danger—and so is the future of the nation! His solution for saving the United States will be of interest to everyone concerned about the current direction of the country.

Add $2.95 shipping and handling for each book.

Please send me: Total
_____ copy (copies) of MAKERS AND TAKERS @ $24.95 _____
_____ copy (copies) of THE TROJAN PROJECT @ $17.95 _____
                    Minnesota residents add 6.5 percent sales tax _____
                            Shipping and handling @ $2.95 each _____
                            Check or money order enclosed for $ _____

Name_____
Address_____
City _____State_____Zip_____

Make check to: American Liberty Publishers
Mail to: American Liberty Publishers, Box 18296, Minneapolis MN 55418

This page may be photocopied